Youth Justice

Youth Justice
Ideas, Policy, Practice

Second edition

Roger Smith

WILLAN
PUBLISHING

Published by

Willan Publishing
Culmcott House
Mill Street, Uffculme
Cullompton, Devon
EX15 3AT, UK
Tel: +44(0)1884 840337
Fax: +44(0)1884 840251
e-mail: info@willanpublishing.co.uk
website: www.willanpublishing.co.uk

Published simultaneously in the USA and Canada by

Willan Publishing
c/o ISBS, 920 NE 58th Ave, Suite 300,
Portland, Oregon 97213-3786, USA
Tel: +001(0)503 287 3093
Fax: +001(0)503 280 8832
e-mail: info@isbs.com
website: www.isbs.com

First published 2007

Paperback
ISBN-13: 978 1 84392 224 7
ISBN-10: 1 84392 224 X

British Library Cataloguing-in-Publication Data

A catalogue record for this book is available from the British Library

Project managed by Deer Park Productions, Tavistock, Devon
Typeset by GCS, Leighton Buzzard, Bedfordshire, LU7 1AR
Printed and bound by T.J. International Ltd, Padstow, Cornwall

Contents

Introduction   ix

1   Lessons from history: the 1980s   1
    The need for perspective   1
    Thatcherism and youth justice   2
    Law and policy: targeting young offenders   3
    The changing face of practice: new paradigms?   6
    Patterns of change: offending and outcomes in the 1980s   11
    The meaning of 'success'   15
    Accounting for 'success'   16
    Messages from the past?   19

2   Where did it all go wrong?   22
    Continuity or change?   22
    Gathering clouds: politicians and populism   23
    Backtracking: laying down the law   26
    Diamonds in the mud: practice in a hostile climate   28
    The Troubleshooter Project and beyond: drawing the line   31
    Bail support: working tactically   32
    Supervision in the community: close control?   34
    'Defensive' practice: messages from the 1990s   35
    A rising tide: 'intended' consequences   36
    Explaining the U-turn   39

3   That same old song? New Labour and youth justice   42
    'Tough on crime, tough on the causes of crime ...'   42
    Social inclusion and crime reduction   43
    Generalised crime prevention   46
    Targeted youth crime prevention   47
    Individualised crime prevention   49
    The end of tolerance – the roots of reform   50
    No more excuses – the road to discipline   52

The Crime and Disorder Act 1998 –
   the micropolitics of social control 57
Further reforms: extending control or muddying the waters? 59
Tightening the grip 61
Counter-currents? 63
The state of policy: coherence, camouflage or confusion? 64

4 Where are we now? Policy and outcomes in youth justice 71
A new landscape? 71
A growth industry: dealing with 'anti-social behaviour' 72
The use of ASBOs 73
The consequences of the ASBO revolution 75
Outcomes and disposals: emerging patterns 77
Looking for patterns: targeting, compulsion and surveillance 80

5 Inside the machine 83
Between policy and practice 83
National objectives and National Standards:
   prescribing good practice? 85
The Youth Justice Board: mouthpiece or mediator? 94
YOTs: all at sea? 101
Corporatism: construct, constraint or catalyst? 107

6 Making it happen: practice in the new century 109
Creative tensions or routinised control? 109
First impressions – procedural change 110
Making the best of our ASSETs? 112
New orders – redesigning practice? 115
The Referral Order: moving restorative justice centre stage? 123
Meanwhile, back at the 'heavy end' 125
New orders: recipe for success or 'korrectional karaoke'? 127

7 Nothing gained? 131
How can we judge success or failure? 131
Young black people and institutionalised discrimination 132
'It's different for girls ...' 137
Ships in the night: victims of crime and youth justice 143
Claiming success: a cautionary note 148
The Nero effect 153

8 Theorising youth justice 156
The art of the possible 156
The practicality of theory 157
Targeting the young: the source of all ills? 159
Frustrated ambitions? 163
The reality of youth crime 165
Explaining youth crime? 166

The locus of power: ideologies and structures   170
Foucault and the techniques of justice   176
The limits of functionalism   178
Youth justice: the value of theory   180

9   The consumer view   **182**
What do we want from the youth justice system?   182
The victim's perspective   183
The community: conflicting needs or common agendas?   187
Youth crime and black and minority ethnic groups   193
'What about us?' Young people's views   197
The answers are complex   202

10   Making sense of it all: looking ahead   **203**
Another fine mess?   203
The product of converging interests   207
Managing 'risk'   209
Looking ahead: an alternative framework   210
The way ahead: working at different levels   217
Oiling the wheels: the 'mezzo' level   220
The search for progressive practice at the 'micro' level 225
Lessons from elsewhere   228

Notes   **231**

Bibliography   **233**

Index   **251**

Introduction: false dawns, new starts and missed opportunities

Motives and aspirations

Returning to the start of a second edition has, of course, led me to reconsider the message as well as the content of the first version of this book, in order to address the need for revisions and updating. In brief, I still believe that the analysis set out previously has largely been borne out by events, although it offers little satisfaction to make this claim. Youth justice is, indeed, increasingly characterised by a culture of control and an atmosphere of suspicion and hostility towards children and young people. This is best illustrated by developments at opposite ends of the penal spectrum. The 'tragic' consequences of an excessive reliance on custody (Bright 2002) have been starkly and depressingly documented for us by Goldson and Coles (2005), while, at the other end of the scale, the absurdity of the ASBO has also come to represent a particularly graphic indictment of current policy and practice (Burney 2005).

Indeed, the machinery of the youth justice system seems to have developed a distorted logic and momentum of its own, producing ever more expensive, irrational and counter-productive practices and outcomes. Interventions are supposed to be directed towards 'preventing youth crime', and yet they rely consistently on punitive and custodial measures which are acknowledged to be criminogenic. Policy is claimed to be 'evidence-based', shaping practice on the basis of 'what works'; so why does it largely ignore the lessons of recent decades and other jurisdictions which demonstrate the value of informal, problem-solving and inclusive solutions? And what is the meaning of 'youth justice', when its provisions persistently fly in the face of criticisms from human rights organisations which condemn our failure to meet acceptable standards in the treatment of children and young people?

On a personal level, my feelings of frustration and disappointment are compounded by my own experience as a practitioner and manager, working with young offenders in a setting where many positive lessons were learned. From that particular context, I have been able to draw the conclusion that a liberal and humane approach to youth justice is both achievable and desirable; it may even be acceptable to the community in general, contrary to the fears of some. We need not reach for the 'big stick' as a matter of course. However, many of the gains made during the 1980s have been lost subsequently, and I suppose that my motivation for writing this book lies partly in a desire to understand the reasons for these reversals, and to begin again to think about the possibilities and prospects for progressive practice in youth justice. The appearance of conviction and inevitability about many aspects of current practice may appear daunting, but it can surely be no more the case now than it was for those working in what was then 'juvenile justice' under the Thatcher government of the 1980s. Optimism is needed as much as clear thinking and liberal views, in order to begin to sketch out and develop renewed possibilities for dealing 'justly' with the crimes of the young in the present era.

In practical terms, the book is constructed in three parts in order to demonstrate the potential connections between past experience, present challenges and future prospects. In taking this approach, I hope to be able to demonstrate the necessary connections to be made between 'ideas, policy and practice', as the title suggests.

Changing times?

The recent history of youth justice provides evidence of some remarkable contrasts in approach, as well as some key continuities (for example, the persistence of the sentencing 'tariff'), and thus offers a good starting point for considering present-day experience and the possibilities for change.

The first part begins with an assessment of 'juvenile justice' (as it then was) in the 1980s, when an avowedly right-wing and authoritarian government (Gamble 1988) presided over one of the most benign and liberal periods ever witnessed in the treatment of young offenders. The increased use of informal measures of intervention (diversion) was paralleled by a substantial decline in the use of custody, alongside the emergence of a thriving body of 'intensive' non-custodial programmes of supervision. These trends may be explained in a number of ways, as Chapter 1 demonstrates, including the creativity of practitioners, economic expediency and political circumstances. Important lessons to be taken from this era include the value of imaginative 'bottom up' initiatives, the necessity of a coherent 'minimum intervention' strategy, the importance of political astuteness and the erroneous nature of many assumptions about public opinion.

The following chapter illustrates, in stark contrast, the increasingly high profile of youth justice in the 1990s, and the associated loss of control for those involved in developing effective policies and interventions. Instead, youth crime became a political football, and fell prey to populist gimmickry. This decade witnessed a period of radical retrenchment, characterised by the depressing and misleading slogan 'prison works' (see Chapter 2). That this assertion is unsupported by any evidence but still became conventional wisdom captures the essence of a period epitomised by a spirit of prejudice, ignorance and hostility towards young people in general, and young offenders in particular. The practical consequences were dramatic. Even as crime rates were reported to be falling, there was a significant increase in the use of custody for young people. The professional skills of youth justice practitioners were neutered, and the principled 'systems management' of the 1980s was replaced by a technocratic managerialism with no principles or independent rationale (Goldson 2000b).

The change of government in 1997 led to a much trumpeted reform programme, crystallised in the Crime and Disorder Act 1998 which is the focal point of Chapter 3. The incoming government sought to locate its youth justice policies under the broader umbrella of crime prevention, which led to a multi-faceted strategy incorporating communities, 'at risk' groups and known offenders. In this way, innovations in youth justice could be identified as forming part of a broader 'joined up' approach to neighbourhood renewal and social inclusion.

However, the immediate impact of the new measures put in place did not represent an unambiguous change of direction. The political preoccupations with 'quick wins' and public approval ensured that the prime concerns of the new administration were to look tough and to focus on simplistic measures of efficiency and effectiveness, while overlooking the continuing impacts of discriminatory systems and the excessive use of punitive measures. The rhetoric of radical reform also created unrealistic expectations of dramatic short-term gains. Of itself, this generated all sorts of demands, which appear to have resulted in a series of contrived outcomes and misleading claims (see also Chapter 7). The internal logic of these pressures has led to an ever-increasing reliance on micro-management and systems of control which are bounded by the requirement to produce immediate and tangible results. In concentrating on these superficial outcomes, however, it will be shown that more fundamental principles and key values are lost or compromised. The appearance of success has become all that matters (Pratt 2000).

This second edition of the book will also supplement this discussion with a commentary on the most recent manifestations of these trends (Chapter 4). In particular, the intensification of the government's drive to produce safer communities by controlling the behaviour of young people will be illustrated by reference to the increasing reliance on Anti-Social Behaviour Orders, the preoccupation with responsible parenting, and the highly prescriptive Intensive Supervision and Surveillance Programme. Despite these measures, and in some cases because of them, the custody rate remains far too high, and the mistreatment of young people in custody represents a continuing stain on the nation's character (Goldson and Coles 2005).

The machinery of control

In the second part of the book, I will go on to consider the implications of the New Labour reform programme in more detail, focusing on the three levels of policy, delivery mechanisms and practice. One of the advantages of evaluating the kind of detailed reform programme put in place since 1997 is that it generates a massive amount of policy documentation, research evidence and practice evaluations.

Thus Chapter 5 undertakes a detailed exploration of the initiatives put in place to deliver the government's aims. For example, the National Standards for Youth Justice (Youth Justice Board 2000, 2004a) are subjected to detailed scrutiny, as is the performance of the Youth Justice Board. In addition, the impact of the establishment of Youth Offending Teams as the primary delivery vehicle will also be considered. This chapter concludes that these developments collectively represent a significant extension of 'corporatism' (Pratt 1989) and 'managerialism' (Clarke *et al.* 2000), but that these are not uniform in their impact. Contradictions between aims and principles are likely to lead to unplanned and unpredictable outcomes, while opportunities for managers and practitioners to act creatively in the interest of progressive practice remain available 'between the cracks'. Lipsky's (1980) notion of 'street-level bureaucracy' remains a helpful reminder of the residual power of practitioners themselves.

Chapter 6 moves from the level of strategy and structures to consider the implications of the extensive reform programme for youth justice practice. It is possible here to draw on an extensive body of evaluative material generated by the effort to assess the initial impact of the Crime and Disorder Act 1998. This material demonstrates an emerging pattern of 'routinised control' which subsumes practitioners' professional disciplines and distinctive areas of interest in the demands of a highly prescriptive and centralised political agenda. Alongside this narrowing of the scope and opportunities for imaginative and locally relevant practice, it is possible to identify a degree of dissonance between the claims of efficacy made by leading politicians and policy-makers on the one hand, and the detailed evidence on the other, which has proved stubbornly resistant to the drawing of neat and reassuring conclusions. This chapter concludes that the relatively modest achievements documented are demonstrative of the inadequacies of an over-centralised and interfering approach. By contrast, a greater recognition of the potential for local initiative, practitioner independence and, indeed, a readiness to take risks are all prerequisites for improvements at the level of service delivery.

At this point (Chapter 7), the claims of 'success' made by the government will be subjected to more extensive scrutiny. The outcome measures put in place (such as a reduction in time taken to process offences) are found to be largely superficial and unconvincing. Other claims of improved outcomes, such as a reduction in reoffending rates, have proved difficult to sustain and methodologically suspect (Bottoms 2005). Indeed, the main conclusion to be drawn from the evidence overall is that the 'toughening up' of the youth justice system originating in the early 1990s is continuing apace. More young people have been drawn into the formal networks of control, at an earlier age, for more minor transgressions (Jennings 2002), and, with the advent of ASBOs, for behaviour which falls short of being a crime at all (Burney 2005; Squires and Stephen 2005). The predictable consequence of these developments is a progressively more punitive pattern of interventions, supported, as it is, by the legislative expansion of sentencing options (or other measures of control).

As a result, more young people have experienced periods in custody, while a rather wider group have been subjected to various forms of community punishment and control which also have an increasingly intrusive impact on their lives. In addition, the nature of these new measures has also had broader implications, to the extent that they have impacted on certain groups, such as young women and young black people, in discriminatory and oppressive fashion.

Rethinking/reshaping youth justice

The final part of the book is concerned with developing a theoretical and practical basis for alternative forms of youth justice which are fair, just and progressive. In order to contextualise my prescriptions for change, Chapter 8 will take a step back and explore the outline of a theoretical framework for understanding our longstanding concerns with the intertwined issues of young people and social disorder. The problematic nature of 'youth' itself is taken as the starting point, with a discussion of the issues of socialisation and control in the context of adolescent transitions. The tensions and challenges of young people's experiences will be explored, drawing on Merton's (1957) model of 'adaptation', and contextualised by an analysis of social exclusion and marginalisation.

These experiences will, in turn, be related to broad structural questions of power, legitimacy and control, which will consider the place of law and the judicial system in constructing young people's behaviour as problematic. On this basis, it will be suggested that the prevailing 'technologies' of control which are manifested in the machinery of youth justice represent a way of depoliticising and routinising highly specific objectives in terms of securing young people's compliance to social norms (Foucault 1979). The particular forms of identification, assessment and targeted interventions observable in youth justice systems are thus able to lay claim to being scientifically based, empirically justifiable and therefore normal and acceptable.

Chapter 9, however, takes a rather different starting point, which is represented by the experiences and aspirations of a number of 'stakeholder' interests, who may be said to have a legitimate concern with the delivery of youth justice practice, including victims, young people and ethnic minority groups. Indeed, these apparently disparate interests can be seen to share a number of common reservations about the shortcomings of what has conventionally been provided. In short, they all appear to share a concern that the system simply 'doesn't work'. Not only is this perception widely held, but there also appears to be substantial common ground for the development of workable alternatives, based on principles of negotiation, rights and social inclusion. Youth crime is complex and multi-faceted, and therefore it necessitates a range of sensitive, creative and flexible responses, it seems.

In the concluding chapters, I will take up these questions by sketching out some ideas for the future development of appropriate responses to the issue of youth crime. The current position is restated at this point, in order to establish a baseline from which we can begin to make progress. A series of principles is set out which, in my view, form the essential underpinning to a credible, coherent and just system for dealing with the problematic behaviour of young people. These are then operationalised in two ways: firstly, by considering examples of good practice which are in place currently within the national context and internationally; and, secondly, by articulating new initiatives in policy, organisation and practice which are needed to give them substance.

Overall, the conclusion to be drawn is that youth justice needs to be characterised by a commitment to social as well as criminal justice. Problem-solving approaches, minimum intervention, rights and social inclusion need to be prioritised rather than routinised mechanisms of surveillance, monitoring and control.

1. Lessons from history: the 1980s

The need for perspective

The choice of starting point for a historical review is always likely to be seen as arbitrary in some respects. This is no less the case in the present context, because the interest in the problem behaviour of young people can be traced back over centuries, if not millennia (Pearson 1983). It is equally clear that recurrent themes and challenges have been identified over the course of time (see Thorpe *et al*. 1980, for example). There is, therefore, a need to offer some justification for the decision to begin this story around the beginning of the 1980s.

To begin with, it is important to strike a balance between the 'foreshortening' effect of considering only the present and the recent past, on the one hand, and the tendency to disregard history as no longer relevant to today's concerns, on the other. It may be thought, for example, that to concentrate on the past 25 years may be to over-emphasise essentially ephemeral recent developments (such as the *relatively* small recent decline in officially recorded crime figures, set against their inexorable rise over more than a century (Home Office 2001b: p. 19).

On the other side of the argument, it might be suggested that an extended historical account has little to offer by way of contemporary insights or practical assistance to hard-pressed agencies and practitioners who are faced with ever-changing demands from an increasingly complex and highly technological operating environment. Effective delivery may seem to be a somewhat higher priority than an appreciation of arcane debates about the antecedents of the modern youth justice system.

Nevertheless, we must start somewhere, and in addition to the purely pragmatic justification of focusing on what we know about, there are other, rather more positive, reasons for turning our gaze back to the beginning of the 'age of diversion' in 1980. This has been a time of significant change in policy and practice, with a number of major pieces of legislation, a keen continuing public interest, a variety of imaginative and influential practice and policy initiatives, and perhaps a broader sense of uncertainty and upheaval associated with the transition to the new millennium.

While some of these themes remain common to the whole 25-year period, there is another sense in which this is a useful timescale to consider for present purposes. This relates to the clear and dramatic contrasts which can be drawn between the experiences and practices of the 1980s and those of the 1990s (and beyond) in youth justice (formerly 'juvenile justice' – even the essential terminology has changed!). Taking this approach, we will have the opportunity to consider what are the lessons to be learned from these divergent experiences, for practitioners, for provider agencies, for policy-makers and for academic interests (see Haines and Drakeford 1998). Having established the demarcation between practice in the 1980s and subsequent developments as the critical point of comparison, we should also note that this implies the rejection of certain other potential 'turning points' such as the change of government in 1997 (which, I shall argue, primarily signalled a frenetic period of 'radical rebranding').

Clearly, in the light of wider historical and social factors, it would be unwise to claim that any era in youth justice can be portrayed in terms of an absolute break from its predecessors or successors, but it is still the case that a comparative approach will offer a helpful framework for our efforts to clarify just what has been going on in youth justice recently.

Thatcherism and youth justice

In looking back to the 1980s, it is almost inevitable that we will be inclined to make some simplistic assumptions about the Thatcher era, and the likely consequences for youth justice policy and practice of an explicitly ideological right-wing government. This was a time when the social and political divides appeared stark, and the sense of 'us' against 'them' (whichever side you identified with) was a constant factor in the field of social welfare. Much of the political rhetoric of the time was confrontational, and was directed towards dealing decisively with what were perceived to be fundamental threats to core social values. Repeated references were made to 'the enemy within' (Milne 2004), alongside calls to rebuild and reinforce key institutions such as the family (Gamble 1988). This reflected a highly ideological project on the part of the Thatcher government which left no room for weakness, sentimentality or compassion. It could only be anticipated that this perspective would exert a comparable influence on policy and practice in relation to young offenders.

The polarised and dramatic rhetoric of the time was paralleled by a number of significant events that appeared to provide concrete evidence of the radical political and social project being undertaken. Thus the Falklands' War (1982), the Miners' Strike (1984–5), the denial of poverty and restructuring of welfare benefits (1988), the Poll Tax (Community Charge, 1989) and the Child Support Act (1991) all bore the hallmark of this definitive restatement of 'traditional' values.

The emphasis on the essential character of 'Britishness', the integrity of the family, economic self-sufficiency and personal responsibility all seemed to add up to a coherent and unified position, with little room for acknowledging diversity, taking account of disadvantage or excusing wrongdoing (Gamble 1988). Confrontation between the agents of the state and marginalised groups became a recurrent feature of the decade, with major outbreaks of social unrest recorded in 1981 and 1985, in particular (Davies 1986). The 'riots' and the response to them were also characterised by the impression of racialised conflict and the perception that young black people represented a direct threat to social order and moral stability. In this divided and often oppressive political context, then, the 1980s might not seem likely to have offered much encouragement for the development of creative and liberal initiatives in the sphere of youth crime.

Law and policy: targeting young offenders

Not only was the broader policy arena one of increasing toughness and authoritarianism, but there was also evidence of a punitive shift in the specific area of youth justice at the start of the decade. On taking office in 1979, the Conservative government took action to put into practice its stated intention to establish a 'short, sharp, shock' regime in two detention centres for 14–17-year-olds (Conservative Party 1979). This 'experiment' was subsequently extended to other custodial settings, and eventually to all detention centres (Pitts 1988).

This mood was also reflected in the White Paper *Young Offenders* (Home Office, 1980). In the language of contemporary debates, this represented a victory for those who believed in 'justice' and due process, rather than 'welfare' models of intervention (which had been influential in the 1970s; see Thorpe *et al.* 1980). The notion of individual responsibility and just deserts appeared much more in keeping with the ideology of the Thatcher era, although it also gained support from more liberal critics of the role of 'treatment' in youth justice (Morris *et al.* 1980). While many had been arguing for an end to the confusing melange of overlapping welfare-oriented and tariff-based disposals that characterised the existing system (attributable to the partial implementation of the Children and Young Persons Act 1969), there was nevertheless a real sense of apprehension about the potential consequences of the measures signposted by *Young Offenders* and enacted under the Criminal Justice Act 1982.

Specific measures that crystallised these concerns included the Night Restriction Order and the Supervised Activity Order which both sought to exercise a closer degree of control over young offenders subject to community sentences (and over their supervisors in the social work and probation services), thus intensifying the coercive aspects of intervention.

Alongside these measures, the 1982 Act introduced a new sentence of Youth Custody to replace the indeterminate Borstal regime, and the Residential Care Order to offer courts a greater degree of control over what was ostensibly a 'welfare' disposal. The overall objective of these reforms seems to have been to cement in place a shift from a rehabilitative agenda towards an emphasis on just deserts, deterrence and control. This was an important change because

3

it set the tone for practice at all levels of the justice system over the ensuing years, even if the outcomes were, in the event, not what might have been predicted. We can anticipate subsequent developments by observing that the challenge was now to determine at what point in the tariff of disposals a particular response was merited, rather than to pay close attention to 'tailoring' services to address individual needs or correctional aims.

Alongside the measures introduced at this time, however, the government also initiated a programme that turned out to be at least as significant, if not more so. The Thatcher government had a clear agenda of reducing the role of the state, both in terms of taxation and expenditure, and in the extent to which it should intervene in everyday life, and this was reflected even in its approach to youth crime. It has been suggested that the government agenda was driven, at least in part, by a concern to reduce the cost of imprisonment (Pitts 1988).

At the same time, the concern to ensure that the punishment should fit the crime led logically to a recognition in *Young Offenders* that the use of custody itself should be subject to certain limits, and partly as a consequence, the then Home Secretary (William Whitelaw) promised to supplement courts' powers by 'broadening and strengthening existing non-custodial provisions [in order to] assist the courts to avoid a custodial sentence except where one is absolutely necessary' (Nacro 1987: 11). Thus in 1983 the Department of Health and Social Security launched its intensive Intermediate Treatment initiative (DHSS 1983), providing a sum of £15 million over three years for the development of alternatives to custody. The aim was to create an additional 4,500 places in the community for the supervision of young people convicted of serious offences. As Hudson (1987) has put it, the era of 'net-widening' (the 1970s) was to be succeeded by a period of 'net-strengthening' whereby community sentences would be expected to compete with custodial options to demonstrate comparable levels of toughness and control over young people's activities.

Further evidence that the government was seeking to balance cost saving against punitive interventions was offered by subsequent policy initiatives, including notably the influential Home Office Circular 14/85 on 'cautioning', which actively promoted increased use of disposals short of prosecutions in non-serious cases, including both cautions and informal action by the police. This development was consistent with the intentions of *Young Offenders*, which argued that 'juvenile offenders who can be diverted from the criminal justice system at an early stage in their offending are less likely to re-offend than those who become involved in judicial proceedings' (quoted in Nacro 1987: 15). The 1985 Circular underlined this message and encouraged the use of a range of options for offenders to make amends, including involvement in local youth activities, making an apology, direct or indirect reparation or voluntary supervision. The aim was to secure commitment to the principle of targeted intervention operating at the minimum level necessary to deal with the offence; thus even formal cautions should be avoided where informal alternatives were appropriate. It should be noted at this point that this guidance also provided early legitimation for a shift towards restorative practices in youth justice.

The combined effect of these policy initiatives, stemming from the 1980 White Paper, has been described as one of 'bifurcation' (for example, Pickford 2000), whereby government can get 'tough and soft simultaneously'. The definition of a relatively small group of offenders as 'dangerous and threatening' enables a clear distinction to be made between them and the great majority of those who transgress as merely wayward, misguided or 'easily led'. By adopting this strategy, the government of the time could maintain its reputation as being tough on crime while at the same time actually encouraging a less coercive approach for relatively minor infractions, thereby keeping costs down and relieving pressures on the criminal justice system.

By the latter part of the 1980s, the government felt able to take this strategy further with the publication of the Green Paper, *Punishment, Custody and the Community* (Home Office 1988), which reiterated its twin-track approach. Stating that a custodial option would be the right disposal for many offenders, and emphasising the government's commitment to crack down on both violent crimes and lenient sentences, this document also commented that:

> for other, less serious offenders, a spell in custody is not the most effective punishment. Imprisonment restricts offenders' liberty, but it also reduces their responsibility; they are not required to face up to what they have done or to make any recompense to the victim or the public. (Home Office 1988: 1)

Interestingly, the idea of paying for one's crimes literally also fitted with the prevailing market ideology, it would seem.

The phrase 'punishment in the community' was utilised to allay any concerns that offenders might be getting off lightly, while emphasis was also placed on the correctional and restorative aspects of the proposed strategy. Indeed, it seemed that the government was keen to extend to offenders of all ages some of the ideas associated with its initiatives in the area of youth crime.

These ideas found their eventual realisation in the Criminal Justice Act 1991. It has been argued that this piece of legislation represented the epitome of the 'due process' approach to dealing with young offenders (Haines and Drakeford 1998). Provisions (applying to all ages) such as unit fines, compensation orders and the de-emphasising of previous convictions in sentencing were examples of a philosophy that sought to introduce a greater degree of equity into the system, while maintaining a focus on dealing with the offence rather than the offender. In some senses, though, this appeared to represent a break with conventional assumptions associated with the sentencing tariff. Indeed, it could be seen to reflect a concern with resolving the immediate problems associated with a specific offence at the expense of well-established principles such as deterrence or retribution.

The changing face of practice: new paradigms?

The relationship between policy and practice is never straightforward, and the notion of 'unintended consequences' is well-established in the criminal justice field (Cohen 1985). Not only are there examples of unplanned outcomes of policy initiatives, but there are also plenty of cases where policy change has no real influence on practice at all. During the 1980s, however, it seems that the dynamics of this relationship were reversed, with practice developments effectively determining new directions in policy. Among these can be identified the emergence of diversion as an influential strategy, and the refocusing of Intermediate Treatment (IT) to offer a genuine 'alternative' to custody. As we shall see, despite their rather different origins and points of impact, these practice innovations shared a number of key features, including a common commitment to 'minimum intervention', a 'systems management' perspective and a focus on resolving offences rather than classifying and dealing with offenders.

Diversion

Cautioning as a strategy for dealing with relatively minor offences by young people had been one of the options available to criminal justice agencies (primarily the police) since the 1960s, and an extension of this approach was encouraged as early as 1968 by the White Paper *Children in Trouble* (Home Office 1968). Following an initial increase in cautioning rates at this time, however, usage remained fairly static until the early 1980s, when further rises were to be observed, apparently as a result of local practice innovations (Nacro 1987).

Much of the growth in the use of cautioning and other forms of diversion can be linked with changes in practice led by areas such as Devon and Cornwall, Hampshire and Northamptonshire (Nacro 1987). The emergence of a comprehensive diversion strategy in Northamptonshire, in particular, has been acknowledged as a major development in youth justice, and one which has exercised a considerable influence on subsequent policy initiatives (Audit Commission 1996, for example).

The first manifestations of this strategy were the Juvenile Liaison Bureaux (JLBx) established in Wellingborough and Corby during 1981. A further JLB was introduced in Northampton in 1984, and the scheme was eventually extended countywide. The project arose from a collaboration between senior members of police and social services who agreed that the existing systems and processes for dealing with youth crime were both inefficient and ineffective. The agreed aims for the JLBx were:

1. To divert young people, wherever possible, away from the penal and welfare systems into informal networks of control, support and care.
2. To avoid the imposition of those forms of penalties and welfare intervention which tend to aggravate the very problem they seek to reduce.

3. To enable the agencies to respond to delinquent behaviour in ways which will reduce re-offending and enable young people to become responsible adults.
4. To encourage the normal institutions of society to respond constructively to adolescent behaviour (Hinks and Sloper 1984).

As the operational vehicle for achieving these aims, the JLBx were established as arm's-length multi-agency teams (including representatives of police, social services, education, probation and the youth service) with a responsibility for responding to all police reports of alleged offences by young people and seeking alternatives to prosecution.

The impact, in purely statistical terms, was dramatic. The Wellingborough JLB, for example, saw an immediate halving of the prosecution rate for alleged young offenders, from 40 per cent to 19 per cent (Thorpe 1984), and this was replicated throughout Northamptonshire (Stevens and Crook 1986). By 1992, the JLBx were reported to have received 2,399 reports from the police during the year, relating to 1,389 young people. Only 9 per cent of those referred were prosecuted (Bell *et al.* 1999). The reduction in the numbers processed had a consequential impact throughout the system. Thus the effective lengthening of the tariff and the substantial reduction in the number of court hearings led to a significant decline in the number of custodial sentences. At the same time, agencies were freed to devote attention to those more serious cases giving rise to real concern. Evaluations have also suggested that the Northamptonshire approach to diversion is associated with reduced rates of offending (Stevens and Crook 1986; Kemp *et al.* 2002).

Not only did the JLBx have a demonstrable impact in terms of headline figures, but they also represented a significant change in practice, in terms of the ways in which the offences of young people were addressed. In effect, there was a shift in focus from the offender and her/his characteristics to the offence and its consequences (Bell *et al.* 1999). To some extent, this reflected emerging theoretical and ideological preoccupations with behaviour and its impact rather than the attributes and circumstances of the offender; this shift can also be associated with the ensuing interest in principles of restorative justice (Johnstone 2002).

At the time, this trend could be seen as an attempt to move away from increasingly sterile arguments about the relative merits of 'welfare' or 'justice' approaches to dealing with youth crime and to develop a new paradigm (Kuhn 1970) based around the principles of diversion (Smith, R. 1987). This paved the way for more informal, less prescriptive and more pragmatic responses to offending which sought to deal with the specific issues arising from each incident on its own merits. The JLBx quickly built up a repertoire of interventions both to deal with the impact of the offence and to address the implications for the offender. These included a range of reparative options, both direct and indirect, the development of activity programmes, attempts to resolve school exclusions and short-term programmes focusing on the nature and consequences of unacceptable behaviour.

Interventions along these lines were based on an agreed set of principles:

- the reasons for the intervention must be clear, explicit and have positive consequences for the offender or injured party;
- intervention should be directed towards resolving offences informally and treating the offender as a 'normal' adolescent;
- minimum appropriate intervention should be used;
- intervention should aim to increase the amount of community involvement and create a greater tolerance and understanding of the problem of juvenile crime;
- concern should be shown for the injured party as well as the offender. (Bell *et al.* 1989).

Offences should be dealt with in ways which were both meaningful and relevant to those concerned. In one case, for example, in Corby:

> A number of young people became involved in burglaries of shops, clubs and other premises in a particular area of town. The sums involved, of damage and stolen property, put thoughts of compensation out of the question. As an alternative they were invited to contribute to a mural being painted at the under 5's centre in the neighbourhood. This work was carried out to everyone's satisfaction and under no compulsion. The offenders were not prosecuted. (Smith, R. 1987)

The JLBx, then, developed over a number of years a systematic form of 'negotiated justice' (Abel 1982) which appeared to meet the needs of the community, victims, the statutory agencies and young offenders. This approach, indeed, seemed to achieve a broad consensus of support.

Of course, even within this framework, there were times when the intervention strategy did not work to everyone's satisfaction. Sometimes, negotiated arrangements could not be agreed, some compensation settlements were not honoured by young people, and some reoffended. Despite these occasional failures, the JLBx were successful according to most conventional measures. Reoffending rates were relatively low, with some 30 per cent of those initially reported by the police offending again, and only 10 per cent offending on more than three occasions, according to an evaluation completed in 1990 (Bell *et al.* 1999). In addition, assessments of 'user satisfaction' suggested that, for the most part, offence victims did not feel exploited and were happy with the efforts by young people to make amends (Dignan 1992).

In addition to the various measures developed for operational evaluation, the JLBx (and their successor organisations) were also extensively researched (Thorpe 1984; Cheetham 1985; Reynolds 1985; Blagg *et al.* 1986; Davis *et al.* 1989; Smith, R. 1989; Dignan 1992; Hughes *et al.* 1996; Kemp *et al.* 2002). Not all of these studies produced positive findings, with particular concerns expressed over two issues: the emergence of 'administrative justice', and the interests of offence victims. It was argued, for instance, that in some cases questions of guilt or innocence might be 'fudged' to the disadvantage of young people alleged but not proven to have offended. In other words, young people might be encouraged to admit offences (and thus improve crime detection rates) in exchange for a caution or informal warning, rather than contest the matter.

At the same time, pressure for results might also lead to undue influence being exerted on victims to become involved in unhelpful reparation processes; as a result, they might experience undue stress, or perhaps find their rights to compensation compromised (Davis *et al.* 1988, 1989). While it must be acknowledged that there were potential risks of this kind, most of the studies cited found only limited grounds for criticism. Dignan (1992), for example, found that victims' interests were generally respected and were not subordinated to those of offenders, and the general reduction in formal proceedings suggested that there was little evidence of 'net-widening' in the sense of young people being criminalised unnecessarily (Blagg *et al.* 1985).

Intensive Intermediate Treatment

The other area of youth justice to experience major change in the course of the 1980s was the form of intervention which had been known as Intermediate Treatment (IT) since the 1960s, but whose aims and scope had been poorly defined up to that point. The earlier preventive orientation of the programme was largely superseded by the changes instigated by the Department of Health and Social Security in 1983 (DHSS 1983; Smith, D. 1999). The government of the time took the view that IT should become tougher and more demanding, and that it would thereby meet the requirements of the Supervised Activity Order introduced by the Criminal Justice Act 1982.

This policy initiative coincided neatly with a growing belief among practitioners that welfare-based preventive interventions could be counter-productive, drawing young people into the remit of the criminal justice system without justification (Thorpe *et al.* 1980). According to this argument, the proper focus for youth justice work should be offending behaviour rather than welfare needs. Formal intervention on other grounds would, in effect, be to criminalise young people inappropriately, and may lead to disproportionate and unfair treatment. Practitioners also believed that a more explicit rationale for IT based on the sentencing tariff would also enhance its credibility and assist in achieving the goal of establishing it as a genuine 'alternative to custody'.

As Hudson has observed, the corollary of this was that intermediate programmes would have to offer a sufficiently demanding regime to demonstrate a degree of equivalence with locking children up: 'to be seen by sentencers as suitable…community corrections have to incorporate appropriate degrees of control, and offer the promise of effectiveness in stopping the delinquent behaviour' (Hudson 1987: 153). Programmes that claimed to act as alternatives to a detention centre or youth custody therefore would be likely to include requirements for regular (possibly daily) attendance, regular monitoring ('tracking'), behaviour management activities and possibly also community service of some kind. Associated with this, too, was a commitment to 'breach' and returning to court those participants who failed to comply with requirements. These interventions thus stood in stark contrast to the kind of preventive Intermediate Treatment which had operated previously, incorporating befriending programmes (or mentoring), activities and adventure holidays, a model of practice which has also been replicated more recently in the form of Youth Inclusion Projects and Summer Splash. The £15 million investment by the Department of Health and Social Security in 1983 enabled 110 'intensive' projects to be established through partnerships with voluntary organisations, of which 95 survived beyond the initial funding period (Smith, D. 1999).

Critics have argued that the strategy of promoting IT strictly as an alternative to custody was flawed on a number of grounds. Pitts (1988), for example, suggested that supporters of this approach were effectively endorsing an increasingly authoritarian tendency within the justice system, while Hudson (1987) argued that intensive projects of this nature had 'blurred the boundaries' with custody, and that the experiences of the two had become increasingly similar. In her view, the strategy of trying to reduce the use of custody by mimicking some of its characteristics could not be expected to succeed, purely because custodial places would still remain available, and would therefore be used.

Haines and Drakeford (1998) have subsequently argued that the 'new orthodoxy' that characterised this form of IT, and other interventions with young offenders during the 1980s, tended to focus very narrowly on their offending behaviour, to the exclusion of other legitimate concerns, such as their 'social, family or material circumstances'. According to them, youth justice of this era was characterised by:

- offence confrontation work – reinforcing the unacceptability of offending;
- developing a victim perspective – educating young people into the impact of their offending on victims;
- the offending curriculum – teaching young people how to avoid situations where offending can occur (Haines and Drakeford 1998: 66).

David Smith (1999), however, has suggested that the 'justice model' espoused by those promoting 'alternatives to custody' could also be seen as a form of nihilism on the part of practitioners, who were pessimistic about the potential for any kind of preventive or developmental intervention. As he further observes in this context, the absence of any kind of principled objection to interventions based solely on principles of just deserts also tends to rule out the possibility for practitioners (or others) to advance objections to increasingly repressive regimes on the basis of alternative anti-oppressive values deriving from welfare perspectives.

Nevertheless, the actual outcomes of those initiatives developed in the 1980s lent weight to the pragmatic observation that they could be judged a 'success' (Goldson 1997). Individual programmes were claimed to have achieved positive outcomes in terms of reducing the use of custody and reoffending rates in parallel (Children's Society 1988). Ironically, perhaps, it seems that these successes might be attributable to forms of practice which ran counter to widely held assumptions about the futility of purposeful interventions:

...youth justice workers in the 1980s developed methods of face-to-face work with young people in trouble which were broadly in line with what subsequent research and analysis have suggested is likely to be most effective in reducing offending. This is in a sense paradoxical, since many of these practitioners were strongly influenced by the view that had prevailed since the 1970s that 'nothing worked'. (Smith, D. 1999: 153).

Youth justice practitioners thus appear to have been responsible for a range of successful practices and outcomes almost despite themselves! Haines and Drakeford (1998) support these observations, suggesting that when programmes are devised and delivered in a way that is genuinely 'community-based' they can be effective in reducing offending. It should be noted, however, that claims about the levels of success achieved in the 1980s, at least in respect of reoffending, have to be tempered by the findings of systematic evaluations which suggested very limited improvements in this respect among young people undertaking Intermediate Treatment programmes (Bottoms *et al.* 1990; Bottoms 1995).

Patterns of change: offending and outcomes in the 1980s

The changes in policy and practice within the youth justice system in the 1980s appear to represent a fairly significant break with previous experience. However, it is also important to see this in the context of the general pattern of offending, disposals and outcomes in the course of the decade.

A number of observers have suggested that this was a very distinctive period in terms of the identifiable trends in youth justice (Smith, R. 1995; Goldson 1997; Haines and Drakeford 1998), and it is argued that these developments are reflected in the figures available from official sources – although, equally, these sources should not be treated as the whole story. According to The Children's Society (1993), the 1980s saw unprecedented and parallel declines in the number of known offenders, the use of prosecutions and the custody rate.

For example, the number of young people coming to the attention of the police declined substantially overall, with the exception of 14–17-year-old girls or young women (see Table 1.1).

While part of the reason for the overall fall in the number of known offenders may have been attributable to demographic changes, the rate of juvenile offenders per head of population could also be seen to be in decline, with the period 1980–90 showing a 16 per cent reduction in this figure. In addition, the proportion of all detected offences attributed to juveniles fell from 32 per cent in 1980 to 20 per cent in 1991 (Children's Society 1993).

However, some counter trends were also noted. Some categories of offence such as car-related thefts – commonly associated with young people – were on the increase. Significant geographical variations could also be observed, reflecting an apparent 'north–south divide', with higher rates of offending associated with less affluent northern police areas (Children's Society 1993).

Table 1.1 Number of young people cautioned or found guilty of indictable offences per 100,000 population by age and sex

	1977	1986	1991
Age/gender			
Male 10–13	3,468	2,257	1,817
Male 14–17	7,456	7,076	6,378
Female 10–13	1,029	761	535
Female 14–17	1,553	1,706	1,973

Source: Criminal Statistics England and Wales 1991 (Home Office 1992).

The risks involved in drawing strong conclusions from known (official) offending rates are well-known, and can be illustrated by the observation that a very small proportion of crime comes to the notice of the police, and an even smaller proportion is detected and leads to the identification and processing of offenders. In evidence to the Home Affairs Committee (1993) inquiry into juvenile crime, the Association of Chief Police Officers argued that, far from being in decline, there had actually been an increase in the number of offences committed by young people over the course of the 1980s. This was partly masked, in the association's view, by the increased use of informal disposals and diversionary measures, which meant that offences were being 'cleared up', but offenders were not being formally processed as a result. In other words, the very success of the diversionary strategies of youth justice practitioners might have led to a reduction in the official figure of 'known offenders', which did not reflect the reality of criminal activity but simply a change in agency practices.

In the specific case of girls or young women aged 14–17, where the trend seems to have been in the opposite direction, explanations offered for this anomaly have been fairly tentative, but they might reflect an increasing 'awareness' of 'criminal girls' by the justice system (Worrall 1999). Of course, these figures may also have reflected either changing patterns of behaviour among young women or cultural changes in the way in which they are perceived (Walklate 2004).

Despite the lack of certainty about the meaning of the figures relating to young people's participation in crime, the trends they suggest were mirrored in a more lenient approach to the treatment of young offenders during the 1980s. According to the Children's Society (1993), cautioning rates increased, in accordance with government policy, at precisely the same time as the overall numbers coming to the attention of the justice system were in decline.

Indeed, in the space of just over a decade, the ratio between different outcomes for young offenders had changed dramatically. Whereas in 1977 prosecutions were brought and young people found guilty in 48 per cent of cases dealt with formally by the police, this proportion had declined to just 21 per cent by 1991. While prosecution was clearly the most likely option for older young offenders (those aged 14–16 inclusive prior to the changes introduced by the Criminal Justice Act 1991) at the start of this time-span, this was clearly not the case by the early 1990s. For girls and young women, despite the changes in the pattern of recorded offending, the likelihood of being prosecuted was even more remote (see Table 1.2).

While it is possible at this point to distinguish clearly between male and female young offenders, it is only relatively recently that any serious attempt has been made to identify patterns of crime, victimisation and outcomes according to ethnicity. Although racism has been identified as a determining factor in a number of studies, even in the context of practices around cautioning and informal disposals (Landau and Nathan 1983, for example), official figures shed little light on this issue until the latter part of the 1990s when section 95 of the Criminal Justice Act 1991 imposed a requirement on criminal justice agencies to take race and ethnicity into account when reporting on their activities.

Despite this omission, the general picture seems to be that progressively fewer young people were being brought before the courts, both proportionally and in absolute terms over this period of time. In addition, at the point of sentencing, courts were observed to be making an increasing number of supervision orders, in line with the policy of promoting intensive community programmes (Children's Society 1993). According to Haines and Drakeford (1998), the use of community-based supervision increased from 15 per cent to 20 per cent of all court disposals between 1980 and 1990. This was not achieved uniformly, however, with the proportion of custodial sentences initially remaining fairly stable, but the net effect over the whole period appears to have been a displacement of custody by a range of community alternatives. The implication here (with resonance in the current era of Intensive Supervision and Surveillance Programmes) is that 'net-widening' can be avoided where an effective systems management strategy is applied.

Table 1.2 Changes in the numbers of young people cautioned or found guilty of indictable offences 1977–91 (000s)

	1977	1986	1991
Cautioned			
Males 10–13	39.4	26.3	21.0
Males 14–16	31.3	43.6	41.0
Females 10–13	14.0	8.7	6.3
Females 14–17	10.5	14.9	14.8
Total	95.2	93.5	83.1
Found guilty			
Males 10–13	19.2	6.1	2.3
Males 14–17	59.8	37.7	17.2
Females 10–13	2.4	0.5	0.2
Females 14–17	7.6	3.7	2.2
Total	89.0	48.0	21.9

Source: Criminal Statistics England and Wales 1991 (Home Office 1992).

Changing patterns in the detection and processing of young offenders therefore had a cumulative effect in reducing the numbers being committed to custody, with quite dramatic consequences (see Table 1.3).

At the apex of the youth justice process, then, the use of custody declined by around 82 per cent over this ten-year period. On the basis of this evidence alone, it might be concluded that the reputedly hard-line Thatcher government was, indeed, 'soft on crime' (Smith, R. 1995).

At each key decision point, changes in policy and practice appear to have combined to reshape the treatment of young people and their offending behaviour in a dramatic and perhaps unexpected manner: (1) fewer young people were the subject of formal interventions by the police; (2) a much greater proportion of those processed were being cautioned; (3) substantially fewer in number were being prosecuted; (4) relatively more community-based court disposals were being administered; (5) and so, fewer young people, numerically and proportionally, were being incarcerated. The cumulative effect of these changes was thus progressively intensified. Significantly, the consequences were not just limited to minor offences or less experienced offenders:

> ...if more and more minor and younger offenders are being diverted from formal prosecution then it is increasingly the older and more serious offenders who appear in court...If there were no changes to courts' sentencing behaviour, then an increase in diversion would be likely to lead to a proportionate increase in more severe sentences. But this did not happen in the 1980s...juvenile justice practitioners were not just successful in reducing the custody rate, they were even more successful in reducing this rate for a relatively older and more serious cohort of offenders. (Haines and Drakeford 1998: 60)

Table 1.3 Numbers and percentages of young people aged 14–16 processed by the justice system and the use of custody 1981–91 (000s)

	Cautioned/found guilty (A)	Sentenced to custody (B)	(B) as a percentage of (A)
Year			
1981	113.7	7.7	6.8%
1986	99.8	4.4	4.4%
1991	75.2	1.4	1.8%

Source: Criminal Statistics England and Wales 1991 (Home Office 1992).

Interestingly, this comment attributes this outcome to the efforts of practitioners, and their ability to manage the system in such a way as to influence crucial decisions at all points in the justice process.

Despite the appearance of dramatic achievements, we should be careful about the distorting effects of choosing particular timeframes for our analysis. As David Smith (1999) observes, for example, the custody rate in 1996 was lower than that of a decade previously, indicating that the patterns and outcomes attributed to the strategies adopted during the 1980s may be something of an oversimplification. To characterise the 1980s simply as the 'decade of diversion' would be to obscure other trends and developments relevant to the changing shape of youth justice, such as the persistence of regional variations and institutional racism, and the impact of wider social and political developments. Despite this cautionary note, the available evidence suggests a clear shift towards less intrusive, more informal, more community-based and more inclusive responses to the offending of young people.

The meaning of 'success'

The important task here for those concerned with achieving and sustaining a fair and effective youth justice system is to unravel the possible reasons for the achievements of the 1980s and thus to draw out possible lessons for policy, management and practice in another era.

Perhaps the proper place to start is the clarification of what we mean by 'success'. As already noted, the headline figures suggest a parallel reduction in offending rates, formal sanctions and the use of custody during the 1980s. For those concerned with pursuing reductionist or abolitionist agendas, these figures represent positive outcomes purely in their own terms. However, evidence of success according to wider criteria is more equivocal.

The most extensive and sophisticated evaluations of practice innovations, epitomised by the Cambridge Intermediate Treatment study (Bottoms 1985), found evidence only of a very small influence on patterns of re-offending for some types of intensive programme (see also Audit Commission 1996). These findings are supported by other more localised studies, which appear to show that carefully targeted programmes might be expected to reduce offending rates at the individual level (Children's Society 1993). This chimes with the rather more intuitive conclusions of many practitioners who feel that their own interventions have led to positive outcomes in specific circumstances where they believe that they have been able to 'make a difference' (Smith, R. 2002).

Despite these indications, the overall impact of community-based interventions on offending rates appears somewhat limited (Haines and Drakeford 1998). In addition, other indicators of 'success' are even more open to question. During the 1980s and at least up until the latter half of the 1990s, crime rates continued to increase, at least according to victim surveys (Mirrlees-Black *et al.* 1998), in contrast to the official figures which suggested a reduction in youth crime, as we observed earlier. This contradiction may at least partly be accounted for by the continuing paucity of police clear-up rates (Audit Commission 1996). It did not seem that diversionary strategies had freed up capacity in order to solve more challenging cases!

Equally, public perceptions of the level of risk and danger presented by young people remained high (Home Affairs Committee 1993). Pearson (1983) argues that fear of the young is almost endemic to society, suggesting that an over-dramatised sense of threat is always close to the surface in public and media consciousness. As others have observed, this is of particular concern because of the cumulative effect of juxtaposing negative stereotypes, for instance in the case of African-Caribbean young men (Haines and Drakeford 1998; Goldson and Chigwada-Bailey 1999). The successes of the 1980s were not accompanied by a parallel reduction in the over-representation of this group at all points in the youth justice process, including, most significantly, the custodial population (Gordon 1983; Pitts 1988), despite evidence that they are no more likely to be involved in crime than the general population (Graham and Bowling 1995).

So, in seeking to account for the apparent successes of the 1980s we must be a little circumspect. The significance of those achievements which have been documented may, for instance, have appeared more dramatic to those working within the system than to others with a more objective view. The emphasis on one key outcome (the reduction in the use of custody) may have obscured the need to consider other interests whose priorities might be rather different (Haines and Drakeford 1998). It is the limited nature of this consensus about what represents progress which may help us to understand the subsequent fragility of what was gained during this particular decade.

Accounting for 'success'

Despite the provisional nature of the achievements documented here, it may nonetheless be helpful to set out in a little more detail some of the reasons for the dramatic changes identified, not least because this may offer some positive clues for the development of similar strategies in future. It is probably best to think in terms of a multiplicity of factors combining to create a favourable climate for the liberalisation of youth justice from the early 1980s onwards. Thus contextual factors such as the political ethos, enabling factors such as policy shifts and delivery factors such as practitioner commitment should all be seen as contributing towards the momentum for change that developed over time.

Political influences

As already noted, the period from 1980 to 1990 coincided with the heyday of the Thatcher government, driven by an ideological commitment to right-wing free-market principles (Gamble 1988). Despite (or perhaps because of?) this, a number of the ideas associated with this perspective proved favourable to a liberalising agenda in youth justice.

To begin with, the government's commitment to cutting state spending pointed towards a need to cut down on expensive interventions, including custody. As Rutherford (1992) has observed, the declining use of secure accommodation in the local authority sector from 1981 onwards is one example of this budget-driven agenda.

In addition to cost-cutting aspirations, other political factors could also be seen to have an impact. Whether it was coincidental or not, most of the Home Secretaries of this era were relatively liberal by inclination, despite their obligatory declamatory performances at the annual party conference. They and their colleagues did not seem uncomfortable with considered arguments in favour of reductions in the use of punitive measures, so long as they could cloak these in hard-line rhetoric (Home Office 1988).

John Patten, Minister of State at the Home Office, for example, stated: 'I think there is now a fairly wide consensus about what the response to juvenile offending should be…formal intervention should be kept to the minimum consistent with the circumstances and seriousness of each case' (Patten 1988). There is also a sense in which these concerns with saving money and minimal intervention fitted with another central tenet of Thatcherism which was the concept of 'laissez-faire' (Fox Harding 1997), whereby the state should resist intervening in civil society unless absolutely necessary. This principle, in turn, is also consistent with the phenomenon of 'bifurcation', identified previously as a significant characteristic of the justice system (Bottoms 1977). Thus state intervention in what were identified as relatively minor cases should be avoided, while coercive and intrusive measures should be reserved for those responsible for the most serious infringements, where an authoritarian response would carry more weight, both substantively and symbolically.

A more cynical interpretation of the 'rolling back' of the state (Gamble 1988) in this context might be that the Conservative government (representing largely middle-class and less urban areas) was relatively uninterested in those forms of crime and anti-social behaviour which seemed particularly prevalent and damaging in more working-class and highly populated parts of the country (predominantly represented by Labour politicians). This was certainly a view expressed subsequently by the Labour opposition (Straw and Michael 1996), and is also consistent with the arguments of the school of thought known as 'left realism', which sought to refocus interest away from the offender in isolation to a concern with the impact of crime on already disadvantaged neighbourhoods. It was argued that: 'responsibility for "trivial" or "secondary" crime is hived off from the police, and, in effect, thrown back upon those sectors of society who have the greatest need for responsive and effective policing' (Kinsey et al. 1986).

Policy change

Unusually, youth justice policy during the 1980s showed a high degree of consistency. Thus the principles of minimum intervention, proportionality and punitive sanctions where necessary which informed the White Paper *Young Offenders* (Home Office 1980) at the start of the decade were to be found in much the same combination in its counterpart *Crime, Justice and Protecting the Public* (Home Office 1990b) ten years later.

These principles could be seen to flow from the dominant political themes of the time, and were translated into specific measures. For instance, the Criminal Justice Act 1982 set clear limits to the use of custody, to be reserved for extreme circumstances, while also introducing more intensive forms of supervision in the community, maintaining the emphasis on punishment and control. In this sense, 'bifurcation' became a much more explicit feature of youth justice strategy. Pitts (1988) has drawn attention to the irony by which the intensive Intermediate Treatment initiative launched by the government in 1983 (DHSS 1983) was planned to provide exactly the same number of community places (4,500) as the initial Home Office projections for the increase in the use of custody following implementation of the 1982 Act. In fact, the increase in demand for the use of custody did not materialise. Indeed, this may have been, in part, a consequence of the more explicit demarcation drawn between minor and less experienced offenders, on one hand, and those whose offending careers were more entrenched on the other. As a result, an important part of the rationale for the 'short, sharp, shock' regime offered by detention centres was lost. This was compounded by a critical evaluation of their performance and impact (Thornton *et al.* 1984), and their use declined rapidly, leading to their abolition following the Criminal Justice Act 1988.

Equally, other policy developments such as the formal endorsement of cautioning in 1985 (Home Office 1985) were consistent with the emphasis on minimum intervention and the targeting of resources at the 'heavy end' of youth offending. The Home Office advised that prosecution should not be the norm for young offenders, but should be used only where the 'public interest' required it (Home Office 1984). Indeed, the consistency between the various policy initiatives of this period led to suggestions from some that this represented 'the end of the argument' about youth justice policy (Smith, R. 1989).

Practitioner-led initiatives

The 'permissions' offered by the policy developments of the early to mid-1980s were eagerly seized upon by practitioners in a number of areas, and at different points in the justice process (see, for example, Smith, R. 1989; Rutherford 1992; Children's Society 1993; Haines and Drakeford 1998; Smith, D. 1999; Goldson 2000a). While this favourable political climate is an important factor, the achievements of the 1980s overall owe a lot to the energy and commitment of a large band of practitioners and managers who exploited the opportunities available to them. This is an important point, because it provides a safeguard against the mood of paralysis and pessimism (Eadie and Canton 2002) which might otherwise infuse the field of youth justice when the going gets tough, as it does periodically. Examples of successful local initiatives include the establishment of a 'custody-free zone' in Hampshire (Rutherford 1992), the Juvenile Liaison Bureaux in Northamptonshire which saw the county ascend rapidly from the bottom to the top of the 'diversion' league table (Stevens and

Crook 1986), and the parallel reductions in reoffending and the use of custody achieved by voluntary sector IT projects (Children's Society 1988).

While these initiatives tended to develop independently, they came to share a number of characteristics over time. They tended to operate fairly strict 'gate-keeping' criteria in order to avoid 'net-widening' and target interventions only at those young people whose behaviour warranted them. This principle was clearly based on previous research, which indicated that ill-defined and overlapping objectives would suck into the system young people whose behaviour alone did not necessitate formal action (Morris *et al.* 1980; Thorpe *et al.* 1980). In addition, it was at around this time that youth justice began to emerge as a discrete area of practice, with specialised knowledge and a committed workforce, and with a degree of distance established from conventional probation or social work structures (Haines and Drakeford 1998). Thus a distinctive location and operational identity emerged for those involved in delivering youth justice, even though much practice depended on inter-agency or cross-sector partnerships. Indeed, it has been suggested that this 'blurring' of agency roles was a deliberate part of the emerging strategy (Smith, R. 1999). As a result of these developments, intervention became increasingly offence-focused, which, according to some, meant that important welfare issues were excluded from consideration (Haines and Drakeford 1998).

Nevertheless, the fact that youth justice initiatives shared such distinctive characteristics also contributed to another important feature of their success, namely their capacity for 'system management'. The establishment of integrated specialist teams with a clearly-defined area of responsibility meant that it was possible to develop a measure of control over the youth justice process by creating a unified knowledge base, and creating a single locus for key decisions about disposals, interventions and resource allocation. This development, in turn, made it easier to deliver a coherent system-wide strategy directed towards the reduction of punitive or excessive interventions. Those areas of the country with a coherent approach to systems management of this kind appear to have been able to deliver very dramatic and significant results, leading to the subsequent observation that what was, in fact, emerging was a form of 'justice by geography' (Children's Society 1988).

Messages from the past?

While it is clear that present-day youth justice practice is influenced by rather different political and ideological agendas, it is still of some value to consider what lessons might be drawn from earlier experience (Pitts 2002).

The evidence of radical change and positive achievements associated with the 1980s remains persuasive, although there were some shortcomings in evidence, too. For example, the predominant strategy was simply too narrowly based in the view of some analysts: 'The 1980s juvenile justice new orthodoxy was essentially based on an anti-custody philosophy...In other words, it was the avoidance of custody for young people that justified and gave meaning to the actions of juvenile justice workers' (Haines and Drakeford 1984: 74). According to this line of argument, this one objective, combined with an increasingly sophisticated approach to systems management, rendered youth justice practice rather simplistic and sterile. As David Smith also suggests, the belief that intervention of any kind would be at best ineffective and at worst actually destructive may have led to a rather tokenistic view of direct work with young people, whatever its apparent objectives: 'Their belief that nothing worked meant that some workers came to believe that it did not matter what they did, as long as they did little of it' (Smith, D. 1999: 153). The consequent problem appears to have been that those who took this stance had very little to offer by way of principled arguments against new demands imposed with changes in the overall direction of youth justice policy. It became very difficult to defend forms of intervention for which practitioners themselves had little enthusiasm, and in which they did not really put much faith.

Against this argument it must also be noted that the 'anti-custody orthodoxy' was not all-encompassing. Within the wide range of initiatives developed during the 1980s there was a variety of new models of practice which did, indeed, take a much more positive view of their own efficacy and value. For example, the diversion projects developed in Northamptonshire were not restricted simply to reducing the number of young people prosecuted. Their stated objectives also incorporated the prevention of further offending and promoting reparation (Dignan 1992). These objectives were reflected in practice, and a range of what would now be seen as 'restorative' interventions (Johnstone 2002) was put in place.

Examples of innovative practice could also be observed among the Intermediate Treatment projects developed as alternatives to custody (Children's Society 1988), which offered a range of 'active and participatory' programmes and helped young people to 'develop their problem-solving skills', for example (Smith, D. 1999). Thus, even those who criticise the apparent nihilism of the diversion movement recognise that it would be too simplistic to dismiss the achievements of the time on these grounds alone (Haines and Drakeford 1998). There is no doubt, though, that some youth justice initiatives did come to be driven primarily by the aim of modifying the existing tariff and *reducing* custody (Stevens and Crook 1986), as opposed to the rather more positive aim of developing new forms and principles of intervention and thereby *replacing* punitive measures with sustainable alternatives (Smith, R. 1987). The principal weakness of a pure reductionist strategy is that it offers no defence against those who argue simply that 'prison works' (Howard 1995), because it offers no clear set of alternative principles for intervening to deal with the problems associated with offending behaviour. On the other hand, it should be noted that the 1980s did witness a substantial amount of innovative activity on the part of practitioners, which may still carry important implications. For example, new approaches to promoting inclusion for young offenders were developed, offending behaviour programmes were devised, reparation became a routine aspect of diversionary programmes and efforts were made to engage communities in understanding and responding to the problems of youth crime.

Importantly, as we shall see, it is the emerging lessons about developing new models of intervention which were inclusive and restorative, and which were not dictated by narrow concerns with justice, due process, the tariff and the 'numbers game', which, in reality, offer a way forward for practitioners and their agencies in the circumstances of today.

2. Where did it all go wrong?

Continuity or change?

As already observed, the choice of starting points and transition dates reflects implicit assumptions about the shape of history and the key events which punctuate it. In this respect, the insertion of a dividing line between the 1980s and the 1990s is conscious and deliberate. It does seem to me that there is strong evidence of a quite dramatic shift in the shape and nature of youth justice in England and Wales, which can be dated to the early 1990s. This view is shared by a number of other commentators (Goldson 1997; Haines and Drakeford 1998; Pitts 1999), although it is fair also to point out that others think more in terms of continuities (Hudson 1996; Smith, D. 1999; Muncie 2000; Pickford 2000).

In taking the former position, the present account also adopts the view that the changes evident from this point on were not positive, and in fact represented a substantial rolling back of previous gains. Some important achievements were undone and crucial ideas lost. From this perspective, this can be identified as a period of 'unlearning'. While it is clear that many of the drivers of these changes can be located outside the justice system itself, the consequences can be identified quite clearly in terms of changes in practice and outcomes, as we shall see. However, the aim of this book is not to provide an account simply of poor practice, since this would be to miss the point that many of the influences and circumstances which lead to negative outcomes do not lie within the direct control of practitioners. Indeed, even in adverse conditions, there remain some important examples of positive interventions which should be acknowledged as such. Overall, though, a picture will emerge of a youth justice system in retreat, where historical susceptibilities to self-righteous populism (Hall *et al.* 1978; Pearson 1983) have proven yet again to be the Achilles heel of competent and committed youth justice practice.

Gathering clouds: politicians and populism

As we have seen, the 1980s culminated in a series of policy changes which seemed to provide an effective and durable underpinning for contemporary achievements in youth justice practice based on principles of minimum intervention and offence resolution. Home Office Circular 59/1990 (Home Office 1990a) once again endorsed the use of measures short of prosecution to deal with offences by children and young people, even in the face of some resistance from police and magistrates. At the same time, the White Paper *Crime, Justice and Protecting the Public* (Home Office 1990b) endorsed the further development of alternatives to custody, extending some of the principles applying to young offenders to adults as well.

The White Paper made explicit (and politically expedient) commitments to the 'punishment' of more offenders in the community, and it was dismissive of the reformative value of custody. Instead, it continued to pursue the 'bifurcation' strategy (see previous chapter) of establishing clear demarcations between serious offences (violence, domestic burglary and sexual offences), and those other lesser offences which could be dealt with effectively by way of community sentences. These principles were incorporated in the Criminal Justice Act 1991, which set out a new framework for the administration of disposals: 'Arguably, the CJA 1991 represented the first time that a British government clearly enshrined in a piece of criminal justice legislation a single coherent sentencing philosophy and policy' (Haines and Drakeford 1998: 77).

This approach was described as one of 'just deserts', with outcomes being proportionate to the offence(s) committed, with no account being taken of either prior criminality or personal circumstances (aggravating or mitigating factors). In one sense, this appeared to be no more than an extension of the offence-based perspective that had informed much practice in the preceding decade.

This assimilation of sentencing principles for young and adult offenders also facilitated some other changes introduced at this point, such as the rationalisation of the Youth Court (for those under the age of 18, defined as children under the newly ratified UN Convention on the Rights of the Child) and the extension of some 'adult' sentences (such as Community Service Orders and Combination Orders) to those aged 16 and over.

The emergence of a general consensus about the aims and delivery of youth justice also led to other changes of emphasis. The guidance issued with the 1991 Act promoted a greater degree of inter-agency cooperation to enable the new procedures to work effectively and coherently. For some, indeed, the new legislation represented the high point of the emerging orthodoxy 'around the desert-based approach to sentencing' (Haines and Drakeford 1998: 84). Specific examples of this trend could be found, for example, in the replacement of welfare-oriented Social Inquiry Reports with more offence-focused Pre-Sentence Reports to assist courts in their sentencing decisions. Similarly, there was identified an emphasis on court disposals such as bind overs to emphasise 'parental discipline and control' at the expense of social factors (Macmillan 1998). Indeed, it has been suggested in some quarters that it was this very erosion of concern with social and environmental factors that laid the foundations for the increasingly punitive turn of the 1990s and beyond (Haines and Drakeford 1998). This is ironic in light of earlier arguments which had suggested that it was an inappropriate emphasis on welfare concerns which had led to an increase in controlling and institutional responses to young people's offending behaviour in the 1970s (Thorpe *et al.* 1980).

In any event, the 1991 Act had barely become law before it ran into a barrage of intense criticism. The fragile penal consensus was broken. A number of factors appear to have contributed to this eventuality, including the increasing public and political sensitivity to the issue of youth crime around this time. While it is a little too simplistic to attribute every twitch in the penal apparatus to a political reaction to public concern and media campaigns, there is no doubt that these are perennial influences on policy and practice in the youth justice arena. Specifically, the early part of the decade saw a number of events combine to generate a climate of instability and retrenchment. Even as the achievements of the 1980s appeared to have been cemented in place, trouble was brewing.

First, a change in key political personnel occurred, with the replacement of Margaret Thatcher as Prime Minister by John Major, and the appointment of a new Home Secretary, David Waddington, acknowledged as more right-wing than his predecessors. It seemed, indeed, that he was not fully supportive of the new legislation, even during its passage through Parliament, emphasising its punitive elements and contradicting the previously stated aim of reducing the prison population (Macmillan 1998).

Second, the early 1990s was a period when rioting became a matter of public concern, with outbreaks in Cardiff, Oxford and North Shields, for example. Although rioting was by no means a newly discovered phenomenon, there were distinctive aspects to this particular set of occurrences. For instance, they appeared to take place in predominantly white areas, unlike previous disturbances during the 1980s, in areas with a much higher black population such as Handsworth, Brixton or Toxteth. Explanations for the 1990s outbreaks could perhaps more easily attribute 'criminal' rather than 'political' motivations to them.

Third, it appears that there was coincidentally a 'sophisticated campaign' initiated by influential figures in the police to focus on 'persistent offenders' – the small minority reported to be responsible for the great bulk of serious criminal behaviour. This campaign appears to have shared overlapping concerns with those generated by the riots of the time, for instance over 'joy-riding', and as a result, perhaps, a number of individual young offenders gained national notoriety, including a 10-year-old from Hartlepool (Brown 1998), 'Rat Boy' from Tyneside and a number of other similarly lurid characterisations.

The police provided more reasoned support for their arguments to the Home Affairs Select Committee that, in spite of falling numbers of young offenders, offending *rates* were actually on the increase – 54 per cent up between 1980 and 1990 (Children's Society 1993). In addition, the police reported concerns that a large number of offences were being committed by young people while on bail (up to 40 per cent of all offences in Northumbria, for example).

Fourth, the courts rapidly came to resent the limits placed on their sentencing powers by the 1991 Act (Hudson 1996). In particular, the requirement to focus almost solely on the current offence limited their ability to escalate sentences for persistent offenders (the very category that was the subject of the police campaign noted above). The requirement to base their decisions primarily on the 'seriousness' of the offence was seen as unacceptable political interference in the independence of the judiciary (Goldson 1997), and it seemed somewhat counter-intuitive, given prevailing views about the need to respond more severely to repeated acts of defiance, whether for reasons of deterrence or 'exacting the price' of crime.

The fifth reason advanced by many for the dramatic shift of direction in youth justice was the killing of the toddler James Bulger by two boys aged 10 and 11. However, while this traumatic event definitely added impetus to the punitive turn, and influenced specific measures such as the abolition of *doli incapax*,[1] it was not, as is sometimes assumed, the originating factor, coming as it did early in 1993.

Finally, and also of continuing relevance, was the emergence of a political consensus at last between the two leading political parties about being 'tough on crime'. This can perhaps be linked to the involvement of ambitious political 'heavyweights' on both sides (Kenneth Clarke as Home Secretary and Tony Blair as Shadow Home Secretary), each anxious to make a reputation for himself and to establish popular support around the issue for their own party.

In 1993, shortly after James Bulger's death, the Prime Minister, John Major, said that: 'Society needs to condemn a little more and understand a little less.' This slogan has come to symbolise the conventional tone of political pronouncements in relation to youth crime, it may be thought. Writing in the *Daily Mail* at around the same time, Kenneth Clarke argued that: 'The courts should have the power to send really persistent, nasty little juveniles away to somewhere where they will be looked after better and where they will be educated' (*Daily Mail* 22 February 1993). Later in the year, in a bid to gain the political high ground, his opposite number Tony Blair observed: 'No one but a fool would excuse the commission of a crime on the basis of the offender's upbringing; and no one but a bigot would ignore the impact of that upbringing on the individual's behaviour' (*Daily Express* 31 August 1993). Despite the acknowledgement of the influence of external factors and the aspirations for better outcomes for young offenders, these statements were clearly designed, first and foremost, to attract public support for a tough and essentially punitive stance on youth crime. Little attempt was made to add any real depth to the discussion about social causes and effective interventions. Such posturing has, indeed, tended to become the norm in political debates about the problem of youth crime.

One immediate consequence of the rush to denounce the liberalisation of the justice system was the Aggravated Vehicle-Taking Act 1992, which was the government's response to the apparent epidemic of 'joy-riding' associated with the riots referred to previously and a reported increase in car crime (Home Affairs Committee 1993; Children's Society 1993). This, indeed, was one of the early examples of the kind of 'knee-jerk' single-issue legislation which has become an increasingly familiar characteristic of the British legislature. Much of this has resulted in precipitate, poorly targeted and sometimes simply unworkable solutions – the Child Support Act 1991 being perhaps the classic example, although the more recent spate of anti-social behaviour legislation shares many of the same features.

The government also announced plans to tighten up on persistent young offenders on a wider scale. Within months of abolishing custody for 14-year-olds under the 1991 Act, Home Secretary Kenneth Clarke was announcing plans to create 200 new places in Secure Training Centres, which could be utilised for children as young as 12:

> The Government are determined to continue to strengthen the powers of the courts to deal with persistent offenders. We must also take measures to tackle the problem on a broader front...The secure training orders will be different from anything that has ever been provided before. (House of Commons Debates, cols 139–140 2 March 1993)

Interestingly, such claims that new measures are unique and groundbreaking have also become a feature of recent policy developments, regardless of historical precedents. (The proposed Secure Training Centres had much in common with Detention Centres, abolished only five years previously, as we have seen.)

Backtracking: laying down the law

The government's U-turn took more concrete shape with the passage of the Criminal Justice Act 1993, which explicitly reinstated the power for the court to take account of offenders' previous criminal records by simply inserting two words into section 1(2) of the 1991 Act, so that rather than only 'one' other offence 'one *or more*' offences 'associated' with the current one could be considered as part of the sentencing process. Other aspects of the 1993 legislation also revealed the government's intention to create a more punitive framework for dealing with crime, including the provision (section 66(6)) that offences committed while on bail should be treated as an 'aggravating factor' in determining sentences. This represented another dimension of the reversal of the earlier consensus that interventions and disposals should be based almost exclusively on dealing with the current offence; the idea of the 'tariff' was reasserting itself.

Just in case there should be any doubt about where all this was heading, the incoming Home Secretary, Michael Howard, speaking to the 1993 Conservative Party conference, proclaimed that 'prison works' (Rutherford 1996). He advanced two justifications for this: that prison protects the public from 'murderers, muggers and rapists', and that it also acts as a deterrent. He did not make any claims for the reformative, rehabilitative or correctional powers of custody. Not only did this stance signal a new legislative onslaught, but it also demonstrated that political decisions about crime and justice were unlikely to be unduly influenced by the evidence available, for example in relation to the efficacy of custody (Rutherford 1996). The following year saw two further attempts to reverse the achievements of the 1980s, at either end of the youth justice process.

At the lower end of the scale, the tone was set by revised advice on cautioning. Home Office Circular 18/94, pushed through against professional advice, effectively put a stop to repeat cautioning, except in very tightly defined circumstances. This measure also sought to ensure that the nature of the offence would also be taken into account, and that 'serious' offences would automatically result in prosecution. Effective multi-agency strategies, such as that developed in Northamptonshire, were perceived to be under threat: 'Although previous Home Office circulars on cautioning…had positively encouraged the police to consult with multi-agency partners…this circular went a long way in retracting this policy commitment' (Bell *et al.* 1999: 99).

The net (widening!) effect of this policy shift was always likely to be an increase in the numbers of young people being formally processed and taken to court. As always, it seems that whereas liberalising initiatives need copious evidence to demonstrate that they 'work' (Burnett and Roberts 2004), moves in a punitive direction can be determined on the basis of hearsay or whim, as seems to have been the case here. Macmillan (1998), for example, suggests that this particular step was prompted by a BBC television programme, in which a young offender spoke of a caution being meaningless, and in which police and magistrates speculated about a link between increased use of cautioning and higher crime rates.

At the same time, but entirely consistently, the Criminal Justice and Public Order Act 1994 did, as promised, expand the range of custodial options. Courts were to be given the power to make Secure Training Orders on 12–14-year-olds for up to two years, of which half would be served in the newly constructed Secure Training Centres. Establishing these institutions as part of the prison estate rather than under children's legislation appeared to put the government in breach of the Beijing Rules on the administration of juvenile justice (United Nations 1985), to which the UK is a signatory. This was no deterrent to Mr Howard; neither was the projected cost of the new centres, estimated at £75 million in capital expenditure and £20 million annual running costs (Children's Society 1993).

The 1994 Act also extended the scope of section 53 of the Children and Young Persons Act 1933,[2] and gave powers to the courts to pass longer sentences on 10–13 year olds for a wider range of offences than previously. Maximum sentences for 15–17-year-olds were doubled, from 12 to 24 months, and it was made easier for courts to override the presumption in favour of bail established by the Bail Act 1976.

Not satisfied with this substantial shift towards a youth justice regime dominated by a punitive spirit, the Home Secretary proceeded to announce yet further plans to confront criminal behaviour. Despite the absence of any evidence to support their efficacy, he became a convert to the American model of 'boot camps', and announced their introduction to the UK in February 1995.

The same year a further document emerged from the Home Office, promising tougher forms of 'punishment in the community' (Home Office 1995). This was entirely consistent with the government view that punishment should be the motif for all measures to deal with young offenders, and it included plans for the expansion of forms of 'community restraint' such as electronic tagging and curfews.

For youth justice practitioners, this kind of shift has tended to pose difficulties over the years. This is largely because of the risks associated with efforts to negotiate an acceptable space for positive interventions. These are reflected in the uncertain nature of the 'trade-off' between applying more intrusive conditions and requirements on the one hand, and achieving 'credibility' as genuine alternatives to custody on the other. Put another way, at what point does an acceptable compromise become an abdication of principle? This kind of dilemma has confronted those seeking to develop progressive practice in the shadow of the justice system for a very long time, and at least since 1982 and the introduction of Supervised Activity Orders (Pitts 1988). The very nature of compromise renders it difficult to argue, in principle, against the implementation of increasingly stringent conditions in a hostile climate. Despite this, the underlying weakness of this position remains, namely that 'alternatives to custody' clearly cannot be equated to forms of incarceration, with the result that these could still be portrayed as a 'soft option' as they were at this time by the Home Secretary (Muncie 1999).

The strategy of the Major administration was defined by the legislative changes of 1994, and represented a move to increase both the flow and the intensity of the processing of young people by the formal justice system. More young people would be drawn into the process, on the presupposition that pre-court diversion had failed to prevent offending, and at the same time courts were to be enabled and encouraged to use custody more freely, not just as a last resort, but because it 'works'. Even in the last throes of this Conservative government, this approach was extended by the Crime (Sentences) Act 1997, which included provisions to extend curfews yet further, and to 'name and shame' convicted juvenile offenders for the first time.

As noted, a number of distinct factors can be seen to have contributed to this 'punitive turn' (Goldson 2005), but the cumulative effect was to create a new 'feel' to the youth justice system as a whole, typified by one commentator as 'revenge justice' (Macmillan 1998).

Diamonds in the mud: practice in a hostile climate

For those involved in delivering youth justice services, the speed and intensity of the policy reversals of the early to mid-1990s felt like being hit by a juggernaut, with a complete negation of many of the principles on which their practice was based. The consensus between different stakeholders in youth justice had evaporated, and there appeared to be little room for manoeuvre in the face of policies which enthusiastically embraced the principle of punishment, irrespective of cost, efficacy, international obligations or moral considerations.

Not only was the political climate increasingly hostile to inclusive and welfare-oriented practice, but there was also a sense in which organisational and structural changes were impacting on services at the same time. This can partly be attributed to contextual factors which ensured that attention and, indeed, resources were directed elsewhere. It may be that the achievements of the 1980s contributed to an assumption that the battle for progressive youth justice was won, and for hard-pressed local agencies money and personnel could be redeployed, for instance into child protection, or towards the implementation of community care (in 1993). In addition, the substantial investment of money and energy represented by the 1983 IT initiative had gradually tapered off, and the 100 projects established under that programme were either wound up or incorporated into mainstream services (Smith, D. 1999). There is perhaps something also in the argument that the nature of the task had changed, from one of developing and proving the value of new forms of intervention, to one of 'managing' these interventions as part of established practice. Some (for example, Muncie 1999) have argued that this shift is also consistent with wider trends towards 'managerialism' in the delivery of public services, which can be seen as part of the Conservative legacy, stemming back as far as 1979. Indeed, Pratt (1989) has argued that even the debates between 'welfare' and 'justice' positions were themselves merely a smokescreen for the emergence of a 'corporatist' agenda, which was primarily concerned with efficient, effective (and cheap) service arrangements.

This emerging influence was associated with new forms of public management, which emphasised common strategic and organisational characteristics rather than substantive differences of purpose or service context, so offering one rationale for the parallel development of multi-agency partnerships in youth justice as in other areas:

> By the 1990s such corporate, multi-agency strategies were to become subsumed within a much broader process of public sector managerialization. This...has generally involved the redefinition of political, economic and social issues as problems to be managed rather than necessarily resolved. (Muncie 1999: 288)

A further development, which resulted in more explicit expectations of those responsible for direct practice, was the initial publication of National Standards for the Supervision of Offenders by the Home Office (Home Office 1992). This set in motion a conveyor-belt which periodically delivers a new or revised set of standards almost as a matter of course (Youth Justice Board 2000, 2004a). The consequences have been highly significant in terms of the imposition of centralised constraints and procedures on practitioners, albeit in the name of consistency, fairness and good practice.

A major issue to emerge from these developments is the sense in which youth justice appears to have been depoliticised. The challenge becomes one of finding the best and most effective way of delivering an agreed package of assessments, service management, record-keeping and intervention, which is based on universal principles of best practice. The scope for alternative perspectives and professional discretion becomes extremely limited in this context: 'Social issues were depoliticised. Policy choices were transformed into a series of management decisions. Evaluations of public sector performance came to be dominated by notions of productivity, task remits and quantifiable outcomes' (Muncie 1999: 288). Accounts of practice began to portray this kind of preoccupation, being more likely to highlight improvements in efficiency and 'system management' than the development of new models of intervention or the promotion of social justice through service developments. Thus the Children's Society (1993) reported an inter-agency initiative in South Wales that had claimed, as success indicators, a 'speeding up' of the judicial process and a reduction of offending while on bail. Another initiative mentioned in the same report listed as its principal achievement the adoption of a comprehensive approach to managing the youth justice system, with no mention of substantive outcomes beyond this. Although these achievements may have some merit, they can only be seen as meaningful targets within a broader strategy to promote crime reduction or social inclusion.

In a context of policy reversal and creeping managerialism (Clarke *et al.* 2000), practice innovations took on a rather different aspect to those of the previous decade. They were no longer inspired by a vision of minimum intervention, informal justice, reconciliation and community cohesion; rather, they took on a tactical and defensive character at best. Nevertheless, there were initiatives put in place which sought to modify the worst consequences of the punitive agenda. These interventions were largely confined to the voluntary sector, with organisations such as the Howard League and The Children's Society taking the lead (see, for example, Ashton and Grindrod 1999; Moore and Smith 2001; Moore and Peters 2003). Both were explicitly committed to ending the use of custody for children, and sought to promote and preserve their rights in the youth justice context. In this sense, they represented a spirit of continuity with the 'anti-custody', justice-oriented movement of the 1980s identified by Haines and Drakeford (1998). Unlike providers located within statutory agencies, they did not experience the same constraints of rationalisation and prescription, and they began to develop a role as defenders of the key elements of a 'liberal' approach to youth justice. Thus they sought to find ways of protecting and promoting the interests of children and young people at the most acute pressure points, specifically targeting the arbitrary and discriminatory use of custody. This, it was suggested, helped to compensate for one of the shortcomings of the existing multi-agency strategies:

> The current orthodoxy…is inclined towards holistic and multi-agency approaches…but there has been a tendency for those who are working with children who are at risk of entering the penal system to regard their involvement as being at an end if a child is remanded or sentenced into prison custody. (Ashton and Grindrod 1999: 170)

The Troubleshooter Project and beyond: drawing the line

Ironically, the Troubleshooter Project was inspired by the realisation that the number of 15-year-olds remanded to custody in England and Wales was at an all time low, around 25 at the time the project was planned (Ashton and Grindrod 1999), and this offered an opportunity to achieve the symbolically important target of reducing this figure to zero. This objective was supported by one of the provisions of the Criminal Justice Act 1991, section 60, which, when implemented, would have ended the use of prison remands for 15- and 16-year-olds, replacing these with remands to local authority secure facilities where necessary (Moore and Peters 2003).

Concern for the well being of young people in custody had also been heightened by the occurrence of a number of prison suicides among young people at around this time (Children's Society 1993). The Troubleshooter scheme, then, was conceived at the high-water mark of the movement to replace custody for young offenders with alternative welfare-oriented disposals. The numbers of those affected had fallen to such an extent that this now seemed a feasible objective.

Despite these high hopes, even as the project itself got under way in the autumn of 1993, the tide had already turned. As we will see again in relation to sharp changes of direction in sentencing practice, it seems that custodial figures are particularly susceptible to shifts in the public mood and policy agendas. By June 1991, the number of 15-year-olds remanded to custody had risen to 102 as the impact of riots and concern about persistent offenders took effect; by June 1993, the comparable figure was 126, but, even after the launch of the Troubleshooter Project, the escalation continued, with 278 15-year-olds being subject to custodial remands by June 1997. Thus it seems that far from being 'one last push' to secure the abolition of remands to custody for this age group, the new initiative found itself struggling to stem a rapid increase in their use.

The project itself was established with five key objectives: to 'rescue 15-year-olds from prison custody', to provide them with support and advocacy while in custody, to assist youth justice agencies, to monitor outcomes and to promote good practice (Ashton and Grindrod 1999). The first phase of the scheme was implemented at Feltham Young Offender Institution and Remand Centre. Project staff were able to meet young people as soon as possible after reception, both pre- and post-sentence, in order primarily to establish grounds for seeking an alternative non-custodial disposal. Intervening directly in this way enabled the scheme to identify shortcomings in existing processes, as well as providing positive support for the negotiation of alternative placements. From its inception, the Troubleshooter Project was able to secure the release of significant numbers of young people, largely by remedying process failings. Some young people were found to have been remanded to custody illegally, some were let down by agencies which did not offer alternatives despite their responsibilities for young people's welfare, and in some cases custodial remands were made because there were no alternatives. Associated with its role in securing non-custodial outcomes, the project was also able to draw attention to a related problem, that of institutional discrimination on grounds of ethnicity. Black and Asian young people were found to be substantially over-represented in both remand and sentenced custodial populations, and by intervening at this point, the project was also able to take a proactive role in identifying and challenging this (Ashton and Grindrod 1999: 177).

Building on the initial work of the Troubleshooter Project, The Children's Society established the National Remand Rescue Initiative, from January 1997. This sought to extend the support and advocacy function in relation to new admissions to custody to a wider range of institutions, including local authority secure establishments, and to include 16-year-olds within its remit. The scheme also attracted Youth Justice Board funding from December 1999 (one condition being that the project's name was amended, so that it became the National Remand *Review* Initiative – rather less politically challenging, perhaps), and was further extended to include provision for 17-year-olds.

The standard model of practice for the extended scheme was to arrange to meet and assess young people received on a secure remand, and to identify whether or not alternative disposals could be pursued, whether on welfare or judicial grounds. In this respect, the project attempted to make use of the 'vulnerability' provisions introduced by the Crime and Disorder Act 1998, intended to protect 15- and 16-year-olds identified as being at risk if placed in prison custody. The initial assessment could thus lead to a number of strategies to obtain alternative placements: enabling young people to challenge the legal basis for a remand to custody, liaising with other agencies to gain support for alternative placements or taking on a direct advocacy role to remind agencies of their legal and moral obligations. Intervention thus took place on three levels – correcting system failures, addressing young people's needs and promoting their rights. In its first three years, Remand rescue dealt with 1,666 cases of 15- and 16-year-olds on remand, and of these 32 per cent were released as a result of this intervention (Moore and Smith 2001). By the time the initiative ended in July 2002, over 1,200 children and young people had been 'removed' from secure remand, and the number of 15–17-year-olds on remand in prison establishments declined from 803 in January 1997 to 506 in July 2002 (Moore and Peters 2003).

Bail support: working tactically

Another example of the kind of strategic intervention that was developed in the 1990s was 'bail support'. As we have already observed, the emergence of fears about 'persistent' young offenders and associated changes in government policy created a climate in which courts became increasingly reluctant to grant bail, irrespective of the presumption in its favour created by the Bail Act 1976. Prompted by evidence of a rapid increase in the use of custodial remands (Nacro/ACOP 1995), programmes were put in place to increase courts' confidence in the alternatives. Local schemes were developed such as the Manchester Youth Bail Support Project which began in 1996, and was extended to the entire Greater Manchester area in 1999. This project was the product of a wide-ranging inter-agency and inter-sectoral partnership, including probation, social services and The Children's Society. The aim was to deliver 'individually tailored programmes to provide support and supervision to young people, addressing in particular the grounds for potential refusal of bail' (Moore and Smith 2001: 67). In common with the Troubleshooter Project, this initiative was established to develop *individualised* and *less restrictive* interventions focusing on key decision points, where alternative options may not be fully explored otherwise.

The Manchester programme was targeted at young people who would otherwise be refused bail; it was not the intention to increase levels of surveillance and control over those who would, and should, have been granted bail as a matter of course. The overarching aim of the scheme was to reduce the numbers of young people remanded to any form of secure setting, including both custody and local authority secure accommodation. In order to achieve this, however, it was accepted that there would be a need to provide a comprehensive bail support package acceptable to the courts. The project thus aimed to provide the courts with an assessment of risk, need and suitability for the support programme on the basis of which specific, tailored interventions would be made available. These might include: measures to provide some certainty that the young person would return to court at the end of the bail period; family support; counselling; educational opportunities; and offence reduction work. As a further step to provide reassurance to the courts, they would be provided with progress reports and evidence of successful completion. In addition to this, the project also provided for a formal breach procedure, to be enforced where necessary. As we can see from this, this particular initiative felt constrained to operate defensively, in order to secure cooperation and support from the courts.

Following its inception, the scheme was subject to an intensive evaluation during 1998. Over this period 136 referrals were made to the programme and 102 young people were accepted. Of these, only 51 were granted bail on condition that they attend the programme, with 39 of the remainder being remanded to custody and three to local authority accommodation (Moore and Smith 2001). From these figures, it seems that the scheme may well have targeted its interventions fairly effectively at those most at risk of being remanded to secure settings. This is of particular importance, given that the intrusive nature of the programme itself, and the breach arrangements, clearly presented a risk of 'net widening', that is drawing in and subjecting relatively minor offenders to more coercive treatment than indicated by their offences. Of concern also, even at this stage, was the evidence that black and Asian young people were relatively less likely to be both recommended for and accepted onto the scheme.

A total of 37 young people completed the programme during the evaluation period, of whom 8 (22 per cent) either breached the attendance requirements or reoffended and were taken into custody. The remaining 78 per cent all completed the programme without being locked up. For those where a final outcome was recorded, 63 per cent of those completing the programme satisfactorily did not receive a custodial sentence. The project could thus claim a degree of success in securing young people's compliance and avoiding custodial outcomes. Similar schemes were developed elsewhere in the 1990s, and likewise, their emphasis was on containment, compliance, personal development and the prevention of further offences (Audit Commission 1996). The South East Kent Bail Support Scheme, for example, was 'offered as a condition of bail to all those under 18 years who risk having bail refused. It aims to satisfy the courts that remand to custody or local authority accommodation is unnecessary, provided the young person complies with the rules and requirements of the scheme, and to offer appropriate control within the community' (Audit Commission 1996: 31).

Although these programmes were clearly targeted and demonstrated a degree of success in diverting individual young people from custody, the problems for this kind of defensive and focused initiative arise from their limited ability to influence ideas, policy and wider systems. That is to say, while they may be able to demonstrate significant levels of 'success' according to their own internal criteria, they may actually be achieving very little within a broader context of increasing control and intrusion. Indeed, the net effect, at a time of 'system shift' towards more coercive paradigms, may be that a range of such interventions become progressively applied to minor and less experienced young offenders, thus resulting in the very 'net widening' (Scraton 2003) that their targeted approach seeks to avoid (Nacro Cymru/ Youth Justice Board 2001).

Supervision in the community: close control?

The increasingly explicit punitive agenda of government in the 1990s also influenced the response of those who sought to develop effective alternatives to custody post sentence, usually resulting in stronger and more restrictive supervised activities imposed as additional requirements of Supervision Orders. The Audit Commission (1996) provides an example of one such programme, with young people required to attend for 30 or 60 days. Attendance was reported as being strictly monitored with two failures resulting in an automatic return to court for breach proceedings. The programme's content comprised five 'compulsory modules', covering: offending behaviour; social skills; numeracy and literacy; job search/education; and substance abuse and HIV. Other optional components were also offered, including the ubiquitous 'constructive use of leisure time' and information technology.

In providing a strict and explicit correctional framework, this project could be said to be meeting the concern of the government of the time to ensure that the controlling aspects of community supervision programmes were enhanced. By the middle of the decade, there were 'over 150 diversionary community programmes operating in England and Wales designed to address offending behaviour through victim awareness, anger management, drug awareness and positive leisure schemes' (Muncie 1999: 283).

Ironically, however, the example cited by the Audit Commission did not appear to be fulfilling the aim of providing a direct alternative to custody.

Only 38 (25 per cent) of 153 young people considered suitable for this particular scheme were accepted onto it. Of the remainder, only 34 (22 per cent) received a custodial sentence, while the rest were made subject to a range of less punitive disposals, including supervision or probation orders without conditions attached (29 per cent), and in some cases fines or even conditional discharges. Not only was this project relatively unsuccessful at persuading the courts to make use of it, but it also seemed to be some way from offering a pure alternative to custody given the diversity of outcomes recorded for potential participants. Indeed, for those not at risk of custody, but who subsequently breached the conditions of the programme itself, the result might have been an increased risk of being locked up. We cannot draw too heavily on one example (even one cited, rather surprisingly, as an illustration of 'good practice'), but it does at least illustrate quite sharply the point that a strategy of intensifying 'punishment in the community' (Hudson 1996) is hard to justify in any sense if it cannot demonstrate that it is genuinely acting as an alternative to custody.

'Defensive' practice: messages from the 1990s

The general pattern of changing practice in the 1990s suggests some emerging themes. First, there are some encouraging messages: despite disparaging comments from some quarters (Haines and Drakeford 1998), the 'anti-custody' philosophy of much youth justice practice does appear to have survived the political onslaught of the Conservative government. Second, a concern with promoting children's rights appears to have become stronger if anything, perhaps encouraged by the increasing prominence of international standards as represented by the UN Convention on the Rights of the Child (United Nations 1989) and the Beijing Rules (United Nations 1985). Third, it is possible to identify a growing recognition of discrimination within the criminal justice sphere and a commitment to address this at the level of practice, reflected in the stated objectives of schemes such as Right Track in Bristol, which aimed to tackle both individual injustices and structural inequalities in the administration of youth justice.

There is also a sense in which the programme content of the projects identified retained a concern to promote the personal and social development of young people in trouble. This aspirational element of practice is important, not least because it coincides with young people's own ambitions to achieve a good education, to obtain rewarding employment or to attain other personal goals (Graham and Bowling 1995). Thus, the aim of structured interventions to offer these opportunities appears to have been relevant to young people in a very practical way.

Despite these positive observations, there are also clearly some harder lessons to be learnt from the experiences of this period. Notably, the acceptance of the language and some of the requirements of the 'punishment' agenda made it difficult to offer principled opposition to increasingly intrusive and controlling forms of community discipline. In a sense, this is to pose the question in terms of 'how much punishment should we administer to young offenders?' as opposed to whether or not a punitive approach is appropriate at all. Thus alternative discourses and intervention strategies, such as enabling young people to 'grow out of crime' (Rutherford 1992), became progressively more difficult to sustain. In addition, the loss of flexibility resulting from explicit and mandatory programme components led to greater difficulty in adjusting interventions to meet the changing circumstances or welfare needs of young people. Indeed, the 'welfare' discourse itself became increasingly muted in this historical phase.

There was a continuing sense, too, of interventions being shaped and limited by the challenge of operating on someone else's turf, and according to rules imposed from elsewhere. For example, despite its success in individual cases, the Troubleshooter/Remand Rescue/Remand Review scheme could only function within a framework which treated custody as the norm. In this respect, advancing 'special case' arguments for some young people to secure their release also implies a tacit acceptance that where no such arguments apply the use of custody is legitimate and justified. In other words, the very existence of special projects of this kind may help to validate the use of incarceration in general.

Similar consequences also derive from the increasing flexibility of 'alternative to custody' programmes and the greater emphasis on breach procedures, where failures to comply, even those falling short of reoffending, may expose young people to more punitive responses.

A rising tide: 'intended' consequences

How, then, did the changes in policy and practice identified impact on the delivery and outcomes of youth justice over the course of the 1990s? And, to what extent is it possible to identify consistency between policy and practice in this decade, given that during the 1980s at least, political rhetoric and experiences 'on the ground' were somewhat at odds?

As far as it is possible to rely on official sources, it appears that the diversionary trends of earlier years were sustained until about 1993, when the pattern of disposals changed abruptly. At this point, indeed, it seems that a policy 'U-turn' (Moore and Peters 2003: 2) had an almost immediate impact on the behaviour of the judicial apparatus. This was not, it would seem, related in any clear-cut fashion to changing patterns of offending, especially given the very small proportion of offences that were identified as coming to the attention of statutory agencies (19 per cent), or the even smaller proportion (3 per cent) leading to formal action of any kind (Audit Commission 1996).

General trends in the incidence of crime may help to provide a context for our analysis of changing practices in youth justice, although this relationship is, indeed, problematic for a number of reasons. Estimates of the level of offending from both official records and surveys of the general population suggest that this reached a high point in the early 1990s (Home Office 2001b). Recorded crimes, for example, rose from 4.5 million in 1990 to 5.6 million in

1992, although by 1998/99 they had declined again to 4.5 million annually, at which point new counting rules took effect. The revised figures after this date suggest that the crime rate had levelled out over the next two years. However, it is extremely difficult to extrapolate from these headline figures any meaningful estimates of the proportion of offences carried out by children or young people, although the Audit Commission (1996) estimated that, based on the relative proportion of known offenders under the age of 18, this figure can be put at around a quarter. Subsequent estimates have suggested a rather higher figure than this, at just over a third (Budd and Sharp 2005). Of course, we know too that the profile of offences committed by young people is also likely to be different from that of adult offenders, given differences in culture, lifestyle and opportunity (Budd *et al.* 2005).

At the same time as the rate of offending appeared to stabilise, detection rates were falling, while police also continued to make use of informal warnings in some cases (Home Office 1996). The net effect was a reduction in the proportion of young offenders who were the subject of formal action (cautions or prosecutions) over the course of this ten-year period (Home Office 2001b). This is not the same, of course, as suggesting that the number of offenders decreased in reality, or that we can infer anything about wider patterns of behaviour (Muncie 2004). It does mean, however, that a pattern emerged of progressively fewer young people coming to be processed formally by the machinery of the justice system.

For those who were cautioned (replaced in June 2000 by Reprimands/ Final Warnings) or prosecuted, there were significant changes in the pattern of disposals. In common with other trends, cautioning as a proportion of outcomes increased to its highest level in the early 1990s for all age groups and for both sexes (Home Office 2001b: 105), but then declined steadily to the year 2000 (see Table 2.1). Cautioning rates, too, fell for all categories of indictable offences between 1990 and 2000, except criminal damage and robbery.

With the rate at which children and young people were proceeded against falling, and the cautioning rate moving in the same direction, the net effect was that the number of cautions administered was dropping quite sharply over this period.

Table 2.1 Cautioning rates (offenders cautioned as a percentage of all those cautioned or found guilty) 1990–2000

Year	Males			Females		
	10–11	12–14	15–17	10–11	12–14	15–17
1990	95	84	53	99	93	73
1992	96	86	59	99	96	81
1994	95	81	56	100	94	77
1996	94	77	51	99	91	72
1998	91	72	48	97	88	67
2000	86	68	43	95	86	63

Source: Criminal Statistics England and Wales 2000 (Home Office 2001b).

On the other hand, the *number* of those aged 10–17 being taken to court for indictable offences was on the increase. After an initial decline in this figure from 66,000 in 1990 to 60,000 in 1993, there was a steady rise to 81,000 by 2000. While the overall number of those being dealt with by way of formal proceedings did not change substantially, the balance had clearly shifted very significantly, towards a much greater relative emphasis on prosecutions rather than pre-court disposals.

This change was paralleled by a much greater use of the most punitive options by the courts, with an increase in the rate of custodial sentencing over the period 1990–2000, from 10 per cent to 15 per cent of all disposals in respect of 15–17-year-old males, and (a threefold increase) from 2 per cent to 7 per cent for 15–17-year-old females. In numerical terms, these trends are even more striking, with an increase from 3,600 to 5,200 for young men, and 100 to 400 for young women in this age group.

For 12–14-year-olds, custodial options had only been available at the start of the decade under section 53 of the Children and Young Persons Act 1933 in respect of the most serious of offences. With the introduction of Secure Training Orders from 1997, this became a much more widely used form of disposal. Importantly, this also illustrates the lesson that, whatever safeguards are in place, if a punitive disposal is available, it is likely to be used, sometimes with enthusiasm. By 1994, for instance, the percentage of sentenced 12–14-year-old boys sent to custody had decreased to an insignificant amount (but not zero) but by 2000 this had increased again to 6 per cent, of which 4 per cent was represented by Secure Training Orders (repackaged as Detention and Training Orders under the Crime and Disorder Act 1998) (see Table 2.2). Females in this age group were also now receiving custodial sentences where they had not previously (2 per cent in 2000).

In short, the 1990s, and particularly the latter part of the decade, saw a rapid reversal of the 'double gain' identified in the previous decade (Haines and Drakeford 1998). Previously, diversionary strategies had reduced the numbers of young people coming to court, and at the same time greater availability

Table 2.2 Custody rates (percentage of children and young people receiving custodial sentences as a proportion of all those sentenced) 1990–2000

Year	Males			Females		
	10–11	12–14	15–17	10–11	12–14	15–17
1990	0	2	10	0	0	2
1992	0	3	11	0	0	2
1994	0	0	14	0	0	4
1996	0	1	16	0	1	4
1998	0	2	15	0	0	6
2000	1	6	15	0	2	7

Source: Criminal Statistics England and Wales 2000 (Home Office 2001b).

and use of alternative to custody schemes had reduced the proportionate use of custody, achieving a kind of multiplier effect across the system as a whole. However, these achievements were thrown precisely into reverse by the end of the 1990s: fewer young people were being diverted from court, and as a greater proportion were being dealt with by the courts, so the higher rate of custodial sentencing again had a compound effect, accelerating the trends towards a more punitive regime.

At the same time, there were also big increases in the use of community sentences (Supervision Orders, for example), but these were at the expense of other lower-tariff disposals, such as fines and discharges (Home Office 2001b). Such trends looked certain to be further exacerbated with the effective removal of the Conditional Discharge as an option for anyone who had previously received a Final Warning by the Crime and Disorder Act 1998.

The cumulative evidence from this brief review of trends in the exercise of police discretion and courts' sentencing behaviour suggests that the youth justice system did take an increasingly punitive turn from the early 1990s onwards, and that this shift was not modified in the short term by the change of government in 1997. Alongside this, another important message becomes apparent for those engaged in managing and practising within the youth justice system. This is, that it is of considerable importance to retain an awareness of how the 'system' as a whole operates, and how its various elements interact. Good practice in one context can easily be negated elsewhere, either as a result of 'unintended consequences' (Thorpe *et al.* 1980) or because of deeper changes which effectively transform the whole working environment – so that, for example, legitimate and sound diversionary practices are undertaken with increasingly inexperienced offenders responsible for more and more minor offences.

Explaining the U-turn

In order to try to sketch out what is possible and achievable in youth justice in the current era, it is important to seek to make sense of the contrasting experiences of the 1980s and 1990s, albeit that some authors have taken the view that the continuities between the two are more significant than any evidence of significant change.

Hudson (1996) has argued that the outcomes observed can best be seen as a reflection of broader and deeper historical trends reflecting ideological transitions, and the emergence of 'actuarial regimes', geared to assessing and managing the risk represented by potential offenders. The debate in these terms is simply one of developing the most effective mechanisms of surveillance and control. This is no more than an instance of the perennial contest between 'penalising and normalising responses to crime' (see also Garland 2001, on 'inclusionary' and 'exclusionary' criminologies). Hudson argues that the 'technologies' of intervention advocated by each perspective are similar, but that the 'actuarial' solution (Smith, R., 2006) is more widely accepted (and acceptable): 'Who could argue against policies and practices designed to help people avoid suffering from criminal victimization' (Hudson 1996: 154).

Thus, she argues, once the youth justice arena had been 'depoliticised' as a result of the emergence of the 'back to justice' consensus of the 1980s, the way was opened for the development of a segregating and repressive form of justice based purely on calculating and then acting to reduce the possibility of future offending. Inequalities of money and power and offenders' personal and social circumstances are irrelevant to this kind of strategy. Offender characteristics are reinserted into the calculative process only as a means of determining future risk and calibrating sentencing decisions. The successes of the 1980s can thus be seen as essentially illusory and counter-productive, serving only to prefigure the increasingly repressive practices that followed.

Haines and Drakeford (1998) similarly argue that a continuing commitment to an 'anti-custody' philosophy remained in evidence, but that this was increasingly out of step with the punitive mood of the time. Muncie (1999), too, has suggested that some strands of thought and practice have remained fairly constant, reflected in the growing influence of 'corporatist' (Pratt 1989) and authoritarian strands in the treatment of young offenders: 'One notable feature of English youth justice in the 1980s and 1990s has been a consistent copying of punitive measures from America' (Muncie 1999: 298).

Others have seen continuities across the decades associated with the development and refinement of a penal strategy based on 'bifurcation' (Pickford 2000). The change over this period, by this account, was a consequence of the improvement in techniques for making a clear distinction between minor offences committed by relatively inexperienced young offenders, and other criminal acts perpetrated by those who represent serious and/or persistent threats to the community. The enhanced capacity to make this judgement clearly and effectively provides for a more sophisticated approach, which is then reflected in the nature and severity of the disposals administered. In other words, it may be that over this period youth justice interventions simply became better 'targeted'.

One example of the implications of this kind of approach arises from the conclusion reached by the Audit Commission (1996; see also Home Office 2001a) that cautioning could be shown to be progressively less effective than prosecution (in the sense of reducing reoffending), which lent support to the government's subsequent discouragement of repeat cautioning, cemented in place by the Crime and Disorder Act 1998. Despite the fact that the evidence in support of this conclusion is limited and untested (see Audit Commission 1996), it has become an accepted truth.[3] The narrow concern with reoffending and the certainty applied to this kind of predictive measure both seem to indicate the kind of 'actuarial' shift suggested by Hudson (1996).

On the other hand, some commentators have suggested that there are significant discontinuities between the 1980s and 1990s which contain important lessons for the future development of youth justice. Goldson (1997 1999), for example, takes the view that the events of the early 1990s represent a dramatic about-face in both ideology and practice in dealing with youth crime. Thus the abandonment of the central elements of the Criminal Justice

Act 1991 and the commitment to redevelop custodial regimes for 12–14 year olds seemed to represent 'a death blow to the non-interventionist delinquency management strategies of the 1980s' (Pitts 2001b: 17). The government's backsliding is attributed to a combination of factors, which together created the conditions for a 'moral panic', with the result that a 'reactionary U-turn was launched which rapidly dismantled the successful practice orientation of the previous decade and set a harsh new tone in relation to state response to children in trouble' (Goldson 1997: 79). The evidence for this, in Goldson's view, is the renewed commitment to locking up children in direct defiance of the UN Convention on the Rights of the Child, which the government itself adopted only in 1991. Indeed, the UK government has been repeatedly criticised for failing to honour its obligations in relation to 'juvenile justice' by the UN Committee responsible for overseeing the Convention (Harvey 2002).

To some extent, the judgement as to whether this was a period of rapid reversal or underlying continuity is a matter of interpretation, as Cohen (1985) has reminded us. As he put it, histories of the criminal justice system can readily be characterised according to one of three paradigms: 'uneven progress', 'we blew it' or 'it's all a con'. Indeed, it is likely that a rounded analysis will draw on all three (see Chapter 7). There is no doubt that the 1990s did witness significant changes in the political climate, with the two leading parties seeking to outbid each other in appearing 'tougher' on youth crime, and that the promulgators of earlier youth justice policies had, indeed, 'blown it'. At the same time, and it would seem at least partly as a consequence, there was an observable change in the way in which young offenders were processed. While David Smith (1999) warns us to take care not to overstate arguments based simply on the evidence of outcomes, the coincidence of political agitation and more punitive practice cannot be entirely accidental, and does form an important backdrop for thinking about future directions in the way we deal with young people in trouble.

At the same time, the evidence of continuities is also worthy of note, because it reminds us of other, more deep-rooted challenges which may persist. For instance, creeping 'corporatism' (Pratt 1989), the continuing emphasis on offence-focused interventions and the persistence of the sentencing tariff (on which the 1991 Act foundered) suggest that the organisation and realisation of youth justice practice may also have a surprisingly consistent feel about them, even in the light of significant contextual changes. We should not, however, allow this last observation to lull us into the seductively reassuring assumption that external events or changing policies have no material bearing on the capacity of agencies and practitioners to sustain consistent and effective interventions, or that there is no need to be aware of and respond to such developments.

3. That same old song? New Labour and youth justice

'Tough on crime, tough on the causes of crime …'

Although this quotation has become something of a cliché, it is nonetheless (and perhaps because of this), a valid starting point for a consideration of the New Labour project in the area of youth justice for a number of reasons. Firstly, it is indicative of a wider trend towards 'soundbite' politics, whereby persistent, substantial and complex social problems can apparently be diagnosed and solved in a matter of seconds. But, in addition, the author of the quotation in 1993, Tony Blair, was writing as Shadow Home Secretary; as he moved on to become Prime Minister, he carried with him a substantial interest in, and influence over, policy in relation to young people and their behaviour. Further, it was the elision of personal responsibility and social inclusion implied by this one utterance which appeared to encapsulate a distinctive and coherent 'New Labour' position on youth crime. Historically, the party had been seen as electorally vulnerable in this area, and this formed the centrepiece of a politically driven campaign to challenge and overturn traditional Tory dominance in this area of policy. Events since that point, especially since New Labour came to power in 1997, must be seen in light of this attempt to establish hegemony over this high-profile and sensitive issue.

Central to this political strategy was the linking of criminal behaviour with its antecedents and underlying causes, rooted in the dynamics of 'social exclusion', apparently. As time passes, however, there is less and less evidence of an explicit attempt to sustain this connection by government ministers (see, for example, 'Crackdown on yob culture', BBC News 28 November 2000). In 1993, though, writing in the *New Statesman*, Mr Blair made an explicit connection between individuals' personal responsibility for their offences and the social circumstances which could be seen as contributory factors.

Importantly for an analysis of the youth justice system, this link between the context of offending and the criminal act itself should lead us to consider specific measures to deal with crime only as one aspect of a wider strategy to deal with criminogenic influences, such as poverty, family problems, educational disadvantage, neighbourhood decline and other aspects of social exclusion. From this perspective, it might be suggested that criticisms of the youth justice system under New Labour in isolation are misleading in that they do not take account of the 'joined up' nature of the policy agenda (Clark 2002). On the other hand, as we shall see, it may be that, rather than coherence between different aspects of policy, what is in fact in evidence are contradiction and conflict.

Indeed, the extent to which the various elements of New Labour's social policy programme are complementary or contradictory is an important question. The aim of this chapter is to provide an account both of the broader policy canvas, particularly in relation to the aim of reducing crime by tackling social exclusion (Social Exclusion Unit 1998, 2002), and of the developing picture in relation to the specific area of youth justice, so that the issue of consistency or conflict can be considered more fully.

Social inclusion and crime reduction

In many ways, the approach adopted by the incoming Labour government in 1997 reflected a well-established consensus which linked the incidence of youth offending with a number of predisposing factors, including various forms of social disadvantage, including 'inadequate parenting', 'lack of training and employment', 'unstable living conditions' and 'drug and alcohol abuse' (Audit Commission 1996). The new government established the Social Exclusion Unit (SEU) immediately in order to develop an integrated strategy to address these issues, both in their own right and as contributing factors to other social problems. The SEU's initial findings suggested that there are clear links between a range of individual and collective difficulties which produce a compound effect, generating a pattern of 'social exclusion' concentrated within certain communities and in specific geographical areas:

> The poorest neighbourhoods have tended to become rundown, more prone to crime, and more cut off from the labour market. The national picture conceals pockets of intense deprivation where the problems of unemployment are acute and hopelessly tangled up with poor health, housing and education. (Social Exclusion Unit 1998: para. 1)

Given the interrelationship between these aspects of disadvantage, as well as their significance in their own right, the benefits of developing coherent strategies for addressing them appeared self-evident. It was argued that this would be a break with tradition:

> Above all, a joined-up problem has never been addressed in a joined-up way. Problems have fallen through the cracks in Whitehall Departments or central and local government. And at neighbourhood level, there has been no one in charge of pulling together all the things that need to go right at the same time. (Social Exclusion Unit 1998: para. 7)

Further support for this kind of integrated approach was offered by earlier evidence which suggested that tackling one type of social problem might generate benefits across a range of areas of need, producing a 'virtuous circle' of mutually reinforcing gains. The experience of the Headstart (High/Scope) programme in the USA has long been taken as demonstrating that good quality early years services for parents and children can generate improvements against a number of social goals, including improved educational attainment, higher employment levels and reduced levels of offending (Schweinhart 2003). Thus the major investment which followed in family support and improving parenting through the Sure Start programme (£1.4 billion up to 2003/04; Social Exclusion Unit 2001a) is at least partly held to be justified by the anticipated contribution to a future reduction in youth crime (Sure Start 2000).

Equally, high rates of teenage pregnancy, school non-attendance, unemployment and neighbourhood decline are all seen as interwoven according to this analysis, so that they are individually and collectively associated with increased crime rates:

> The 'joined-up' nature of social problems is one of the key factors underlying the concept of social exclusion – a relatively new idea in British policy debate. It includes low income, but is broader and focuses on the link between problems such as, for example, unemployment, poor skills, *high crime*, poor housing and family breakdown. (Social Exclusion Unit 2001a: para. 4)

Closer analysis of the connection between wider aspects of social exclusion and youth offending seemed to offer confirmation of this analysis. For example, it has been noted that offending is strongly associated with 'non-attachment to school' and lack of 'parental supervision' (Graham and Bowling 1995). High crime areas are also observed to demonstrate characteristics of *compound social dislocations* – that is, an accumulation of social problems alongside crime, including drug-misuse, family violence, teenage pregnancy, children taken into care, and school failure ...' (Hope 1998, p. 53). At the same time, it is noted that these are *areas of concentrated poverty ... Here, low-skilled* and otherwise disadvantaged youth often fail to gain access to the primary labour market. Such conditions bring together vulnerable victims and potential offenders...' (Hope 1998: 52). As we shall see subsequently (Chapter 7), the evidence of these findings also seems to confirm the relevance of well-established sociological explanations of crime among young people who are denied conventional opportunities to achieve and prosper (Merton 1957).

The conclusion drawn by the Social Exclusion Unit, and indeed by government itself, was that a systematic response to the problems facing many disadvantaged groups and neighbourhoods needed to recognise and address these issues in a coherent and integrated manner. It would not be sufficient to address specific issues in isolation since this would be likely to result in partial, inefficient and inadequate outcomes. As the Prime Minister concluded, shortly after taking office: 'Joined up problems demand joined up solutions' (Blair 1997). Combined with a belief in the efficacy of early interventions, this implied a systematic approach to preventing social problems, including the occurrence of crime, by investing in the collective well-being and life chances of the community as a whole. It could thus be argued that these broader initiatives had as much to with achieving the objective of 'preventing offending' as the specific measures to which the government had committed itself in its initial policy pronouncements on youth crime (Home Office 1997a, 1997b).

Despite the overarching aim of addressing interconnected social problems, however, the emerging policy initiatives appeared to demonstrate a rather more multi-faceted approach, with generalised measures being complemented by a series of rather more specific interventions. Thus the Social Exclusion Unit set out to focus on a series of discrete areas of concern, as did the various government departments with particular areas of responsibility (see, for example, Social Exclusion Unit 1999b, 2002). Indeed, as the overall strategy developed, it appeared that the government's objectives of prevention and inclusion were being pursued on three distinct levels – general social programmes, targeted schemes for 'at risk' groups and individualised interventions directed at those known to be offenders or troublemakers (see Table 3.1).

Table 3.1 Government youth crime prevention initiatives

Level	Generalised	Targeted	Individualised
Object of intervention	Disadvantaged neighbourhoods, problem populations, 'crime' in general	'At risk' groups, marginalised young people	Known offenders, anti-social individuals
Methods of intervention	Family support, community development, education and training	Leisure schemes, project work, employment schemes, learning opportunities	Offending behaviour management programmes, surveillance, restrictions of freedom
Intervention programmes/mechanisms (*examples*)	Sure Start, Connexions, Neighbourhood Renewal Programme, inclusive education	'On Track', Youth Inclusion Programme, Community Safety Partnerships	Final Warning programmes, ISSP, ASBO, bail support
Outcome targets	Long-term overall reduction in crime figures	Medium-term, area based, reduced rates of reported crime	Short-term, stop/reduce/ prevent individual offending

Generalised crime prevention

Over the course of its first two terms in office, New Labour put in place a wide range of initiatives directed at various aspects of social exclusion with a more or less explicit link to the perceived risk of crime, including truancy and school exclusion, neighbourhood renewal, teenage pregnancy, youth unemployment and children in care (Social Exclusion Unit 2001a, 2003). For instance, the initial focus on education led to a series of measures designed to promote education for all and to accommodate those who might otherwise become marginalised. Sure Start was one concrete example of this, as we have already noted, but there were a number of other developments aimed at enhancing the capacity of the education service to be truly universal in its coverage.

For instance, a series of initiatives was introduced to tackle school exclusion and truancy at a cost of £300 million over the period 1997–2001, keying in with the government's wider emphasis on educational achievement. This programme included the establishment of Learning Support Units, additional places in Pupil Referral Units and the addition of incentives to encourage schools to 'hold on' to students at risk of exclusion. In addition to these broadly supportive measures, however, the government also brought in a number of specific (targeted) schemes to emphasise the *responsibilities* of children and parents in this context, including 'truancy sweeps', to be negotiated between local education authorities and the police, which involved an extension of police powers in December 1998.

It was subsequently reported that 'in York, when truancy sweeps were launched in 1999, youth crime fell by 67 per cent, and in parts of Newham, car crime fell by 70 per cent' (Social Exclusion Unit 2001a: Annex B, para. 16). Here, the link between promoting positive educational outcomes and preventing youth offending is made quite explicit, and the reduction in youth crime is advanced as one of the major justifications for getting young people back into school. Interestingly, however, subsequent research has questioned the ease with which a causal connection between school exclusion and youth crime has been assumed (Berridge *et al.* 2001; Hodgson and Webb 2005). Even though this is clearly identified as a 'joined-up problem' (Berridge *et al.* 2001: 48), patterns of cause and effect are complex, and thus simplistic responses are unlikely to provide a complete answer.

Concerns about the implications of unemployment for young people were also addressed quite early in the SEU's lifespan (Social Exclusion Unit 1999a), and this led to the establishment of the Connexions Service.[4] This was set up as a universal programme, unlike other initiatives, such that every young person would have access to information and assistance in making key decisions about the transition into further education or training and the world of adult responsibilities. Connexions was launched in the year 2000 with a spending commitment of £420 million, to:

> provide information, advice, support and guidance to all teenagers through a network of Personal Advisers based in schools, further

education colleges and elsewhere. The service has a range of ambitious targets to improve participation and achievement in education and training, and to reduce drug abuse, offending and teenage pregnancy rates. (Social Exclusion Unit 2001a: para. 5.22)

Once again, the explicit link is made between the overall programme objective and a series of apparently connected social problems, including, of course, youth crime. Thus even a universal programme such as Connexions was partly to be judged according to its achievement in reducing offending. Indeed, evidence from early pilots suggested that this was a realistic aspiration:

Thirteen Connexions pilots have already demonstrated how a Personal Adviser can make a real difference. There are examples within the pilots of young people at risk being pulled back from the brink of chaos and set up to achieve greater success in later life. (Social Exclusion Unit 2001a: Annex E, para. 3)

Within the wider programme, specific funding was also earmarked to improve educational opportunities for young offenders (Social Exclusion Unit 2001a). This reflected an attempt to create logical coherence between broader inclusionary policy goals and the initiatives put in place, whether universal, targeted or individualised.

The government also promised a 'revolutionary approach' to the problems of disadvantage and deprivation in specific neighbourhoods. This would be triggered by the creation of a £900 million Neighbourhood Renewal Fund, and programme targets included improved educational attainment and reductions in crime, specifically domestic burglary (to be cut by 25 per cent over the period 2001–05).

The National Strategy for Neighbourhood Renewal (Social Exclusion Unit 2001b) set out to provide substantial funding for the benefit of entire communities on the assumption that focused universal provision of this kind would provide mutually reinforcing gains, improving the quality of life generally at the same time as producing measurable achievements such as a reduction in crime and anti-social behaviour.

Targeted youth crime prevention

As well as seeking to achieve a reduction in levels of crime as one of a series of outcomes from generalised measures, the New Labour government also sought to develop a more focused range of targeted programmes, seeking to address those young people 'at risk' in various ways. Some of these were pragmatic developments of schemes already in place, such as drug education and crime prevention in schools, Safer Cities projects and other existing initiatives, focusing on bullying, graffiti and vandalism (Home Office 1997b). Some were quite specific and appeared designed to attract popular support, such as the 'local child curfew', proposed by the new government with the dual aim of protecting children in particular areas from the risk of harm and preventing 'crime and disorder' (Home Office 1997b: 16).

These ideas were supplemented by other strategies aiming to promote a more 'joined up' approach at local level, including a new requirement for local authorities and the police to work together to reduce crime and improve community safety (through the establishment of Crime and Disorder Reduction Partnerships). Specifically, it was stated that 'the Government expects that measures to tackle youth crime will figure wherever that is a problem locally' (Home Office 1997b: 10). Government set the framework but made it clear that local strategies should be tailored to meet local needs in this respect.

Additional funding was provided by government to address the issue of young people 'at risk' of offending through other policy streams aimed at specific target populations. On Track was one such development, launched in December 1999 and aiming to put in place a range of preventive options for children aged 4–12. The suggested menu of interventions included 'home-school partnerships, home visiting, parent training, structured pre-school education and family therapy' (Children and Young People's Unit 2002).

In an approach that carried echoes of the 'Catch 'em Young' ideas espoused by the Conservative government of the early 1980s and of the early pioneers of Intermediate Treatment in the late 1960s, On Track's aims were to ensure that 'children at risk of offending are identified early and they and their families provided with consistent services through the child's development' (Children and Young People's Unit 2002). Similar aspirations are associated with the Youth Inclusion Programme, set up to target 'the most disaffected young people in the 13 to 16 age range' (Morgan Harris Burrows 2001: 1). The objectives of this initiative, launched in 2000, was to identify the 50 young people at greatest risk of offending in the highest crime areas in England and Wales, and to include them in a variety of activities alongside other young people, including holiday schemes, sport, after-school projects, informal education and social skills training. The initial results from the YIPs were said to be highly encouraging (Morgan Harris Burrows 2001), with a 32 per cent fall in crime reported in Doncaster and 14 per cent falls in Gateshead and Wrexham where schemes were in place. Subsequent follow-up suggested that these initial achievements had not been sustained, with project areas actually experiencing an increase in recorded crime, even though arrest rates declined among the 'top 50' young people at risk (Morgan Harris Burrows 2003: 14).

Further development of this kind of approach is evidenced by schemes such as 'Splash', initiated by the Youth Justice Board in 2000 to provide summer activities for young people at risk – borrowing, it seems, from the much-praised French model of the *étés jeunes* (Pitts 2001b). From 2003, the idea of targeting potential young offenders reached a new level of sophistication with the development and piloting by the Youth Justice Board of Youth Inclusion and Support Panels, multi-agency groups established to develop creative strategies for diverting those most at risk from involvement in criminal activities and enabling them to make better use of 'mainstream services'.

In a quite different context, the teenage pregnancy initiative prompted by an earlier SEU report (Social Exclusion Unit 1999b) also made links to youth crime:

A module on sex and relationships for young offenders has been developed as part of the Life Skills package with the Prison Service. The Sex Education Forum has produced supporting materials. The sexual health education course for young offenders will be rolled out from April 2001 … (Social Exclusion Unit 2001a: Annex D, para. 8)

The assumption here appears to be that promoting a sense of personal responsibility in one aspect of one's life may contribute to a broader embrace of pro-social behaviour. It also points to an underlying concern about the apparent 'joined-upness' of social problems, in that it becomes possible to apply quite damning generalisations to those whose behaviour may be a cause of concern in just one respect. In this sense, it might even become easier to find validation for the notion of a composite 'underclass', sharing a catalogue of inadequate characteristics and undesirable behaviours (Murray 1996).

Within the broader framework of the government's generalised strategy, these targeted schemes appear to demonstrate a degree of internal coherence, being based on the principle of systematically identifying those most likely to offend according to common characteristics and then providing intervention programmes which seek to reincorporate them to mainstream activities, providing opportunities for personal growth and development, social integration and achievement. While there have been criticisms of the negative connotations of 'targeting' (Percy-Smith 2000), and the empiricist assumptions underlying 'administrative' approaches to tackling deep-rooted structural problems (Clarke *et al.* 2000), these programmes do appear to have offered both a substantial investment and a clear commitment to the principles underlying an inclusive approach to crime prevention among young people.

Individualised crime prevention

However, in tandem with the broadly inclusive measures detailed above, the government also initiated a series of preventive measures that focused on specific individuals identified as offenders and troublemakers, reflecting a concern with social control and containment rather than social inclusion, it would seem. From the start, New Labour's White Paper *No More Excuses* (Home Office 1997b) proposed a range of options under the heading 'Effective Intervention in the Community' that aimed to identify and address children and young people identified as being 'at risk' of offending, and their parents. Thus 'the child safety order is designed to protect children under ten who are at risk of becoming involved in crime or who have already started to behave in an anti-social or criminal manner' (Home Office 1997b: 15). Presumably here the word 'protect' is intended to imply the words 'from themselves'! The proposed order (aimed at children below the age of criminal responsibility, it should be stressed) would allow courts to require children to comply with specific instructions, such as 'to be home at certain times' or to attend 'a local youth programme', with the option of instituting care proceedings for failure to comply[5].

This measure would be complemented by the parenting order under the government's proposals, which could require parents to attend specific training programmes as well as requiring them to secure the good behaviour of their children. The justification put forward for this provision was that 'inadequate parenting is strongly associated with offending – in a Home Office study,[6] 42 per cent of juveniles who had low or medium levels of parental supervision offended, but only 20 per cent of juveniles with a high level of supervision' (Home Office 1997b: 12).

As we have seen subsequently, this strategy has been further intensified, most notably through the various mechanisms of surveillance, prohibition and enforced compliance. Thus, for example, known and persistent young offenders have been subjected to greater scrutiny through the introduction and subsequent extension of the Intensive Supervision and Surveillance Programme (Beaumont 2005), put in place with an explicit commitment to reduce reoffending (Youth Justice Board Press Release 18 March 2004). At the other end of the spectrum, of course, the invention, extension and enthusiastic promotion of the Anti-Social Behaviour Order, and its associated paraphernalia such as the Acceptable Behaviour Contract, has focused on those whose behaviour is problematic, but who may not have been made the subject of criminal proceedings (Burney 2005). Interestingly, the growing concern with the anti-social behaviour of the young has also led to the development of 'targeted' measures, such as the Dispersal Order (introduced by the Antisocial Behaviour Act 2003), and the extension of curfew provisions to include children up to the age of 16 (Criminal Justice and Police Act 2001), with the aim of providing blanket protection from crime and anti-social behaviour to specific areas.

Thus the New Labour government's youth crime prevention strategy could be argued to have three distinct elements, one with a focus on the social factors associated with crime, developed as an integral element of an overarching social inclusion agenda; one that aimed to target and intervene with certain populations or communities known to be 'at risk' of becoming involved in crime or anti-social behaviour; and one to address potential and known perpetrators directly by imposing a range of measures of containment and control on them and their parents. These latter options would, of course, be supplemented further by the extensive range of criminal sanctions also put forward under the government's developing reform programme for youth justice, to which we shall now turn.

The end of tolerance – the roots of reform

The central project of tackling youth crime, which formed such a significant element of the incoming government's overall project in 1997 and continued to do so thereafter, can be traced back to a number of emerging strands, linking political expediency, research evidence and direct experience. These elements coalesced to form a purportedly coherent and politically attractive change strategy, which was set out in detail in the White Paper *No More Excuses* (Home Office 1997b).

It had become increasingly apparent over a number of years that the impact of young people's behaviour was a major issue of social concern, which necessarily forced it up the political agenda. 'Left realists' had argued that the attribution of 'criminality' should not be seen simply as the consequence of the imposition of state control on young people in particular, but also as a feature of the everyday experience of most communities, and especially those experiencing other social disadvantages (Lea and Young 1984; Kinsey *et al.* 1986). Not only do the official figures fail to recognise a huge number of unreported offences, but these are also likely to affect certain sectors of the population disproportionately, with poorer people demonstrably more likely to be burgled and young black men more likely to experience violent assaults, for example (Lea and Young 1984: 22). The fact that these constituencies were seen as being 'Labour' led to a significant reappraisal of the party's response to the issue of crime. The victimisation of specific groups, such as women and ethnic minorities, and the concentration of specific types of crime in poorer areas, were seen as requiring a range of proactive responses in order to demonstrate a commitment to social justice:

> Law and order … is a radical issue. It is an issue for the poor and the old, least able to resist the impact of crimes that … may appear trivial. It is an issue for ethnic minorities suffering racial harassment and racial attacks. It is an issue for women suffering … male harassment and violence … All these social groups, despite their many differing interests, have a common interest in combating crime. (Kinsey *et al.* 1986: 73)

This realisation, driven initially by academic research, found echoes in the direct experience of Labour politicians, national and local, notably those 'from working class backgrounds' (Taylor 1981). They tended to represent those very areas that were experiencing the multiple impacts of a series of social disadvantages, including the kind of 'intra-group' (Lea and Young 1984) crimes that compounded the sense of injustice and abandonment that they felt. This recognition, combined with Labour's traditional vulnerability to the accusation of being 'soft on crime', led to a significant reappraisal during the party's long period in opposition from 1979 to 1997.

The first clear signs of a shift in emphasis emerged with Tony Blair's contributions to the debate in the prevailing climate of moral panic in the early 1990s (Blair 1993). Moves to develop a new and credible centre-left position on crime, and particularly youth crime, were further intensified with the promotion of Jack Straw to the position of Shadow Home Secretary in 1994. It seems that his willingness to take action in this area derived at least partly from his own history and experience. He had been brought up in relative poverty, and he had been made particularly aware by his own constituents of their concerns about crime. As a result, he found less room for excusing the act of offenders than might have been expected, perhaps. A visit to New York in 1995 enthused him with the idea of 'zero tolerance' policing (Newburn and Jones 2001). According to the principles of this approach, any and all signs of anti-social behaviour and community disintegration must be tackled swiftly and resolutely (Kelling 1998). This message was relayed bluntly, and with a distinct shift of emphasis away from the causes of crime and towards its manifestations:

> In conjunction with tackling the underlying causes of crime, the community has a right to expect more responsible and less anti-social behaviour from its citizens. That means less intimidation, bullying and loutish behaviour on the streets and in our towns and city centres. (Straw 1995, quoted in Charman and Savage 1999)

These clear statements of intent were quickly translated into policy commitments prior to the forthcoming General Election, at least partly to neutralise the Conservatives' perceived electoral advantage in this area of the political landscape (Pitts 2001b). Thus by 1996 the language of 'blame', 'responsibility' and 'punishment' had been purposefully introduced into the rhetoric of Labour politicians. In seeking to take the initiative, the party's document on youth offending stated that:

> Recognising that there are underlying causes of crime is in no way to excuse or condone offending. Individuals must be held responsible for their own behaviour, and must be brought to justice and punished when they commit an offence. (Straw and Michael 1996: 6)

Equally importantly, the historical concerns of Labour to prioritise children's welfare (in the Children and Young Persons Act 1969, for example) were now being de-emphasised: 'The welfare needs of the young offender cannot outweigh the needs of the community to be protected from the adverse consequences of his or her offending behaviour' (Straw and Michael 1996, quoted in Goldson 1999: 9). The contrast with Labour's commitment to address offending behaviour *by* meeting welfare needs under the 1969 Act could not be starker.

The consequences for government policy when New Labour took power were evident. Youth offending would be dealt with directly in its own right, and at face value. It was subsequently noted that 'the (re)politicization of youth crime has ushered in a new agenda moulded and fixed around the imperatives of punishment, retribution and re-moralisation' (Goldson 1999: 9).

No more excuses – the road to discipline

The consequences of this concentrated focus on youth crime policy and its separation from other policy developments are of some interest, not least because they begin to reveal some of the fault lines in the emerging change agenda. There was, for example, a clear distinction evident between youth justice initiatives and the incoming government's broader social inclusion programme, reflected in the different ways in which crime prevention was to be addressed, as we have observed previously. The incoming government argued that these elements of its overall portfolio would effectively complement each other, and that therefore there would be no adverse consequences to its measures to 'shake up' the administration of youth justice.

No More Excuses, published shortly after New Labour took office, was a swift and confident statement of intent, setting out a detailed vision for the future of youth justice, and claiming to represent a clean break with the past. In fact, this was a significant underestimation of the historical continuities incorporated into the new programme, for example proposals for the 'tagging' of young offenders were directly inherited from the previous administration. It may appear that the political need to appear different and innovative may have sometimes led to a degree of overstatement in this respect. Nevertheless, there seems no doubt that there was a genuine attempt to set out a distinctive philosophy by the new government, and the White Paper itself made a strong bid to achieve radical change, claiming to herald a 'root and branch reform of the youth justice system', in the words of the Home Secretary's introduction (Straw 1997).

Of particular significance was the pronouncement that the principal aim of the youth justice system should be purely and simply to prevent offending, thus explicitly making the connection between wider and more generic 'preventive' programmes (Social Exclusion Unit 2001) and the range of measures being pursued in the specific field of youth crime and anti-social behaviour.

The aim of preventing youth offending would be achieved, according to the White Paper, by the realisation of a number of key sub-objectives, including the requirement for offenders and their parents or carers to take responsibility for their behaviour, the development of early interventions with first offenders and pre-delinquents, more effective administrative procedures,[7] and improved partnerships between youth justice and other relevant agencies. These aims set the parameters for the planned reform programme, and it should be noted in passing that they bear some of the characteristics of the strategies of control identified by authors such as Foucault (1979) and Donzelot (1979). Thus the incorporation of parents as agents of control was anticipated by Donzelot's concept of policing *through* the family, and the establishment of extended networks of agencies with the common objective of controlling crime finds echoes in Foucault's 'carceral archipelago' which extends networks of power and discipline throughout the community and social institutions. The emerging focus on early intervention could also be seen as a manifestation of this kind of tendency, extending mechanisms of control to earlier stages of young people's lives, but also into a wider range of family and community settings (Smith, R., 2001).

In order to allay fears about the extension of state control in this way, the government sought to perform the same reductionist sleight of hand as attributed to Foucault himself (Garland 1990). That is to say, potential conflicts between different types of intervention and competing objectives are not addressed or simply dismissed:

The Government does not accept that there is any conflict between protecting the welfare of a young offender and preventing that individual from offending again. Preventing offending promotes the welfare of the individual young offender and protects the public. (Home Office 1997b: 7)

Apart from conjuring up rather worrying rationalisations for draconian measures along the lines of 'we're only doing this for your own good', this also sidesteps the potential challenges of aligning two quite distinct (and sometimes contradictory) policy goals. However, taken at face value, it represents a significant achievement in terms of justifying a range of interventions across all aspects of young people's lives. It also bridges the gap between 'rights' and 'responsibilities' quite nicely, implying that one is dependent on the other and that they are mutually reinforcing (Jamieson 2005). It is only a short step from this position to the argument that failure to meet one's responsibilities should, indeed, lead to consequences in terms of loss of entitlements:

It is wrong that young people who do not respect the opportunities that they are given, by committing crimes or behaving anti-socially, should benefit from the same opportunities as the law-abiding majority. (Kelly 2005: 1)

The subsidiary aims associated with the prevention of offending in the White Paper also indicated a more proactive, intensive and intrusive approach. The responsibilities of parents and young offenders would be reinforced; punishment would be determined according to either the seriousness or the persistence of young people's offending; interventions would be administered swiftly; and young people would be expected to face up to the consequences of their behaviour (Home Office 1997b: 8).

Glossing over any possible contradictions between these aims, *No More Excuses* proceeded to elaborate the proposed intervention strategy in more detail. Interventions would be carefully graded according to the level and nature of young people's criminality (Foucault 1979; Smith, R. 2001).

Pre-delinquent prevention

Thus, for example, at the pre-delinquent stage, parental responsibilities could be reinforced through programmes of education and guidance (again see Donzelot 1979). For a 13-year-old who did not attend school, for example, 'a parenting order might be imposed which required his [sic] parents to attend training and included additional requirements that they ensure his attendance at school …' (Home Office 1997b: 14). As well as the extension of control by proxy through the enhancement of parents' role in supervising and controlling young people's behaviour, the White Paper also proposed more specific forms of community-based intervention, signalling that 'disposals should focus on changing behaviour as well as punishment' (Home Office 1997b: 15). The Child Safety Order, for instance, would incorporate specific requirements relating to school attendance and other aspects of the child's behaviour.

More widely, child curfews were proposed, which would be applicable to entire streets or neighbourhoods, with the aim of providing 'an effective immediate method of dealing with clearly identified patterns of anti-social and disorderly children who are too young to be left out unsupervised late at night' (Home Office 1997: 16). These supposedly preventive measures were thus targeted at pre-delinquents by definition, extending the scope of the youth justice system into areas of behaviour management previously beyond the reach of the criminal law. The blurring of the distinction between prevention and crime control in this way has subsequently led to a considerable expansion of policy measures and enforcement activity in respect of behaviour by young people (and others) which gives cause for concern but is not necessarily criminal (Burney 2005; Squires and Stephen 2005). Among these measures can be numbered the extension of curfew orders, the enhancement of Anti-Social Behaviour Orders through a series of legislative changes, the introduction of Dispersal Orders and the extension of parenting orders to apply to children's behaviour in school (under the Antisocial Behaviour Act 2003).

Responses to early offending

Moving up the scale and beyond the offending threshold, the government sought to put in place a range of more stringent, but finely graded, interventions, including Reprimands for minor first offences, then Final Warnings should an individual offend on a second occasion. Unlike previous disposals available at this point in the justice process (cautions and informal action by the police), these measures were explicitly tied to the notion of a sentencing tariff, available once and once only, and in the case of the Final Warning, to be accompanied in most cases by planned programmes of correctional intervention with the young person concerned (Youth Justice Board 2002). In this respect, the processes of assessment and targeted intervention outlined can easily be equated with the vision of systematically organised and calibrated mechanisms of discipline set out by Foucault (1979), whereby the form and extent of intervention is closely matched to the specific offender. Of course, at this point, the practicality and legitimacy of such a strategy was not in question.

As the seriousness and persistence of young people's offending behaviour progressed, the government envisaged a further series of similarly tailored measures, intended to address the specific issues relevant to the individual's distinctive profile and characteristics. This creates a sense of continuity and integrity to the continuum of interventions to be made available under the new regime. For example, the proposed Action Plan Order was designed to ensure that carefully constructed programmes, involving a choice of options from a broad menu, could be put in place depending on the circumstances and behaviour of the particular young offender, but still with the overall aim of discouraging him/her from reoffending.

Interestingly, and apparently as something of an anomaly, it was in this middle range of proposed new interventions that the government introduced the idea of a new kind of disposal, the Referral Order, which would incorporate a rather different set of 'restorative' principles, based on notions of resolving the problems caused by the offence and making amends in some way to the victim.

Prevention at the 'heavy end'

In order to ensure overall system coherence, the government proposed to apply the same overarching preventive goal to disposals targeted at the most serious and persistent young offenders. There would thus need to be a new framework for penal facilities, with changes both in the scope and purposes of secure institutions. New regimes would be developed, with greater emphasis on the constructive use of time spent in custody, and positive support for achievement and progress:

> The Government believes that a custodial sentence should not be an end in itself – it protects the public by removing the young offender from the opportunity to offend, but the fundamental aim of both custodial and community sentences, in line with the aim of the youth justice system, should be to prevent offending. (Home Office 1997b: 19)

Pursuing this logic, *No More Excuses* asserted that sentences should be closely related to the nature of the offence and should reflect concerns about both the seriousness and persistence of offending. Custodial regimes should be appropriately designed to provide a disciplinary framework which would encourage compliance while also promoting future good behaviour. Thus the planned Detention and Training Order should incorporate a degree of flexibility, in terms of regime, sentence length and release date, in order to maximise the prospects of discouraging further offending. Post-sentence supervision and surveillance would be designed to achieve the same objectives, with sustained evidence of acceptable behaviour being rewarded with reduced levels of surveillance and restrictions.

Out of this series of proposals emerged a number of consistent themes, characterised by the overriding concern to put in place effective mechanisms for controlling and reducing offending by young people. In taking this approach, the government conveyed a belief in its capacity to design and establish accurate and consistent methods for identifying problematic behaviour, assessing and itemising risk factors, and on this basis constructing appropriate correctional programmes tailored to each offender. This reflects the influence of the belief in principles of technological efficiency and 'modernisation' which were evident across the range of New Labour's policy agenda, including youth justice (Newburn 1998). In this respect, the White Paper's proposals reflected the managerial and procedural ethos of the time (Clarke *et al.* 2000). Throughout the youth justice system (and beyond), the government's plans could be seen to represent a quasi-scientific 'carceral continuum', which:

> covers the whole social body, linked by the pervasive concern to identify deviance, anomalies and departures from the relevant norms. This framework of surveillance and correction stretches from the least

irregularity to the greatest crime and brings the same principles to bear on each. (Garland 1990: 151)

The Crime and Disorder Act 1998 – the micro-politics of social control

Following the publication of *No More Excuses*, the government moved fairly quickly to translate its proposals into legislation, more or less without revision, and in the face of considerable concern from practitioners and organisations in the field (Crowley 1998, for example). The Crime and Disorder Act was passed in 1998 and most of its provisions had come into force by June 2000.

The Act itself built on the proposals in the White Paper directly, particularly in areas such as the creation of inter-agency arrangements to plan, implement and oversee local youth offending services. The establishment of Youth Offending Teams, local inter-agency partnerships and statutory plans to tackle youth crime were all put on a statutory footing. The Act thereby created the structures to enable a corporate (Pratt 1989) approach to be pursued.

In addition, the Act put in place a series of mechanisms and procedures which set out detailed and prescriptive means of implementing the government's stated policy objectives. This might be expected from a source which has repeatedly demonstrated faith in its capacity to 'micro manage' public service delivery (Jessop n.d.). For example, the requirements relating to the assessment of young offenders (and alleged offenders at the pre-trial stage) have led to the development and revision of the ASSET form (in various formats), with the aim of providing an accurate tool for precision measurement of offenders' characteristics and likelihood of reoffending (see Baker *et al.* 2005, for example).

Beyond this, the Act can be seen as quite precise, too, in linking specific interventions to the circumstances and offending careers of individual young offenders. The room for judgement, creativity or professional discretion appears to be quite restricted, for both practitioners and judicial decision-makers. Thus the progression through Reprimands and Final Warnings for early stage offenders is tightly prescribed and leaves little room for manoeuvre, as some Youth Offending Teams have found (Pragnell 2001), and despite evidence which suggests that discretionary use of alternatives to prosecution generated significant benefits over the years (Stevens and Crook 1986; Smith, R. 1987; Kemp *et al.* 2002).

The Crime and Disorder Act also sought to exclude the possibility of administering a Conditional Discharge in cases where a Final Warning had previously been administered. The subsequent introduction of the Referral Order as a mandatory disposal for a first court appearance (in nearly all circumstances) under the Youth Justice and Criminal Act 1999 compounded this arbitrary fettering of judicial discretion. In these ways, the new legislation cumulatively represented the construction of a:

> Continuous gradation of the established specialized and competent authorities ... which, without resort to arbitration, but strictly according to the regulations, by means of observation and assessment, hierarchized, differentiated, judged, punished and moved gradually from the correction of irregularities to the punishment of crime. (Foucault 1979: 299)

Thus a process is put in place which, by treating every infringement in the same way and as part of an unbroken continuum, blurs the distinction between different forms of behaviour, and arguably has paved the way for the further criminalisation of forms of problematic or unusual behaviour which would not have previously come within the remit of the justice system. By contrast, ironically, the distinction between misdemeanours (*délits*) and criminal acts (*crimes*) remains embedded in the French system of justice (Ministère de la Justice 2001).

However, we can see just such a process of gradation and progression, from the pre-criminal to the most serious of crimes, set out in the detailed prescriptions of the Crime and Disorder Act (and subsequent legislation):

1. Protective orders are established to deal with the anti-social actions and potential actions of those individuals (or groups of young people) identified as at risk of offending at the pre-delinquent stage: the Child Safety Order, the Curfew Order, the Parenting Order, the Anti-Social Behaviour Order and now the Dispersal Order.
2. Progressive pre-court disposals, accompanied in some cases by correctional interventions, are made available only to those in the early stages of offending careers: Reprimands, Final Warnings and the Referral Order (determined by the court but not treated as a conviction if successfully completed).
3. A range of options available to the courts or repeat offenders once the previous disposals have been exhausted. These incorporate both traditional and newer disposals, but the sense of progression up the sentencing tariff remains clear and unavoidable: discharges (only available in a limited range of circumstances), fines, the Reparation Order, the Attendance Centre Order, the Action Plan Order and then the Supervision Order, and for 16–17-year-olds, Community Punishment and Rehabilitation Orders[8] (with the possible addition for serious and persistent offenders of additional requirements such as the Intensive Supervision and Surveillance Programme in the last two cases). While there are some additional requirements (such as Curfew Orders) which can be attached to any of these core sentences, this does not appear to detract from the central principle of a graded, targeted and progressive sentencing structure.
4. Custodial sentences that form the apex of the penal pyramid. It is the use and form of custody that sets the standard by which the youth justice system in general should be evaluated. Thus we can observe recurrent themes: progression, detailed risk-based assessment and the purported application of specifically tailored correctional programmes: the Detention and Training Order, and the Section 90/91 Order[9] – although, in practice,

the Prison Inspectorate and others have shown that the performance of the various regimes is rather more uniform (uniformly oppressive, that is – see Goldson 2002; Joint Chief Inspectors 2002; Goldson and Coles 2005).

More recently, the principle of a strict progressive tariff has been thrown into question as a result of a further re-evaluation of youth justice policy (Home Office 2003b), which has suggested, for example, extending the availability of the Referral Order and replacing the full range of community sentences with one umbrella option, the Action Plan Order, within which other interventions ('fines, reparation and a range of other specified activities'; Home Office 2003: 7) could be incorporated. Whether this represents a pragmatic, managerially driven rationalisation of an increasingly crowded menu or a more fundamental rethink of the philosophical rationale for the tariff remains to be seen, however.

Further reforms: extending control or muddying the waters?

Following the passage of the Crime and Disorder Act in 1998, the government continued to seek improvements and refinements in this area of policy. Despite the apparent ideological and operational coherence of this initial reform package, and despite pragmatic arguments for allowing the new measures to 'bed in', there has, in fact, been a plethora of further developments. While it may be possible to propose theoretical arguments for this constant search for change and innovation, for example in the reflexive nature of modernity (Giddens 1991; Beck 1992), the challenge remains for analysts and practitioners to make sense of what is going on, and, indeed, to make it work.

The referral order – the advance of restorative justice?

The first significant reorientation of the government's strategy following 1998 came with the introduction of the Referral Order the following year. The order had been signposted by *No More Excuses* and it put in place a means for young offenders to be dealt with outside the conventional sentencing framework on their first court appearance. If pleading guilty, they should be referred to a 'youth panel' for their offence(s) to be addressed through the application of the principles of 'restorative justice' (Johnstone 2002; Newburn and Crawford 2003). Although these principles have, naturally, been the subject of some debate (Dignan 2005, for example), according to the White Paper itself these were:

- *restoration:* young offenders apologising to their victims and making amends for the harm they have done;
- *reintegration:* young offenders paying their debts to society, putting their crime behind them and rejoining the law abiding community; and
- *responsibility:* young offenders – and their parents – facing the consequences of their offending behaviour and taking responsibility for preventing further offending. (Home Office 1997b: 32)

This attempt to provide a rationale for the government's preferred model for the Referral Order seemed somewhat eclectic, and at the same time glossed over a lively and continuing discussion about the nature of restorative practice (Haines 2000). For the moment, however, the important observation is that it was this interpretation which informed the subsequent legislation and its implementation.

Thus, on an admission of guilt, a young person would be referred to the youth panel,[10] and s/he and her/his parents would be required to attend a 'panel session', with others in attendance, including the victim and any other relevant participants. The panel itself would be representative of the community, and would therefore reflect 'lay' rather than judicial interests. Legal representation would not be allowed, in order to ensure that the panel itself was able to engage 'directly' with the young offender.

The proposal for the new order suggested that a 'contract' should be drawn up between the panel and the young person, setting out the requirements to be placed on her/him and her/his parents. These would 'always include an obligation to make *reparation*. This might be achieved through a letter of apology or a direct meeting with the victim; by putting right any damage caused by the offence; or through financial compensation' (Home Office 1997: 32). Reparation could also be made to 'the community' where direct methods were deemed inappropriate, for instance if a victim declined to become involved. In addition, the contract might be expected to include requirements to participate in specific activities, such as counselling or drug rehabilitation, unpaid community work or educational provision. The agreement might also specify that the young person should not participate in certain activities, or visit particular places. According to the White Paper, although the court would have no control over the content of the programme, it could determine the length of time for which it should apply (between three and twelve months), subject to three-monthly progress reviews by the panel.

These proposals were enacted, virtually unchanged, by Part I of the Youth Justice and Criminal Evidence Act 1999 (itself subsequently consolidated in the Powers of Criminal Courts (Sentencing) Act 2000), so that referral to a 'youth offender panel' became mandatory on a young person's first court appearance (and admission of guilt), except where the court might intend to impose a custodial sentence (or hospital order), or deal with the matter by way of an absolute discharge. Thus, on the one hand, the youth offender panel and the Referral Order were established as central features of the youth justice system, to which virtually every young person appearing in court for an offence would become subject. But, on the other hand, clear limits were imposed on its intrusion into the established judicial structures and procedures, in that the order would only be available at this point in the young person's offending career (with limited exceptions in the case of further offences while subject to the order).

In addition to these constraints, the issues of compulsion and failure to comply also pose some questions in relation to Referral Orders. Although highly punitive sentences are not imposed as a matter of course when offenders do not attend, fail to agree a contract, do not comply with the contract or reoffend (Crawford and Newburn 2003: 140), additional sanctions are available to the courts in these circumstances. This, along with the fairly standard menu of interventions on offer, may indicate that the young offender's experience of the Referral Order may be little different from that of other forms of disposal. So, while the Referral Order apparently moves restorative ideals centre stage, it:

> represents both a particular and a rather peculiar hybrid attempt to integrate restorative justice ideas and values into youth justice practice. It does so in a clearly coercive, penal context that offends cherished restorative ideals of voluntariness. (Crawford and Newburn 2003: 239)

Tightening the grip

Despite the apparently innovative approach offered by the Referral Order, many other aspects of the 'radical shake-up' (Straw, quoted in Pitts 2001: 46) of youth justice heralded by New Labour seemed more to be a matter of repackaging. The changes introduced by the Crime and Disorder Act represented an intensification of the processes of criminalisation and punitive actions against young people, at all levels of the justice system. This process was accompanied by a steady flow of florid rhetoric from successive Home Secretaries (Jack Straw, David Blunkett and Charles Clarke) as well as the Prime Minister. In one such example, the support of the electorate was courted in the following way:

> One of the biggest challenges we face is how to deal with young offenders who believe that their age makes them untouchable, who flout the law, laugh at the police and leave court on bail free to offend again. The public are sick and tired of their behaviour and expect the criminal justice system to be able to keep them off the streets. (David Blunkett, Labour Party Election Broadcast 24 April 2002)

While the sceptical observer might note that this says little for the reform programme already undertaken by the self-same administration, of greater significance is the persistence and consistency of this kind of reputedly authoritative pronouncement which can only serve to reinforce a hegemonic (Gramsci 1971) view of what is the problem and what are the solutions.

A series of policy documents and legislative measures followed, informed by and to some extent also validating these politically driven arguments (Home Office 2001a; Home Office 2003a; Home Office 2003b). For example, the government's review of the entire criminal justice system, *Criminal Justice: The Way Ahead*, issued in 2001, proposed a series of changes focusing on the restriction, containment and surveillance of young offenders, including the introduction of more intensive community supervision programmes, tighter surveillance and monitoring of bailees (Home Office 2002a), and increased availability of places in custody. In announcing the new Intensive Supervision and Surveillance Programme (ISSP) with funding of £45 million from April 2001, the emphasis on control and rigour was made clear:

> The Youth Justice Board is making grants to around fifty YOTs [Youth Offending Teams] (or groups of YOTs) for each to work with 50–60 hardcore repeat young offenders a year.

> An ISSP will last at least six months for each offender. It will combine close surveillance by the police and other agencies with a highly structured intensive daily programme tackling the causes of offending. During the first three months the supervision programme will be for at least five hours a day on weekdays with access to support during the evenings and weekends. The whereabouts of each young offender on the programme will be checked at least twice daily with 24 hours a day, seven days a week surveillance where this is necessary. Techniques may include electronic tagging, voice verification …, tracking …, and intelligence led policing. (Home Office 2001a: 32)

Clearly, here, the focus is entirely on surveillance, containment and crime control and there is no consideration of any underlying factors linked to the young person's offending, or the issues of need and personal and social development.

The ISSP was launched initially in 41 areas of England and Wales, and subsequently its coverage was extended to young people on remand, thus ensuring that a highly intrusive programme would be imposed on young people prior to conviction or sentence. By 2003, plans were afoot to expand the number of ISSP places to 4,200, three-quarters of which would be available post-conviction (Home Office 2003b). Although ISSP was promoted by the Youth Justice Board and others as an 'alternative to custody' (Nacro 2005), this number was actually in excess of the total number of young offenders in custody at the time, strangely.

In addition to the ISSP, proposals were included in *Criminal Justice: The Way Ahead* for a further extension of courts' powers 'to refuse bail to youngsters with a history of committing or being charged with imprisonable offences' (Home Office 2001a: 32). This appeared to represent a further toughening of the government's position and a clear dilution of the commitment to the underlying presumption in favour of bail, established in principle by the Bail Act 1976. This proposal was implemented by section 130 of the Criminal Justice and Police Act 2001, which enabled courts to impose a 'security requirement' where a young person had a 'recent history' of repeat offending, and where in the court's opinion they must be kept in a secure setting to prevent the commission of further offences. Earlier restrictions based on the seriousness of the alleged offences, or the level of risk posed to the public, were effectively removed by these new powers. As the supporting guidance stressed: 'the courts have not previously had the power to remand into secure detention those young people who have committed, or who are alleged to have committed, repeated offences of a less serious nature' (Home Office 2002b: 2).

In addition, the same piece of legislation provided courts with the additional power to require 'electronic monitoring' (tagging) of young people on bail or remanded to local authority accommodation (sections 131 and 132).

Finally, in this bundle of measures to 'strengthen' the youth justice system, the government made a commitment 'over the next five years to build 400 additional secure training centre places, providing intensive supervision and high quality programmes for young people in custody' (Home Office 2001a: 32). Presumably these were partly intended to offset the need for 600 places in local authority secure units to accommodate the increased numbers of young people detained on remand (*Guardian* 16 April 2002).

If these measures are to be seen as part of a coherent programme, then there can be no doubt that government initiatives targeted at *individuals* involved in crime or anti-social behaviour represent a strategy of intensifying levels of control and restriction of liberty, whether in community-based forms of intervention or in secure settings. This, as we have seen (Chapter 1), stands in marked contrast to earlier commitments to minimise the use of custody and other punitive measures, thus continuing the trends originating in the 1990s of eroding the safeguards for young offenders, especially at the younger end of the age scale.

The catalogue of prescriptive and restrictive initiatives continued unabated, indeed, with the introduction of further legislation, including the Criminal Justice Act 2003 and the Anti-social Behaviour Act of the same year. In both cases, the trends were similar. Yet more powers were provided to the police, courts, youth justice services and others to impose requirements on children and their parents across a range of activities and settings. Thus, under the former (sections 322 and 323), it became possible to attach Individual Support Orders to Anti-Social Behaviour Orders, in effect to impose compulsory intervention programmes on young people whose behaviour might not necessarily have constituted an offence. In addition, powers to make Parenting Orders were also to be extended to be available in cases where Referral Orders were made on young people (section 324), thus further compromising the 'restorative' principles underpinning this particular disposal.

Burney (2005: 37) comments that the Anti-social Behaviour Act incorporated a 'raft of new controls' on parents, and incorporated a 'rag-bag' of proposals based on the preceding White Paper *Respect and Responsibility* (Home Office 2003a), including the ability to impose curfews on children under the age of 16.

Measures such as this have repeatedly drawn criticism from practitioner and associated interests, notably the National Association for Youth Justice, which complained that the Criminal Justice Act 2003 represented a missed opportunity to ensure that criminal justice for children in England and Wales reflects international standards of fairness and decent treatment.

Counter-currents?

Despite the overall impression of an increasingly punitive character to the youth justice system, there were some indicators that alternative considerations might have some part to play in the development of policy and practice in this area. Thus, in parallel with the government's wider strategy for improving services for children (DfES 2003), further proposals were put forward for youth justice (Home Office 2003b, 2004). Given the government's aim of developing integrated service frameworks and information systems for all children (the *Every Child Matters* initiative: DfES 2003), and given the acknowledged links between the needs of children and their problematic behaviour, it became incumbent on the agencies and policy bodies associated with youth justice to make some kind of response, although the impression created was that this was rather grudging.

Nevertheless, the policy paper *Youth Justice: The Next Steps* indicated some recognition of the interplay between child welfare and concern about offending behaviour:

> Alongside ... proposals ... to tackle the risks faced by children early in life, the Government considers it essential to tackle the problems caused by, and the needs of, those young people who do become involved in crime ... (Home Office 2003b: 3)

In addition, there was some suggestion of a softening of the government line in a number of key areas of practice, with the proposal that 'diversions from court should be used wherever possible' (Home Office 2003b: 4), and that Intensive Supervision and Surveillance should be 'the main response to serious and persistent offending' (p. 7), subsequently clarified as representing a 'robust alternative to custody' (Home Office 2004b: 10). Despite these apparent concessions, the document came in for considerable criticism because it made no real attempt to make links between the issues of offending and children's needs (Family Rights Group *et al.* 2003), and because it insisted on preserving the youth justice system as a separate entity. Despite the requirement to cooperate imposed on different agencies concerned with children, including YOTs, by the ensuing Children Act 2004 (section 10), it remains to be seen whether this will impact on structural arrangements or working practices to any substantial degree. The government's response to consultation on its fairly limited proposals for reform (DfES 2004) suggested that even these may have been too ambitious, and it quickly backtracked on the idea of extending pre-court diversion any further.

The state of policy: coherence, camouflage or confusion?

At this point it might be helpful to take a step back and reflect on the meaning and impact of changes in youth justice policy as developed by the New Labour government over a period of nearly ten years in office. While there is no direct or unproblematic connection between policy and outcomes as earlier chapters have already shown, we will be able to reflect on the interaction between policy, structures, practice and outcomes in what follows.

The first question to consider here is that of the *intent* of the government's activities in the field of youth justice. As we have already observed, this is a highly politicised and contentious subject, and it is one on which the Labour Party has historically felt itself to be vulnerable, and therefore a certain amount of political manoeuvring might be expected. It is on this basis that we might ask the question as to whether the government is actually committed to some of the draconian measures introduced or merely wishes to appear 'tough on crime'.

For example, the government has sought to distinguish between measures which are intended to reduce crime by improving the quality of life and promoting social inclusion on the one hand, and those which are targeted at specific individuals and groups whose behaviour is problematic, on the other. These various initiatives are then presented as coherent and compatible parts of an integrated overall strategy (Home Office *et al.* 2002: 30). According to Prime Minister Tony Blair, a political consensus had emerged, based on a common understanding that while offending cannot be excused and must be dealt with firmly, 'tackling the root causes is essential' (Blair 2002). This recognition, he has argued, underpins a comprehensive programme of reform, which forms part of a virtuous circle. Summer activity programmes, which promote children's development and encourage responsible behaviour, are mirrored by action to target anti-social behaviour and impose tougher sanctions for 'street crime'. These in turn form part of a wider package of measures intended to 'deliver a fair balance between the rights of victims, witnesses, the rest of law-abiding society and the defendant' (Blair 2002). He added that:

> Re-balancing the system means tackling the causes of crime – striving to give everyone in our society the rights and the opportunities they need to avoid a life of crime.
>
> It means tough legislation – backed up with police on the streets – to reduce crime and anti-social behaviour and reinforce people's responsibility to society.
>
> It means bringing our courts into the twenty-first century and making sure that they serve victims and witnesses as well as they serve defendants.
>
> And it means sentencing that keeps the public safe from the most dangerous prisoners, and which rehabilitates those who can be diverted from reoffending. (Blair 2002)

Vision statements of this kind have been further elaborated in a series of policy documents, stemming from the mid-1990s through the period of New Labour's term in office, including *No More Excuses*, *Justice for All* and *Respect and Responsibility*. In addition, there has been a heavy emphasis on criminal justice reforms in the government's legislative programme. At the same time, this panoply of authoritarian reforms of justice systems and processes is matched by an almost equally extensive range of policy and spending initiatives which are intended to promote community well-being and prevent crime (see Table 3.2).

Of course, there is a difference between simply presenting a series of disparate measures as a coherent and unified programme and being able to demonstrate that this is the case. This is clearly a pertinent question in this context.

Firstly, it has been suggested that the overall 'managerial' tone of the government's approach to policy-making reflects a misunderstanding of the structural nature of the problems being addressed. For example, Pitts has argued that dealing with superficial 'manifestations' of poverty is unlikely to provide real or lasting solutions to the 'structural economic and political problems at the heart of social exclusion' (Pitts 2001b: 147). In other words, the New Labour government's approach has focused primarily on symptoms rather than causes of social disadvantage and crime. As a result, intervention strategies have focused on easily identifiable and measurable 'risk factors' which have, at best, only a partial relationship to the causes of offending behaviour (Pitts 2001a). Thus concerns with 'social exclusion' are translated into programmes which are designed to manage and eradicate only its visible representations, in the form of '[poor] "parenting", "truancy", "drug abuse", "homelessness", "low income" and the like' (Pitts 2001a: 9). As a consequence, initiatives to tackle these issues such as 'truancy sweeps' are based on, and indeed reinforce, causal assumptions which are not based in concrete evidence. Indeed, to some extent, these approaches actually divert attention away from more plausible explanations of disadvantage and anti-social behaviour. Managerial indicators of performance, objectives and outcomes serve only to gloss over and obscure key questions about both the purpose and efficacy of the strategies adopted. The attempt to deal with symptoms in the form of 'risk factors' means that:

we are little nearer understanding the causes of youth crime and our choice of methods of intervention must remain haphazard. In the event, this, by no means insignificant, problem has been resolved by a process of political and scientific attrition. (Pitts 2001a: 9)

Table 3.2 'Tough on crime, tough on the causes of crime' – the government's integrated strategy

Tough on crime	Tough on the causes of crime
Catching and convicting criminals	Sure Start
Prosecuting and rules of evidence	Neighbourhood Renewal
Review of the criminal courts	Children's Fund
What works (prison service reform)	Raising standards (education)
A better deal for witnesses	New Deal(s)
Anti-social behaviour measures	Anti-Drugs Coordination Unit
Stronger sentencing powers	Youth activity programmes

Thus the 'consensus' identified by Prime Minister Blair appears to be based on an unwillingness to ask awkward questions about the nature and origins both of social exclusion and one of its manifestations in the form of youth crime.

Associated with these concerns about the limitations of a programme based on managerial assumptions is the fear that dealing with social problems by way of a 'targeted' approach will itself result in a number of unintended consequences. These interventions may, indeed, run counter to the intentions of more generic, universal services. There are likely to be problems with both the techniques of 'targeting' and the consequential impact on those individuals and communities who are highlighted in this way. It is, as Percy-Smith puts it, very difficult to find sufficiently accurate and sensitive tools to 'identify individuals, groups or areas who should be the focus of targeted actions' (Percy-Smith 2000: 18). In addition, because these mechanisms are crude, people are inevitably going to be wrongly classified, with some alleged troublemakers being targeted incorrectly and others, whose behaviour may be more problematic, being missed. Indeed, it may be that subjective concerns about what is problematic come to determine apparently *objective* decisions about what is acceptable and unacceptable, especially in an era of increasing concern with the anti-social as well as the criminal (Squires and Stephen 2005: 202).

As the Audit Commission (1996: 58) acknowledges, there is 'no way of predicting accurately which individuals are going to offend'. And, as Pitts (2001b) reminds us, 'risk factors' linked to youth crime operate in quite different ways depending on the context. Furthermore, apart from the practical difficulties associated with identifying just which individuals and groups should be the subject of particular interventions, there may be other counterproductive consequences. The result can be the exacerbation of 'negative perceptions of particular areas or groups' (Percy-Smith 2000: 18). This, in turn, can generate additional problematic consequences, such as racial stereotyping and generalised discrimination against communities and neighbourhoods. The risks of these 'unintended' outcomes of youth justice policy are of real significance, given the recognition that young black men are overrepresented at all stages within the justice system.

Alongside the practical limitations of policies based on identifying 'at risk' populations and individuals, we should also be aware of some of the broader implications of the contradictions inherent in government policy. The rhetoric of social inclusion, and its associated universal policy measures, are consistently undermined by the intensified focus on those individuals and groups who are calculated to represent a threat, having either been identified as offenders or as displaying the potential to offend. Labelling theory (Becker 1963, for example) has for many years offered us an understanding of the potential consequences of setting individuals apart on the basis of certain ascribed attributes, and yet it seems that policy has frequently not taken account of this. The process of singling out those who appear to represent a threat and concentrating interventions on them may in effect create a self-fulfilling expectation, whereby their response is to live up to the label applied to them. At the precise time of writing, the chair of the Youth Justice Board has graphically illustrated this concern, expressing fears about the 'Mark of Cain' which some young people will carry with them while subject to Anti-Social Behaviour Orders spanning their entire childhoods (*Independent on Sunday* 22 April 2006). Squires and Stephen (2005) have also provided a very helpful illustration of the way in which such labelling processes impact on young people's lived experiences.

On top of this concern, the tendency has been for governments to infuse criminal justice policy with a set of assumptions about the progressive nature of sanctions. Thus New Labour made it clear from the start that interventions would be intensified as young people progress through the stages of offending careers, moving on to become 'persistent young offenders' (Home Office 2001a: 31). This is clearly cemented in place by provisions for punitive sanctions should young people be found in breach of Anti-Social Behaviour Orders, and in the stipulation that there should be a strict limit of one Reprimand followed by one Final Warning, with any subsequent infraction leading almost automatically to prosecution. Underpinning this adherence to a progressive system of disposals were concerns that 'offenders are returning to court again and again without seeing an appreciable increase in the severity of punishment they receive' (Home Office 2001a: 21). Despite the claim that its overarching objective is the prevention of offending, the youth justice system appears in this respect to be shaped by more conventional and well-established preconceptions, such as the sentencing tariff (Hudson 1996), with each successive offending episode warranting an intensification of the mechanisms of scrutiny and control (Foucault 1979), with a corresponding diminution of interest in the 'causes of crime' as far as that individual is concerned.

This brief summary of the anomalies incorporated into New Labour's youth justice policy is intended to demonstrate that claims to offer a seamless and integrated approach (DfES 2003), while superficially attractive, tend to be wide of the mark. In fact, in certain key respects there are intense and fundamental contradictions at the heart of this government's project. Notably, the use of an increasingly diverse array of mechanisms to identify and target problematic individuals is likely to run counter to other, more benign, measures promoting social solidarity and inclusion, and apart from the problems of individual injustice and discriminatory practice which are likely to arise, this must surely also fail to meet the managerialist objectives of efficiency and effectiveness in policy delivery.

Given that the New Labour policy agenda for youth justice clearly lacks 'coherence', how else might we explain its emergence in the form taken? Some (Burney 2002, for example) may have taken the view that the aim of the incoming government in 1997 was to appear 'tough' without actually following this through. Indeed, the limited use of certain orders made available under the Crime and Disorder Act 1998 (such as Curfew Orders,

ASBOs and Parenting Orders) suggested that there might be some truth in this assumption. But this belief was firmly dispelled by the then Home Secretary, Jack Straw, when he strongly urged local agencies to make more use of their powers (BBC News 28 June 2000). More broadly, in the light of the continuing emphasis on measures of scrutiny and control, within the ambit of a progressive and increasingly punitive sentencing structure, it is difficult to see how other principles apparently espoused by policy-makers can gain much influence. There is thus little space on the agenda for innovative ideas based on, say, principles of restorative justice, or, ironically, for a systematic approach to the prevention of offending. The glimpse of an alternative justice model offered by the Referral Order (Crawford and Newburn 2003) appears to be no more than this, given its limited and highly prescribed role within the overall framework of youth justice disposals. Whyte (2000), for example, has contrasted the role of the Youth Offender Panels in England and Wales with their nearest counterparts in Scotland, the Children's Hearings, and finds that:

> attempting to define young people in criminal terms alone is an ineffective form of classification with limited predictive validity in terms of getting positive results. (Whyte 2000: 187)

This, however, is a major problem for the Referral Order, which is implemented in the shadow of the court, where a range of sanctions awaits those who fail to comply and where the tariff limits its application to one (and not necessarily the most appropriate) point in the young person's offending career. Whereas the Scottish Children's hearings have had a primary concern for the child's welfare,[11] such a concern is absent from the Youth Offender Panel's formal remit. Even where restorative principles are pursued, 'there is potential for tension between the YOP and the youth court if the former is following a restorative justice philosophy and the latter is more inclined to punishment' (Bentley 2000: 216).

The sense of confusion which emerges from the rather different aspirations to be found at varying points in youth justice policy has been compounded by other developments such as the publication of the *All Wales Youth Offending Strategy*[12] (Youth Justice Board and Welsh Assembly Government 2004) which reintroduced a strongly welfarist strand to the arena, stating that: 'Young people should be treated as children first and offenders second' (p. 3). Indeed, Muncie (2002: 156) argues that it is impossible to find a pure ideological strand in legislation and policy (see Chapter 4).

Despite this complex and sometimes contradictory melange of ideas, policies and practices, it is nonetheless difficult to avoid the overriding impression that scrutiny, behaviour management and the restriction of young people's freedoms lie at the heart of New Labour thinking in this area. A continuing torrent of high-profile pronouncements on 'tough new penalties' (Youth Justice Board 2001), 'tackling crime' (Blunkett 2002), 'cracking down on anti-social behaviour' (Blair 2002) and 'nipping in the bud' disruption to communities (Charles Clarke, BBC News 27 September 2005) are best summed up as 'an attempt to peddle simplistic, but politically acceptable, solutions to remarkably complex social, economic and cultural problems' (Pitts 2001a: 14).

4. Where are we now? Policy and outcomes in youth justice

A new landscape?

As we have already observed, it is not routinely the case that policy statements or even legislative changes lead straightforwardly and directly to the kinds of outcomes intended. Thus we should not necessarily expect the purportedly radical changes introduced by New Labour to have produced exactly the kinds of results to which the government aspired. However, unless we believe that policy is totally irrelevant, we must also assume that it has some bearing on developments, and that there might be some evidence of this in the concrete outcomes identified. In light of this, the aim here will be to set out some of the more significant changes (and continuities) identifiable in youth justice following its initial overhaul in the late 1990s, and in the context of further policy developments subsequently.

In some ways, the important question is whether practice has followed policy changes or has merely adapted its public facade while, in fact, demonstrating a great measure of continuity with previous patterns of intervention and outcomes. Considered in this light, we may begin to glean some important observations about both the highly politicised nature of the territory of youth justice and the implications in terms of the latitude available for genuinely radical or alternative developments in practice.

In order to achieve this, I will first consider some of the 'new' policy initiatives which appear to have resulted in a new array of outcomes, especially at the early and pre-criminal stages of young people's 'offending' careers, and then I will focus on the evidence of practices and outcomes demonstrated by official accounts available from government and other organisations such as the Youth Justice Board. This brief overview will then provide the basis for discussions in subsequent chapters about the extent to which practice has become more heavily circumscribed in a number of ways, while also, ironically, opening up a range of possibilities for innovation.

A growth industry: dealing with 'anti-social behaviour'

It is perhaps an indication of how rapidly things can change that one of the leading authorities on the government's anti-social behaviour strategy took the view early in its development that it was little more than a smokescreen – an opportunity for the government to look 'tough' while, in practice, little would be done to intervene in respect of minor acts of criminality or social nuisance (Burney 2002; Smith, R. 2006).

Government had responded to calls from communities and local authorities to provide greater powers to tackle anti-social behaviour through section 1 of the Crime and Disorder Act 1998, supported by some hard-hitting ministerial rhetoric. This was 'a triumph of community politics over detached metropolitan elites' (Home Secretary Jack Straw, 8 April 1998, quoted in Burney 2002: 471). The aim was to provide measures which would give a range of local agencies powers to control and prevent behaviour short of a crime which was causing significant neighbourhood disruption. Although these were not targeted solely on young people, provision was made for action to be taken against them within the legislation and supporting guidance (Burney 2002: 474).

The Anti-Social Behaviour Order was implemented in April 1999, although initial take up was fairly low, with only 466 orders being made in the first two-and-a-half years (Burney 2002: 475). Significantly, however, 58 per cent of these were made on under-18s. In addition, even at this stage, there was clearly a wide variation in their use geographically.

Any thought that government might merely have introduced these measures as a form of posturing was dispelled by the enthusiasm which has been shown for ASBOs by a succession of ministers, including further legislation to extend their use, for example through the Police Reform Act 2002 and the Anti-Social Behaviour Act 2003. As early as October 1999, the Home Secretary wrote to local authorities reminding them that the order had been introduced at their instigation and urging them to make greater use of it (Burney 2005: 32). Both Jack Straw and then his successor, David Blunkett, continued to promote ASBOs, culminating in the announcement that: '"ASBO Ambassadors" would be despatched to those areas deemed not to be making sufficient use of the orders' (Squires and Stephen 2005: 74).

Although the ASBO was introduced as a civil power, a number of aspects of its operation appear to blur the distinction between civil and criminal disposals, and it seems clear that this distinction has little value in the minds of the ministers concerned. So, an easy elision began to be made between anti-social and criminal behaviour, implicitly justifying punitive measures of control in both instances:

> The anti-social behaviour of a few damages the lives of many. We should never underestimate its impact. We have seen the way communities spiral downwards once windows get broken and are not fixed, graffiti spreads and stays there, cars are left abandoned, streets get grimier and dirtier, youths hang around street corners intimidating the elderly. The result: crime increases, fear goes up and people feel trapped. (Blunkett, Foreword to Home Office 2003: 2)

As Burney (2005: 167) argues, the changing nature of ASBO usage presaged by these remarks may also reflect a transformation in its purpose and impact. Thus it is important to review the way in which this relatively recent adjunct to the range of state measures of coercion has been used.

The use of ASBOs

As Squires and Stephen (2005) point out, the basis for the use of measures such as ASBOs is somewhat uncertain, allowing for a 'range of activities' to be included within the definition of anti-social behaviour (p. 38). On one day, 10 September 2003, no fewer than 66,107 incidents were recorded by more than 1,500 organisations. However, of these, more than half were already defined as criminal acts. This substantial element of double counting suggests that:

> ASB comprises not a new range of problems to which modernity has lately become subject but rather a range of very familiar crimes and disorders defined largely by reference to a new range of enforcement processes. (Squires and Stephen 2005: 38)

The substantial overlap between criminal behaviours and the vague and extensive list of other issues of concern, such as 'loud music' or 'climbing on buildings' (Home Office 2004: 4) suggests very wide scope for interpretation in the application of legislative powers in this area. As a result, there is a 'large area of enforcement leeway' (Squires and Stephen 2005: 38), with the process of enforcement itself acting to apply the label 'anti-social' to a particular form of behaviour (which thereby also justifies its use).

Understandably, perhaps, in the light of this there has been considerable variation both over time and by geographical area in the processes of obtaining and implementing ASBOs thus far. Initial findings (Campbell 2002) suggested that ASBOs were not being granted in very large numbers (see above), but that they were very rarely refused on application to magistrates courts (only 18 (4 per cent) turned down between April 1999 and March 2001). In addition, in the early days of implementation, the great majority of orders made were on young people (74 per cent aged 21 or under), prompting the comment that:

> This bears out the common perception of ASBOs as largely combating anti-social youth. (Campbell 2002: 8)

Interestingly, too, for younger recipients ASBOs were far more likely to be administered to young males than females (a ratio of 14:1 was reported; Campbell 2002: 9). Applications were received almost equally from police and other agencies, and the most common concern was about behaviour committed as part of a 'gang'. At least 18 different types of behaviour were targeted, including some which were clearly 'criminal' (such as assault and racial harassment), and others which may simply be annoying ('noise', or 'public disturbance').

Other observations were also made in this study about the characteristics and antecedents of those made subject to ASBOs. Over 60 per cent of those for whom information was available had 'mitigating factors' which might have contributed to their behaviour (Campbell 2002: 18), and a large number also had previous convictions. This appears to support the view held elsewhere (Burney 2005; Squires and Stephen 2005) that the distinction between anti-social and criminal behaviour has become blurred through the introduction of the ASBO.

Equally, this initial study found that ASBOs were of limited value in terms of achieving the objective of preventing the repetition of problematic behaviour. Of a small follow-up sample, 36 per cent were found to have breached their ASBOs within a year of the order being made (Campbell 2002: 75). For those who were breached for failure to comply with the terms of the ASBO, custodial sentences were administered in 46 per cent of cases, including a number of young offenders. While the numbers were not large, this appeared to indicate the possibility of custodial sentences being made for behaviour falling short of a crime, thus incorporating a 'tariff-jumping' effect, which creates an 'artificially steep and slippery slope into custody' (Squires and Stephen 2005: 109).

Such concerns did not appear to inhibit the government, however, given that it proceeded to widen the scope for obtaining ASBOs and continued to exhort agencies and police to extend their use. Introducing the Anti-Social Behaviour Bill to the House of Commons in 2003, the Home Secretary proclaimed this as:

> very important legislation, which will empower people across the country once and for all to get a grip on the scourge that bedevils their communities: the anti-social behaviour that makes other people's lives a misery. (Blunkett, quoted in Burney 2005: 34)

Dismissing the legislation as based on a 'rag-bag collection' of community concerns and lacking any real definition of 'anti-social behaviour' at its core, Burney further predicts the 'targeting of certain types of problem people, some of whom – beggars, youths – become anti-social simply by being in the street. Linked to this is the theme of sanitised public space' (2005: 36). In light of this, it is of real significance that one of the 'case studies' given great prominence on the relevant government website reflects exactly this kind of scenario (see crimereduction.gov.uk 2006b).

Following their initial slow start, and in response to influential exhortation, ASBOs have become increasingly popular tools, and this is reflected in the statistical evidence. By September 2005, there had been 7,356 orders made, over 1,000 of which were accounted for by one area alone, Greater Manchester (crimereduction.gov.uk 2006a). Additionally, the rate at which orders were being made was increasing, so that the number made in the first nine months of 2005 was greater than for the whole of 2004 (asboconcern 2006). Forty-three per cent of orders were made on young people aged 17 or under. By 2003, the breach rate for ASBOs had reached 42 per cent (asboconcern 2006), although the incidence of multiple breaches often exceeded the number of orders made (*Daily Mail* 14 January 2006).

Investigations by the Youth Justice Board (2004, 2005) suggested that a considerable proportion (36 per cent) of young people were breaching ASBOs made against them in the period June 2000 to December 2002, and of this number, 41 per cent (71) were sentenced to custody. Nevertheless, the YJB concluded that this did not mean that failure to comply was recruiting a 'whole new group' of young people into the prison population, since many of these cases concerned young people who were already likely to be 'considered prolific offenders', with an average of 42 previous offences (Youth Justice Board 2005). Despite this, the Board expressed its concern about both the length and the nature of the restrictions imposed by ASBOs, which were 'quite challenging'.

Given the level of interest and its own commitment, it is perhaps surprising that the government appears to have gone cold at this point on evaluation and dissemination of the impact of ASBOs, with substantial criticism being made of its reluctance to issue up-to-date figures on breaches, for example (asboconcern 2006). This may partly be connected with the parallel concerns emerging about the effectiveness of this 'targeted' measure, with its additional 'tailored' options of Individual Support Orders (introduced under the Criminal Justice Act 2003) and Acceptable Behaviour Contracts; in practice, evidence was beginning to build up of ASBOs being used in a simplistic attempt to control behaviour with complex and deep-seated antecedents (British Institute for Brain Injured Children (BIBIC) 2005; Fletcher 2005). Children with identifiable learning difficulties, for example, appeared to be made subject to orders, regardless of the origins or prognosis of their 'problem behaviour'. Thus, BIBIC found that Youth Offending Teams had identified 35 per cent of those under 17 subject to ASBOs as having a 'diagnosed mental health disorder or accepted learning difficulty'. In one case, a 14-year-old boy with a language impairment and suspected ADHD (Attention Deficit Hyperactivity Disorder) had been subject to an ASBO for two years during which time he had broken its terms on 13 occasions. Despite having committed no additional offences during this time, he had spent a considerable period in custody as a result.

The consequences of the ASBO revolution

The implications of the introduction of the ASBO and other strategies to tackle anti-social behaviour have been discussed more fully elsewhere (Burney 2005; Squires and Stephen 2005), but it is important in the present context to consider a number of problematic consequences of these policy-driven initiatives. These focus on three areas which may be identified as recurrent themes of this book: discrimination and oppression, loss of credibility and net-widening.

Discrimination and oppression

For a number of reasons, the ASBO and attendant requirements are particularly susceptible to the kind of distorting influences that are likely to lead to discrimination and oppression of the most vulnerable groups. For instance, the very terms in which government policy is couched focuses on behaviours associated with young people (Squires and Stephen 2005: 17), rather than the complex and varied picture in evidence from rather more sophisticated attempts to understand communities and disorder (Burney 2005: 81). More specifically, too, identified groups and individuals may come to be targeted because of their very visibility, so that it appears to have become quite common for ASBOs to be made in respect of children and young people with specific conditions such as autism or Tourette's Syndrome (Fletcher 2005). The use of hearsay and third party evidence, and the tactic of 'naming and shaming' those subject to orders (Statewatch 2006) also creates greater opportunities for the 'community' to use orders as a way of carrying out 'vendettas' against individuals (Fletcher 2005: 20; Statewatch 2006).

Credibility

In common with other youth justice measures which appear to be applied rather arbitrarily (such as Final Warning programmes; see Chapter 5), the growing evidence of irrational and often unfair use of ASBOs creates wider problems for the justice system as a whole, since it strikes at the very heart of its claims to rationality and credibility. The excessive length and blanket coverage of some orders renders them both extremely difficult to enforce and liable to the claim that they are simply irrational knee-jerk responses to problems which could have been dealt with in another way. In one case cited by NAPO, a 15-year-old boy with Asperger Syndrome was made subject to an ASBO with the condition that he did not stare over the neighbour's fence, which was a feature of his behaviour (Fletcher 2005: 14). Clearly, this is an inappropriate response to a matter which should be addressed in more measured terms.

An additional problem evident from statistical returns on the use of ASBOs is their very variable use from area to area. This suggests that there is a variable level of commitment to this particular strategy, but it also sheds further doubt on the basis for the use of this sanction, which appears to rely as much on the arbitrary judgement of particular local officials as it does on any more consistent standards of what constitutes unacceptable behaviour.

Net-widening

A perennial concern in youth justice has been the tendency for new disposals, especially at the lower end of the scale, to lead to the incorporation of more and more young people into the justice system and to excessively punitive interventions.

ASBOs, by definition, are intended to be applied where the behaviour causing concern falls short of being criminal, and where its effect on 'one or more' members of the community in terms of 'harassment, alarm or distress' determines the outcome rather than the intent of the perpetrator. This clearly opens up considerable scope for a wide range of activities to become liable to the sanction of an ASBO, as the evidence indicates (Burney 2005; Fletcher 2005).

Not only are young people more likely to be brought within the judicial sphere through this process, but they are also likely to be subject to additional sanctions, imposed through the 'voluntarily' agreed Acceptable Behaviour Contracts (Home Office 2002d) and the court-imposed Individual Support Order (Youth Justice Board 2006b), breach of which may lead to a substantial fine.

Additionally, the consequences of breach of the ASBO itself mean that some young people are liable to receive severe punishments, including custody for behaviour which is neither criminal nor subject to the same standards of proof as apply in criminal matters (Burney 2005: 86).

The net result of the 'ASBO revolution' may well be that this crude, superficial and 'targeted' approach effectively undermines more sophisticated and inclusive measures intended to improve the lives of individuals and their communities. This might help to explain the reluctance of some local authorities to embrace the government's anti-social behaviour agenda in full (Burney 2005: 133).

Outcomes and disposals: emerging patterns

Other evidence for the impact of New Labour's youth justice policies can be sought in the broader range of disposals and outcomes to which young people are subject. While overall crime levels appeared to be falling (Home Office 2005a, table 1.1), those proceeded against and found guilty were steadily increasing in number by 2004. However, the number of young people (aged 10 to 17) being proceeded against for indictable (more serious) offences was declining sharply from its peak in 2001. In addition, the 'cautioning rate' (Reprimands and Final Warnings) was also increasing as a proportion of all disposals from its low point in 2002, although this remained significantly lower than the mid-1990s (Home Office 2005a: table 3.3). The proportion of young people being processed (cautioned or found guilty) was also falling at this point (1,671 per 100,000 population compared with 1,962 per 100,000 in 1998). The overall picture this presents is one of a decline in the rate at which young people were being processed and subsequently sentenced for more serious indictable offences.

Other data produced at around the same time suggested that these outcomes were largely consistent with this wider body of evidence (Budd *et al.* 2005). The 2004 Offending, Crime and Justice Survey found that 26 per cent of young people interviewed said they had committed an offence in the previous twelve months, a figure which has remained reasonably steady over a period of several years (MORI 2002) and possibly over several decades (Bateman 2006). In addition, the annual British Crime Survey has suggested that the levels of crime experienced across the population as a whole have also been falling consistently, with a 44 per cent fall between 1995 and 2004/05 (Nicholas *et al.* 2005: 11).

Against this backdrop, it might be reasonable to expect a general reduction in the use of the range of criminal justice disposals in respect of young people. However, the figures available in relation to sentencing patterns and interventions convey a rather different picture. Bateman (2006) argues, for instance, that a greater readiness to instigate formal interventions at the lower end of the scale has found its parallel in a persistently high use of custody. He confirms that the rate of diversion from court (first through cautions and informal action, and later by way of Reprimands and Final Warnings) declined from 73.5 per cent in 1992 to 55.9 per cent in 2003 (p. 73), leading to a significant increase in prosecution rates over time. He also observes that this was paralleled by a 55 per cent increase in the number of custodial sentences over the same period, reflecting a particularly high level of dependence on this option compared with other European countries (Bateman 2006: 74).

Indeed, the available evidence suggests that the reforms progressively implemented from 2000 onwards had little effect on the use of custody for 10–17-year-olds in England and Wales. In March 2000, there were 2,650 young people from this age group in secure facilities, and by March 2006, this figure was 2,785. While there was some fluctuation over this five-year period (3,175 in October 2002; 2,590 in December 2003), the general impression is one of continuity. Bateman (2005a) and Goldson (2006) have both argued that it is the imperative to appear 'tough' on crime that results in senior figures in government implicitly and explicitly endorsing the use of custody, irrespective of other more considered statements of policy or interpretations of key objectives such as the statutory aim of preventing youth offending (as specified in the Crime and Disorder Act 1998). Thus, for example, it has been repeatedly demonstrated that being imprisoned is closely correlated with the likelihood of reoffending (Goldson 2006: 150), and that this relationship has been sustained even following the establishment of new purpose-built institutions and tailored regimes (Secure Training Centres). A persistent reliance on a comparatively high use of custody appears to fly in the face of the government's claim that its principal objective in reforming youth justice was to prevent offending by young people (Home Office 1998).

At the same time, and perhaps in recognition of this, the Youth Justice Board (2005b) has sought to initiate a reduction in the use of custody for young people:

> The YJB's aim is to work with sentencers through the provision of additional and better delivered alternatives to custody so that the population of children and young people in custody is reduced by 10 per cent, or about 270 places, between March 2005 and March 2008. The YJB believes that this objective is challenging but achievable … (Youth Justice Board 2005b: 11)

While this aim was criticised at the time for being too modest (Children's Society 2004), it represents both a change of direction for the YJB itself and a challenge to the government's indifference to (or even implied endorsement of) the levels of custody prevailing at the time.

In fact, however, the initial impact of this declaration by the YJB was disappointing, given that the number of 10–17-year-olds in custody actually increased by over 100 between March 2005 and March 2006. The Youth Justice Board had clearly anticipated that the introduction of a range of new disposals 'strengthening community alternatives to custody' (Youth Justice Board 2005a: 12) would have an impact. Thus it might be expected that the pattern of disposals for those admitting or found guilty of an offence might change over time. In 2004/05, for example, there were 26,133 Referral Orders made, representing 13 per cent of all disposals for that year. Equally, 3,638 (2 per cent) Supervision Orders with conditions were imposed in the same period, compared with 6,682 (4 per cent) custodial sentences.

Overall, patterns of sentencing over time provide the basis for some important observations (see Table 4.1).

On the face of it, there appear to have been some major shifts in the way in which the offences of young people are dealt with over this period, with a very substantial increase in the number of disposals for both males and females, largely accounted for by the rise in the use of community sentences, especially Referral Orders, since their implementation. At the same time, the number of Conditional Discharges has declined substantially.

Table 4.1 Sentencing patterns 1994–2004 for 10–17 year olds

	1994	1999	2004
Males			
Number of disposals	55,511	79,262	83,413
Custodial sentence	4,561	7,244	5,881
Community sentence	19,456	27,072	47,824
(Curfew Order[a]	0	298	3,624)
(Referral Order[b]	0	0	21,310)
Conditional Discharge	17,240	22,144	7,975
Females			
Number of disposals	6,483	10,898	12,775
Custodial sentences	158	409	444
Community sentences	1,864	3,547	8,891
(Curfew Order	0	22	426)
(Referral Order	0	0	4,812)
Conditional Discharge	3,339	4,590	1,300

(a) Curfew Orders only became available in 1996.
(b) Referral Orders were introduced nationally on 1 April 2002.
Source: Home Office (2005b) Sentencing Statistics 2004.

By contrast, the figures for custodial sentences increased substantially before declining somewhat in the case of males and maintaining the level of increase for females. At the same time, it is noted that sentence lengths have increased in respect of custodial outcomes (Bateman 2006: 74), which accounts for the continuation of what Goldson (2006: 149) terms the 'excessive practices of child imprisonment in England and Wales'.

We can perhaps conclude that the reshuffling of options at the lower end of the scale of disposals has generated a much larger throughput of young people, associated with the reduction in the use of cautions and informal disposals discussed previously, and (so far) to a lesser extent the net-widening impact of ASBOs. While this has, in the main, resulted in the supplanting of one form of disposal, the Conditional Discharge, by another, the Referral Order, it has also helped to fuel the continuation of very high levels of custodial sentencing and the corresponding population of young people in secure facilities.

There is little evidence that the greater range and flexibility of community sentences on offer has had any impact on the use of custody, as the Audit Commission has concluded, for example, in relation to the Intensive Supervision and Surveillance Programme, purportedly introduced as an 'alternative to custody' (Beaumont 2005):

> there is no significant difference between the custody rates in those areas that had ISSPs and those that did not ... This implies that the programme is drawing in young offenders who would otherwise have received community sentences ... (Audit Commission 2004: 44)

Instead, what appears to have been in evidence, following the implementation of New Labour's reforms, is a steady intensification of the level and nature of interventions at all levels of the justice system, from the pre-criminal (the ASBO and ISO), through pre-prosecution (Reprimand and Final Warning), pre-trial (for example, ISSPs attached to bail), community sentences (such as Referral Orders, Curfew Orders and ISSPs attached to Supervision Orders) and custody (post-release conditions, again including ISSPs).

Looking for patterns: targeting, compulsion and surveillance

For some, it might be considered unwise to seek consistent or unilinear patterns from developments in youth justice, since it is a site of competing ideologies and contradictory practices. Muncie, for example, believes that:

> The new legislation has, in the main, augmented, rather than overturned, existing legislation. Youth justice is now an amalgam of:
>
> 1 *Just deserts*
> 2 *Risk assessment*
> 3 *Managerialism*

4 *Community responsibilization*
5 *Authoritarian populism*
6 *Restorative justice.* (Muncie 2002: 156)

As he rightly observes, this list is essentially contradictory. Thus the risk assessment approach epitomised by tools such as ASSET which is essentially forward-looking runs counter to the principle of just deserts which is applied on a retrospective basis in sentencing. Equally, the emerging emphasis on restorative justice encounters significant problems to the extent that it is constrained by the sentencing tariff or associated with measures of surveillance and control.

Despite these contradictions, Muncie believes that there are also common threads running through the 'modernised' youth justice system, such as the emphasis on individual responsibility, controlling behaviour and (quasi-) scientific techniques of risk assessment and performance management. He further observes that:

> At the heart of much of this reimagining of youth justice is a fear of an undisciplined underclass. For observers on the right the underclass is young, homeless, criminal and welfare-dependent, but for some of those on the left the 'underclass' is a pejorative label to describe those who have been systematically excluded from the labour market. (Muncie 2002: 157)

It is New Labour's equally ambiguous response to this perceived social problem which has arguably resulted in the particular pattern of outcomes to be observed in youth justice. The kind of universal and broadly based programmes to tackle deprivation introduced as part of the social inclusion agenda also imply an explicitly interventionist approach. Combined with modernist assumptions about the capacity to identify and anticipate problems, this creates a rationale for specific, focused interventions to correct problems and create positive opportunities where individuals, families and communities are seen to be falling through the net. However, failure on their part to make use of the opportunities provided only leaves them open for the application of more intensive, explicit and coercive measures designed to control and change behaviour. This kind of pattern of intervention can be seen to be replicated in the youth justice system, with broad-based and relatively unintrusive options such as Youth Inclusion and Support Programmes at the pre-problem stage being replaced, first by ASBOs, and then by progressively more intrusive surveillance and control packages, which find their twofold justification in the persistence of individuals' unacceptable actions and the scientific certainties offered by risk assessment and behaviour management techniques.

In essence, then, the changing pattern of disposals and interventions in youth justice can be traced in substantial measure to this belief in the value and efficacy of more intensive, targeted and earlier measures to change the attitudes and behaviour of those who refuse to accept the social contract offered by New Labour, which ties 'rights' and 'responsibilities' increasingly tightly together (Home Office 2003). We therefore observe a greater readiness to intervene early in order to emphasise this linkage and to require young people to adhere to it. The burgeoning number of ASBOs offers evidence of this aspect of the overall strategy. As we progress through the repertoire of interventions, this principle of the conditionality of rights is demonstrated in other ways. Reprimands and Final Warnings, for instance, are only available on one occasion, and Final Warnings are usually administered in combination with intervention 'programmes' which require compliance as evidence of behavioural change. Failure to comply, or a further offence, however, represents a failure to honour the contract with the community, and therefore merits more extensive and intrusive measures, which points the way towards criminal proceedings and sanctions.

It is perhaps unsurprising that the figures considered previously indicate that there has been a substantial increase in the proportion of all young people being formally processed since the mid-1990s; it appears that the new range of interventions available have not supplanted others, but they have taken their place alongside existing options. Where displacement has occurred, it has usually meant that more intrusive disposals have supplanted others which are less so. Thus it appears that Reprimands and Final Warnings have superseded informal action by the police and repeat cautions; Referral Orders have supplanted Conditional Discharges; and ISSPs have been imposed as adjuncts to existing community orders rather than as a true alternative to custody. In some instances, too (breaches of ISOs, ASBOs and other orders, for example), the new options available have actually operated as a form of recruiting agent for more draconian measures, including custody.

It is difficult on this basis to avoid concurring with Goldson's (2006) conclusion that the cumulative effect is one of 'penal expansion' derived 'from a politics of intolerance and punitiveness that has come to frame contemporary youth justice policy' (p. 151). It should be noted, however, that this underlying populist agenda is legitimised by the scientific and managerialist machinery of performance management, risk assessment and behavioural techniques identified by Muncie (2002).

5. Inside the machine

Between policy and practice

The previous chapters explored the policy aims and rationale(s) (Muncie, 2002) associated with the New Labour project, and considered their impact on youth justice processes and outcomes. However, it is also important to make sense of the ways in which pure policy objectives are mediated and reconstructed by way of the procedures and organisational arrangements which create the terrain for practice. We cannot simply assume that policy as set out by government or quangos such as the Youth Justice Board translates directly and straightforwardly into standardised programmes and interventions, and this is so even in a context where it frequently feels as if practitioners are being addressed directly by government, over the heads of responsible agencies and managers. Harris and Webb (1987), in their study of secure accommodation for young people, advanced the proposition that there is a dynamic relationship between each of three levels, the 'macro', 'mezzo' and 'micro'; thus policy originating at the 'macro' level is interpreted, developed, revised and in some cases bypassed or subverted as it is translated into operational guidance and practice itself.

Inevitably, there is a degree of tension between the generalised aims of policy and the practical challenges of making these aspirations 'work' on the ground. Obviously, for example, broad prescriptive statements cannot offer enough detail or precision to inform interventions across a wide range of very different settings. In addition, it is quite likely that some aspects of policy may come into conflict with one another at the point of implementation. Hard choices have to be made, and organisations have to find ways of mediating between competing expectations, such as the imperative to reduce delays as against the requirement to carry out detailed assessments.

We should also expect room to be allowed for variations in the application of policy depending on local circumstances or the specific characteristics of the population. Attempts to apply blanket policies in 'colour blind' fashion will only compound inequalities and discrimination experienced by certain groups (see, for example, Bowling and Phillips, 2002; Feilzer and Hood, 2004). It is also the case that policy is sometimes self-defeating, with a tendency to incorporate its own contradictions and unintended consequences (Muncie, 1999a). For example, the increasing use of formal procedures at the early stages of the justice process (Reprimands and Final Warnings) is in itself likely to lead to administrative complexity and procedural delays, with resultant pressures to find ways of reintroducing informal disposals.

There are, therefore, a number of essentially pragmatic reasons for expecting policy in the form of law and guidance to be developed and modified firstly by agencies and managers and then by practitioners as they are translated into concrete interventions. This, in one sense, is a relatively benign interpretation of the way in which 'bureaucracy' (Weber, 1957) adapts the intentions of the state in order to ensure that they are fair, realistic, practical and deliverable. This in turn provides one criterion by which the machinery of youth justice can be evaluated; that is, it can be judged according to the extent to which it is efficient and effective in delivering the practices and outcomes prescribed by government, such as the 'principal aim of preventing offending by children and young people' (Home Office 1998).

At the same time, there are other, rather less benign interpretations of the mechanisms and procedures put in place for the delivery of youth justice which must also be considered. Muncie (1999b) and Pratt (1989, 2000), for example, have suggested that the increasing emphasis on the apparatus of management and procedural compliance should be seen as part of an emerging pattern of closer and more pervasive forms of control, which themselves bind agencies and practitioners together in a strategy of containment and coercion. This is seen as the:

> 'dark side' of modernity. That is to say, the seeming humanity and rationalist side of punishment in the modern world camouflaged a more intrusive and extensive modality of social control, based around tactics of discipline and surveillance: and at the forefront of such deceptions were the penal experts and the penal bureaucracies. (Pratt 2000: 143)

While Pratt argues that this coercive tendency of the machinery of youth justice might be superseded in time, there is no doubt that contemporary concerns about the impact of 'managerialism' (Clarke et al. 2000) need to be addressed.

Other perspectives on the apparatus of youth justice might offer a rather less functionalist view. It might be felt, for instance, that New Labour's reforms have essentially established a framework of common aspirations (core objectives and targets), within which it is possible to accommodate both situational diversity and the capacity to develop creative and innovative services to address the problems associated with youth crime. As part of this exercise, the establishment of a body such as the Youth Justice Board might be seen as contributing significantly to this function, by acting both as the representative of government and as a source of experience, expertise and new ideas.

The cynical view might be that this sort of arrangement shifts much of the complexity involved in delivering service goals (and, of course, the blame, should things go wrong) outside of government itself. However, by the same token the space is therefore opened up for independent initiatives, innovation and risk-taking. Yet again, this might lead to the incorporation into the government project of professional and policy interests which might otherwise be directly critical of some aspects of the youth justice reform programme. There is a sense here in which the structures for the delivery of youth justice themselves constitute contested territory. It is thus possible to argue that there is 'all to play for', on the one hand, while, on the other, these developments may also be taken as confirmation that significant professional interests have been co-opted by government as one means of extending control into the detailed workings of the system (Foucault 1979). In order to unravel these problematic questions, it is important to consider the evidence, such as it is, arising from the actual development and implementation of the procedures, structures and mechanisms for the delivery of youth justice in the early years of the twenty-first century.

National objectives and National Standards: prescribing good practice?

There are a number of ways in which government has attempted to set the terms for the development of youth justice including the structural prescriptions of the Crime and Disorder Act 1998, but there have also been associated initiatives in terms of the procedures and practices to be followed. Thus the starting point for this analysis will be the attempts to establish prescriptive standards for practice (Youth Justice Board 2000, 2004a). Like many other initiatives, the move towards standard setting is not specific to the post-1997 Labour government but dates back at least to the early 1990s. It was at his point that the criminal justice system began to witness the publication of a range of standards for interventions with offenders (Smith, D. 1999). In particular, the progressive development of National Standards for work with young offenders from 1992 onwards represented an attempt to set clear and consistent expectations as to the levels of control to be applied across the range of interventions. This appears to have been a progressive process, with successive versions of the standards representing an increasing emphasis on behaviour management and a reduced level of concern with meeting welfare needs. The standards thus promote compliance and responsible behaviour on the part of offenders. As Smith points out, by 1995 the needs of young people had been subsumed within the aim of reforming them. Supervision Orders were thus expected:

> To encourage and assist the child or young person in his or her development towards a responsible and law-abiding life, thereby promoting the welfare of the offender. (Home Office 1995, quoted in Smith, D. 1999: 148)

These developments, he suggests, emphasise young offenders' criminality, according them no substantive recognition as children or young people.

In arguing for a creative response to the uniform requirements of practice standards, he urges 'the recovery of forgotten possibilities, memories of social work's past which have been all but eradicated from practice today by managerial diktat and the rule-bound proceduralism of National Standards' (Smith, D. 1999: 163).

Smith's concerns were further substantiated by the progressive hardening of Home Office policy towards enforcement and compliance which promoted greater use of punitive sanctions in cases where orders were breached (Home Office 1997b). Thus, the implementation of tighter and more prescriptive practice standards could be seen as part of a trend towards control and coercion at the expense of a concern with young offenders' personal welfare, delivered within a corporatist managerial framework (Muncie and Hughes 2002).

Have these fears been borne out, then, by the further development of National Standards for Youth Justice (Youth Justice Board 2000, 2004a), issued in conjunction with the Crime and Disorder Act 1998 and associated legislation? In their initial form, these standards undoubtedly set out to create the impression that practice would be driven by a spirit of rigour and certainty. Reiterating the principal aim of the youth justice system (the prevention of offending by young people), six objectives were specified:

- the swift administration of justice so that every young person accused of breaking the law has the matter resolved without delay;

- confronting young offenders with the consequences of their offending, for themselves and their families, their victims and the community and helping them to develop a sense of responsibility;

- intervention that tackles the particular factors that put the young person at risk of offending;

- punishment proportionate to the seriousness and persistence of the offending and which strengthens protective factors;

- encouraging reparation to victims by young offenders; and

- reinforcing the responsibilities of parents. (Youth Justice Board 2000: 1)

The general tone of this corporate document,[13] setting the 'required standards of practice which youth offending teams and others are expected to achieve (Youth Justice Board 2000: 2), was highly prescriptive, and clearly underlined the priorities of punishment, responsibility and behavioural change. While the preamble also made some gestures in the direction of children's rights and avoiding discriminatory practices, these were no more than rhetoric in light of the prevailing ethos of the document.

With a change in the Chair of the Youth Justice Board, there was also something of a change in tone of the second edition of the *National Standards for Youth Justice* (Youth Justice Board 2004a). From this point, practice would be expected to support the 'principal aim' by:

- preventing crime and the fear of crime by ensuring that services are targeted at children and young people at high risk of offending and meet the needs of victims and communities;

- ensuring that young people who do offend are identified and dealt with without delay, with punishment proportionate to the seriousness and frequency of offending; and

- promoting interventions with young offenders that reduce the risk factors associated with offending, increase the protective factors and reinforce the responsibilities of parents. (Youth Justice Board 2004a: 3)

Perhaps this represents a slight shift of emphasis with the insertion of a responsibility to address 'protective factors', although the language of 'targeting', 'risk' and 'punishment' retains a strong flavour of offence-oriented behaviour management.

As previously, the revised standards cover all stages of the youth justice process from preventive work through to custodial provision. They are directed primarily at youth offending teams (YOTs) and secure facilities, but also apply to 'partner agencies', such as the police, education and health departments, who are responsible for collaborating to deliver 'good practice' (Youth Justice Board 2004a: 5). As before, it is of some interest that YOTs are seen as the pivotal organisations in achieving the delivery of National Standards rather than other agencies or strategic bodies. This, again, reflects the wider prescriptive and centralised approach associated with the New Labour project. Government and its 'partners' (in this case the YJB) address practitioners directly.

Preventive work

The corporatist theme is sustained by the standards' references to the importance of YOTs becoming involved in joint initiatives of various kinds, including links with local Crime and Disorder Reduction Partnerships (National Standard 1.1). Specific activities should include delivery of Youth Inclusion Programmes, and interventions alongside Connexions services and Drug Action Teams (1.3). Preventive programmes should target crime-prone neighbourhoods and those young people most 'at risk' of offending (1.4):

> The YOT must manage the process of identifying the 50 young people most at risk of offending [in its area]. (Youth Justice Board 2004a: 10)

In addition, the YOT should develop school holiday programmes to divert young people from crime (Standard 1.7). Here, the definition of preventive activity is restricted solely to the 'factors associated with youth offending', and makes no connections to the broader preventive aims of the wider children's services agenda (DfES 2004).

Remand management

Standards under this heading focus on the requirement to provide a comprehensive service to young people and the courts following arrest and prior to trial proceedings. In some respects, this is the aspect of National Standards which provides most assistance in clarifying the rights of young people (and their parents) in the criminal justice process. Thus requirements to provide appropriate information to parents/carers (Standards 2.5 and 2.9) and young people (2.11) are set out here, as is the stipulation that a parent (2.3) or appropriate adult (2.4) is present for police interviews. It is the YOT's responsibility to ensure that the Police and Criminal Evidence Act 1984 and associated Codes of Practice are followed in the course of police investigations (2.6) and to provide an 'appropriate adult service' where parents cannot attend police interviews.

The appropriate adult 'is not just an observer but has a responsibility to ensure that the young person's rights are upheld at all stages, understands what is going on, and is not the subject of any discriminatory action' (Moore and Smith 2001: 33). This element of the YOT's operation, therefore, incorporates a commitment to children's welfare and the protection of their rights, albeit within fairly limited parameters, through the justice process. This offers an indication that a concern with children's needs remains relevant in some aspects of youth justice practice. The precise nature of appropriate adult practice is rather less clear cut, as research has shown (Pierpoint 2004). There appears to be little consistency in practice across geographical boundaries, with the result that 'the nature of the appropriate adult's role varies and this, in turn, impacts upon the young person's experience of police interviewing and detention' (Pierpoint 2004: 42). As a consequence, it is unclear whether the appropriate adult is, indeed, primarily concerned with children's interests, or with 'due process', 'crime control' or 'crime prevention'.

Work in courts

A newly inserted standard (Youth Justice Board 2004a) draws attention to the responsibilities of YOTs for providing 'high quality services' to courts. This section appears principally concerned with the necessity of providing an efficient administrative service to enable the smooth and timely running of courtroom business, in respect of attendance, provision of reports and liaison with other organisations. Within this, however, there is a brief reference to the responsibility of the YOT for addressing 'vulnerability issues regarding 15- to 16-year-old boys' in the completion of court reports (Standard 3.5); and subsequently for conveying information about 'an enhanced risk of suicide, self-harm or harm to others' to the secure establishment following a custodial sentence or secure remand (3.7).

Assessment

The National Standards document sets out detailed requirements about the approach to assessment to be undertaken by youth justice professionals, which once again is loaded in the direction of identifying 'the risk factors associated with offending behaviour and [informing] effective intervention programmes' (Standard 4.1). Assessments are to be carried out at each stage of the process, and the principal tool for their completion is the ASSET form (in its various versions), pioneered by the Youth Justice Board itself.

While evaluations of the form itself have been, at best, equivocal (Roberts *et al.* 2001; Baker *et al.* 2002; Baker 2004), it has been decisively established as the 'industry standard', with the aim of bringing uniformity to the assessment process. National Standards make this clear, setting out in some detail the procedures for completing and monitoring ASSET forms. The second version of the standards (Youth Justice Board 2004a) offers some limited concessions to the principles of children's rights and welfare concerns in this context, so that detailed assessment must be undertaken if a child appears likely to commit self-harm, for example (Standard 4.5). In addition:

> The young person must be invited to complete the ASSET self-assessment form and be given any necessary assistance to do so. (Youth Justice Board 2004a: 28)

In light of the very prescriptive approach towards assessment set out by National Standards, substantial concerns have been articulated about the threat to professional discretion (Eadie and Canton 2002), and the importance of avoiding treating ASSET as a 'purely bureaucratic document' (Baker 2005: 119).

Work with victims of crime

Consistent with wider developments in criminal justice (Williams 2000), National Standards give a substantial section over to the involvement of victims, especially in respect of 'restorative processes' (Youth Justice Board 2004a: 31). Youth Offending Teams are expected to provide services to victims in the context of their work with offenders. Victims' wishes should be identified, and they should be offered the opportunity to participate in restorative processes (Standard 5.9), which might include receiving information, apologies or reparation. Victims, however, should not be involved simply for the benefit of the offender (5.1), and they should always 'feel safe' (5.9). Victims should only be involved on their terms, and to the extent that they wish, in order to avoid co-opting them to serve the interests of the justice system, it would seem. However, it should also be noted that the focus of the document as a whole remains the processing of reported young offenders rather than the meeting of victims' needs. Thus the challenges for youth justice practitioners of making a cultural shift away from a preoccupation with outcomes for offenders (Williams 2005) may have led to the unhelpful consequence that victims are simply reminded:

> of their secondary status within the process. In this context, victims may see themselves as a 'prop' in an offender-focused drama. (Crawford and Newburn 2003: 228)

Final Warnings

The Final Warning is the most substantial disposal available which falls short of actual prosecution as introduced under the Crime and Disorder Act 1998, and is intended to be administered following an earlier Reprimand should a young person reoffend. It is made clear that the norm will be for those young people to be made subject of a Final Warning to undergo an ASSET-based assessment in the first instance, which will determine the content of any programme of intervention to be provided (Standard 6.6). Such programmes may be restorative (where the victim wants to participate), 'one-off' (where risk of reoffending is low) or a short period of intervention (where the risk is higher). These programmes are therefore focused either on securing reparation or addressing the risk of reoffending. There is no mention of welfare needs or the possible connection between these and the offending itself. In keeping with the broader trends identified elsewhere, this seems to draw a very restrictive line around the work of the YOT in terms of its responsibilities either to consider or to address welfare issues. One long-standing and highly regarded exponent of pre-court diversion asks: 'Why can't we respond to a child in need who also offends outside the criminal justice system?' (Pragnell 2005: 82).

Reports for courts

The standard relating to court (and Youth Offender Panel) reports sets out a very detailed and highly prescriptive format for their completion. Reports must be based on an ASSET assessment (Standard 7.3) and face-to-face interviews with the young person and parent(s)/carer(s) and they should include reference to victim statements and other information from 'relevant sources'. It is stated that:

> The purpose of a Pre-Sentence Report (PSR) is to provide information to the sentencing court about the young person and the offence(s) committed and to assist the court to come to a decision on a suitable sentence. (Youth Justice Board 2004a: 40)

The main foci of Pre-Sentence Reports should be the offence and assessments of the young person and the risk of reoffending, with associated sentencing proposals (7.10). This framework is quite restrictive and has not been adapted to any great extent with the revision of the National Standards. Thus the process of standardisation and the limited scope for discussion of the offender's background and wider contextual factors remain significant influences on the shape and content of reports. Indeed, the preoccupation with meeting the very specific time limits of the youth justice system appears to be a greater priority than the quality of the reports themselves. PSRs must be produced within ten working days for 'persistent' offenders and those meeting the criteria for the ISSP, and within 15 days in other cases (7.9). Furthermore, where the court is considering a 'specific' sentence, it is expected that a 'Specific Sentence Report' (SSR) can be produced 'on the day of request' except where there is no ASSET available (7.12). In addition, again in the interests of expediency, it seems, provision is made for reports to be made 'on a stand down basis' should the court so require (7.14). At least one commentator has found these arrangements somewhat anomalous:

> It is not easy to see how a report prepared at court could properly address the views of the victim (as legally required in the case of a reparation order report), or adequately detail a range of requirements tailored individually to address offending behaviour (as expected of an action plan order report). (Bateman 2005b: 115)

Ironically, in light of this, it is also expected that 'rigorous' arrangements will be put in place for monitoring the quality of reports (7.15), although in the revised version of the document the specific requirement for ethnic monitoring of reports appears to have disappeared (Youth Justice Board 2000, 2004a). Despite the high level of prescription apparent in this aspect of youth justice practice, at least one study has found that 'report writing remains idiosyncratic' (Drakeford and McCarthy 2000: 110), with a significant variation, for example, in the degree to which report providers are or are not prepared to recommend custodial sentences (Bateman 2005b).

Court ordered interventions

The standards also cover the expectations of practitioners responsible for overseeing young offenders subject to community-based court orders,[14] which:

- must be informed by the following objectives:
- provide a rigorous and effective punishment;
- reduce the likelihood of offending;
- rehabilitate the young person; and
- enable reparation to be made to the victim or wider community. (Youth Justice Board 2004a: 45)

(The document simply passes over the potential and, indeed, likely incompatibility of these objectives.)

At the outset, it is acknowledged that the making of an order accords certain rights to young offenders as well as imposing requirements on them (Standard 8.4), so as not to interfere with school, work or religious observance, for example (8.5). However, the substantive detail is again highly prescriptive, detailing the amount of contact to be maintained between the young person and her/his supervisor twice-weekly for the first twelve weeks and once a week thereafter (8.6); precise requirements are also set out for the administration of procedures for failure to comply with the terms of an order. 'Unacceptable' failure to comply will lead to the issuing of a formal warning; on the third occasion breach action must be initiated 'within five days of the most recent failure to comply' (8.8).

Despite this overarching preoccupation with compliance, National Standards do offer some guidance as to the actual conduct of orders, including Referral Orders, given that YOTs are largely responsible for the establishment and administration of Youth Offender Panels (8.17). However, apart from referencing alternative sources (Baker *et al.* undated), they offer little detail of the key components of each intervention or how it should be conducted. For example, 'the Action Plan Order is intended to provide a short, intensive, individually tailored response to offending behaviour and associated risks' (Youth Justice Board 2004a: 52). This appears, if anything, to be a step back from the earlier version which made specific reference to the need for planned intervention to address matters such as parental or carer involvement, substance misuse, healthcare needs, educational needs, experience of discrimination or harm reduction (Youth Justice Board 2000). Welfare issues are, therefore, further marginalised in the delivery of community-based interventions, it would seem. It has been suggested that the preoccupation with compliance at the expense of content also reflects an:

> undue emphasis on the characteristics of effective *programmes*, ... neglecting the evidence about the importance of effective *relationships*. (Batchelor and McNeill 2005: 170)

Intensive Supervision and Surveillance Programmes (ISSPs)

The second edition of the National Standards included a section on the ISSP for the first time, emphasising the programme's 'rigour' and intensity. Thus: 'It combines intensive community-based surveillance with a comprehensive and sustained focus on tackling the factors that contribute to the young person's offending behaviour' (Youth Justice Board 2004a: 65). Specifically, young offenders subject to ISSP receive 25 hours a week 'supervision' for the first three months of any programme (Standard 9.2), reducing to five hours a week subsequently. This element must include the 'core elements' of: education and training; offending behaviour work; reparation; and developing interpersonal skills and family support (9.9), with additional support for specific problems. Alongside the supervision component, young people on ISSPs will be subject to a minimum of two 'surveillance contacts' daily (9.10), which might include tracking, tagging, voice verification, or intelligence-led policing. Programmes must be agreed by all parties, including parents/carers and the young offender (9.14), and enforcement procedures including 'fast-track breach proceedings' are stipulated (9.17).

Interestingly, while the ISSP is clearly centrally bound up with processes of monitoring and compliance, it is also the only community order for which specific elements are suggested which might assist young people and their families in addressing welfare needs. However, it has been suggested (Canton and Eadie 2005: 147) that:

> 'increasing the likelihood of breach by tightening standards may lead to those who are most in need of effective supervision being breached

before they have a chance to be transformed into 'completers'. This might apply particularly to emotionally volatile young people needing to test boundaries ...

Secure accommodation

Since the Youth Justice Board has assumed responsibility for commissioning the provision of secure establishments for young offenders, the Board has taken an active role in developing the standards by which it requires providers to operate. It is in this context, ironically, that the specifications are most explicitly oriented towards the rights and well-being of children and young people. Thus, for example, staff in secure facilities are expected to act openly and honestly 'as a model for young people' (Standard 10.9). On reception into these establishments, young people should be offered a full assessment (10.10), including a detailed health assessment (10.12) and an assessment of the risk of self-harm (10.13). Workers should be allocated to provide 'advice and assistance' to young people (10.16) and the general ethos should promote a sense of dignity and autonomy. Contact with parents/carers 'should be encouraged' (10.31) and constructive activity promoted, including opportunities for education and training. In addition to these positive provisions, there should also be procedures in place to prevent child abuse (10.27) and to enable complaints to be raised without fear of the consequences (10.25).

While the emphasis on humane treatment in custody is clearly of great importance, this also raises significant questions in terms of monitoring and compliance, particularly in light of critical accounts of practice (Goldson and Coles 2005; Carlile 2006).

Work with young offenders sentenced to a detention and training order

As well as the shape and conduct of custodial regimes, the National Standards prescribe the approach to be taken in administering custodial sentences, and those such as DTOs which have both custodial and community elements. Again, it is interesting that the content of these orders is specified in some detail, in terms of young people's entitlements to planned interventions (Standard 11.5) and objective setting, including education, health and accommodation arrangements on returning to the community. The Supervising Officer is expected to act almost as an 'advocate' for the young person to ensure that planned services are actually delivered (11.16), and has a continuing role in pursuing entitlements with the education authority (11.22), health authority (11.23) and other services (11.24) such as Connexions. However, the supervisor is also responsible for ensuring compliance with the terms of community supervision (11.20) and retains the power of breach (11.26).

Section 90/91 supervision

Similarly, for young people subject to custodial sentences in respect of more serious offences, the YOT has a hybrid role, carrying out assessments

(Standard 12.4), liaising between the young person and the community (12.8), sentence planning (12.9), welfare services post release (12.13) and post-release surveillance (12.16). Specifically:

> Given that all section 90/91 offenders will, by definition, have been convicted of serious offences (often involving violence), supervision may need to be especially close and recall action may need to be taken urgently to protect the public. (Youth Justice Board 2004a: 90)

As if to reinforce the message that monitoring and compliance are central to the functioning of the youth justice system this is the concluding stipulation of the National Standards document. By contrast, the Scottish equivalent (Scottish Executive 2002) is far less detailed and less prescriptive, and it encourages creativity and diversity in responding to youth offending.

Considered in this level of detail, there is some evidence that National Standards incorporate a range of different (and often competing) objectives, including broad aspirational aims such as 'preventing crime and the fear of crime' (Youth Justice Board 2004a: 3), as well as acknowledging continuing concerns with the rights and welfare of young people in the justice system, especially in custodial settings, such as the requirement to identify and act to protect 'vulnerable' young offenders (Youth Justice Board 2004a: 20).

On one hand, this does suggest that there remains some scope within the youth justice framework for the promotion of issues to do with young people's general well-being; on the other hand, however, there is also considerable evidence that the standards themselves reflect a dominant preoccupation with control and containment, which may come to fundamentally shape practice. The National Standards document itself is disappointing in this respect, because in acknowledging the rights and needs of children and young people, it does not provide a strong basis for pursuing requirements identified in a range of human rights instruments already available (such as the Race Relations Act 1976 and the Human Rights Act 1998) or international conventions such as the United Nations Convention on the Rights of the Child (UN 1989) or the 'Beijing Rules' on the administration of juvenile justice (UN 1985).

In light of these concerns about the limitations of the framework document for the delivery of fair and effective services in the youth justice context, it will be important to consider in more detail the practical impact of two major vehicles for the delivery of the 'new youth justice': the Youth Justice Board and Youth Offending Teams themselves.

The Youth Justice Board: mouthpiece or mediator?

Under the heading 'Partnership' in its White Paper *No More Excuses*, the incoming Labour government set out its proposals to establish an arms'-length body which would provide 'clear national leadership ... to improve the performance of the youth justice system' (Home Office 1997b: 2). Despite Labour's professed aversion to quangos while in opposition, the attractions of this kind of semi-independent agency were more apparent when in power. It would allow for a concentration of expertise to oversee and bring coherence to the entire youth justice system, including the operation of the courts and the provision of secure facilities. It would be the source of authoritative advice on the setting and monitoring of standards for the delivery of services (see above). It would be well placed to 'identify and disseminate good practice' (Home Office 1997b: 26), and it could provide independent advice to the Home Secretary on possible future reforms and improvements to the machinery of youth justice. This essentially advisory role was 'fudged' to the extent that the proposed body was also to be given direct operational responsibilities, for example for 'commissioning and purchasing ... secure facilities for young offenders' (Home Office 1997b: 26). This could be expected to pose significant challenges in implementation to the extent that the body responsible for setting standards would also be obliged to apply commercial considerations to the allocation of public money in this context.

Nonetheless, the Youth Justice Board (YJB) was duly established under section 41 of the Crime and Disorder Act 1998, and it was additionally provided with grant-making powers for the purposes of developing good practice, as well as responsibility for receiving and evaluating annual youth justice plans to be submitted by local authorities (section 40). This provision, according to Pitts (2001a), put the Board in an extremely powerful position in respect of local providers of youth justice services, with the ability, in effect, to determine the extent to which these plans were acceptable or consistent with national priorities. In effect, the YJB was therefore accorded very substantial influence, both operational and political in nature. It was established in such a way as to be capable of acting as a conduit for the expression of government's desired objectives, while apparently operating as an independent and authoritative expert body. At the same time, it was put in a position of being able to exercise significant influence over key funding decisions.

So, how have these powerful levers (including the responsibility for National Standards discussed previously) been used by the YJB to shape the activities of agencies and practitioners?

Performance management and youth justice plans

The YJB maintains tight control over the preparation of local annual youth justice plans, in a process where sanctions can be applied if plans are unsatisfactory. Thus, for example, where the board specifies a series of national objectives and performance targets, these are likely to be reflected directly in local strategies. For example, in 2001/02, the key objectives set for Youth Offending Teams (YOTs) were:

1. The swift administration of justice ...
2. To confront young offenders with the consequences of their offending
3. Interventions which tackle the particular factors which put a young person at risk of offending

4. Punishment proportionate to the seriousness of offending
5. Encouraging reparation to victims by young offenders
6. Reinforcing the responsibility of parents

(Leicester YOT 2001; Northamptonshire YOT 2001)

Within these broad parameters, more specific performance targets were also set out centrally by the YJB, and as a result, the aims and objectives of individual YOTs were more or less constrained to fit these overarching goals. These initial aims appeared to be procedurally driven, and in some respects quite inappropriate. Thus, the pre-election pledge by Labour to reduce the length of time between arrest and conviction (Straw and Michael 1996) was reflected in the first of these objectives, several appeared to be about holding young people responsible for their actions, and one at least (proportionate punishment) seemed to fall well outside the remit of youth offending services, lying more appropriately with the courts. In these early days of the YJB, there were significant omissions, too, from its list of priorities, including concerns with discrimination in the justice system, protecting the rights of young people, or promoting their well-being, even where welfare needs might actually be related to young people's offending behaviour. Nor is there anything here about promoting opportunities for young people, through education or other forms of activity.

These constraints appeared to have a direct impact in terms of the shape and limitations of local youth justice plans at this point in time. Thus the preoccupation with 'speeding up' youth justice is reflected in the commitment to timely production of court reports, and the reduction of delays in identifying and processing 'persistent young offenders'. The 'provision of information to Police to execute warrants on Persistent Young Offenders' was a priority area of work for one YOT (Leicester YOT 2001: 13).

Equally, the pressure to ensure that young people were 'confronted' with the effects of their behaviour led to a focus on the development of reparation schemes and the establishment of effective monitoring procedures. However, even at this stage, there appears to have been some leeway for local variations. In spite of the YJB's lack of any specific reference to this issue, YOTs were able to identify diversity and discrimination as an area of concern. In one area, it was the intention that: 'all minority ethnic young people in custody are referred to the Black Prisoners Support Group' (Leicester YOT 2001: 17). In addition, the absence of any pressure on the part of the YJB to address welfare issues did not prevent some YOTs from including this kind of objective in their local plans, referring for example to the need to promote young people's access to mental health services (Leicester YOT 2001). This continuing concern to retain the link between justice processes and young people's needs represented a continuing recognition at the level of practice that the two could not simply be disengaged.

Other objectives such as the requirement to achieve proportionate punishment created significant difficulties for the YOTs, firstly because they are only responsible for *administering* some punishments, rather than *imposing* them, which is the job of the courts, and secondly because proportionality is an extremely difficult concept in any case:

Ranking sentences according to seriousness and then establishing a scale of penalties of commensurate severity achieves *ordinal proportionality*, but gives little guidance on *cardinal proportionality*, the overall severity of penalty scales. Put simply, the problem is that deserts theory can help with the graduation of punishments within the most severe and least severe points, but can do nothing to tell us what these anchoring points should be. (Hudson 1996: 45)

Given this fundamental problem for any system for dispensing justice, YOTs appear to have been set an impossible task in this respect. To require them to produce meaningful objectives and targets in the absence of the ability to control sentencing practice or a consensus on what constitutes 'fair' punishment is simply unrealistic. Indeed, it has been argued further that the youth justice system has become less 'proportionate' in its outcomes following the 1998 reforms (Cadman 2005).

Nevertheless, most local plans appear to have sought to comply with this expectation. Some, for example, appear to have taken it as a licence to pursue reductions in the use of custody (Leicester YOT 2001: 25), some were concerned to promote the 'confidence' of the courts in the quality of their assessments and sentencing proposals (Peterborough YOT 2001: 59) and one, at least, continued to promote its historical commitment to 'diversion' by seeking to 'obviate' the need for Anti-Social Behaviour Orders (Northamptonshire YOT 2001: 40). Yet others (Newham and Northumberland YOTs, for instance) appear to have concentrated on developing and promoting more intensive community programmes to work with persistent offenders, such as the ISSP.

Over time, the focus of the YJB's objectives and targets has shifted, and this is of interest for a number of reasons. By 2005, and following changes at its most senior levels, the Board was still acting quite prescriptively, addressing the 156 YOTs and 38 secure establishments in terms of six key targets and the 'levers' to be used to achieve these, under three main headings:

Reducing offending and the use of custody
1 Reduce the number of first-time entrants to the youth justice system.
2 Reduce reoffending by young offenders.
3 Reduce the use of custody.

Improving outcomes for children
4 Improve the assessment of risk and need of young people who have offended, and their access to specialist and mainstream services once these have been identified.
5 Reduce local differences by ethnicity in recorded conviction rates.

Safe and appropriate use of custody
6 Accommodate all girls under 18 years of age in secure establishments that are separate from adults, and replace 250 places for boys, currently accommodated separately from adults but on sites with some shared facilities, with dedicated sites and facilities.

(Youth Justice Board 2005c: 10)

In this way, it seems that the principles and priorities of the YJB may have changed over the course of time. There is clearly a renewed concern with children's welfare and the provision of relevant services, and there is also now an explicit commitment to address the problem of institutional racism in youth justice (see Bowling and Phillips 2002). The form by which the YJB communicates its expectations is little changed, in that it sets precise targets with which it expects YOTs to comply (a 10 per cent reduction in the under-18 custodial population by 2008, for example) and continues to apply explicit performance measures (reducing the use of secure remands, say), but the content of the strategy has been modified. It might thus appear that the ability to prescribe outcomes in this fashion offers positive benefits if utilised benignly, but this conclusion should be treated with care, since it still leaves the Board open to accusations of centralised control and an undue willingness to compromise with government's populist agenda.

Buying influence: the YJB's approach to funding services

Since its establishment in 1999, the YJB has held responsibility for administering a range of budgets and funding programmes on behalf of a number of government departments, but predominantly the Home Office. It has also, as already noted, acquired responsibility for commissioning all places in the under-18 secure estate from April 2000. The way in which these very sizeable funds are distributed is clearly an important indicator of the way in which the Board seeks to influence the delivery of youth justice and promote its own priority aims.

It is evident that money has been directed to almost all levels of intervention, from targeted prevention through to investments in improving the standards of custodial regimes. By 2002, the YJB had already been responsible for funding 70 Youth Inclusion Programmes and over 150 Summer Splash holiday programmes, intended to reduce the likelihood of offending by young people in high-risk areas. In order to make the case for further funding, the YJB was quick to claim success for these initiatives (Youth Justice Board 2001a). By 2004/05, the board had secured additional investment from a range of sources including the Children's Fund, and alongside the (now) 72 YIPs there were 124 Youth Inclusion and Support Panels, 400 Safer Schools Partnerships and '125,643 at-risk children and young people participating in Positive Action for Young People' (Youth Justice Board 2005d: 6), all of which were designed to prevent young people from becoming offenders.

For young people on the threshold of the justice system itself, the YJB made an initial three-year investment in the establishment of bail support schemes (129 by February 2002), which 'offer individually tailored programmes according to the risks and needs of young people on bail. In general, they provide help with education, employment and training, accommodation, social and life skills and work with families' (YJB Press Release 26 February 2002). Early in its existence, the YJB also made £5 million available for the development of the Remand Review Project (see previously), with the express intention of reducing the reliance on custodial remands for young people.

Dedicated funding for bail support came to an end in 2002, however, leaving some doubt as to whether it would be 'embedded' within YOTs and the courts (Youth Justice Board 2005e).

In the context of direct interventions with young offenders and their families, the YJB has also been fairly active in trying to shape practice. It has, for instance, funded mentoring schemes, drug workers (Youth Justice Board 2005c) and accommodation projects. It has also developed and evaluated new measures, such as Referral Orders, parenting programmes, 'intensive fostering' (Youth Justice Board 2005d) and the Intensive Supervision and Surveillance Programme. By 2005, for example, the ISSP was accounting for £32 million (8 per cent) of the YJB budget, and nearly 5,000 young people were subject to the programme (Youth Justice Board 2005c, 2005d).

While the YJB appears to be committed to developing non-custodial options for young offenders (and *alleged* offenders pre-trial), these are often characterised by a greater degree of intrusion and surveillance than had been the case previously. For example, the use of electronic tagging has become one of the means by which ISSPs can be administered, and the rationale for this has been its contribution to controlling a potential threat:

> The ISSP is testimony to the fact that unprecedented levels of supervision, in the form of tagging and otherwise, does protect the public whilst the supervision element looks at the reasons for offending and challenging young people's behaviour. (Youth Justice Board Press Release 26 February 2002)

Welcoming the reported achievements of the ISSP in 2004, the Chair of the YJB made it clear that the programme would remain a central plank in the Board's strategy of promoting tough community sentences which would 'force' young people to face up to the consequences of their crimes (Youth Justice Board Press Release 14 September 2004).

Although seeking to invest in supposed alternatives to custody, the YJB has also invested heavily in the custodial estate. Its initial spending concentrated on improving provision for educational, vocational and personal development (£40 million), but it also put in motion plans to increase the number of places available in secure establishments, proposing to build an extra 400 secure training centre places (Youth Justice Board 2001a). Claiming that it would be able to remove young offenders under 18 from adult prisons, the Board's 2002 budget proposals increased this figure to 600 places.

In fact, only 144 of these places were completed by 2005 (Youth Justice Board 2005f: 5), but the Board also claimed to have made a substantial number of improvements to the secure estate overall, such as the removal of all 15- and 16-year-old girls from Prison Service accommodation ('except in exceptional circumstances'), and improvements in educational provision and specialist after-care for young people with mental health or substance misuse 'problems'.

However, this catalogue of 'improvements' should also not mask a number of other issues of concern. Firstly, and most significantly, as already observed, serious concerns persist about the welfare and treatment of young people in custody (Goldson and Coles 2005; Carlile 2006). Secondly, apparent enhancements in secure living conditions may actually encourage sentencers to view such facilities in a positive light. And thirdly, the level of funding demanded by secure establishments creates a massive imbalance in the spending allocated to youth justice in general – 72 per cent of the YJB's 2005/06 budget of £411.7 million was taken up in this way, for example.

It may be an oversimplification to suggest that there is any degree of consistency about the board's funding strategy, although it is apparent that the notion of 'targeting' and intensification of interventions does seem to represent a common theme, and these are consistent features of spending programmes across the youth justice continuum from preventive services through to community-based alternatives to custody. This might be justifiable, in its own terms, if there was evidence of a parallel reduction in the dependence on the most restrictive sanctions, and custody in particular, but this does not appear to have been the case, with the reliance on secure regimes having remained at a consistently high level, as illustrated in the previous chapter.

Using publicity to lead change?

The YJB has also taken a key role as 'champion' of change in youth justice, with a demonstrable readiness to use publicity as a vehicle for promoting its own agenda. This, in turn, has raised some awkward questions about its structural position and the legitimacy of its role, given that it was established ostensibly as an independent body.

In some respects, the Board has acted clearly as the agent of government, in setting National Standards, for example, and in taking on responsibility for the secure estate. In constitutional terms, this might be felt to be inappropriate, but it also raises significant questions about the extent to which the Board itself has taken on a political function on behalf of government which threatens its integrity and credibility in the field.

Indeed, repeated references in its press releases to the role of the YJB in 'spearheading' the reform programme and in implementing this 'flagship' policy (YJB News March 2000) suggested that there might be some confusion over this issue within the Board itself. Nonetheless, there were some signs that it was prepared to distance itself from current policy from the start, for example over the inappropriate use of custody: 'Short custodial sentences disrupt the lives of young people and make it more difficult to implement effective educational and behaviour changing programmes. They also waste resources' (Lord Warner, Youth Justice Board Press Release 22 August 2001). The YJB's first chair, Lord Warner also took this opportunity to criticise a 'wide [geographical] disparity' in sentencing practice, which 'is inherently unfair'. On the other hand, the Board was paradoxically untroubled by the government's policy of increasing the number of custodial places available (or its own role in this) and by the courts' increasing eagerness to make use of them (Youth Justice Board 2002: 15). Direct spending on expanding the custodial estate is surely more likely to have an impact on its use than countervailing press releases issued during the summer holidays. The YJB's principled position on locking up children was, and remains, ambiguous at best.

The YJB was only established as a statutory body in 2000, but moved quickly to become a significant influence in the field. In taking on this role, its public pronouncements and style of operation have begun to communicate a strategic vision for preventing and responding to youth crime, characterised by central direction, close management, targeting and intrusive forms of intervention. As a consequence, it has been experienced as a source of routinised planning and standardised service delivery, which have narrowed the scope for imaginative and creative professional responses to the problems associated with young people and crime (Eadie and Canton 2002).

Despite these concerns, the Board has shown some signs of pursuing a distinct role, independent of government and representing wider interests. Despite its own somewhat compromised position, the chair came out more strongly in favour of reducing the use of imprisonment, saying 'there are too many kids in custody' (*Guardian* 28 July 2002), and the YJB was also reported to be lobbying government for greater investment in alternatives to custody and crime prevention projects at around this time (White 2002). This assertiveness on the part of the Board was further emphasised by its increasingly strong opposition to the use of short custodial sentences (Youth Justice Board Press Releases 27 January 2003, 4 February 2003), and the withdrawal of sentenced young people from Ashfield Young Offenders Institution (YOI) following a highly critical inspection report (Youth Justice Board Press Release 5 February 2003).

With a change at the helm, the second chair of the YJB also clearly saw it as part of his role to express an independent view when he criticised the processes of net-widening and 'demonisation' associated with the use of ASBOs against young people (*Independent* 23 April 2006). Taken together, these might be seen as tentative emerging signs that the YJB is capable of exercising a degree of independence and drawing on the available evidence to promote soundly based interventions which respect the rights of children and do them no harm.

YOTs: all at sea?

Finally, in considering the new post-2000 terrain of youth justice management and service provision, we must address the emergence and early experiences of the specific implementation vehicle, that is the Youth Offending Teams. The origins of their establishment as multi-agency entities for the delivery of youth justice can probably be ascribed to the convergence of a number of strands in thought and practice. Firstly, there was evidence that previous inter-agency arrangements had worked well, notably the much-researched, well-reported and highly regarded diversion schemes of the 1980s (Smith 1989; Audit Commission 1996; Bell *et al.* 1999). The Northamptonshire model offered grounds for optimistic assumptions that good working relationships between agencies in one area could be replicated elsewhere without too much difficulty. Cautionary notes were sounded, though, by those involved, who stressed that effective partnerships have to be worked for and actively sustained: 'Inter-agency strategy and working in partnership involve complex and dynamic processes which require intellectual, emotional and practical commitments' (Bell *et al.* 1999: 101).

Others have taken a more cynical view of what such arrangements achieve, suggesting that they represent the emergence of a form of 'corporatism' (Davis *et al.* 1989; Pratt 2002). This is no accident, instead representing a:

> third model of juvenile justice ... This sociological concept refers to the tendencies to be found in advanced welfare societies whereby the capacity for conflict and disruption is reduced by means of the centralization of policy, increased government intervention, and the co-operation of various professional and interest groups into a collective whole with homogeneous aims and objectives. (Pratt 2002: 404)

This argument is supported by broader analyses of welfare state formation (Esping-Andersen 1990) which have suggested that corporatism is a common feature of the structure and delivery of state-provided services in general and youth justice in particular (Smith, D. 2000).

The convergence of these underlying tendencies with evidence of the effectiveness of inter-agency practice found further reinforcement in New Labour's diagnosis of social exclusion, as we have already observed, in the sense that it quickly became accepted as a truism that 'joined up problems' require 'joined up solutions'. Thus 'in the past, governments have had policies that tried to deal with ... problems individually, but there has been little success at tackling the complicated links between them, or preventing them arising in the first place' (Social Exclusion Unit 2000: 1). In this sense, then, the establishment of Youth Offending Teams, or something similar, was almost inevitable. They have taken their place alongside an array of inter-agency, inter-professional and inter-sectoral initiatives put in place from 1997 onwards, including Education Action Zones, Health Action Zones, New Deal for Communities, Neighbourhood Renewal Programmes, Sure Start, Connexions, Drug Action Teams and Crime and Disorder Reduction Partnerships.[15]

Building YOTs

YOTs were created by the Crime and Disorder Act 1998 (section 39), with the local authority established as the lead body but requiring the 'co-operation' of the police and health authorities. They were required to include as members:

> at least one of each of the following, namely –
> (a)   a probation officer;
> (b)   a social worker of a local authority social services department;
> (c)   a police officer;
> (d)   a person nominated by a health authority any part of whose area lies within the local authority's area;

(e)   a person nominated by the chief education officer appointed by the
      local authority under section 552 of the Education Act 1996.
                      (Crime and Disorder Act 1998, section 39(5).[16]

Other people could also be recruited to the YOT, depending on local
circumstances. The task of the team would be to 'co-ordinate the provision of
youth justice services' and to deliver the youth justice plan.

In a display of 'corporate' commitment to the principles of joint working,
the guidance on their detailed operation was issued jointly by the Home Office,
the Department of Health, the Welsh Office and the (then) Department for
Education and Employment. It was emphasised that YOTs were 'not intended
to belong exclusively to any one department or agency' (Home Office et al.
1998) and that local authority chief executives should ensure that they were
developed 'corporately'. The YOT manager was seen as having a key role
in bringing together a disparate team, and establishing coherence of purpose
and operational consistency. Where necessary, the principle of partnership
could also be extended to include the voluntary sector, victims' organisations
or the youth service.

Some aspects of service delivery could, indeed, be delivered by other
bodies, 'such as bail support, reparation or mediation work or specified
activities under a supervision order' (Home Office et al. 1998). Guidance also
extended the legislative requirements of the YOT to include a commitment to
preventive work, with a stipulation that at least 2.5 per cent of the YOT budget
should be dedicated to this purpose. The work of the team was further located
within the 'joined up' government social exclusion strategy with explicit links
to other programmes, including crime reduction, Youth Action Groups, school
inclusion initiatives, parenting and family support, drug misuse programmes,
neighbourhood renewal and 'welfare to work'.

Despite the emphasis on links and shared agendas, the guidance also
emphasised the distinctive nature of the YOTs' tasks in practice, with the
advice that the YOT manager could be drawn from any, or none, of the
participating agencies, and ought not to be '"buried" within the management
structure of any of the partner agencies; it is essential that they are able to
engage, as appropriate, with all the relevant local agencies ...' (Home Office
et al. 1998: 14).

Thus a significant degree of independence from local parent agencies
appears to have been vested in the YOT manager from the start, and this
was reflected in their responsibility for the recruitment of team members and
allocation of tasks. Implicit in this is the idea that agencies should not just
be able to second existing practitioners in their established roles, but that
they should adapt their practice to the new structures: 'While the skills that
different professionals bring to the team are likely to reflect their occupational
background, rigid boundaries within the team would be inefficient and limit
the benefits of joint working' (Home Office et al. 1998: 21). However, it is
unlikely that guidance alone can resolve the recurrent tensions to be observed
in simultaneously maintaining a distinct professional identity and contributing
collaboratively to a shared operation with rather different objectives. Indeed,

the guidance itself incorporated some of these dilemmas by going on to specify a number of tasks which would best be carried out by specific professionals within the multi-agency team; for example, police officers were identified as best equipped to carry out victim-related tasks.

And finally, the Home Office guidance also stressed the responsibilities of the YOTs to the Youth Justice Board, including their duties to submit annual youth justice plans for review, as well as their responsibilities for ensuring compliance with legislation, producing monitoring information and arranging training for practitioners.

Floating YOTs

In parallel with the production of YOT guidance, pilot teams were established in nine areas (Nacro 2001), starting in September 1998. Of these, four were given the full range of YOT powers while five were allocated selected responsibilities in order to test specific aspects of the new legislation. The pilots were extensively evaluated, with one large-scale study commissioned by the Home Office (Holdaway *et al.* 2001) and other investigations carried out independently (for example, Bailey and Williams 2000; Burnett and Appleton 2004). The Home Office study reported broadly positive outcomes following some teething problems. YOTs were applauded, for example, for responding to fundamental changes in structures and working practices quickly. They were commended for overcoming initial tensions and for moving towards a collective approach to the task of delivering youth justice services: 'There was a 14% increase in the numbers of staff who, when surveyed, saw the team as having a shared view of work' (Nacro 2001: 2). Similar findings are reported by researchers who took a case study approach to the implementation process, suggesting that, in fact, the dominance of social services staff in the early days of the YOT helped to preserve the 'welfare ethic' of practice (Burnett and Appleton 2004: 50). According to the national survey:

> YOTs have been successful at melding the skills and expertise of members from different agencies to create the possibility of a distinctive culture for the delivery of youth justice. (Holdaway *et al.* 2001: 113)

The pilot stage YOTs were also commended for undertaking a 'systematic approach to case management and for drawing on 'specialist services' to tackle offending behaviour and 'criminogenic factors' in young people's lives. However, closer reading of the report suggests that criticisms could be made of certain aspects of practice. Completed assessment forms were found to be variable and subjective in content, and some aspects of intervention programmes were 'questionable' (Holdaway *et al.* 2001: 33), a finding which has been echoed elsewhere (Feilzer *et al.* 2004; Wilcox 2004). In addition, the national study found that some participants appeared uncommitted to the idea of joint working (somewhat at odds with the individual case study reported elsewhere; Burnett and Appleton 2004), budget disputes persisted and service delivery was paradoxically observed to be both 'formulaic' and 'inconsistent'!

Nacro's overview of the evaluation also notes that pilot YOTs appeared to have little impact on specific outcomes, such as the use of custody for young offenders, apart from a sharp increase in one area which may be viewed as an 'unintended consequence'. However:

> It would be wrong to blame the apparent increase in the use of custody on the new orders since a slight upward trend in the number of custodial disposals was apparent from early 1997. It would be equally mistaken, however, to dismiss the possibility that the changes associated with the Crime and Disorder Act might have helped to intensify the drift in Wessex [the pilot area of Hampshire and the Isle of Wight] towards a more punitive approach towards young offenders. (Holdaway *et al.* 2001: 69)

Independent research into the introduction of YOTs has attributed some of their difficulties to an oversimplistic understanding of the new legislation: 'The [Crime and Disorder Act] is a complex one, capable of being interpreted in a variety of ways. In practice, this presents some difficulties for agency managers in establishing youth offending teams' (Bailey and Williams 2002: 18). It is noted, for instance, that the belief among agency managers in the diversionary potential of the new legislative framework was not widely shared, and, indeed, the early evidence suggested that younger and less experienced offenders were actually being drawn into the justice system (Jennings 2002). Differing perceptions of the likely impact of the new legislation were complemented by continuing wrangles of a more long-standing nature, such as budgetary arguments, contested access to confidential information and the extent to which members of YOTs believed their allegiances lay with parent agencies. Conflicts could be identified on a number of levels: organisational, professional and between practice ideologies (for example, over dealing with 'risk'). These differences of perception could also be linked to questions of professional status, organisational authority and public esteem, which are all likely sources of tension and which affect the extent to which YOT members could truly expect to work in a spirit of partnership and cooperation.

Despite these concerns, the researchers' conclusions were not wholly pessimistic, although they have suggested that there is much to be done to generate effective and productive inter-agency working arrangements:

> The pressure of getting youth offending teams off the ground has meant that practitioners have largely stuck to doing what they know. Only when they have the time and resources to share their expertise and develop new skills will the real benefits of inter-agency work be seen. (Bailey and Williams 2000: 83)

Equally, in the case study referred to above, the consensual view of YOT members was 'cautiously optimistic' (Burnett and Appleton 2004: 51), not least because the very complexity of the new legislation enabled them to pick and choose from the array of differing principles and strategies incorporated within the legislation.

While these studies indicate cautious but positive support for the initial achievements of YOTs in establishing effective working relationships, none seems concerned about the possible limitations of a 'corporatist' strategy. Indeed, Burnett and Appleton (2004: 50) appear to believe that this may offer opportunities to preserve a 'welfare' approach, and David Smith (2000: 129) likewise argues that 'it is at last worth considering the possibility that a more corporate approach would help to deliver [desirable] outcomes'. Reflecting again on the experiences of the 1980s, he reminds us that successful inter-agency projects, like the Northamptonshire Juvenile Liaison Bureaux, were 'in large measure a creation of practitioners', and that the lack of collective organisational commitment can sometimes undermine progressive interventions:

> The Labour government's version of corporatism is based, in large measure, on the kinds of criticism of established practice which youth justice practitioners have themselves made over the years, and it deserves, at least, a serious collective attempt to make it work in practice. (Smith, D. 2000: 142)

Against this positive portrayal of the merits of corporatism, however, we must also set the arguments of those who see it merely as an extension of centralised state control (Althusser 1977) which restricts professional creativity and limits autonomy, enforcing a punitive straitjacket on those who deliver and those who experience youth justice interventions. For some, it is evident that uniformity and control are at the centre of the New Labour project. The government was reported to find 'conflict uncomfortable and threatening and it therefore strives to characterise the new youth justice system it has brought into being as one in which such conflict has been "designed out"' (Pitts 2001b: 142).

In light of this argument, we might expect to find a seamless and internally consistent relationship between the triad of National Standards, Youth Justice Board and Youth Offending Teams, apparently working harmoniously towards the common and uncontentious goal of preventing youth crime. Muncie argues that corporatism is not unique to the New Labour reform programme, but is instead a continuation of well-established trends:

> By the 1990s it was already clear that traditional welfare or justice-based interventions had become peripheral to much youth justice practice. The ... setting of performance targets and the establishment of local audits does indeed suggest a depoliticisation and dehumanisation of the youth crime issue such that the sole purpose of youth justice becomes one of delivering a cost-effective and economic 'product'. (Muncie 1999: 290)

Interestingly, then, these critics actually share with the New Labour government the functionalist assumption that the youth justice system can be, and has been, constructed and delivered in such a way that specific high-level policy objectives can be translated directly into the intended practice outcomes through the implementation of standardised organisational arrangements and precisely specified procedures.

Corporatism: construct, constraint or catalyst?

In summary then, we might draw the conclusion that the machinery of youth justice put in place by New Labour to deliver its reform programme was intended as a unified and centralised system, displaying some of the characteristics of a 'corporatist' or 'managerialist' (Clarke *et al.* 2000) approach. Thus it was observed by one study of YOTs that senior managers from different agencies could be heard to 'parrot' the stated aims of the Youth Justice Board in setting out local aims and objectives (Bailey and Williams 2000: 21), and it is certainly the case that the youth justice plans adhere to the board's template very closely.

Despite this evidence, care must be taken to avoid simplistic conclusions. It is also clear that tensions remain. As we have observed, aspects of the National Standards are contradictory for example, and it is clear that agencies, managers and practitioners still experience conflicts arising from their obligations to honour competing objectives. In addition, research into the use of standardised tools such as ASSET has revealed significant variations in practice (Baker *et al.* 2002). Indeed, it is suggested that the use of such tools should support rather than circumscribe professional discretion (Baker 2005). Tensions can, of course, be creative, and it seems that there remains a degree of latitude for those in practice to apply policy goals and procedural instructions flexibly. Lipsky (1980) has demonstrated that it is almost a 'fact of life' for what he terms 'street-level bureaucrats' to have to adapt rules and procedures to the complex realities within which they operate. Eadie and Canton (2002) suggest that the ideal basis for practice is one which is 'accountable' but also offers substantial scope for the exercise of discretion within this framework.

However much policy-makers might aspire to drawing up coherent and consistent prescriptions for the organisation and delivery of services, there will always remain a degree of uncertainty, both in terms of complex human realities, but also in the sense that prescriptive statements themselves tend to incorporate anomalies. While National Standards might juxtapose the aims of preventing crime, meeting the needs of communities and proportionate punishment as if they are compatible, this is not necessarily the case. 'Proportionate punishment', for example, may even be criminogenic, given the well-established links between incarceration and the likelihood of reoffending (Goldson and Coles 2005: xiv).

So, we may conclude that there is a considerable degree of discord over whether 'corporatism' is beneficial or damaging in its effect on youth justice on the one hand, and on the other whether it actually achieves the kind of monolithic outcomes predicted by its more functionalist proponents and critics. Perhaps we can conclude with the speculation that a corporatist approach of the kind documented here must have a powerful influence on the shape and practices of youth justice, but that this does not offer any certainty as to the justifications for such an approach, and, further, it seems equally likely that it may contribute to the generation of further unplanned consequences such as net-widening through the formalisation of pre-court diversion (Goldson 2000a), the emergence of YOTs as a new agency and the intensification of the punitive aspects of practice through inappropriate targeting of interventions such as ISSP (Audit Commission 2004; Bateman 2005a).

6. Making it happen: practice in the new century

Creative tensions or routinised control?

Following the themes of the previous chapters, it seems that competing portrayals of youth justice are available. In their idealised (Weber 1957) forms, they can be formulated as two diametrically opposed viewpoints. One suggests that the extensive reform programme of the late 1990s and beyond established, perhaps for the first time, a sound and sustainable basis for the delivery of interventions which can be shown to 'work' building on a substantial body of international evidence (Burnett and Roberts 2004). This evidence includes policy analysis (Audit Commission 1996, 2004), systematic reviews (Goldblatt and Lewis 1998), and copious research carried out into the new schemes put in place in parallel with the Crime and Disorder Act (for example, Holdaway *et al.* 2001; Newburn *et al.* 2002; Baker *et al.* 2002; Campbell 2002; Farrington *et al.* 2002; Baker *et al.* 2005; Youth Justice Board 2005e). This body of knowledge, it is believed, provides the soundest possible grounding for the implementation of new models of practice which are most likely to deliver effective outcomes (see, for example, Goldblatt and Lewis 1998). This perspective has clearly taken hold with those at the centre of policy-making in 'contemporary UK youth justice' (Bateman and Pitts 2005: 252).

The critical perspective takes issue with the overwhelming sense of 'certainty' which seems to permeate the 'what works' agenda (Bateman and Pitts 2005) and holds the view that much of the evidence produced is little more than a smokescreen for the development and legitimation of routinised mechanisms of control. Little professional imagination is required, and standardised processes are put in place instead to deliver fixed, measurable and predictable outcomes:

> 'Delivery' has been facilitated by encouraging standardised interventions, reflected in performance targets, to be implemented without deviation, in order, it is said, to avoid the problems of 'implementation failure'...
> (Bateman and Pitts 2005: 252)

Too much reliance is placed on studies which appear to have a distinct vested interest in producing positive findings, it is suggested:

Unsurprisingly, perhaps, the evaluations of mentoring cited by the Youth Justice Board, which is funding over 100 such programmes, are remarkably upbeat, deriving as they do mainly from studies undertaken by members of the US-based National Mentoring Association. (Pitts 2001a: 12)

At the same time, rather less encouraging findings are given rather less public exposure (Wilcox 2004), and in some cases it is suggested that they are simply misrepresented (Green 2004).

In Pitts's view it is not that 'nothing works' – indeed, a wide range of interventions can be shown to have a positive impact with some young people, some of the time (Bateman and Pitts 2005: 257). It is important, however, that these examples of successful interventions are not over-generalised. This is to create unrealistic expectations on the one hand, but it also feeds a prevailing trend towards reducing the available range of interventions to 'a narrow range of correctional techniques' (Pitts 2001a: 12).

Indeed, there appears to be a dual and somewhat contradictory dynamic in play here (Goldson and Muncie 2006a), whereby an apparently increasing reliance on rational practices based on sound evidence is not quite what it seems. When scrutinised in more detail, the evidence of favourable outcomes based on routinised interventions is 'at best, tenuous' (Goldson and Muncie 2006a: 208). At the same time, the certainty and finality of the rationalising 'modernisation' agenda justifies a political strategy organised around the themes of 'toughness', control and behaviour change (Goldson and Muncie 2006a; Smith 2006).

While the reality for those engaged in and experiencing youth justice may be somewhat more complex than these polarised positions might suggest, they do provide a helpful framework within which we can begin to develop a realistic picture of what is happening in the field, and it is against this backdrop that we will review current developments and the changing shape of practice.

A substantial body of evidence has been generated following the New Labour reforms, concerning changed working arrangements, the administration of new orders and practice innovations. Much of this material has been commissioned on behalf of government or the Youth Justice Board, but there is an increasing number of other sources of evidence available, usually drawing on local evaluations and accounts from practitioners and managers themselves.

First impressions – procedural change

In order to avoid concentrating unduly on the high-profile and highly publicised initiatives which have gained considerable attention, the aim here will be to try to gain a flavour of the way the system as a whole has been affected, including procedural changes which may lead to unpredictable outcomes.

Reducing delays

Perhaps indicatively, the first priority for the incoming 1997 Labour government in youth justice was to reduce the length of time for processing alleged offenders. This was, in fact, one of the five key election pledges made by the party. The commitment was based on the arguments advanced by the Audit Commission (1996) that delays were both wasteful of resources and damaging to young people in that they might contribute to the risk of reoffending while diluting the impact of any punishment. By the time of the White Paper *No More Excuses*, these concerns had been crystallised:

> The Government is determined to end these delays. They impede justice, frustrate victims and bring the law into disrepute. And delays do no favours to young offenders themselves; they increase the risk of offending on bail and they postpone intervention to address offending behaviour. The top priority will be to halve the time taken between arrest and sentence for persistent young offenders. (Home Office 1997: 23)

Pilot schemes to put this pledge into effect were established on passage of the Crime and Disorder Act, and a guide was produced on *Speeding Up Youth Justice* (Youth Justice Board 1999). These steps were supported explicitly by National Standards which set limits for the completion of Pre-Sentence Reports (Youth Justice Board 2000, 2004a) and Specific Sentence Reports (Youth Justice Board 2004a: 42). Perhaps surprisingly, the time allowed for reports on persistent young offenders (PYOs) was ten days, whereas for those with a less serious offending history it was 15 days. Thus, somewhat perversely, it was just those more complex cases where the time pressure of YOT practitioners would be greatest.

Such pressures were amplified by the advice given on behalf of the Youth Justice Board, which cited 'unnecessary adjournments between verdict and sentence as one of the five major causes of delay' (PA Consulting 2002). In order to reduce these, requests for Pre-Sentence Reports should be made 'selectively', and these should 'only be considered where a custodial or community sentence is a serious option' (PA Consulting 2002). Even in these cases, 'existing' reports may be acceptable to the courts, rather than taking time to request updated versions.

The concern here must be that professional issues to do with the quality, scope and thoroughness of the assessment process may be subverted by the need to hurry things along to meet externally imposed deadlines. Reviewing a number of pilot initiatives, Ernst & Young (1999) found no evidence of any impact on the 'quality of justice', although, strangely, they do not appear to have considered the implications either for the nature of assessments or sentencing decisions. On the other hand, the team reviewing the pilot Youth Offending teams noted that:

> There is evidence from all of the pilots that the perceived need to speed up the system of youth justice is being treated as an end in itself. This

is having the unintended consequence of jeopardising the attainment of other important objectives. (Holdaway *et al.* 2001: 25)

Among these were found to be 'the need to ensure just outcomes' based on a full and informed understanding of the circumstances of the offence, but also proper attention to the interests of the victim and the 'accountability of the offender'. Although these researchers were not concerned about the impact of a 'corporate approach to the task of sentencing', they remained concerned about the impact of 'fast-tracking', commenting that 'courts have demanded increasingly tight schedules for cases and YOT members have had to accommodate them within workload constraints' (Holdaway *et al.* 2001: 111).

While the Audit Commission (2004) found that the targets for 'speeding up' youth justice were being met and this was broadly welcomed, some concerns were expressed that this may have led to a greater readiness to bring 'too many minor offences' to court (p. 20). Additionally, there appears to be cause for concern about the consequences of rapid processing for those awaiting court hearings for further offences, who may thereby come to be classified as persistent young offenders more quickly than would previously have been the case. Despite the emergence of these issues, the preoccupation on the part of government and the Youth Justice Board remains the narrow and procedural issue of whether or not targets for reducing delay have been met.

Making the best of our ASSETs?

The emphasis on procedural improvements can also be identified in other aspects of the youth justice system, including a more structured approach to the various phases of practice (Baker *et al.* nd). This approach has been epitomised with the introduction and development of the ASSET form, versions of which are available for each stage of the process. As the relevant National Standard puts it:

> All children and young people entering the youth justice system should benefit from a structured needs assessment. The assessment process is designed to identify the risk factors associated with offending behaviour and to inform effective intervention programmes. The Youth Justice Board has developed the *Asset* common assessment profile for this purpose. (Youth Justice Board 2004: 27)

The aims of the ASSET form are identified as being to assist decision-making in practice and to improve management information. Most importantly, the principal 'function of ASSET is to help YOTs assess the needs of young people and the degree of risk they pose and then to match intervention programmes to their assessed need' (YJB, quoted in Roberts *et al.* 2001: 28).

In this respect, ASSET and the assessment process appear to share the principles of other materials, such as the *Framework for the Assessment of*

Children in Need and Their Families (Department of Health 2000) and the *Common Assessment Framework for Children and Young People* (DfES 2006). These documents identify the importance of an integrated approach to assessing children's circumstances and well-being. However, the YJB's guidance also makes it clear that it sees the ASSET form as a management tool, and as a source of data to contribute to a broader understanding of youth offending and to support service planning (Baker *et al.* 2003: 9).

The updated (2006 version) ASSET form (Core Profile) itself runs to 26 pages (although there are shorter versions for specific purposes such as bail assessment and Final Warnings), incorporating basic information about the offenders, including ethnic origin, nature and circumstances of the offence and victim details; but, more significantly, it concentrates on assessing the risks of further offending by the young person.

Practitioners are required to complete an offence analysis and criminal and care histories before going on to complete a detailed rating of the likelihood of further offending, based on categories such as 'living arrangements', 'education, training and employment', 'lifestyle', 'family and personal relationships' and 'motivation to change'. A section is also provided for the identification of positive factors, although these are not scored in the same way. The concluding sections focus on the 'vulnerability' of the young person and the 'risk of serious harm' to others. There is also an accompanying pro forma on which young people are invited to conduct a self-assessment, 'What do you think?' This option has been received positively by practitioners, it is reported (Roberts *et al.* 2001).

Despite this concession in the direction of dialogue and young people's perspectives, the general approach of ASSET can be summarised as a 'tick box' approach, with a heavy emphasis on the negative indicators of risk of offending, which may well predispose practitioners to a narrow and unfavourable view of the young person and her/his behaviour. As a result, it is perhaps unsurprising that it has proved impossible to integrate the assessments undertaken under ASSET with those focusing on children's needs more generally under the *Common Assessment Framework* (Youth Justice Board 2006b, para. 1.3). ASSET is reaffirmed as the primary tool for considering the 'risk of: reoffending, causing serious harm to others [and] vulnerability'.

The ASSET form and procedures have been piloted, revised and evaluated repeatedly (Roberts *et al.* 2001; Baker *et al.* 2003, 2005), while at the same time YOT practitioners and managers have been able to form their own views about its use and value. An immediate dichotomy emerged in the first stage of the evaluation between ASSET as a management tool and as a flexible aid to understanding young people and their behaviour. The initial expectations of the Youth Justice Board that the form would be completed 'fully' and 'on all young people entering the justice system' (Allan 2001) seemed to conflict with the evaluators' view that:

> ASSET was not intended to be used as an inflexible interview schedule or just a checklist to run through with a young person. Whilst there appeared to be some staff using the form in this way, most recognised that this was not a helpful approach. (Roberts *et al.* 2001: 33)

Indeed, at this point eight different approaches to the completion of ASSET were observed, with practitioners often preferring to use it as a 'framework' for interviews rather than a rigid template.

When considering the relationship between ASSET and more traditional approaches to the construction of reports for the courts, practitioners were found to express a range of opinions. Most thought there was some value in the form in that it provided a comprehensive framework to inform the preparation of Pre-Sentence Reports, although some felt that it added little to the process and in fact oversimplified the task of providing an 'individual' picture of the young person (Roberts *et al.* 2001: 38).

While there were some concerns about the appropriateness and relevance of some of the detailed questions included in ASSET, practitioners' main worries related to the value and validity of being asked to use the form as the basis for 'rating the risk of re-offending' (Roberts *et al.* 2001: 45). This aspect of the exercise appeared to many to be arbitrary and unreliable. It also appeared to sit rather oddly with the suggestion that the form was not intended to be used rigidly in this way, but should inform a more considered and flexible approach to information-gathering and assessment.

One illustration of the problems of relying unduly on a rating system such as this was provided when:

> One police officer described how he would always give a rating of 4 [highest risk of reoffending] if a young person admitted using cannabis because this, by definition, meant that they were likely to reoffend. Other colleagues who regarded cannabis use as low risk and low priority did not accept this approach. (Roberts *et al.* 2001: 45)

The concerns of YOT workers about the spurious accuracy of an apparently objective scoring system focused on a number of specific points: uncertainty about what a particular score might mean; lack of flexibility to 'weight' elements which might be more or less relevant in some cases; the negative consequences of finding out more about a young person (especially significant because of the overall bias in this direction of the ASSET document); and possible misuse of aggregated data by the YJB.

These concerns crystallised the tensions implicit in the formulation of a standardised instrument such as ASSET, which confronts professional 'know-how' with a reputedly objective mechanism which can provide better information. The core beliefs of those who see a central place for individual discretion and imaginative decision-making in working with young offenders are thus fundamentally challenged. As a result, YOT staff were found to be making limited use of completed ASSET forms to inform their subsequent interventions. While most of those responding to a questionnaire on the subject stated that they were using ASSET 'in some way' to inform their practice, in group discussions this did not appear to be borne out (Roberts *et al.* 2001: 48) and one despairing respondent commented: 'Nothing is done with completed ASSETs, so what are we doing it for?' (quoted in Roberts *et al.* 2001: 51).

This kind of experience may have underpinned the cynical view of some staff that the main purpose of the exercise was to provide statistical information for the YJB and government. Indeed, the evaluators noted that this may have understated the depth of hostility to ASSET due to the way in which respondents were recruited (Roberts *et al.* 2001: 61). Despite these reservations, however, the YJB pressed on, announcing that 'it would now make completion of the assessment tool a key condition of funding provided by the board' (Allan 2001: 3).

Further experience of ASSET has been equally mixed, with subsequent evaluations suggesting that its use has become more systematic and that this is reflected in an improvement in its ability to predict the likelihood of reoffending (Baker *et al.* 2003, 2005). However, research commissioned by the YJB does appear to have been unduly preoccupied with the predictive accuracy of ASSET; as a result, endorsements of its value may appear somewhat one-sided:

> The results … provide further support for the Youth Justice Board for England and Wales' (YJB) strategy of putting *Asset* at the centre of YOT practice. The data suggest that practitioners and managers can have confidence in using *Asset* as an indicator of risk of reoffending, and also therefore of the level and intensiveness of intervention required to address offending behaviour. (Baker *et al.* 2005: 7)

According to this account, ASSET is able to predict the likelihood of reconviction correctly in 69.4 per cent of cases. It also seems to be the case that changes in ASSET scores over time are correlated with the chances of a young person being reconvicted.

However, this rather narrow account of ASSET's achievements is somewhat undermined by the associated evidence that there is no relationship between the assessment itself and intervention plans (Baker *et al.* 2005: 6). In addition, practitioners have been found to be variable (Annison 2005) and strategic in the way in which they have used the form, such that 'YOT staff may be allocating ratings on the basis of perceived problems' (Baker *et al.* 2005: 6). In other words, ASSET may be used as a post hoc justification for professional decisions rather than a tool to assist in making assessments.

Indeed, the value of ASSET as anything other than a predictive tool is widely questioned (Birmingham Youth Offending Team 2004). In practice, YOTs have found it difficult to use it as anything other than an aid to statistics gathering, leading to a pragmatic and limited approach which 'devalues ASSET in the eyes of practitioners from being a useful tool to a paper exercise' (Birmingham YOT 2004: 37), an observation echoed by the Audit Commission (2004: 74).

New orders – redesigning practice?

While there has been some evidence of routinisation in the initial stages of the youth justice process, as noted above, it is equally important to consider the question of whether there have been any substantive changes in practice following the implementation of a range of new orders from 2000 onwards.

It is an advantage for us that the new interventions have been researched extensively, usually at the pilot stage, so there is good evidence on which to draw. However, both their timing and their content seem to have meant that most of these studies have been ignored by government and the Youth Justice Board. This is no reason, however, for us to bypass the important messages for good practice which have emerged. For example, comprehensive evaluations have been undertaken of the impact of systemic change (Bailey and Williams 2000; Holdaway *et al.* 2001; Burnett and Appleton 2004) and of specific innovations in practice (Newburn *et al.* 2001b; 2002; Gray *et al.* 2005).

The study by Holdaway and colleagues (2001) offers the most comprehensive overview of the new youth justice environment, and examines in some detail the general and specific implications of the 'new disposals' (specifically, the Final Warning, Reparation Order, Action Plan Order, Parenting Order and Child Safety Order). The investigators make it clear that their primary interest is in discovering if and how interventions 'work':

> At many points of [our] report we comment on the importance of evidence-based practice to the routine work of YOT staff. By 'evidence-based practice' we mean work with offenders to reduce offending, the success of which has been demonstrated through rigorous evaluation. (Holdaway *et al.* 2001: 1)

This research is driven by a practical orientation towards ensuring that assessments and interventions are soundly based and consistent. We might thus expect their findings to reflect a pragmatic emphasis on outcomes rather than a more reflective account of process: 'YOT staff should base their work with offenders on systematic evidence of "what works" (Holdaway *et al.* 2001: 1).

We have already considered these researchers' observations and concerns about the YOTs as delivery mechanisms (Chapter 5), and we will now address their findings in relation to direct interventions, which are also linked to some fairly prescriptive views about what constitutes good practice. For example:

> YOTs need to ensure that they are able to offer a sufficient range of meaningful and effective reparative interventions, whether these are intended to meet the needs of individual victims or to ensure that reparation is made to the community at large. Such interventions should be sufficiently flexible to cater for different types of offenders and offences … YOTs need to take particular care to avoid the use of 'tokenistic' or 'formulaic' interventions … (Holdaway *et al.* 2001: 28)

Thus there is a clear emphasis on researching impacts and outcomes from a particular perspective. The research team went on to examine a number of YOT interventions, seeking evidence of their effectiveness in reducing the likelihood of further offending.

Final Warning

The Final Warning has been identified as an important innovation, representing a dual commitment to diverting young people from court by giving them a 'last chance', while at the same time making it clear that further offending will result in criminal proceedings. The Youth Justice Board has also promoted the use of positive intervention programmes to support the administration of a Final Warning by the police, suggesting that such interventions should be made available in 80 per cent of cases (Pragnell 2005). These 'change programmes' would have the central aim of addressing offending behaviour, but should also meet 'the needs of victims' (Holdaway and Desborough 2004: 24). Initial findings suggested a wide variation between YOTs in their use of additional interventions alongside Final Warnings (Holdaway *et al.* 2001: 33), suggesting in the researchers' view that the intentions of the Crime and Disorder Act were not being achieved. However, by 2004/05, 85 per cent of Final Warnings were administered in combination with an intervention programme.

The kind of services provided in this context might include restorative justice, drug counselling, letters of apology, reparation, mentoring, youth club attendance, education support, 'general offence' work and parenting support. It was discovered in the early implementation phase that programmes were usually undertaken within 2.5 months of the Final Warning being administered, of which 74 per cent were completed satisfactorily. However, at this point, there was some concern about YOTs' failure to offer programmes in some instances, or the provision of simplistic standardised responses that might often be unsuitable. Researchers questioned:

> The considerable use of a letter of apology as an element of a change programme ... In some pilot areas, staff dealing with change programmes were requiring all young people to write letters of apology, irrespective of the circumstances ... This is surely inappropriate in many cases and a less than satisfactory way of meeting the needs of offenders and victims. (Holdaway *et al.* 2001: 78)

Concern was expressed about the 'questionable' relationship between 'off-the-peg' change programmes and the specific nature of the offence or the young person's circumstances and perceptions. Additionally, it was suggested that the focus of interventions might be too narrow, and that some offenders at least would benefit from services which were not within the YOT's remit. In some cases, parents' needs for support were not being addressed.

While the research team concluded with positive support for the Final Warning scheme, they raised concerns about whether YOT practice could be seen as sufficiently flexible to address the diverse range of circumstances likely to be encountered in this context. In addition, it seemed that intervention programmes were not linked in any coherent fashion to prior assessments (using ASSET), so that: 'Many offenders with risk factors of relevance have not been referred to projects that could have accepted them' (Holdaway and Desborough 2004: 26).

These concerns have been supported by other findings. Thus one study which claimed that Final Warnings were having a positive effect on reducing re-conviction rates offered no support for the argument that intervention programmes could further enhance this outcome:

> There was no statistically significant difference in further criminal proceeding rates between those who the youth offending team assessed as appropriate for a 'behavioural change programme', those who were assessed as not appropriate, and those who were not seen by the youth offending team. This result calls into question the nature and role of assessment procedures and the programme delivered as part of a final warning during the pilot period. (Hine and Celnick 2001: 1)

Not only are programmes apparently offered on a fairly arbitrary basis, with little justification either in terms of the contents of the assessment or the likelihood of reoffending, but there are also grounds for thinking that the prior administration of reprimands and warnings themselves is fairly erratic (Audit Commission 2004; Pragnell 2005). Thus, in 2002–03, the Youth Justice Board found a regional variation of between 38 per cent and 51 per cent of all disposals resulting in a reprimand or warning (Pragnell 2005: 80), while the Audit Commission (2004: 17) also reports that 'local practice varies. Sometimes several reprimands are given, sometimes the gravity factor system[17] is not used correctly and sometimes Final Warnings are issued to those who had previously received them.'

So, while the YJB (2006a) is able to report that its 80 per cent target has been achieved for Final Warning intervention programmes, it seems far less certain that these are based on reliable assessments targeted on the intended participants and appropriately designed or capable of achieving the desired outcomes, unlike the diversion initiatives of the 1980s (see Chapter 2). The conclusion that, nonetheless, Final Warnings should be supported by change programmes sits rather oddly with the exhortation that we should concentrate only on pursuing 'evidence-based practice' (Holdaway *et al.* 2001: 33).

Reparation Orders

The Reparation Order was incorporated in the Crime and Disorder Act 1998, although it was not without precedent, building on a lengthy tradition of reparative interventions in youth justice dating back at least as far as the 1980s (Smith, R. 2002a). In some ways, then, it might be expected to have a stronger basis than some of the other innovations in the field of youth justice initiated by New Labour. According to Holdaway and colleagues (2001: 35), the Reparation Order needs to be seen as part of a series of interventions introduced since 1998 which incorporate principles of 'restorative justice' (Johnstone 2002) for the first time into the English and Welsh criminal process for young people.

Although initially the government had planned to require courts to consider making Reparation Orders in all cases (Home Office 1997b: 14), the legislation eventually restricted their use to the 'entry level' for dealing with minor offences. Despite this limitation, the new provision would require YOTs to develop their repertoire to include work with victims. Reparation should be arranged where courts required it, and according to the researchers concerned this represented:

> one of the most important and far-reaching cultural changes required by the Crime and Disorder Act ... [A]n essential prerequisite ... is the need to ensure that all who are involved in the imposition and delivery of reparative interventions ... are fully conversant with the restorative ethos that underlies the Act. (Holdaway *et al.* 2001: 36)

Leaving aside this highly questionable final assertion, the evaluation of YOT pilots showed that practitioners and managers had responded positively and creatively to the requirements of the new order, establishing new ways of working to accommodate and respond to the interests of victims. These included the development of 'victim consultation procedures', offering support to victims, the establishment of mechanisms for securing direct reparation and direct and indirect mediation. In addition, offenders could be involved in broader 'restorative' interventions, such as writing letters of apology, undertaking victim awareness programmes and indirect reparation. Clearly, those new forms of practice which required the involvement of victims introduced a changed dynamic in the context of work with young offenders, and it has been voiced as a matter of concern that victims' interests should not thereby become subordinated to those of young offenders or the youth justice system itself (Davis *et al.* 1989; Williams 2000). Most victims who were asked in the course of the YOT pilot evaluation felt that offenders' interests were, indeed, prioritised over their own (Holdaway *et al.* 2001: 81).

Despite this, the researchers expressed a strong preference for continuing to promote victim involvement, particularly in light of an initial low response rate: 'It seems probable that some form of personal contact with victims (either by telephone or by a follow-up visit) is more likely to elicit a positive response than a simple letter, requiring the victim to "opt-in" to the process' (Holdaway *et al.* 2001: 37). It also appears that there is a tendency for victim work to become seen as a distinctive area of responsibility within the YOT, often taken up by police officers on the team, who are assumed to be more victim-oriented and to have more prior experience of such work. This separation is also believed to have been necessitated by the requirements of data protection legislation which restricted the ability of the police to share victim details with YOT colleagues (Dignan 2005: 135). With the ensuing introduction of the Referral Order (see below), this compartmentalisation of roles has become more strongly entrenched, at least in some areas (Smith, R. 2002a). The need to separate responsibilities in this way remains questionable, at least in the experience of the present author (Smith, R. 1989), and has significant implications for the interprofessional model of working exemplified by YOTs.

Even where victims could not (or should not) be directly involved, it was always intended that the reparative activity undertaken by young offenders under a Reparation Order could be 'indirect', meaning 'community reparation'. However, questions can be raised about the purpose and relevance of such activities, especially where they bear little relationship to the original offence:

> It appears easier to set up general reparative tasks, such as the performance of basic conservation work, than ones that are particularly suited to particular types of offences or offenders ... there is a risk that it could degenerate into a somewhat tokenistic response ... (Holdaway et al. 2001: 38)

Generally, the pilot YOTs were found to have established both indirect and direct reparation processes, although there was considerable variation between the areas concerned (Dignan 2000: 11). However, in the early stages this was found to be limited largely to writing letters of apology, of limited value to victims who were largely excluded from prior consultation about this (Dignan 2000: 23). In addition, the political pressures on YOTs to reduce delays (discussed previously) sometimes appeared to override the need to take time to negotiate sensitively with victims and develop meaningful forms of direct reparation. Sometimes, too, it seemed that courts were being overly prescriptive as to the form and content of the Reparation Order itself, irrespective of the difficulties in ensuring compliance (Dignan 2000: 27). Such pressures clearly affected YOTs' ability and willingness to spend time and effort establishing flexible and sensitive forms of 'mediation' as a means of bringing offenders and victims together to resolve the issues relating to an offence, and to facilitate direct face-to-face apologies.

Similar difficulties were reported by the investigators responsible for the wider evaluation of the YJB's restorative justice projects (Wilcox 2004). Here, too, the pressure to reduce delays and the rigidity of court procedures had a discernible impact on practice, with the result that easier options such as 'community reparation' and written apologies became the norm, irrespective of their value. In the light of these problems, it is perhaps not surprising that YOTs were observed to be turning to other options, such as victim awareness exercises, designed to 'challenge' the young person's offending behaviour. These enabled the incorporation of established forms of activity, with which practitioners were more familiar. Thus in one case:

> The standard programme is based on a cognitive behavioural approach, but this can be adapted if necessary to encompass anger management or drug therapy. In other areas, the victim awareness programmes are mainly linked with victim empathy and apology exercises. (Holdaway et al. 2001: 39)

While it would be unfair to extrapolate too much from these early findings, it seems clear that these interventions under the terms of a Reparation Order had little to do with the ostensible aim of requiring offenders to make amends to their victims. At the same time, it is also apparent that the order has become established as an occasional sentencing option, used by the courts on 3,635 (3.3 per cent of all court disposals for young offenders) occasions during 2004/05 (Youth Justice Board 2006a), with relatively low reconviction rates (Williams 2005).

While both Williams (2005) and Dignan (2002, 2005) recognise the important steps taken to take account of the victim perspective, they also identify a number of problems arising from the specific manner in which the Reparation Order has been implemented. These include: the status and treatment of victims; the pressures of time and the impact on processes of consultation and negotiation; the extent to which certain 'reparative' activities are meaningful; the consequences of compulsion; and the routinisation of a form of intervention at the expense of individual circumstances and needs:

> Even before they were introduced, the restorative potential of these reparative measures had been assessed in very modest terms ... But as a result of the implementational problems ... it is clear that even this limited potential was not fully realised. (Dignan 2005: 136)

The Action Plan Order

The Action Plan Order is a central element in the New Labour reform programme. The intention was to create a short-term intervention that would allow for 'individually tailored' programmes to be provided for young offenders 'at an early stage', with the aim of tackling the causes of their offending (Home Office 1997a). The order would effectively offer a flexible framework, within which a range of more or less specific requirements could be incorporated, such as compliance with 'educational arrangements', reparation, participation in specified activities, or avoidance of certain areas (Home Office 1997a). Initially, it was noted, the Action Plan Order was intended not to replace but to supplement other sentences, although there did appear to be a tendency for this option to displace the Attendance Centre Order to some extent, which is perhaps unsurprising given that attendance centre requirements are offered as one component of the Action Plan Order (Home Office 2000). Even at this point, there seems to have been some confusion as to the relationship between the Action Plan Order and the sentencing tariff. While for Holdaway and colleagues (2001) there was no intended relationship, this is clearly at odds with the guidance issued in support of the Crime and Disorder Act:

> The action plan order is ... intended to be imposed for relatively serious offending, but it is also intended to offer an early opportunity for targeted intervention to help prevent further offending. Courts may wish to consider the action plan order when a young person has *first* been convicted of an offence serious enough for a community sentence. (Home Office 2000: 4)

Despite the apparent constraints on its use, the Action Plan Order was well received by courts and youth justice staff alike. Courts appreciated the opportunity to specify programme content as well as the duration and type of order. In addition, it was reported that young offenders and their parents/ carers also welcomed the structure and clarity offered (Holdaway *et al.* 2001: 41). By 2004/05, Action Plan Orders were made on 5,318 occasions by the courts, and the possibility of extending their use as a matter of policy was also being considered. By 2003, the Home Office had announced a plan to replace the nine juvenile non-custodial sentences with 'just one, a broader Action Plan Order' (Home Office 2003: 6).

In delivering the Action Plan Order, the approach taken by YOTs has been to offer a 'core programme' with other elements added as appropriate to the specific circumstances. The typical core programme includes elements that appear at other points and under other orders, such as the attendance centre requirement mentioned earlier, addressing the consequences of offending behaviour, victim issues and work on family and relationships. Additional requirements which might be added include mentoring, reparation and involvement with motor projects.

The overlap with other parts of the repertoire of disposals is particularly noticeable in the context of reparation, with the same form of activity potentially available to young offenders subject to Final Warnings, Reparation Orders, Action Plan Orders, Supervision Orders and Referral Orders. This congruence is associated with the growing interest in restorative interventions, it is suggested (Crawford and Newburn 2003: 17).

The distinctive programme elements are combined to form an overall package, which was found to involve about 25 hours of input from the YOT (Holdaway *et al.* 2001: 42), although there was also considerable variation in the content and delivery of the order. The response from participants was found to be generally positive by evaluators, except where victims felt that they were not being well served.

The evaluation team was critical, however, of the approach they observed in some areas which was attributed to staff with prior youth offending experience bringing 'old ways of working' with them and turning Action Plan Orders into 'mini-supervision orders' (Holdaway *et al.* 2001: 42). This is not what the legislation intended, according to this perspective. Both the 'menu' of activities and the individualised nature of the programme are reminiscent of the content of conventional interventions such as Supervision Orders stretching back over a considerable period (see, for example, Children's Society 1988, 1993; Audit Commission 1996). In this sense, the models of intervention observed could be characterised as essentially 'correctional', despite the emergence of a stronger insistence on reparative activity in law and guidance. Indeed, this aspect of the order has come under criticism for being 'mechanistic' (Williams 2005: 214).

On the other hand, observation of the work of YOTs also suggests that there does, remain a strong 'welfare' element in much of what is undertaken under the terms of an Action Plan Order. It could, in fact, be construed as a compressed attempt to deliver some of the needs-based interventions associated with Supervision Orders, including family support, assistance with accommodation or addressing the problems arising from school exclusion

(Smith, R. 2002a). If this is the case, clearly it would be unhelpful for courts or even the YJB to be overprescriptive in determining the content of orders.

The Referral Order: moving restorative justice centre stage?

Although it was only introduced in 1999 by the Youth Justice and Criminal Evidence Act[18], the Referral Order quickly became a central element in the reshaped terrain of youth justice. Like other reforms of that period, the new order was extensively piloted and evaluated before its full implementation in April 2002 (Newburn *et al.* 2001a, 2001b, 2002; Earle and Newburn 2002; Crawford and Newburn 2003).

The place and significance of the order is guaranteed by its location at a specific point in the sentencing tariff. On a first conviction, courts are required to make a Referral Order on a young offender, except where a custodial sentence is being considered. In some ways, this represents another means of achieving the objectives of the Action Plan Order, but with the additional benefit that the conviction is spent once the order is completed.

The effect of the Referral Order is to transfer the responsibility for the intervention to a Youth Offender Panel, consisting of a YOT member and two independent people. The task of the panel is to agree and then oversee a 'contract' with the young person, specifying a programme of requirements to be met during the period of the order (3–12 months). Like the Action Plan Order, the Referral Order 'may include' one or more of a by now familiar list of requirements: reparation, mediation, community service, school/work attendance, 'specified activities', attendance at specified times and places, avoidance of specified places or people, and compliance monitoring (section 23, Powers of Criminal Courts (Sentencing) Act 2000).

The supporting guidance (Home Office 2001c) emphasises the centrality of the victim to the process, and makes it clear that her/his involvement is expected: 'It is essential that all victims be given the *opportunity* to become involved in the referral order process, and to facilitate their involvement where they do wish it' (Home Office 2001c: 22). Victims should be enabled to attend Youth Offender Panel meetings, so that they can express their views about the offence and their expectations of the offender. The guidance suggests that a contract should be agreed at this meeting, and that this will 'always include an element of reparation' (Home Office 2001c: 35). Other elements of the agreed programme will depend on factors 'leading to the offending behaviour'. In this context it appears that the 'principal' aim of the youth justice system, the prevention of youth crime, has been subsumed under the principle of achieving restorative interventions, although this also begs the question of how we define 'restorative justice' itself (Haines and O'Mahony 2006).

Evaluation of the Referral Order in the initial implementation phase was broadly favourable. Thus key features such as the Youth Offender Panels gained a positive welcome:

> Possibly the most encouraging result to date is the fact that within a year YOPs appear to have established themselves as deliberative and participatory forums in which to address a young person's offending behaviour. (Newburn *et al.* 2001b: x)

Over 1,100 orders were made in the eleven pilot sites in the first nine months of operation. Most were for six months or less, although subsequent experience suggests that this was not the case everywhere (Smith, R. 2002a). Because of the way in which the legislation was framed, many orders appear to have been made for traffic offences, and it has been suggested that up to 16 per cent of cases coming to the panel could be classified as 'minor' (Crawford and Newburn 2003: 111).

In terms of the panels' operation, researchers found that offenders complied with the requirement to attend in virtually every case examined, but that victim participation was quite low (13 per cent), and in only 28 per cent of cases was any victim involvement observed (Crawford and Newburn 2003: 185). Thus a central plank of this new disposal appears not to have been put into place effectively in these early stages. By 2004, in one area at least, there was little sign of any increase, with under 9 per cent of victims attending initial panel meetings in Leeds (Crawford and Burden 2005: 35); national standards were blamed for imposing unrealistic deadlines.

Despite this drawback, panels were reported to be agreeing contracts with young offenders in nearly all cases (97 per cent), with some form of reparative activity being the most common element of the programmes agreed (41 per cent). Most contracts had a relatively limited number of stipulations, so there were fewer instances of requirements appearing such as 'addressing educational issues' (8 per cent), 'exploring career options' (7 per cent) and addressing offending behaviour (7 per cent). It must be observed here that these are fairly familiar elements in the youth offending correctional repertoire. Of the distinctively reparative measures identified, community reparation and letters of apology figured most prominently, which may be unsurprising in view of the very limited evidence of direct victim participation. In addition, panel meetings seem to have been fairly successful in obtaining expressions of regret from young people, with around two-fifths offering apologies in the course of panel meetings (Newburn *et al.* 2001b: 29), although in the absence of victim attendance it might be wondered: to whom?

The implementation of programmes agreed with the panel is supervised by the YOT, subject to reports to 'progress panels', which are convened to assess compliance and to consider any need for contract variation, to refer young people back to court in cases of unsatisfactory progress, or to agree that the contract has been fulfilled. The initial evaluation found a non-completion rate of 26 per cent, with non-compliance or reoffending being the main reasons for this (Newburn *et al.* 2001b: 12). Subsequent investigation revised this figure slightly (to 25 per cent, Crawford and Newburn 2003: 139), although it was also clear that success rates were much higher for shorter orders and for 'less serious offences' (Crawford and Newburn 2003: 140). In terms of other conventional measures of success, the one-year reoffending rate[19] for young people subject to Referral Orders has been put at 44.7 per cent (Whiting and Cuppleditch 2006: 18), higher than for pre-court disposals, and lower than for other disposals by the court. It is hard to say, however, whether this reflects anything other than 'differences in the characteristics of offenders given each disposal' (Whiting and Cuppleditch 2006: 8).

The overall picture of the early experiences of the Referral Order is therefore rather uneven. Early studies suggested a considerable degree of enthusiasm for the new disposal (Newburn *et al.* 2002), and a willingness to incorporate a victim perspective and 'restorative' aims into practice (Crawford and Burden 2005). However, a number of concerns also emerged fairly quickly. It seemed (Smith, R. 2002a) that the formal requirements of Referral Order contracts often reflected rather familiar forms of intervention, with only a relatively limited use of a wider reparative repertoire (Crawford and Burden 2005: 37). Much of the activity undertaken took the form of 'community reparation' (44 per cent of cases, in one study; Holdaway *et al.* 2001), which is not necessarily clearly or closely linked to the offence committed and seems more consistent with the Community Service Order in practice. Beyond this, concerns have been expressed in several quarters that the new disposal has both displaced other sentencing options and resulted in interventions 'disproportionate' to the original offence. The Audit Commission (2004: 20) suggests that one in four Referral Orders are made for minor offences, and Burnett and Appleton (2004: 54) also report examples of orders being made for minor infringements when the young person concerned had not even been subject to an earlier warning. By 2004/05, Referral Orders had largely displaced other 'first-tier' court disposals (Youth Justice Board 2006a). As one YOT member is reported to have said:

> This is processing young people when a conditional discharge would have been sufficient ... Intensive supervision with overloaded contracts to address lots of issues which are resource intensive should be reserved for higher risk offenders, in line with 'what works' principles, not low-risk one-time offenders. (Quoted in Newburn *et al.* 2001b: 61)

Meanwhile, back at the 'heavy end'

So far we have concentrated on the new range of orders and other options for young offenders subject to pre-court disposals, first-tier and relatively low-level 'community' penalties. At this point, however, it will also be helpful to consider the changing practice environment in relation to more serious or 'persistent' offenders. Notable in this respect has been the advent of the Intensive Supervision and Surveillance Programme (ISSP) launched in 2001, targeted at those persistent young offenders who are estimated to be responsible for 25 per cent of all youth crime (Graham and Bowling 1995), and at the same time focusing on those police areas 'worst affected by street crime' (Youth Justice Board Press Release 30 April 2002).

ISSPs were made available as attachments to Supervision Orders, Community Rehabilitation Orders, the community element of Detention and Training Orders and as part of a bail supervision package. Young people are eligible if they are:

... charged with or convicted of an offence and have previously:

Been charged, warned or convicted of offences committed on four or more separate dates within the last 12 months and received at least one community or custodial penalty;

In addition, young offenders can also qualify for ISSP if they are at risk of custody because:

The current charge or sentence relates to an offence which is sufficiently serious that an adult could be sentenced to 14 years or more;

Or they have a history of repeat offending on bail and are at risk of a secure remand under section 130 of the Criminal Justice and Police Act 2001.

(Youth Justice Board, letter to ISSP managers 19 June 2002).

The YOT is responsible for delivering the 'intensive supervision' element of the ISSP, involving 'structured programmes' of at least 25 hours per week for the first three months of the programme. Supervision then continues at 'reduced intensity' of one hour a day during the week. Throughout the order, additional 'support' will be available during evenings and weekends (Gray *et al.* 2005: 23).

The ISSP programme content should incorporate five core modules (education and training, restorative justice, offending behaviour, interpersonal skills, and family support), with ancillary options based on individual circumstances and local resources, including drug or alcohol work or 'constructive leisure/recreation' (Gray *et al.* 2005: 24). In addition, those on ISSPs should also be subject to at least one form of direct surveillance, which might take the form of 'tracking', 'electronic tagging', 'voice verification' or 'intelligence-led policing' (see Chapter 3). These elements of the programme could be contracted out to private providers of security services, although overall responsibility for compliance and decisions about breach action would rest with the YOT (Home Office 2002a: 11).

The framework and delivery requirements for the ISSP are highly prescriptive, leaving little scope for the exercise of professional discretion by practitioners. The overall aim is clearly to provide a demanding programme which will reassure courts and the public that it is an 'effective' alternative to custody. By 2005, ISSP had 'become recognised as the most robust and innovative community-based programme available for persistent and serious young offenders', based on 'what works' research and backed up by 'strict enforcement' (Gray *et al.* 2005: 7).

Despite this fanfare, the results reported for the programme itself were somewhat equivocal at best. Indeed, detailed research has failed to demonstrate any real achievements (Moore *et al.* 2004; Gray *et al.* 2005). ISSP, although increasingly popular with the courts, has had a negligible influence on custody rates, with no difference being detected between those areas with and without ISSPs (Gray *et al.* 2005: 8). Indeed, there were concerns about 'net-widening' and the displacement of less intrusive community disposals instead. In terms of reoffending, the positive falls in frequency (39 per cent) and seriousness (13 per cent) of ISSP participants' subsequent offending were matched by the comparison group, suggesting nothing more than 'regression to the mean' (Gray *et al.* 2005: 9). At the same time, reconviction rates for the ISSP were very high, 91 per cent over the two-year follow-up period. The positive achievements of ISSP, instead, seemed to focus on the broadly positive view of the programme of both young people and their parents and the capacity of providers to identify and focus on welfare needs, partly as a result of the intensive nature of the programme (Gray *et al.* 2005: 125). In light of these rather limited indications of success, however defined, it is unsurprising perhaps that ISSP has come in for trenchant criticism (Green 2004).

Indeed, the conclusion to which we are drawn is that, like the other new orders considered here, ISSP offers nothing more than an intensified version of a fairly well-established correctional programme which may nod in the direction of recent developments such as restorative justice, but otherwise has failed to transform the youth justice terrain.

New orders: recipe for success or 'korrectional karaoke'?

It may help here to take an approach to the New Labour reform programme based on Weber's (1957) 'ideal types', which utilise idealised versions of possible alternative constructions of events in order to enable us to make an informed judgement about the extent to which these represent 'reality'.

In terms of the 'new youth justice', then, we are able to set the 'official' version against other perspectives which may take a rather more critical view. For example, the public presentation of the reform programme suggests that it is seamless, coherent and comprehensive, based on the best evidence about effective interventions. At the same time, dramatic levels of success have been claimed (Youth Justice Board 2002), at least initially.

The administrative and procedural framework for these achievements is provided by the machinery in place to reduce delays and to provide a standardised basis for assessment and planning (the ASSET form). Thus it has been possible to develop an effective predictive method to inform decisions about appropriate interventions. ASSET is capable of correctly determining the likelihood of reoffending in almost 70 per cent of cases:

> This means that offenders who are most likely to continue to offend can be identified at the earliest stage and steps can be taken to prevent it with confidence. More than any other aspect of the reformed system, this tool, properly used, is capable of preventing further offending. (Youth Justice Board 2002: 9)

The comprehensive nature of ASSET thus means that a wide range of factors contributing to the potential risk of reoffending can be identified, and utilised as appropriate to determine the most suitable intervention package, selected from a recognised menu of effective measures.

The multi-professional nature of the YOT means that a 'case management' approach can be adopted, with the skills of the relevant team member being brought to bear as required (Holdaway *et al.* 2001: 112). Practical interventions can be explicitly and directly linked to the evidence that identifies certain factors in young people's background, attitudes and personal characteristics as criminogenic (Graham and Bowling 1995; Youth Justice Board 2002). For example, where a young person's offending can be linked strongly to drug involvement, as indicated by the relevant section of the ASSET form (Baker *et al.* 2005), the YOT health worker can be involved in developing a suitable treatment programme (Holdaway *et al.* 2001: 112). The team member concerned will also be able to draw on the resources of the parent agency to support this intervention.

The flexibility and range of services available means that this intervention (or any other selection from the YOT menu) can be incorporated into the response targeted at the individual young person, at any point in their offending career, from Final Warning through to ISSP (and beyond into custodial and post-custodial support). In other words, the primary determinant of the specific intervention applied is whether or not it contributes to the 'primary aim' of preventing (re)offending, rather than its place in the sentencing tariff. In this way, questions of surveillance, control and restrictions of freedom are only relevant to the extent that they contribute to the overarching goal of reducing crime.

To complete this virtuous circle, evidence has been adduced, mainly on the part of the Youth Justice Board, to suggest that this systematic approach to young people's offending has, indeed, impacted favourably on reoffending rates. Initially, sharp falls in reconviction rates were reported, as compared to what might have been predicted (Jennings 2002, 2003). Even though doubt has been cast on these findings subsequently (Smith, R. 2003; Bottoms 2005; Bateman and Pitts 2005), more modest levels of improvement are still claimed (Whiting and Cuppleditch 2005). Similar achievements are claimed for specific disposals, too. The rate of further proceedings for those subject to Final Warnings has been reported as 6 per cent better than expected (Hine and Celnick 2001); a re-offending rate of 49 per cent for the Reparation Order has been highlighted (Youth Justice Board 2002); and it is repeatedly claimed that the 'new' orders (Reparation Orders, Referral Orders, Action Plan Orders) have demonstrated better outcomes than rather more traditional interventions (such as Supervision Orders). Referral Orders are highlighted as particularly successful, with no further offences reported in 60 per cent of cases within a year of the order being made and 69 per cent of contracts honoured in full (Holdaway *et al.* 2001: vi). Similar achievements were claimed for new pre-trial Bail Support Schemes (Youth Justice Board 2002). Although ISSP has clearly not been able to sustain this impression of undiluted achievement, it is nonetheless maintained that its 'basic elements of intensive contact, supervision and parallel surveillance' have had a positive effect, in the opinion of those involved (Gray *et al.* 2005: 124).

As a counterpoint, a number of observers have taken a much gloomier view of what has (or has not) been achieved by the New Labour reforms (for example, Goldson 2000b; Jones 2001; Muncie 2001; Eadie and Canton 2002; Pitts 2003; Goldson and Muncie 2006a). Claims of effectiveness for particular programmes are found to be misplaced, suggesting that the standardisation of practice referred to previously might not be as securely grounded in the evidence as claimed. Indeed, it is possible to discern a common pattern, but 'we are witnessing the emergence of a "one-size-fits-all" national (correctional) curriculum for offenders in prison and the community …' (Pitts 2001a: 11). This is not justified by clear evidence of effectiveness but by other preoccupations, such as the need to appear 'tough'. In addition, a one-sided approach to developing a consistent and standard model of intervention misses the important point that this will nonetheless be experienced and acted upon differentially by the young people on which it is imposed (as a 70 per cent predictive accuracy rate surely indicates). It is also arguable that the experience of intervention will become characterised essentially by 'surveillance', 'prohibition' and 'incapacitation' as these elements become more central to youth justice practice. Drawing attention to the emphasis on control in the ISSP, one observer suggests that 'it is inconceivable that this move will not undermine still further the capacity of YOTs to deliver the "holistic" regimes which were their original raison d'être' (Pitts 2001a: 13). It is interesting in light of this to note the frustration of YOT staff at being unable to meet young people's requirements in the context of ISSPs because of the limited availability of resources to meet their needs (Gray *et al.* 2005).

The problems with the new measures available post-1998 are twofold, according to this perspective. First, a standardised range of programmes is developed, to be 'dropped into' the framework offered by any specified disposal but for which there is little by way of evidential support. Routinisation of this kind actually appears to inhibit practitioners in their aspirations to address young people's needs in context. Second, and partly as a consequence of these shortcomings, a variety of coercive mechanisms are put in place to ensure that programme components are delivered. Young people's noses are metaphorically held as the medicine is forced down on the assumption that it is good for them. To extend the metaphor, however, research has already shown (Hine and Celnick 2001; Gray *et al.* 2005) that placebos work just as well. The consequence, however, is that coercion and monitoring come to dominate the agenda at the expense of other possible objectives, including reform, rehabilitation or restoration. This is evident in quite mundane ways at the point of delivery, for example in the way that home visits have been supplanted by requirements to attend office appointments as directed, and to be subject to breach proceedings in the event of non-compliance. At the same time, the threat of further penalties will almost certainly compromise young people's motivation, commitment and sense of personal responsibility.

The obvious divergence between contemporary characterisations of youth justice presents some very acute challenges for those engaged in direct work with young people in trouble. In the real world of practice, of course, the task may not have changed to any great extent over the years. Practitioners still need to work creatively and constructively with young people whose behaviour is problematic, negotiating the tensions and contradictions that arise:

> Wherever practice is tightly prescribed, practitioners will repeatedly discover that an uncritical application of the rules would be oppressive and unfair. Reflective youth justice workers draw on their knowledge and skills, but also give expression to their values. They are guided by awareness of the constraints upon young people, and of the differential impact of 'the same' penalty on those who they supervise. They continue to offer opportunities to change even when these appear to be rejected. Throughout, they respect both substantive and procedural justice, working openly and honestly with young offenders and with their managers. If workers behave officiously or take enforcement action prematurely, this not only constitutes poor social work, but is also reductively ineffective and unjust. (Eadie and Canton 2002: 23)

The question which remains for us is whether the reform programme at the turn of the twenty-first century could be said to facilitate or inhibit this form of sensitised practice. The available evidence appears to suggest the latter.

7. Nothing gained?

How can we judge success and failure?

As we have seen, the context is one of a substantial and rapid reform programme, starting in 1998 and continuing over a number of years. These reforms have impacted on all aspects of the youth justice system, including legislation, policy guidance, national standards, strategic and operational delivery mechanisms, and front-line management and practice. They have been driven forcefully from the centre, by the Home Office and the Youth Justice Board, and at the core has been the one overarching objective 'to prevent offending' by young people (Youth Justice Board 2002: 8). At the time of writing the second edition of this book much of the reform programme has been operational for several years, and claims of success in relation to this principal goal (and other outcomes) have been articulated for some time (for example, Home Office *et al.* 2002: 29; Audit Commission 2004; National Audit Office 2004). More recently, however, the tone has changed somewhat, and by 2005 the Youth Justice Board was reporting 'mixed results' (Youth Justice Board 2005d: 4). While modest reductions in reconviction rates were noted, significant concerns were reported in other areas, such as the limited achievements of educational programmes for young offenders and the continuing high use of custody.

Behind these observations lie further questions with which the youth justice system will have to engage. In particular, the reliance on just one measure of overall achievement is both risky and narrowly framed. Inevitably, the youth justice system, its processes and outcomes are about more (and less) than the rate at which young people offend. It is important, for instance, to consider the impact on a number of constituencies whose own objectives may not be equated simplistically with the patterns of youth crime as represented in official statistics and complex calculations (for example, Jennings 2002; Whiting and Cuppleditch 2006). For example, fear of crime and public confidence do not have a straightforward relationship with rates of crime, whether these are measured by official records or crime surveys (Home Office 2001b). The rate of offending by young people, in turn, has only a passing relationship with the youth justice system, which itself deals only with a small fraction of all offences (Audit Commission 1996; Home Office 2001a). It may seem, then, that this system, itself, is not ideally equipped to take a leading role in preventing crime. In other words, we must be very careful to distinguish between measures designed to address 'youth crime' and the policies and practices represented by the youth justice system, which plays a much narrower and more specific part in the overall scheme of things.

Given these observations, it may be more sensible to consider a range of aspects of the impact of youth justice practices, of which the attempt to secure a reduction in the rate of offending is but one. As we have observed, this has been effectively acknowledged by the Youth Justice Board itself (2000, 2004a) – for example by including in National Standards a series of objectives that modify the principal aim of reducing offending. These include: reducing the fear of crime; providing services to children and young people, victims and communities; avoiding delay in processing young people who offend; proportionate punishment; and interventions to address risk factors, promote protective factors, and reinforce parental responsibility (Youth Justice Board 2004a: 3). In addition, it is pointed out that the rights of children should be protected and interventions delivered 'fairly, consistently and without improper discrimination, in a way that values and respects the cultural and racial diversity of the whole community' (Youth Justice Board 2004a: 4).

In reality, maintaining the pure aim of reducing crime by young people is an impractical objective for the youth justice system; on the one hand, it does not deal with most youth crime (Audit Commission 1996), and on the other, additional objectives are incorporated into the standards framework set for the delivery of interventions. Thus a wider range of outcomes must inevitably become part of the agenda when we come to consider the meaning and impact of the youth justice system, particularly when we consider the contested nature of statistical measures such as recorded levels of offending (Muncie 1999).

In order to develop a broader picture, it will be helpful first to consider the implications for specific groups, and then, drawing on these observations, to reframe the wider question of just what the New Labour reforms have achieved.

Young black people and institutionalised discrimination

Broadening the scope of our concerns about impact and effectiveness in youth justice, it becomes possible to consider questions about outcomes rather differently. Are young people's rights protected, for example? And what are the consequences if they are not?

In particular, the issue of 'race' and discrimination has been a persistent theme, reflected in efforts to identify the processes associated with both over-representation of black young people in the justice process and the oppressive treatment to which they may have been subjected. It seemed at one point as if these problems were being addressed, for instance following the inquiry into the death of Stephen Lawrence, with the government accepting without question 56 of the 70 recommendations made (Bowling and Phillips 2002). Notably, the inquiry had, for the first time, identified 'institutional racism' as endemic in the practices of the police and other organisations responsible for the delivery of criminal justice (Macpherson 1999). Partly as a result, the Race Relations (Amendment) Act 2000 was introduced, applying anti-discrimination principles much more explicitly to public services than had previously been the case. For instance, some of the immunities applying to chief police officers in this respect were removed. Other legislation also appears to support the aims of this measure, including the Human Rights Act 1998 and the earlier requirements for ethnic monitoring (introduced under section 95 of the Criminal Justice Act 1991). These provisions have been criticised for being relatively weak (Bowling and Phillips 2002), but there is at least a greater degree of openness about discriminatory processes and outcomes (Barclay *et al.* 2005; Home Office 2006).

Despite a number of attempts at progressive reform, there is continuing evidence of unequal treatment of young people from ethnic minorities (Feilzer and Hood 2004). Specifically, a detailed study carried out on behalf of the Youth Justice Board found a series of points of concern, including:

- the higher rate of prosecution and conviction of mixed-parentage young males;
- the higher proportion of prosecutions involving young black males;
- the greater proportion of black and Asian males ... remanded in custody before sentence ...;
- the slightly greater use of custody for Asian males;
- the greater use of restrictive community penalties for Asian and mixed-parentage males ...;
- the much greater proportion of mixed-parentage females who were prosecuted;
- the substantial variations in outcomes between Yot areas (Feilzer and Hood 2004: 27).

Indeed, it has been argued that attempts at reform themselves may have continued to mask the effects of deep-rooted racism and discriminatory practices, with the result that the impact has inevitably been limited:

> Racial oppression may be real, morally repugnant, and pervasive, but when the new managerialism takes it on, it becomes little more than a dysfunctional organisational residue amenable to the kinds of administrative techniques developed to solve many other kinds of 'human resource' problems. (Pitts 2001b: 137)

The process of transforming a major social evil into a legal-rational problem has produced limited gains in the past, and, as Pitts observes, it does little to address underlying attitudes and structural influences.

Consistent with this analysis, the experiences of young black people in the justice system continue to reflect discriminatory practices and oppressive outcomes. We should perhaps recall that, at the start, identified patterns of offending are broadly similar. Despite some apparent variations, overall there appears to be no difference in the propensity of black or white males aged 10 to 25 to commit offences, it is suggested (Barclay *et al.* 2005: 8). Self-report evidence appears to show some variation, but on the whole, black children are less likely to offend than white children, while those of mixed heritage are slightly more likely to say that they have offended (Armstrong *et al.* 2005: 19). This kind of pattern has been consistent over time, as has the finding that young people of Asian origin are much less likely to say that they have been involved in criminal activities (Graham and Bowling 1985; Armstrong *et al.* 2005). As a consequence, it has been concluded that 'the answer to the question as to why black (young) people are over-represented in the … system as "subjects" is likely to lie somewhere other than with their rates of "participation in offending"' (Goldson and Chigwada-Bailey 1999: 54), a viewpoint with which others concur (Barclay *et al.* 2005: lv).

The evidence of the overrepresentation of young black people at each stage in the process, from first contact in the street all the way to custodial sentencing, produces the impression of an integrated chain of progressively intensified discriminatory interventions, described by Goldson and Chigwada-Bailey (1999) as a 'multiplier effect'. As they point out, this comes into operation from the point at which young black people encounter the justice system. This has been a persistent feature of their experience:

> In England and Wales in 1993–4, 25 per cent of all stop and searches were of ethnic minority populations … Nationally black and ethnic minorities are five times more likely to be stopped and searched than white people. (Muncie 1999: 233)

Again, in 1999, black people were more likely to be 'approached by the police' – 28 per cent as compared with 24 per cent of white people, and this was especially so for young black males (where the ratio was a third as compared with a quarter). At the same time, a much smaller proportion of those from ethnic minorities were likely to report that they had been treated 'well' by the police (Clancy *et al.* 2001), and substantial proportions of all minority ethnic populations believe that they are likely to experience discrimination within the justice system (Barclay *et al.* 2005: 18).

Despite the impetus given by the Stephen Lawrence inquiry, there has been little change over time. By 2003/04, for example, it was found that black people were 6.4 times more likely to be stopped and searched than the white population, and Asian people 1.9 times more likely to be dealt with in this way (Barclay *et al.* 2005: 9).

At the next stage in the process, the proportion of black people arrested for 'notifiable offences' in 1999/2000 was four times higher than for the white population (Home Office 2001: 19). By contrast, a relatively smaller proportion of black people who were arrested were subsequently dealt with by way of cautions – 11 per cent as compared with 16 per cent of white people. More detailed analysis of the picture relating to young offenders suggests that this pattern persists, but with important variations. Thus 'pre-court disposals' (Reprimands or Final Warnings) appear to be much more likely to be made in cases involving young Asian people (32 per cent) than white (24 per cent) or black (19 per cent) young people, or especially those of 'mixed parentage (9.5 per cent), resulting in 'the odds of a case involving a mixed-parentage youth being prosecuted [being] 2.7 times that of a white youth with similar case characteristics – an indicator of unfavourable treatment' (Feilzer and Hood 2004: 17).

Decisions by the Crown Prosecution Service and the courts are reported to 'reflect decisions made at earlier stages of the criminal justice process including charging, cautioning and also the circumstances of the offence' (Barclay and Mhlanga 2000: 1). In this way, initial distortions are merely confirmed by apparently neutral decisions made at later stages of the process. This highlights one of the most contentious areas of debate about racism in criminal justice. On the one hand, it is suggested that the system itself does no more than reflect inequalities in the wider society, producing unequal outcomes because of the greater likelihood of black people becoming criminalised for a variety of external reasons (Muncie 2004: 271). However, it is also suggested that the system itself compounds these inequalities, either by adopting a 'liberal rhetoric of equality and rights' which takes no account of prior social discrimination, or by incorporating further discriminatory attitudes and practices of its own.

Taking the former view, for example, Barclay and Mhlanga argue that 'the ethnic group of the suspect was not found to be a predictor of post-arrest decisions' (Barclay and Mhlanga 2002: 2). They suggest that arrests of young (under 22) black and Asian people are less likely to lead to a conviction than those involving young white people. The overrepresentation of young people from ethnic minorities at the entry point to the justice system appears to be modified but not overcome by principles of due process. Barclay and Mhlanga (2000: 1) conclude that it is 'not possible' to say whether differences in outcome 'reflect the result of discrimination in the criminal justice system'.

This does illustrate the potential complexity of a system-wide analysis, but evidence of unevenness in the processes applied should not necessarily undermine the broader conclusion that the system itself reveals discriminatory tendencies. The Commission for Racial Equality is reported to have found that decisions to prosecute are weighted against young black people (Goldson and Chigwada-Bailey 1999: 65), which might account for the greater proportion of this group whose cases lead to discontinuances or acquittals (Feilzer and Hood 2004: 17). Other findings appear to show that outcomes are weighted against certain ethnic groups. Higher proportions of black and 'mixed-parentage' young people are remanded in secure conditions; higher proportions of these groups are sentenced to custody, and higher proportions of black young people receive longer custodial sentences (12 months or more), suggesting significant levels of unequal treatment at key decision points. Thus it is observed that 'there were, at various points of the processes, differences that were consistent with discriminatory treatment' (Feilzer and Hood 2004: 27).

The evidence from large-scale surveys is consistent with more localised findings, too. The Manchester Youth Bail Project, for example, was able to demonstrate that black and Asian young people were progressively screened out of the programme (Moore and Smith 2001). Of 136 referrals in the first year of the project, 29 (21 per cent) were from ethnic minorities; of the 102 accepted for the bail support programme, 17 (17 per cent) were from these groups; of the 52 then granted bail on condition that they attend, only six (12 per cent) fell into this category. While these six all went on to complete the programme successfully, this example illustrates quite well an institutionalised selection process which is constructed according to supposedly objective criteria but which still produces discriminatory outcomes.

More graphic evidence of the discriminatory impact of impersonal and apparently objective decision-making processes has been demonstrated by the experiences of those involved with remands to custody. Of the 650 referrals to the Howard League's *Troubleshooter Project* from December 1993 to June 1996, '45 per cent were ... Black or Asian' (Ashton and Grindrod 1999: 176). This is not an isolated finding; in 1999, '16.2 per cent of children and young people remanded in HMP and YOI Doncaster; and 31.2 per cent of those similarly remanded in HM YOI and RC Feltham were Black' (Goldson and Peters 2000: 15). These findings are echoed in the survey carried out by Feilzer and Hood (2004: 78) which found that a significantly higher proportion of black young people were remanded in secure conditions.

At the point of sentencing, the position, according to research evidence, is a little less clear. Earlier studies are reported to have shown an independent 'race' effect on court disposals (Goldson and Chigwada-Bailey 1999: 65), although more recent findings are more complex. In the most detailed study of its kind, 'no evidence was found that either black or mixed-parentage males were, once the characteristics of their cases had been taken into account, more likely to receive a custodial sentence than white males ... they were treated, if anything, more leniently' (Feilzer and Hood 2004: 166). Nonetheless, there was a greater likelihood that black males would receive longer custodial sentences than white males from the Crown Court.

In this context, we must also bear in mind the evidence of racism and mistreatment experienced by black young people once they are detained in custody (Wilson 2006), graphically underlined by the inquiry into the death of Zahid Mubarak (Keith 2006).

Studies have consistently shown that young black people in particular are disproportionately represented in the custodial population (Barclay *et al.* 2005: 14); these figures might partly be accounted for by antecedent factors (such as the nature and circumstances of the offence), but they are also attributable to the 'amplification' effect of the justice system itself:

> The empirical evidence demonstrates the existence of both direct and indirect discrimination in the criminal justice process. (Bowling and Phillips 2002: 241)

It is argued that some aspects of the reform programme instituted by New Labour may actually intensify the discriminatory impact of the justice system. These include the introduction of new and finer 'nets' in the form of

Reprimands, Final Warnings and the Referral Order. The tendency to 'over-charge' young black people may be intensified through the formalisation of these lower-tariff interventions, for example. In addition, the increasing use of targeting and surveillance techniques, the Foucauldian mechanisms highlighted in previous chapters, are likely to result in relatively poorer areas where minority ethnic groups are concentrated becoming subject to more intensive scrutiny, given what we already know about the unequal use of stop and search powers. To many communities, however, this is just 'business as usual'. Research into the lived experiences of young black people in and around the justice system seems to confirm this:

> They [police] just stop you all the time – sometimes two or three times a day. They just make up a reason, usually it's drugs, sometimes stealing. (Male 16, quoted in Sharp 2006: 8).

The result is a systematic sense of unfairness and unequal treatment:

> As a consequence, British black and Asian people feel angry, unsafe and insecure. The 'double whammy' faced by these communities is that they are widely seen by the police and prison services as problematic, suspicious and, sometimes, simply criminal. (Bowling and Phillips 2002: 255)

Against this bleak backdrop, the limited initiatives taken by the Youth Justice Board seem relatively insignificant. The development of specialist mentoring schemes, for example, may reflect a genuine attempt to address concerns about discriminatory treatment (see, for example, Leicester Youth Offending Team 2001). The YJB has also produced a 'toolkit' to assist YOTs in planning and monitoring their own efforts to avoid discriminatory practices (Youth Justice Board 2004b).

However, the targeting of crime 'hotspots' and those 'at risk of offending' ('the fifty'; Morgan Harris Burrows, 2001) for preventive programmes may intensify the experience of being under scrutiny, and the targeting of areas with relatively high minority populations for initiatives such as ISSP might also be potentially discriminatory, given the existing propensity to subject certain groups (Asian and mixed-parentage males) to more intensive community penalties (Feilzer and Hood 2004: 20).

'It's different for girls ...'

In order further to unpick the sense of uniformity which sometimes pervades the youth justice system, it is also helpful to consider the position of girls and young women, given that this is a world dominated numerically and ideologically by masculinity (Walklate 2004). There has been much debate about the reasons for their differential involvement in offending and criminal justice processes, without a substantial measure of agreement.

To start with the question of their offending behaviour, it seems that the involvement of females in crime is lower than that of males, according to both official statistics and self-report findings, in both the nature of offences and intensity. Thus just over a third of females report having committed an offence 'ever', as compared with rather more than half the male population (East and Campbell 2000); on the other hand, males are responsible for three times as many offences overall, and five times as many 'serious' offences (Graham and Bowling 1995). In respect of young offenders, in 2004/05, males were responsible for 81.6 per cent of offences leading to 'a disposal of some sort', compared with 18.4 per cent committed by females (Youth Justice Board 2005a). Although the peak age for offending is similar (MORI 2004; Budd *et al.* 2005: 10; Home Office 2005a), the rate declines more quickly from this point for females (Home Office 2001b: 101; Budd *et al.* 2005: 11). Despite the imbalance in recorded and reported patterns of crime between males and females, it should not be overlooked that significant numbers of offences are committed by girls and young women (Youth Justice Board 2005a: 4), so the role of the youth justice system in this respect is a matter of considerable interest.

An analysis of the pattern of offending suggests that girls and young women are more likely to be involved in certain property offences such as theft and handling stolen goods as a proportion of their overall offending, and less likely to commit burglary and robbery (Budd *et al.* 2005: 14). On the other hand, violent offences account for 56 per cent of the offences reported by 10- to 17-year-old females, as compared with 57 per cent of offences committed by males. It appears that the pattern of offending behaviour of young females is little different to their male counterparts according to their own accounts, but simply of lesser intensity. However, when it comes to official processes, it appears that while females are less likely to be proceeded against for serious offences, they are relatively more likely to be charged with crimes of violence or theft/handling (Feilzer and Hood 2004: 153).

Taking a different view, over an extended period the relative level of criminality of girls and young women appears to be on the increase. From 1981 to 1999, there was a decline in the number of 'known' young male offenders from 7,000 to 5,400 per 100,000 population, while over the same period, the equivalent figure for females went up from 1,300 to 1,400: 'Thus, although there remains a substantial decrease in the proportion of offenders among males (23 per cent), there has been an 8 per cent *rise* in the proportion of females found guilty or cautioned' over this period of time (East and Campbell 2000: 22). From 1999 to 2004, there was a further decline in the proportion of known male offenders across the age range (10–17), while again, the rate for females stabilised or increased slightly (Home Office 2005a). Explanations for these disparities have postulated changing patterns of behaviour among girls and young women, or changing attitudes (Muncie 1999; Worrall 1999; Bowling and Phillips 2002), but it is important to recognise the complexity of possible interactions between these factors and others, including the gendered nature of the construction of criminal justice (Walklate 2004).

Despite these notes of caution, it is undeniably a matter of considerable interest to reflect on the way in which the youth justice system deals with those female offenders who come to its attention. Again, the lessons of history are that there have been persistent disparities in the ways in which young males and females have been dealt with by the criminal process. For example, cautioning rates have consistently differed. In 1990, 84 per cent of 12–14-year-old boys were cautioned, as compared with 93 per cent of girls of the same age. By 2000, the last year in which cautions were available, these figures had fallen to 68 per cent and 86 per cent respectively. By 2004, with the introduction of Reprimands and Final Warnings, this position had stabilised, with 67 per cent of boys reported for offences in this age range dealt with by these means and 87 per cent of girls (Home Office 2005b). While both the proportions going to court have increased over time, the pattern revealed by the cautioning figures is repeated here, with females being relatively more likely to receive lesser sentences and less likely to be sent to custody (see also Feilzer and Hood 2004) (see Table 7.1).

Despite the disparity, we can also see from this that the trends over time have shown a narrowing of gender differentials, with the proportion of females in this age range sentenced to custody increasing despite a relative fall for males. The *number* of girls and young women being locked up has almost tripled over this period. This may be attributable to some extent to the availability of a new sentence, the Detention and Training Order, which has extended the custodial options available to the courts for young female offenders.

Worrall (1999) helps to provide a context for these fairly dramatic shifts with the ironic observation that the Conservative government's 1990 White Paper envisaged the abolition of custody for all females under 18, noting that 'the 150 or so girls in custody could be dealt with quite adequately by the "good, demanding and constructive community programmes for juvenile offenders who need intensive supervision"' (Worrall 1999: 29). As she observes, however, this opportunity was not taken at the time, and the increasingly punitive climate of the 1990s swept up young women as readily as their male counterparts. Indeed, she suggests, things may actually have got worse for females, because they have been seen as becoming increasingly criminal and

Table 7.1 Gender and custodial sentencing 1994–2002

		1994	2004
Males 10–17	All sentences	55,511	83,413
	Custody	4,561	5,881
	%	8.2%	7.1%
Females 10–17	All sentences	6,483	12,775
	Custody	158	444
	%	2.4%	3.5%

Source: Home Office (2005b), Sentencing Statistics 2004.

more violent. Thus, she notes, in 1996 an intemperate newspaper editorial proclaimed this trend as fact, and since then the media portrayal seems to have remained consistent. In 2002, the *Daily Mirror* ('Hell child' 16 May) was quick to condemn a 'tearaway girl of 16 with 38 convictions for assaulting police'. Interestingly, the newspaper also reported that this young person had received a Secure Training Order at the age of 13, and a further eight-month custodial sentence at 14 – rather illustrating the futility of imprisonment, it would seem.

Worrall argues that media responses of this kind should be seen as part of a pattern, amounting to a 'moral panic' targeted at the supposed consequences of women's liberation. In other words, the apparent increase in the criminal behaviour of young females is attributed to their rejection of traditional gender stereotypes. However, she also claims that there has been little supporting evidence of a dramatic increase in female offending rates. The number of known offenders among girls aged 10–17 declined steadily during the latter part of the 1990s, for instance, while the *rate* of offending by girls and young women was observed to fluctuate (East and Campbell 2000: 21). Worrall (1999) has expressed concern that these trends have not been reflected in the use of custody, with a persistent increase in the number of girls and young women locked up between 1992 and 1996. This pattern has continued subsequently, too (Home Office 2001b, 2001c; Home Office 2004b; Gelsthorpe and Sharpe 2006). In one sense, this may be a form of 'bifurcation' (Bottoms 1977) in the justice system, whereby minor offences and those less likely to threaten well-established stereotypes (such as shoplifting) result in females committing this type of offence being treated relatively leniently, while more serious and counter-stereotypical offences might lead to more severe forms of punishment. On the other hand, the trend towards harsher treatment for girls and young women has not been found to alter the prevailing position whereby, whatever the nature of their offending, 'females were treated more leniently than their male counterparts' (Feilzer and Hood 2004: 168).

Despite this observation, the broader move away from a welfarist approach to young people's offending coupled with a 'small increase in girls' crime' might largely account for the 'increasing criminalisation of, and punitiveness towards, them' (Gelsthorpe and Sharpe 2006: 58). In other words, because female offenders have historically been more likely to benefit from welfare-oriented interpretations of their behaviour, the increasingly punitive and behavioural orientation of criminal justice processes is likely to have a particularly acute impact. Coupled with increasingly dramatic media images of female delinquency (Gelsthorpe and Sharpe 2006: 55), this has resulted in:

> the abandonment of traditional welfare-oriented approaches to girls' delinquency and their replacement by an increasing desire to criminalise, punish and lock [them] up. (Gelsthorpe and Sharpe 2006: 57)

There is thus evidence of an increasingly and disproportionately harsh regime for dealing with young female offenders, particularly those whose offences are judged to be serious, and this is, in turn, exacerbated by the treatment they are likely to receive in custody. As Worrall (1999) points out, girls in prison are likely to have experienced damaging and traumatic episodes at some point in their lives, possibly in the form of violence or sexual abuse, and custodial establishments are poorly placed to respond (see HM Chief Inspector of Prisons 2004, for example).

To what extent, then, have the reforms of recent years affected the way girls and young women, in particular, are dealt with by the youth justice system? As already noted, the changes introduced have done little to stem the increasing use of harsher disposals (including custody) for young female offenders, and in this respect they appear at least as vulnerable as male offenders in a punitive moral climate, and perhaps more so for the reasons already outlined. As we have noted the number of 10–17-year-old females sentenced to custody increased from 158 in 1994 to 444 in 2004, a 181 per cent increase (Home Office 2005b).

In this context, the failings of the 'new youth justice' might perhaps be explained by the relative 'invisibility' of female young offenders (Walklate 2004), with the result that their needs have simply been overlooked. According to the Youth Justice Board 'the ... typical young offender [is] male, white, aged between 14–16, excluded from school and [has] committed five or more types of offence' (2002: 2). Targeted interventions, even those in the community such as the Youth Inclusion Programme, will by definition contain a very small proportion of females 'at risk', and even from this point of intervention, the programmes offered are unlikely to be designed for them; this is an issue, like ethnicity, which is not adequately addressed in evaluations of the YIP, for example (Morgan Harris Burrows 2001, 2003).

At the other end of the spectrum, where girls and young women are held in custody, the Chief Inspector of Prisons has been observed to express repeated frustrations over the failure of policy to take account of their specific circumstances. Although responsibility for the secure estate for those under 18 was transferred to the YJB in April 2000, the initial response was inadequate:

I am ... concerned about young females, including juveniles, for whom the YJB and the Prison Service have not yet made the same arrangements as they have for young males. I was appalled to find 17 year old girls on remand in HMP Holloway with sentenced adult women ... (HM Chief Inspector of Prisons 2001: 10)

The YJB (2001a) subsequently made a commitment to put things right in this respect. However, these concerns were only amplified when the succeeding Chief Inspector began to visit particular institutions. At Eastwood Park Prison, the inspectorate considered:

The treatment and conditions of the 12 under-18s held with 411 18–21 year olds in D wing. They exhibited, in acute form ... chronic problems ... This is an extremely vulnerable and disturbed group of young women: 'It was impossible not to be struck by the profound personality disturbance and mental health problems that many presented and by the inappropriateness of prison, or indeed any other custodial placement, for them'. (HM Chief Inspector of Prisons 2002: 4)

In the early days of reform, then, girls and young women were clearly not well-served, and they were left to cope with the consequences of harsh sentences in a hostile climate (see also Goldson 2002, for an insight into the personal impact of being locked up).

The Youth Justice Board did not meet its initial commitment to ensure the removal of all females under the age of 17 from prison custody by the end of 2003, continuing to rely on Secure Training Centres (Youth Justice Board 2005f), where mistreatment remains a problem (Carlile 2006).

Despite this gloomy picture, it is important also to recognise that there remains space and scope for 'good practice' in youth justice, and it may therefore help to consider one example of an effective attempt to address the specific needs of young women who offend in the community:

Case study

Abi is a 17-year-old white female living independently. She was referred to the Youth Offending Team in June 2001 after receiving a Final Warning for an offence of Taking a Vehicle Without Owner's Consent.

At the initial assessment the YOT officer was made aware that Abi had been self-harming (cutting) and had suicidal feelings. An immediate mental health assessment was made by the YOT Primary Mental Health Worker who made a swift referral to the CAMHS Young People's Team. Abi was seen by Psychiatrist within 36 hours and later diagnosed with a borderline Personality Disorder.

The primary mental health worker co-ordinated work around coping skills, support networks and cognitive behavioural interventions (interpersonal effectiveness, emotion regulation, distress tolerance). The case manager co-ordinated other interventions (offence focused work, employment and housing) and towards the end of the order Abi was referred to our YJB funded Mentoring Programme.

At the exit review Abi was praised for her co-operation and non-offending ... support networks were identified. She no longer needs the support of the primary mental health worker ...

(Prior to the YOT Final Warning scheme, Abi's complex needs would, in all probability have gone unnoticed until she re-offended or self harmed).

(Leicester YOT 2002: 95)

On the other hand, the *Daily Mirror*'s 'Hell Child' appears to have received little by way of supportive community-based intervention. Perhaps recent moves towards '"equitable justice" between girls and boys' (Gelsthorpe and Sharpe 2006: 50) have led to a tougher view of behaviour which defies accepted norms. Arguably, the relationship between gender stereotypes, moral panic and the punitive turn is a powerful factor in determining the responses of agencies and institutions to the problems of girls and young women who do offend.

Ships in the night: victims of crime and youth justice

A third and increasingly influential group of stakeholders in youth justice are those people who become victims of the crimes of the young. They are clearly significant in a context of heightened political interest in their needs and wishes:

> Victims of crime are a politically popular group, and an increasingly powerful one. Politicians have been quick to take account of these facts, and the balance between offenders and victims has altered correspondingly. (Williams 2000: 176)

As already noted, this climate has led to a number of government initiatives and it has clearly influenced implementation mechanisms such as the National Standards. From the onset, New Labour's commitment was explicit, with the aspiration to create 'a system ... which commands the confidence of victims' (Home Office 1997b: 29), which then became translated into a framework of law and policy which required that 'the needs of victims of crime are respected and prioritised' (Youth Justice Board 2000: 2).

Thus specific measures such as Reparation and Referral Orders were put in place to ensure that offenders were required to make amends to their victims in some way. In addition, a range of other disposals were also constructed in such a way as to facilitate similar activities, including the Final Warning, Action Plan Order and Supervision Order. The clear victim-orientation of the reformed youth justice system would be further buttressed by the requirement in the preparation of Pre-Sentence Reports for consideration to be given, in every case, to 'what is known about the impact of the offence on any victim, and assessment of the offender's awareness of the consequences to self, family and any victims' (Youth Justice Board 2000: 16). Similarly, the ASSET form specifically draws attention to the victim's perspective.

In addition, the National Standards (Youth Justice Board 2004a: 31) include an entire section on the appropriate involvement of victims in the justice process.

The infusion of every aspect of youth justice with an emphasis on the victim perspective has inevitably had a strong influence on the approach of Youth Offending Teams. Leicester YOT, for example, quickly engaged in a number of initiatives in this area, in conjunction with Final Warnings, including 'victim empathy sessions, letters of apology, supervising short periods of reparation [and] 4 Restorative Justice Conferences ...' (Leicester YOT 2002: 49). Subsequent targets included the incorporation of 'Restorative Justice Principles' in all Final Warnings, which would be reflected in increased victim involvement and measured by enhanced levels of victim satisfaction with the outcomes of any intervention.

This is one early example which is representative of broader developments, with the Youth Justice Board undertaking a substantial additional investment in establishing a series of 46 'totally new restorative justice projects'. These projects worked with over 6,800 young people, 63 per cent of whom were referred as part of a Final Warning or Referral Order programme (Wilcox 2004: 5). While it is important to avoid conflating 'restorative justice' solely with interventions to support victims, there is no doubt that victim participation was a key aim of this initiative. It is therefore reasonable to consider the question of what has been achieved through the drive to place victims at the centre of the process.

In fact, the evidence suggests that the level of victim involvement in youth justice practice has been variable, and this is partly because of the range of local arrangements put in place. Indeed, it is fair to say that diversity was encouraged in the initial stages, in order to promote innovation and improved practice (Wilcox 2004: 15). Nevertheless, evaluations have suggested that there has been a clear preoccupation with the means by which victims are supported and involved. On this criterion, however, achievements must be judged as limited. For example, the most common form of intervention identified in the YJB's restorative projects was 'community reparation (35 per cent)', and although over half (53 per cent) of victims participated 'to some extent', this usually amounted to no more than agreeing to 'their views being made known to the offender, ... to receive a letter of apology, or [making] some suggestion as to the kind of reparative activity the offender could undertake' (Wilcox 2004: 7). Even though the YJB itself proclaimed this as evidence of a significant advance (in contrast to the rather more measured view of the evaluators; Wilcox 2003: 31), this has not been borne out to any great extent by the work of those evaluating the Referral Order, who found that:

> The involvement of victims and in particular their attendance at panel meetings across the pilot areas has been both lower than was originally anticipated and significantly lower than comparative experiences from restorative justice initiatives around the world. (Newburn *et al.* 2002: 41)

The researchers observed that: 'in the absence of significant victim attendance there are obvious concerns that victims' issues are insufficiently represented' (Newburn *et al.* 2002: 43).

The key issue here is that a system whose primary purpose is to process young people who are found to have offended will almost inevitably struggle to find appropriate ways of involving other interests, especially those of victims, although some have taken a rather more positive view of developments in this area (Williams 2005).

For those victims who do get involved, there may be positives to be gained from the experience. They are reported to have found YOP meetings generally helpful, and feelings of 'hurt' and fear can be addressed through these forums. On the other hand, subsequent follow-up was not always regarded as favourably, with a 'significant' number of victims disappointed not to receive any expression of apology or remorse from the young offender at any point in the process. Evaluators of the pilot schemes took the view that these problems were largely technical and administrative problems which could be resolved over time. They base this argument on the underlying goodwill and commitment to the Referral Order, expressed throughout the youth justice system, from magistrates to youth justice staff, to community panel members and victims, and even to parents and young offenders themselves (Newburn *et al.* 2002, p.62; Crawford and Newburn 2003: 178). Their conclusions are positive:

> The issue of victim involvement is, in essence, a problem of implementation rather than a problem of principle. Indeed, the majority of the general principles underlying referral orders appear both to be capable of being operationalised in practice and to receive high levels of approval from all the major participants. In a short period of time referral orders have gone from being an interesting set of proposals to a genuinely robust set of working practices that, notwithstanding some of the tensions identified…, look set to have a considerable impact on the youth justice system in England and Wales. (Newburn *et al.* 2002: 63)

This is perhaps a surprising conclusion in light of what is known already about victim involvement and reparative interventions. As Haines (2000) has observed, despite the general enthusiasm for measures such as compensation, community service and other means of 'making amends', formal and highly structured mechanisms such as the YOPs have not been particularly successful in the past. He argues that the evidence, if anything, steers us away from this kind of routinised practice to approaches which are more flexible in addressing victims' concerns. The potential mismatch between the expectations of victims and the willingness or capacity of young people to make restitution will render the formal panel setting a particularly difficult site to resolve such tensions. For example, victims' demands for compensation may be impossible to meet in full for young people who simply cannot afford what is being sought, and indeed this is echoed in the findings of the YOP researchers (Newburn *et al.* 2002: 46). The conclusions drawn from research are that the low level of victim participation is a matter of concern, and this may partly be associated with the inflexibility of the 'criminal justice establishment' when it comes to implementing more victim-oriented policies (Crawford and Newburn 2003: 214). Integrating victims into the process presents both practical challenges and real questions about 'what kinds of victims, under what circumstances, are more likely to benefit from active participation in restorative programmes and how best to facilitate this' (Crawford and Newburn 2003: 241).

Other models have been tried in the past with a degree of success, and it may be worth reminding ourselves of their distinctive characteristics. Evaluations of the Northamptonshire Juvenile Liaison Bureaux in the 1980s also found a valid place for reparative interventions, based on a flexible and negotiated response. In other words, there was no overbearing pressure to apply 'restorative' solutions where they were unsuitable:

> the Bureaux … have come to use reparation only in situations where all parties are able to benefit rather than where it merely responds to social pressures to treat (or punish) delinquent behaviour. (Blagg *et al.* 1986: 135)

In relation to this, it is interesting to observe the additional constraint imposed by the timetable for interventions set by the National Standards (see Youth Justice Board 2004a: 49), with which Youth Offending Teams found it difficult to comply (Newburn *et al.* 2002: vi). As Williams (2000) has observed, the pressure to deal with young offenders increasingly quickly has created further obstacles to the principle of prioritising victims' needs.

Williams sees this as part of a wider tendency for victim interests to be subsumed under the wider demands of youth justice reform. He contrasts the approach in England and Wales to that of New Zealand, for example:

> A youth justice system based on conflict between the prosecution and the defence remains substantially unaffected by the additions of reparation as an extra sentencing option. In New Zealand, the formal criminal justice system is largely by-passed by restorative processes which replace court hearings. In England and Wales, however, these processes are 'bolted on' to an otherwise unchanged retributive sentencing system. (Williams 2000: 189)

According to this analysis, reparation merely becomes part of the sentencing tariff, representing an imposed forfeit as opposed to an agreed settlement, whereby the young offender really 'means' her/his apology or gesture of compensation. Victims' interests are in danger of being exploited 'cynically', according to this view, simply 'to improve the presentation of punitive criminal justice policies' (Williams 2000: 189).

Haines and Drakeford (1998) have taken this argument even further, claiming that 'victim-oriented' restorative actions need to be distinguished from 'offender-oriented' restorative practices and dealt with outside the constraints of the youth justice system itself, which should focus on reintegrative work with the young offender rather than 'work which is carried out for the benefit of the victim' (Haines and Drakeford 1998: 234). In their view, the emphasis on the victim distorts the purpose of youth justice processes, while such approaches cannot be shown to be effective in any case. The consequence of this is that: 'A primary requirement of any restorative approach or practice that aimed to be child-appropriate ... would be that it put the child first' (Haines and O'Mahony 2006: 121).

Williams similarly argues for a clearer distinction between the treatment of offenders and victims, although he does not reject the notion of victim-offender reparation, arguing instead that it must be relocated at the 'front end' of the justice process. It should be based on a 'fundamental' change of attitudes towards victims, marginalizing courts and other penal processes, and it should provide time and space for the development of consensual 'restorative solutions' to the problems created by young people's offending behaviour (Williams 2000: 190).

Williams (2005) has subsequently expressed rather more positive views about the influence of the reform programme, suggesting that 'greater sensitivity' and 'awareness' (p. 215) of victims' needs and interests is now evident. On the other hand, he notes, progress has been 'patchy' and there remains cause for concern that the new restorative measures may have resulted in 'net-widening' and 'up-tariffing' of young people who offend.

Overall, despite the greater recognition of victims' issues in youth justice, there remain serious concerns. Indeed, we should perhaps consider whether it is reasonable to expect a process which is essentially about dealing with those young people brought to justice also to be geared effectively to meet the interests of another overlapping constituency. In view of this, it must remain questionable to seek to engage victims to contrive apparently successful outcomes. While it is clear that for *some* victims, where the process works effectively, outcomes are broadly positive, this cannot be generalised to suggest that victims' interests in general are well-served (Crawford and Newburn 2003: 12). In fact, one study has concluded that: 'Much reparation appeared to relate more clearly to the needs or desires of the young person rather than the nature of the offences or the involvement of the victim' (Crawford and Burden 2005: 37).

It is perhaps also worth reminding ourselves of the bigger picture – the vast majority of victims of crime are simply not touched by the justice system. Something less than half of all crimes are reported to the police, and just over half of this number are recorded by police as crimes (Mirrlees-Black *et al.* 1998). Of this subset, in 1999–2000, only 14 per cent resulted in a caution or conviction (Home Office 2001b). It thus appears at best that a victim is matched with her/his offender in no more than 3.5 per cent of all cases. As we have also observed, in a very substantial proportion of cases before the Youth Offending Panel there is no real engagement between offender and victim where they are 'matched'. Taking these observations into account, if we are to make any claims about the efficacy of the 'new youth justice' in serving the interests of victims, we must therefore be very modest indeed. In essence:

> Restorative justice, which emphasises restitution and other forms of reparation from the offender to the victim, seems ... to have nothing much to offer the majority of crime victims. It shares this limitation with every other criminal justice intervention. Hence, it might be argued that, if our priority when a crime is committed is really to restore the victim, we should not waste our energy trying to reform the criminal justice system. What is needed is not so much an alternative form of criminal justice, but an alternative to criminal justice. (Johnstone 2002: 78)

Changing perceptions and changing the experience of victims will therefore require wider-ranging reforms than the introduction of the Referral Order (Crawford and Newburn 2003: 212).

Claiming success: a cautionary note

Having identified some of the ways in which youth justice reforms have clearly failed to meet the needs of some key interests, it may now be helpful to set these shortcomings against wider claims of progress and successful outcomes. In being critical of the achievements of reform, I do not want to belittle the continuing enthusiasm and achievements evident in the work of youth justice practitioners, who continue to strive to make the system work. For example, one experienced practitioner commented to me that she maintained an active belief in the importance of using the machinery available to address the welfare needs of young people who offend, illustrating this with reference to a particular intervention. There is clearly still scope for 'good practice', even where the general picture is somewhat bleak (Smith, R. 2002a).

Nevertheless, we must, I think, be critical of the reform programme overall, not least because some of the claims made since its initial implementation in 2000 have been overstated and, at the same time, politically exploited (see, for example, Youth Justice Board 2002). Before addressing the more fundamental question of whether the reformed system is indeed delivering 'youth justice', it will be instructive to address the question of whether it has achieved some of the specific targets and objectives specified by government and by the YJB (Home Office 1997b; Youth Justice Board 2000).

By highlighting as a key election pledge a commitment to halve the time between arrest and final disposal for 'persistent' young offenders from 142 to 71 days, the incoming Labour government had clearly signalled its priority target in terms of the justice process. Amid much fanfare, this was reported to have been achieved by August 2001, with a figure of 65 days being reached by March 2002 (Youth Justice Board 2002), despite some regional variations. This figure was more or less sustained subsequently, at least until 2005, although it had crept up to 73 days by March 2006 (Pandya 2006: 2).

This achievement could be said to be a product of the managerialist approach identified previously, whereby success is judged in terms of meeting quantifiable targets and 'outputs' (Everitt and Hardiker 1996). The extent to which these results contribute to more substantial or lasting achievements, such as the 'principal aim' of reducing youth crime, is much more difficult to assess. On the other hand, there are other questions to ask about the 'unintended consequences' of an initiative such as the reduction of delay. Early evaluations appeared to be quite relaxed about the consequences for the quality of justice delivered (Ernst & Young 1999), but others appear to have been more critical (Holdaway *et al.* 2001; Shapland *et al.* 2001; Kemp *et al.* 2002). Concerns were expressed, for example, by YOT members in response to the stricter deadlines for the submission of reports regarding the effect on standards of practice (Shapland *et al.* 2001: 67). Others have found a greater likelihood of prosecution because of the effect of limited timescales in constraining police discretion (Kemp *et al.* 2002: 13). The pressure to complete cases might also, as already noted, mean that less attention is paid to the interests of victims, as well as offenders, especially in complex cases (Holdaway *et al.* 2001: 27). So, the perceived benefits of bringing 'spree' offenders to justice more quickly might be compromised by other unhelpful outcomes:

It may be helpful to remember that fast-tracking is best regarded as a means of achieving the aims of increasing the accountability of offenders, reducing the risks of reoffending, and meeting the needs of victims, rather than an unyielding end in its own right. (Dignan 2000: 3)

Ironically, the reduction of delays may of itself contribute to the creation of 'persistent young offenders' (PYOs) because of the impact of 'splitting' files relating to separate offences. As a consequence, young people who commit more than one offence are more likely to achieve the figure of four separate court proceedings necessary to qualify as 'persistent' (National Standard 7.9, Youth Justice Board 2004: 41). Whether this might be offset by the reduced likelihood of reoffending while on bail (Audit Commission 2004: 33) or by strengthening 'the link between the offence and its consequence' (Holdaway *et al.* 2001: 27) remains unclear.

Aside from the impact of speeding up youth justice, wider claims of efficacy have also been made for other aspects of the reform programme (Hine and Celnick 2001; Jennings 2002; Youth Justice Board 2002; Whiting and Cuppleditch 2006). It has been claimed, for example, that Final Warnings have had a significant impact on reducing the level of re-convictions (Hine and Celnick 2001). Thus 'on a like with like basis' the rate of further proceedings for those subject to Final Warnings was initially reported as being 6 per cent better than might be expected (30 per cent compared with a predicted rate of 36 per cent; Hines and Celnick 2001: 1). This finding is based on a comparison of reoffending rates in 1998 under the previous cautioning regime and those for young offenders issued with warnings in the pilot areas for the youth justice reforms.

In fact, rates of both further proceedings and reconvictions were found to be higher than previously for those subject to Final Warnings (Hine and Celnick 2001: 16, 20), but this was attributed to the combined impact of the cessation of repeat cautioning and the changing characteristics of the Final Warning subgroup (a greater number of males, older age profile, more previous proceedings). Once these differences are taken into account, it was suggested that Final Warnings were more effective than previous pre-court disposals in reducing the rate at which young people were reported for further offences, especially for the 16+ age group. Further proceedings here are used as an indicator of 'programme effectiveness' (Hine and Celnick 2001: 14). However, they are only a 'proxy' for reoffending, since the rate of further proceedings will be influenced by other factors, such as 'police, crown prosecution and court practice', as well as 'clear up and cautioning rates' (Hine and Celnick 2001: 14). Over this initial period (1998–2001), for example, detection rates were falling, partly as a result of changes in police recording methods, and the proportion of cases discontinued by the Crown Prosecution Service was rising (Home Office 2001b). Other potentially distorting aspects of the transition from one system to another were not explored by this study, such as the extent to which informal disposals previously used by the police might have been replaced by formal pre-court disposals (Reprimands or Final Warnings). There is some evidence to support the view that historically widespread informal responses (Evans and Ellis 1997) were supplanted by formal procedures on the introduction of the new disposals (Kemp *et al.* 2002), and this may throw some doubt on any exercise seeking to draw precise comparisons between the Final Warning cohort (with apparently greater numbers of prior offences) and those subject to previous police interventions (whose prior offending may not have been recorded officially). Certainly, given changes in both procedures and recording methods, there must be some doubt that 'like' really was being compared with 'like' in this evaluative exercise. It is probably unwise, for example, to rely on a presumption that Final Warnings occur at a later stage in criminal careers than cautions had done previously (Hine and Celnick 2001: 5).

In addition, this evaluation found no effect on reoffending rates of intervention programmes put in place to accompany warnings. Indeed, indiscriminate use of these was questioned:

> Firstly, evaluation of work with adult offenders shows that intervention with offenders with a low risk of reoffending can result in increased reconviction rates ... Secondly, reconviction studies (including this one) show that a large proportion of offenders receiving a first caution do not reoffend, suggesting that intervening too early could be a waste of resources. (Hine and Celnick 2001: 35)

Despite this cautionary note, the Youth Justice Board took a rather different view, arguing both that the initial impact of Final Warnings was 'variable' (Warner 2001: 1), but that 'research shows that an intervention programme at the Final Warning stage is one of the most effective ways of diverting an individual from criminality' (Youth Justice Board 2002: 10). Unfortunately, this was just one early example of a recurrent pattern.

The selective reading of the available evidence became a feature of the Youth Justice Board's pronouncements in the initial stages of its existence, which both undermined its own credibility and confused efforts to understand the complexities of the interactions between the machinery of youth justice, young people and others involved. This tendency has led to strong complaints from some evaluators of youth justice innovations. For example:

> It was ... of concern to find that the YJB had reported the results ... in its Annual Review in such a way as to imply that the restorative justice schemes had reduced crime ... Bearing in mind the clear caveat we had made ... such comments were not only highly selective, but could not be said to be based on reliable evidence. (Wilcox 2003: 30)

A particularly striking example of this 'selectivity' concerns the repeated claims of dramatic falls in the levels of reoffending by young people. In the summer of 2002, the YJB claimed that 'even before full national roll-out the youth justice reforms in 2000 cut predicted reconviction rates by nearly 15 per cent' (Youth Justice Board Press Release 9 July 2002). This claim was based on a study comparing 1997 reconviction rates with those of a cohort of young people proceeded against in July 2000. The stated reduction of 'nearly 15 per cent' was arrived at by deducting the 'raw' reconviction rate for this cohort

(26.4 per cent) from the 'predicted' rate based on the outcomes for the 1997 sample (30.9 per cent), and calculating the proportional difference between these figures; in other words, this was the most dramatic possible construction of these figures. By 2003, this purported reduction in reconviction rates was even higher, based on the same calculation, reaching 22.5 per cent between 1997 and 2001 (Jennings 2003). These remarkable figures subsequently became highlights of a number of key national policy documents (Home Office 2003; National Audit Office 2004).

This is unfortunate, to the extent that it may offer spurious justification for changes whose success is actually much more debatable. Further and more responsible consideration of these startling findings has led to rather more modest claims, in fact. Indeed, the study on which the claims were based acknowledged some methodological problems, such as the fact that the results were skewed by comparing two very different populations (pre- and post-reforms), which would make it difficult, for example, to adjust for the substantial 'increase in reprimands and final warnings which would be likely to result in lower reconviction rates' (Jennings 2002: 9). In addition, a number of other commentators have drawn attention to further methodological shortcomings (Smith 2003; Bateman and Pitts 2005; Bottoms 2005). For example, the exclusion of 'pseudo-reconvictions' (further proceedings related to offences committed before the first disposal taken into account – likely to have increased because of the practice of 'splitting files; Shapland *et al.* 2001) and those subject to custodial sentences (a figure which was increasing over the period in question; Home Office 2001b) are likely to have contributed to a reduction in the relative proportion of further proceedings for the later (post-reform) sample. In addition, a number of changes in procedures and recording methods are also recognised as being likely to have reduced the recorded reconviction rate, which the initial study itself acknowledged would have lowered the 'headline (sic!) improvement rate from 14.6 per cent to between 11 and 12%' (Jennings 2002: 10).

In addition, these figures appeared to take no account of the external influences which might have influenced the 'inputs' to the youth justice system, such as possible changes in the use of informal disposals by the police (Pragnell 2005). Aside from this, the question of the 'gearing effect' of the relationship between crimes committed and the rate of proceedings against individual young offenders should be taken into account, especially in light of the general reduction in crime rates reported during this period on all accepted measures (Home Office 2001b: 27). It is difficult, too, to separate out the impact of specific youth justice measures from the impact of other socio-economic factors and wider policy changes. Muncie argues that 'changes in law enforcement and in what the law counts as crime preclude much meaningful discussion over whether youth crime is forever rising (or indeed falling)' (Muncie 1999: 17).

As Bottoms (2005) observes, the Home Office (Reconviction Analysis Section, RDS-NOMS) has subsequently acknowledged some of the methodological problems with the earlier reconviction studies. He suggests rather that there was an initial 2.5 per cent reduction in 'juvenile re-offending' from 1997 to

2001, but little change from that point (Bottoms 2005: 11). By 2006, the Home Office had revised its approach to take the year 2000 (the point at which the reform programme was substantially implemented) as its baseline, and from this point it was calculated that 'the actual one-year re-offending rate' for those receiving disposals (pre-court sanctions and court disposals) of some kind in 2004 was 41.3 per cent, against a 'predicted rate of 41.9 per cent' (Whiting and Cuppleditch 2006: 1). It still appears that a larger decline can be observed to have occurred in the years 1997–2000, however.

Within this overall picture, some interesting variations can also be noted, leading to a degree of 'ambiguity' (Bateman and Pitts 2005: 257). It seems that reoffending rates are more likely to have declined following pre-court and lower-tariff disposals, while the 'more substantial community penalties register a slight increase in re-offending' (Bateman and Pitts 2005: 257; Whiting and Cuppleditch 2006: 9).

The picture is further confused by the evidence of what young people themselves say about their offending behaviour. According to self-report surveys, offending rates among young people are fairly constant (MORI 2004: 14). Despite occasional variations between years, over time there is a considerable degree of consistency, both among 'mainstream' young people (those in mainstream schools – around 26 per cent) and 'excluded young people' (60 per cent). What is also clear is that most offences committed by young people, and indeed most young people who offend, do not come to the attention of the criminal justice system. Thus it has been reported that 26 per cent of young people aged 10 to 25 surveyed in 2004 said they had committed an offence in the previous year (Budd *et al.* 2005: i), but only 3 per cent had been arrested (not necessarily all offenders, of course), and just 10 per cent of those who reported committing a 'serious offence' had been arrested, of whom half had been to court (Budd *et al.* 2005: vi). This is consistent with earlier evidence that 6 per cent of young people who offended stated that their most recent infraction came to official notice. It is also of note that 47 per cent of this group say that being caught and punished has little or no deterrent effect, as opposed to 44 per cent who say that it does stop them from reoffending (MORI 2002: 19).

The evidence from large-scale surveys of young people tells a rather different story from conventional criminal statistics, it would seem. Patterns of crime are not shifting dramatically, according to their own accounts, and the impact of sanctions is not a particularly significant factor in promoting desistance. We might perhaps conclude that the sensationalist claims made in the early days of the post-2000 reforms were misleading at best, and certainly missed the point.

The Nero effect

At this point, it is important to turn our attention once again to other changes in the way in which young offenders are processed by the justice system, which are at least as significant in terms of its overall impact.

Indeed, the starting point for this discussion is the same reconviction study upon which the Youth Justice Board based its unsustainable claim of massive reductions in reoffending rates (Jennings 2002). We are alerted to one key issue by the reported reduction in predicted reconviction rates, from 33.7 per cent in 1997 to 30.9 per cent in 2000 (p. 5). This suggests, even allowing for changes in recording practices, that the cohort of young people dealt with as offenders immediately following the implementation of reforms was considerably less 'criminal' than its predecessors. Confirmation of this trend is also provided by the subsequent self-report survey which reported an increasing proportion of young people being caught and dealt with for offences (MORI 2002: 21). The immediate impact of the new youth justice system may therefore have been increasing criminalisation of young people. At the same time, as we have already observed, intervention programmes, at whatever level, were becoming more intrusive, as witnessed, for example, by the increase from 52 per cent to 70 per cent in the use of Final Warning programmes from 2000 to 2001/02 (Youth Justice Board 2002: 11), despite the evidence questioning their value (Hine and Celnick 2001).

Following a path mapped out by Foucault (Smith, R. 2001), the level and intensity of interventions at all stages of the process appeared to be increasing, with the implementation of demanding Referral Order contracts (Fionda 2005), increasingly wide-ranging Action Plan Orders and, of course, the Intensive Supervision and Surveillance Programme. Young people are accelerated up the 'tariff' by attracting the label 'persistent young offender' earlier in their offending careers and in relation to less serious offences, evidence of failure to comply with programme requirements is subject to more rigorous breach procedures, thresholds for punitive sanctions are widened (Goldson 2006: 144) and the consequence is, of course, a persistently high level of custody.

In sum, then, the available evidence suggests a decline in the rates of offending from around 1995 on all commonly used measures (Home Office 2001b: 27). This is not necessarily supported by young people's own accounts (MORI 2002; Budd et al. 2005), although Bateman (2006: 69) points out that this might be the case over a longer timescale. While credit for reducing levels of offending is attributed to the youth justice reforms (Audit Commission 2004), the evidence to support this is shaky – the start of the trend towards lower crime rates pre-dated the reform programme and the published evidence in support of these claims is at best equivocal (Hine and Celnick 2001; Loxley et al. 2002; Crawford and Newburn 2003; Gray et al. 2005).

What we are able to conclude is that younger, less serious offenders are being drawn into the formal justice system, which is even more noteworthy given the overall decline in the number of young people being processed as offenders – a fall of over 10 per cent between 1998 and 2000, for example (Johnson et al. 2001), a reduction which has been more or less sustained since (Home Office 2005a). Despite this, the balance between those dealt with by relatively less severe means such as cautions (Reprimands and Final Warnings since June 2000) and those sentenced by the courts has tipped towards the more punitive end of the scale. Between 1994 and 2004 the ratio between the number of cautions and court disposals declined from 2.4:1 to 1.3:1, and this changing relationship was not affected by the transition from cautions to Reprimands and Final Warnings. Indeed, it was not intended to, given the apparent distaste for 'repeat cautioning' (Kemp *et al.* 2002).

This progressive 'toughening up' of the youth justice system is also apparent at subsequent stages in the process. More lenient disposals such as discharges and fines were displaced from the start by 'community sentences' (Johnson *et al.* 2001) and the Referral Order. An apparent decline in the number of custodial sentences for 15–17 year olds in 2000 was offset by an increase in sentence lengths (Johnson *et al.* 2001: 11; Youth Justice Board 2002: 15). As we have observed, the increase in the use of custody prior to 2000 has largely been sustained since, with the April 2006 figure for the under 18 population in secure facilities standing at 2,819, or 4 per cent higher than on the comparable date in 2000. As Goldson (2006: 145) observes, there have been increases in the number of children sent to custody, in sentence lengths and in 'long-term detention'. As a result 'greater use of penal custody for children is now made in England and Wales than in most other industrialised democratic countries'. Measures such as the ISSP have signally failed to impact on these high levels, and their place as an 'alternative to custody' must be in doubt.

Thus, despite the vast array of changes in youth justice since 1997, there is little evidence of any significant impact on young people, on the behaviour of the courts or on other key stakeholders, including victims of crime. The available findings suggest an intensification of disposals targeted at increasingly minor and less experienced young offenders, while the injustices experienced by particular groups such as those from ethnic minorities (Bowling and Phillips 2002) and the shoddy and oppressive treatment administered to those in custody continues unabated (HM Chief Inspector of Prisons 2001; 2002; Bright 2002; Goldson 2002; Goldson and Coles 2005; Carlile 2006; Keith 2006).

In some quarters, it might be thought that a greater level of activity and a greater intensity of intervention might simply be indicative of a more responsive and committed approach to youth justice – a sign that the crimes of the young are, indeed, being taken more seriously than in the past (Blair 2002; Blunkett 2002). On the other hand, serious questions must also be raised about the consequences of this intensification. There has clearly been a diminution of the rights of children, with collateral evidence of harmful treatment in custody and persistent inequalities in the way in which certain groups are treated, especially those from black and minority ethnic communities.

At the same time, the propagation of a much broader range of interventions based on those who present a 'risk', whether or not they are offenders (Smith, R. 2006), is both economically wasteful and inconsistent with other policy aspirations intended to promote social inclusion and a sense of community cohesion. Far from generating social solidarity, these measures cement into place a sense of difference and 'otherness' (Garland 2001). The price of an apparently more certain approach to dealing with unacceptable behaviour by young people is far too high, both financially and, more importantly, in human terms.

8. Theorising youth justice

The art of the possible

Having spent some time setting out the 'state of play' in youth justice, it will now be worthwhile to take a step back and reflect on the theoretical context and whether that offers any insights into the possibilities for progressive practice in the current era. The preceding overview of contemporary developments suggests that there are very substantial grounds for concern, in that youth justice provision in England and Wales has managed to achieve the dual failures of being both ineffective, in its own terms, and simultaneously repressive in its impact. The very limited gains that may be identified are hard-won successes, usually carved out of the granite of system inertia by imaginative and persistent practitioners and managers. These gains have been achieved in spite of, and not because of, the reforms initiated in the late 1990s/early 2000s.

If we are to make progress more systematically, there is a task to be undertaken in terms of explaining how and why the youth justice system is constructed in the way it is, and the assumptions and ideas that inform service delivery. What, in short, are the ideological underpinnings for the prevailing obsessions with surveillance, risk assessment, containment and punishment? At the same time, it will also be important to gain a better understanding of the ways in which these underlying beliefs are translated into a prescriptive, target-driven and managerialist delivery system.

Answering these questions should, in turn, provide us with a platform from which we can begin to consider the question of what we want from youth justice and how we can achieve it. This will be extended through consideration of the perspectives of a range of stakeholders, including victims (see also Chapter 7), young people, ethnic minorities and 'the community' (Chapter 9). The aim will be to bring together our theoretical analysis with the aspirations of those affected 'on the ground' in order to set out what is conceivable, practicable and desirable in terms of youth justice services. We may, on this basis, be able to sketch out some of the key elements of a system which 'does what it says on the tin', that is, delivers justice to young people (see also Goldson and Muncie 2006).

The practicality of theory

For many people involved in the day-to-day construction and delivery of youth justice in practice, theory may seem irrelevant, unimportant or simply an unaffordable luxury. So, the first task here is perhaps to justify making the effort to dig deeper and seek out abstract themes and principles which might provide some form of coherent understanding. On the other hand, the evidence of failure and wasted effort set out previously seems to indicate that it might be useful to try to unpack the question of how to achieve effective interventions a little more fully. Of course, this in itself poses a major challenge – just what do we mean by the idea of effectiveness in youth justice, and how do we know what is indeed 'working'? As Bateman and Pitts (2005, p. 251) observe, this is never a straightforward question:

> Instead of asking 'what works' we probably need to ask:
> *What kind of interventions have what kind of impact upon what kinds of people under what kinds of circumstances and why?*

The establishment of a single priority objective by the government, that is, the prevention of youth offending, might appear to go a long way to resolving our difficulties, but this is far from the case, and we must try to ascertain what assumptions are built into even this deceptively straightforward aspiration. The implicit theories that underpin everyday strategies, policies and practice are no less theoretical because they are treated as 'givens' and thus not articulated or laid open to critical scrutiny.

To illustrate this point, it may be helpful to offer two extreme examples of how to 'prevent' youth crime, both of which would, ironically, provide much greater certainty than the strategies pursued to this point. First, the legal framework could be amended simply to decriminalise any and all actions by children and young people – not so far-fetched if we recall that a Labour government came very close to initiating this process in 1969. Nor is it so remarkable if we take a wider perspective, and recognise that the age of criminal responsibility is typically much higher in other European countries, and is, indeed, 18 in some (Fionda 2005).

On the other hand, we might conceive of the institution of a system of 'preventive detention' which would ensure that no child or young person had the opportunity to offend. Again, we can observe elements of this approach in a range of crime reduction and anti-social behaviour initiatives, including the Dispersal Order, where police officers refer to themselves as 'child-catchers' (Smithson 2003: 17).

Finally, we could dispense with youth crime by effectively eradicating the concept of youth itself or childhood as a phase in which differential treatment is necessary. Likewise, we can observe aspects of this perspective in the abolition of the rule of *doli incapax* under the Crime and Disorder Act 1998, and the 'adulteration' of young people's miscreant behaviour, as Muncie and Goldson (2006) put it.

The fact that all these ideas are to be found incorporated in youth justice practices (even if not in the 'here and now') suggests that there are both a very wide range of alternative perspectives and a substantial degree of pragmatism and complexity at play in reality, based on the interplay between a series of beliefs about what is desirable, possible and acceptable.

Dominelli (1998) makes the point that interventions in social welfare are 'compelled to maintain the link between theory and practice', and this is equally true of youth justice. It is not simply a technical or managerial exercise (Bateman and Pitts 2005: 251) in delivering prescribed interventions, but rather a product of multi-faceted and often conflicting or contradictory ideas and beliefs (Muncie 2001). These underlying assumptions must, therefore, be laid open to analysis and critical evaluation, especially if we wish to consider the prospects for change and the potential for progressive practice in dealing with youth offending.

In seeking to develop a plausible account of how youth justice has taken the form that it has, it will be helpful to consider a number of different 'levels' of analysis, corresponding to the distinctive contexts which shape the system itself. In one sense, this might be seen as drawing a distinction between the 'what' (the definition of the problem), the 'how' (the machinery for addressing it) and the 'why' (the underlying rationale), although, of course, these are also inevitably interlinked.

As already indicated, Harris and Webb (1987) have offered a helpful framework in their analysis of power in the context of 'juvenile justice'. They characterise the levels of analysis in terms of the 'macro', 'mezzo' and 'micro' (see also Chapter 3). Within this framework, the 'macro' is represented by the state and its place in determining the shape and orientation of the machinery of intervention. This is, in their view, the origin of a series of core contradictions between the aims and purposes prescribed and the professional culture and principles of 'expert' service providers. They suggest that it is these tensions which lie at the heart of many of the difficulties experienced by those responsible for delivering services:

> Motivations and fine feelings are heavily circumscribed by social function, and in the conflict between competing ideologies of state bureaucracy and professional autonomy lies the source of some of the frustrations regularly experienced by the workers themselves. (Harris and Webb 1987: 3)

Their characterisation of the mezzo level concentrates on the nature and functioning of welfare and justice agencies themselves as mediators in the interchange between state and professional interests. According to them, it is important to recognise that it is at this level that interpretation, adaptation, negotiation and even, sometimes, obfuscation and deception bring together idealised and centrally determined demands with the diverse and challenging realities of delivery in an unpredictable and sometimes intractable environment. This process of seeking accommodation between the ideal goal of predictable social order and messy reality is, for them, 'in part a reflection of the practicalities of managing people who have already proved to be unmanageable' (Harris and

Webb 1987: 102), This fits, too, with Lipsky's (1980) analysis, which suggests that there is a necessary process of interpreting generalised instructions and objectives in terms of local circumstances.

At the micro level, where youth justice work is actually carried out, they suggest that practice appears to be disparate, disorganised and simply incomprehensible to those who are its objects, that is young offenders. This is largely a consequence of the attempts at the macro and mezzo levels to apply oversimplistic solutions to complex circumstances. Harris and Webb draw attention to one aspect of this, 'routine individualisation', whereby standardised instruments and procedures are applied uniformly in ways which fail to take account of difference and diversity, leading to the creation of anomalies and illogical outcomes. For them, this was epitomised in the indiscriminate use of Supervision Orders as a tariff-based sentence, irrespective of the offender's background or the nature of the offence. In the empirical study which informed their observations, '58 per cent of "not serious" and 70 per cent of "serious" cases received two-year orders, apparently as a routine disposal' (Harris and Webb 1987: 118). Their argument is that this is part of a process by which the 'inherent instability' which characterises all aspects of youth justice is played out in a series of ordered interactions and compromises which produce the impression of regularity and 'fit' while also leading to arbitrary outcomes. The process ensures that the appearance of rationality and order is maintained, and this sustains the conditions by which 'the game itself continues' (Harris and Webb 1987: 3). Cicourel's (1968) earlier work also provides a detailed account of the way in which routines and procedures make sense of and create an internal logic to account for and deal with variable and problematic circumstances.

While this analysis offers some important insights into the internal mechanisms of youth justice, albeit based on evidence from earlier periods in time, we should also recognise from it the value of linking theoretical insights addressed to different aspects of a generalised subject, such as 'youth justice'. In order to pursue this aim, three critical questions will be considered here in turn, before we turn to some of the broader emergent themes which might suggest commonalities. First, we will consider the 'micro' question of problematic youth – why are young people in England and Wales, at least, viewed as the source of a whole range of social ills? Second, we will address the nature of justice, and why the problems of disorder and unacceptable behaviour should be seen in the way they are, particularly at the 'macro' level of the state and other powerful institutions. And, finally, we will revisit the issue of the 'mezzo' level mechanisms which link these and ensure that youth justice is delivered in the form that it is (see also Chapter 3).

Targeting the young: the source of all ills?

Why are societal concerns about disorder and threat focused largely on the behaviour of young people? Given that the recorded incidence of criminal activity is rather more evenly distributed across the age range, and that young people are as likely to be victims as offenders, why should there be this degree of concern about children as perpetrators of crime? Why, in short, are we afraid of the young?

The highly specific and selective nature of these concerns is encapsulated by the observation that much of what we know and believe about childhood and adolescence is culturally determined. Jenks (1996), for example, has argued that 'adolescence' is a peculiarly Western phenomenon, representing the playing-out of the specific social, cultural and economic determinants that are influential in modern developed societies. Anthropological evidence offers strong support here, with contributors such as Benedict (1961) and Erikson (1995) identifying very wide cultural variations in the ways in which transitions from childhood to adulthood are managed and experienced. Such variations indicate that the nature of adolescence is substantially determined by the context and by the institutions and beliefs operating in any specific social milieu:

> Undoubtedly each culture ... creates character types marked by its own mixture of defect and excess; and each culture develops rigidities and illusions which protect it against the insight that no ideal, safe, permanent state can emerge from the blueprint it has gropingly evolved. (Erikson 1995: 168)

Adolescence does not appear to be fixed or constant and this has prompted some authors to suggest that it can only be construed as one of the products of the interplay between broader social forces. Thus, for observers such as Willis (1977) and Davies (1986), the experience of being young and growing up is fundamentally influenced by the requirement to socialise the next generation of wage earners, producers and family members. The cultural patterns and practices of young people themselves, such as 'working-class counter-school culture' (Willis 1977: 2), make sense primarily as part of a process by which 'labour power' is reproduced, and young people are socialised into a particular work ethos, coming to terms, not without struggle, with their place in the socio-economic structure. This is not necessarily a straightforward or exclusively one-way process, in that the attempt by the state and other institutions to regulate and reproduce the next generation of producers is both contradictory in itself, and is mediated by the distinctive thoughts, attitudes and experiences of children and young people.

Against this, though, the purposes of the powerful who shape interventions with young people are primarily to secure the creation of a future generation that meets the needs of and sustains existing social relations:

> Youth policies were ... designed to satisfy some powerful sectional (especially class, gender and racial) interests. As the rawest and least valuable recruits to a given social order, the young had to be socialized, schooled, trained and ultimately contained – if necessary [according to a senior civil servant] 'in terms more or less unpalatable' to them. (Davies 1986: 116)

Corrigan (1979), too, in his study of young people 'doing nothing' in Sunderland, has linked changes in the experiences of youth to parallel changes in social structures and the shifting demands of living in a 'capitalist society'. Thus young people are to be brought up both to accept their place in the order of things, but also to be ready to adapt in response to economic and social transitions. Young people are therefore increasingly educated to be 'flexible' in order to adapt to changing jobs and work patterns over the course of their lives in employment. This might be related to the experience of the 1980s and 1990s, whereby they were required first to 'equip themselves with the abilities sought after in the fast-food industry and then ... get on their bikes and ... price themselves into work' (Haines and Drakeford 1998: 8). One aspect of their 'educative' (Gramsci 1971) experience is provided through their interactions with criminal justice agencies. This may be one of the more explicit aspects of a broader process of socialisation, whereby young people learn their proper place and the limits of what is acceptable. To them this may have no obvious origin or justification:

> The power of the police is seen as virtually total by the boys ... The police, like the teachers, are a group of people with power that do some very strange and arbitrary things; their power is massive and has to be coped with, if not obeyed. (Corrigan 1979: 137)

Furthermore, the control that is exercised is not connected in these youths' perceptions to specific instances of wrong doing. It is more the case that specific boundaries are being drawn around their behaviour in order to create a sense of the 'natural order' of things and to ensure conformity. Indeed, this is part of a broader pattern of institutionalised control (Cohen 1985). According to Jeffs (1997), these parallel developments are not purely coincidental. A range of centralised and directive education initiatives, such as home-school contracts, citizenship education and attendance league tables, serve essentially the same purpose as explicit measures of social control such as 'tagging' and the imposition of strict parental liability:

> the role of the police and the role of the education system are parallel here, because they are both attempting to change the styles of living of people who ... are seen as threatening ... (Corrigan 1979: 139)

The Dispersal Order can be seen as a concrete contemporary expression of this project. Young people clearly feel that the objective is to limit their freedoms: 'They only go for the kids, they don't go after the adults. They think we're easier. We're easier to target aren't we?' (young person quoted in Smithson 2004: 13).

The machinery of criminal justice is one of a series of mechanisms which shape the experiences and expectations of young people, which are collectively geared towards creating a spirit of acceptance and compliance with social norms. However, as Muncie (1999) reminds us, it is important to note, too, that the social roles for which young people are being prepared are also mediated by distinctions of ethnicity and genders, with specific implications for young black males, for example. Webster (2006: 42) discusses the specific processes of racialised 'marginalisation' in this respect.

The preoccupation with controlling and channelling the behaviour of the young is linked to a functionalist concern to ensure that they are effectively socialised to meet the requirements of the dominant social order, it seems. Jeffs (1997) has suggested that there is a 'plethora' of government policies covering education, housing, income maintenance and youth crime which, taken together, indicate 'the resolve on the part of the government to control those identified as the underclass. In particular, they have exhibited a willingness to adopt increasingly authoritarian policies to control and manage the young poor' (Jeffs 1997: 160). The apparent need to provide control and guidance might partly stem from an understanding of young people as 'unfinished', that is going through a process of 'transition' (Walther 2006), and thus likely to behave inappropriately or in ways which are threatening to the status quo (Davies 1986). As a result, terms such as 'youth' or 'adolescent' can easily 'conjure up a number of emotive and troubling images. These range from notions of uncontrolled freedom, irresponsibility, vulgarity, rebellion and dangerousness to those of deficiency, neglect, deprivation or immaturity' (Muncie 1999: 3).

However, while concerns about the behaviour and attitudes of the young arise partly because they have not yet been fully prepared for their allotted roles as responsible and productive (or reproductive) members of society, it is also the case that the socialisation process itself is inconsistent, leading to tensions and contradictions. As Willis (1977) has observed, the demands placed on young people by social institutions themselves may not always point in the same direction, and there has never been a time (a 'golden age') when youth transitions were 'really smooth and unproblematic' (Vickerstaff 2003: 269). MacDonald argues that their own emerging personal 'survival' strategies compel young people to develop a range of responses to economic pressures and 'chronic insecurity'. Clearly, their own background and characteristics will also be a factor in this process. 'Normal' expectations may fall foul of acute exclusionary processes (Webster 2006: 41).

Young people can thus be expected to behave in differing and conflicting ways in order to comply with a variety of social expectations within their own specific circumstances; for example, they may be encouraged to take relatively passive roles as 'consumers', sharing 'the mainstream aspirations and values of the wider society' (Webster 2006: 41), whilst they are also encouraged to take an active and entrepreneurial role as 'producers' (Smith, R. 2000), but with 'few bridges or connections' (Webster 2006: 41) to enable them to achieve this goal.

At the same time, 'it is, of course, an absolute requirement for the existing social system that the same standards, ideologies and aspirations are not passed on to all' (Willis 1977: 177). This will, in turn, lead to a series of conflicting dynamics within the processes of transition for young people. For example, the complex expectations of masculinity appear to require young males to be dynamic, competitive and ambitious on the one hand, while on the other, attributes such as being challenging or aggressive are discouraged. In this context, Webster (2006: 41) suggests that a 'racialised "exaggerated masculinity" grows by way of compensation against humiliation and anticipated school "failure" ...'.

Young people on the margins may also be encouraged to aspire to increased spending power, with increasing material aspirations, while at the same time confronting the constraints of the labour market, which, as MacDonald (1997: 106) puts it, frustrates their hopes 'for sustainable family lives and respectable futures'. Transitions in such circumstances are problematic, often resulting in 'interconnected' difficulties extending over a considerable period of time (Webster *et al.* 2004: 35).

Recognising these conflicts and constraints can bring us closer to understanding the relationship between the sources of power and the institutional structures which represent dominant interests on the one hand, and the behaviour of the young in response to the 'mixed messages' they receive on the other.

Frustrated ambitions?

In seeking to account for the behaviour of young people, it may be helpful to reflect on the insights offered by a rather older sociological source (Merton 1957), who constructed a 'typology' to make sense of the differing ways in which individuals adapt to social norms, depending on their circumstances, influences and personal attributes.

At the heart of this model is the distinction between 'goals' and 'means', which Merton then uses to demonstrate that there is a variety of potential combinations of these factors, with differing implications for attitudes and behaviour (see Table 8.1).

Thus, for example, if an individual shares the dominant goals of a given society, and possesses and exercises the institutionalised (socially accepted) means to achieve these, then that person is demonstrating social conformity. However, a number of other patterns of adaptation are possible, including 'innovation'. In this mode, the individual shares the dominant goals but adopts other than institutionalised means to achieve these. Merton (writing

Table 8.1 A Typology of Modes of Individual Adaptation

Mode of adaptation	Culture goals	Institutionalised means
Conformity	+	+
Innovation	+	−
Ritualism	−	+
Retreatism	−	−
Rebellion	±	±

Adapted from: Social Theory and Social Structure (Merton 1957: 140)

in the United States) observed in this respect that 'contemporary American culture continues to be characterized by a heavy emphasis on wealth as a basic symbol of success, without a corresponding emphasis on the legitimate avenues on which to march towards this goal' (Merton 1957: 139). The 'innovative' response to this contradiction might therefore be demonstrated by way of resorting to some form of acquisitive criminal activity. Merton suggested, too, that there would be a distinctive class bias to such patterns of behaviour, for obvious reasons, in that the 'lower strata' will have fewer opportunities to achieve financial success through the labour market:

> Specialised areas of vice and crime constitute a 'normal' response to a situation where the cultural emphasis upon pecuniary success has been absorbed, but where there is little access to conventional and legitimate means for becoming successful. (Merton 1957: 139)

Although this framework helps to account for acquisitive crimes (such as theft, fraud and shoplifting), it may be somewhat less effective in relation to other forms of criminal activity (see, for example, Soothill *et al.* 2002). Nevertheless, it remains of considerable use in demonstrating that accepted social norms can, of themselves, act as prompts to rational forms of adaptive behaviour which are, at the same time, socially unacceptable. So, the crimes of the young can, in part, be attributed to rational choices made in a context of social inequality and unattainable aspirations. As we have seen, Webster's (2006) analysis of 'race', youth crime and justice indicates that there remains a strong commitment to conventional norms among marginalised groups, while Craine's (1997) ethnographic analysis suggests that 'alternative careers' in the illicit economy are a response to 'triple failure'. In this study, young people were found to be constructing viable but unlawful alternatives, where:

> They had 'failed' educationally, 'failed' to secure post-school employment, 'failed' to 'get into' working-class adulthood through employment, even after participation in a succession of government schemes and special programmes. (Craine 1997: 148)

Indeed, illegal alternatives might prove considerably more lucrative for some (Webster *et al.* 2004: 20). At least some of the behaviour of young people defined as criminal might therefore be a by-product of the social pressures and conflicting expectations they encounter and the means by which they adapt to these. Merton's framework can also offer us some insight into other routes into criminality, such as drug use ('Retreatism').

While this framework can begin to offer ways to account for specific forms of youth offending, we must also accept that this behaviour can be experienced by others as unpleasant and unacceptable. As MacDonald (1997) points out, it is a matter of concern that crimes committed by young people are likely to have an adverse impact on their own communities: 'The social and financial costs of acquisitive and more random and violent criminality ... cannot be dismissed' (MacDonald 1997: 184).

The reality of youth crime

While it has been recognised that both 'youth' and 'crime and disorder' are socially constructed (Muncie 1999), it must also be acknowledged that, however defined, some of the behaviour manifested by young people is problematic, anti-social or simply unpleasant. The work of the 'left realists' in criminology was instrumental in bringing this challenge to the fore. The problem of youth crime is not just a consequence of 'labelling' (Becker 1963) or the impact of oppressive forms of social control (Lea and Young 1984). The behaviour of young people can be genuinely damaging, oppressive in its own right and frightening to individuals and communities which may already be disadvantaged in other ways:

> Criminologists have come to realise the essentially contradictory nature of crime, economically, socially and politically ... Radical criminology ... notes quite urgently that there is a substantial element in street crime which is merely the poor taking up the individualistic, competitive ethos of capitalism itself ... (Lea and Young 1984: 116)

In concurring with Merton, Lea and Young identify young people as a prime source of much of the offensive behaviour that gives rise to fear and hostility within neighbourhoods, and also accounts for the apparent popularity of governmental anti-social behaviour initiatives.

They have also controversially argued that there may be a racial dimension to this, in that young black people might be responsible for a disproportionate amount of crime, or at least certain types of crime, in effect 'compounding the oppression' of victims (Pitts 2001b). There is some support for this claim in one self-report study (MORI 2004: 26), but Gilroy (2002: 66) argues that this must not be allowed to generate global assumptions that 'blacks are a high crime group' (see Chapter 7) or provide any justification for racist practices in dealing with offending behaviour. As Webster (2006) points out, the processes of 'racialisation' and 'criminalisation' are complex socially determined dynamics and should not be taken out of context.

Nevertheless, the recognition of the impact of crime in contributing to the suffering of disadvantaged communities has had much to with the contemporary refocusing of thinking and policy in this area, with priority being given to tackling directly the behaviour that creates problems in communities. While there has been a tendency to seek simple solutions to these issues at the policy level, there has also been a corresponding move to try to account for the 'situated' nature of crime and its antecedents. Once we accept that patterns of behaviour, including criminal activity, are differentially distributed, it then becomes possible to focus on the question of why this should be the case. Structural accounts, by contrast, do not provide localised explanations for diversity of experience or behaviour, nor do they offer much help in achieving specific, deliverable solutions. After all, we are reminded, not all young people who are disadvantaged become criminals:

> This more realist approach to the delinquency of young men is a useful antidote to the excessive social constructionism which has pervaded liberal criminology ... It also reiterates the importance of appreciating the way that socially constructed aspects of identity – particularly those informed by gender, class and race – help shape the cultural survival strategies of young people ... some young men, sharing apparently similar social attributes [as those who do] do not attempt ... delinquent solutions ... (MacDonald 1997: 192)

Subsequent investigation into offending pathways by MacDonald and colleagues (Webster *et al.* 2004) did, indeed, identify a number of situational variables which appeared to affect 'persistence' and 'desistance', including 'sustained employment', 'family support' and family formation.

Not only does this refocusing of concern about the crimes of the young help to provide the basis for more nuanced explanations, but it also has substantial pragmatic value. It has paved the way for a shift of thinking on the social democratic left to the effect that it is important to respond directly to public calls to 'do something' about crime and disorder, and it also implies that there may be practical and immediate 'commonsense' means available to achieve this, through, for example, addressing the source of problems within families, that is 'poor child-rearing practices and weak parental control' (Pitts 2000: 10).

Explaining youth crime?

In light of these developments, structural explanations of youth crime have proved less attractive to policy-makers and opinion-formers. Much attention has been given recently to the task of specifying as precisely as possible the factors associated with[20] young people's criminal behaviour which are rooted in their experiences, circumstances and characteristics.

Farrington's work in this context is recognised as seminal. He has identified a number of specific factors associated with a propensity to offend by young people, including:

- low income and poor housing;
- living in 'deteriorated' inner-city areas;
- a high degree of impulsiveness and hyperactivity;
- low intelligence and low school attainment;
- poor parental supervision and harsh and erratic discipline;
- parental conflict and broken families (Farrington 1996).

Similarly, Rutter and colleagues have suggested a range of conditions associated with 'anti-social behaviour', including:

- individual characteristics, such as 'hyperactivity', 'cognitive impairment', 'temperamental features' and a 'distorted style of social information processing';

- psychosocial factors, such as the nature of parenting, family discord and parental depression;

- population-wide influences, such as the mass media, school ethos and behaviour and 'area differences' (Rutter *et al.* 1998).

Further work to bring together knowledge about the relationship between youth crime and contingent factors was commissioned by the Youth Justice Board (Anderson *et al.* 2001), and this broadly supported these findings, suggesting that factors could be grouped under family, community, school and personal headings. These meta-analyses suggest that the relationship between characteristics, circumstances and crime is complex and 'uncertain' (Anderson *et al.* 2001: 24). They also suggest that such factors operate at a number of different levels, so that it is unwise to focus unduly on any one of these, whether individual characteristics at one end of the spectrum or socio-economic factors at the other. Nevertheless, because a number of distinct relationships can be evidenced, it is possible to draw out implications for policy and practice.

Farrington (2002), for example, argues for the development of initiatives directed at securing behavioural change at the individual level, school improvement programmes, parental education and 'enriched' services for the early years. He also argues more broadly for 'community-based programmes against crime' following the *Communities that Care* model (France and Crow 2001). Rutter and colleagues (1998) also share his enthusiasm for early prevention initiatives such as the Perry Pre-School Project, 'parenting enhancement', school-wide interventions and the 'early treatment' of problem behaviour. They caution, however, that 'focusing on high-risk samples will miss a substantial number of offenders' (Rutter *et al.* 1998: 24), a conclusion echoed by Anderson and colleagues (2001: 25), and raising questions about aspects of the 'preventive' approaches represented by selective strategies such as the Youth Inclusion and Support Programme.

While these analyses are of considerable value and demonstrate the importance of empirical research in criminal justice (if properly used), they have also been the source of considerable subsequent confusion, notably over the necessary distinctions between 'predictors', 'risk factors', 'antecedents' and 'causes' – identifying a relationship between certain indicators and offending behaviour is not the same as demonstrating that there is a specific uni-directional causal relationship between them: 'Even the most elaborate predictors of individual offending devised by criminologists have always over-predicted the incidence of crime alarmingly' (Pitts 2001b: 82). Indeed, proponents of meta-analyses concur with this point:

There are methodological as well as ethical difficulties attached to using current knowledge of risk factors to target individual children 'at risk'.

Multi-factor 'prediction' instruments may be relatively accurate but only apply to a small number of children, missing most of those who go on to commit offences. Those that use a narrower range of factors have been apt to identify significant numbers of children as 'high risk' who do not go on to commit offences. (Anderson *et al.* 2001: 25)

However, the necessary degree of caution contingent on these observations is not always apparent in the response of 'politicians, policy wonks, "opinion formers" and some youth justice managers and professionals', who draw simplistic conclusions about the use of predictive instruments to 'target, and then eradicate, youth crime' (Pitts 2001b: 82). Evidence of this elision is apparent in the work of bodies such as the Social Exclusion Unit which has specified a number of factors which are given causal status:

Most juvenile prisoners have experienced a range of social exclusion factors, which may have contributed to their offending behaviour. These include:

- low educational attainment;
- disrupted family backgrounds;
- coming from a black or minority ethnic background;
- behavioural and mental health problems; and
- problems of alcohol and/or drug misuse. (Social Exclusion Unit 2002: para. D6).

Attempts to generate a comprehensive empirical account of the factors associated with certain types of behaviour are important, not least because they have formed the basis for much of recent government thinking. However, it appears that this evidence has been drawn upon selectively. Muncie argues, for example, that the government's preoccupation with parenting stems from the association between the nature and quality of family life and the likelihood of offending by young people. As a consequence, policies and intervention strategies are explicitly designed to address these 'presenting' problems:

New Labour's acceptance that crime runs in certain families and that anti-social behaviour in childhood is a predictor of later criminality has opened the door to a range of legislative initiatives which target 'disorderly' as well as criminal behaviour. (Muncie 2000: 23)

Similarly, the justification for the introduction of measures such as ASBOs is provided by the need to tackle behavioural problems such as 'impulsiveness and hyperactivity'. Indeed, this selective approach has been further reinforced by the emphasis on behavioural programmes across the range of youth justice interventions emerging from the Youth Justice Board (2002). However, implementation of a range of projects focused on behavioural change produced little evidence to justify this (Feilzer *et al.* 2004).

As Muncie notes, a shift of focus, which would be supported by the evidence from meta-analyses, to include 'social' factors, such as poor housing and unemployment, might lead to a rather different emphasis in policy and practice. Despite this, the primary foci of youth justice interventions remain the individual and the family (parents):

> Parental training and a range of behavioural and cognitive interventions are considered to be most effective ... In such ways the targets of social crime prevention have invariably become individualised and behavioural. Primary attention is given to responding to the symptoms, rather than the causes of young people's disaffection and dislocation. (Muncie 2000: 26)

The argument here is that New Labour's youth crime strategy relies unduly on a narrow focus on specific 'high-risk' groups and the superficial manifestations of social problems with deeper roots; this is reflected in specific measures such as the crusade against street crime in 2002, the anti-social behaviour bandwagon and the promotion of technological measures of control (see also Foucault 1979) such as 'tagging' and 'voice recognition' systems.

On the other hand, the evidence from detailed empirical studies suggests that the range of factors associated with youth crime are connected in various ways and as a consequence that we should not overlook the part that social and structural factors play, even in (perhaps especially in) the practice setting. Leonard (1984) has demonstrated the links between social forces and individual personalities. The individual is 'moulded, inculcated or penetrated by the institutions and activities of the social order and the ideologies which inform and legitimate them' (Leonard 1984: 116) in much the same way as Merton (1957) suggests as we saw earlier. The deviant behaviour of individuals must therefore be seen as the product of multi-faceted, interactive and dynamic processes. Criminality emerges as the outcome of a complex interplay of social and ideological forces and personal experience: 'contradictions within and between the economy, the family and the state, connecting to the highly variable experience of specific individuals, provide space for avoidance, resistance and dissent' (Leonard 1984: 116). Specific anti-social acts, which may be reprehensible in themselves and which may or may not be defined as 'criminal', cannot be understood or dealt with solely in terms of their immediate manifestation. Attempts to deal with the offending (and offensive) behaviour of young people only on the basis of what is immediately known and observed represent, at best, a partial solution. At worst, as we know, they may generate further problems, such as reoffending.

Ironically, as Christie (2000) has commented, forms of 'individualised' intervention (which in fact apply 'generalised' assumptions) serve at the same time to 'depersonalise' explanations of youth crime:

> A political decision to eliminate concern for the social background of the defendant involves much more than making those characteristics

inappropriate for decisions on pain [punishment]. By the same token, the offender is to a large extent excluded as a person. There is no point in exploring a social background, childhood, dreams, defeats ... (Christie 2000: 163)

For present purposes, this raises further questions about the nature of formal responses to the crimes of the young and the extent to which these 'miss the point'. In order to understand the interaction between 'youth justice' and young people we must give further consideration to the way in which institutional policies and practices are constituted and how these lead to forms of delivery that simultaneously decontextualise and problematise the behaviour of young people identified as potential or actual offenders.

The locus of power: ideologies and structures

Much attention has been given to the question of power and its relationship to ideologies of crime and disorder. The exercise of social control is a source of continuing academic fascination and debate (see Garland 2001). Authorities such as Cohen (1985) have made major contributions in this field, and there is widespread acknowledgement that it is an important underpinning of an adequate understanding of youth justice (for example, Goldson 1997; Scraton and Haydon 2002; Goldson and Muncie 2006). The key question here is the relationship between state power, the maintenance of social and moral order and the specific machinery of the justice system itself. Clarke (2002), for example, suggests that the courts and other state institutions are constituted in such a way as to carry out aspects of this mediating function, helping to establish the legitimacy of processes which underpin a particular set of social relations. It is their ascribed status and authority which provides them with the justification for imposing sanctions on individuals and their families, both as a direct means of controlling their behaviour and as a way of reinforcing the legitimacy of the system of norms and rules upon which they are based. The institutions of justice therefore have a kind of self-validating quality.

As we have already observed, the rationale underlying the youth justice system is probably derived from persistent concerns about the uncertainty of youth transitions and the associated threat to the maintenance and reproduction of social order. For Clarke (2002), the fear of disorder and unruly youth is endemic, having been observed in historical accounts of unrest for at least 'the past three centuries'. Pearson (1983), too, has provided evidence that modern society has been persistently troubled by fear of its young people, who become routinely problematised. Often, he notes, there are racist overtones as well. Cohen's (1972) *Folk Devils and Moral Panics* graphically illustrated the way in which fears take hold and are reified, contributing to an almost constant sense of threat among the population in general, magnified to the extent that the very social fabric appears to be at risk.

While there are grounds for recognising that the processes of transition might generate a range of challenging behaviour, there is also considerable evidence to support the argument that the perceived threat is amplified. In other words, whatever the nature of young people's behaviour, additional forces are at play in generating more pervasive fears. The media, for example, have a part to play in shaping such perceptions, and this is inevitable, given their role in creating shared meaning. However, the media are only part of a wider process of creating consensus and shared belief systems:

> Social reality is experienced through language, communication and imagery. Social meaning and social difference are irretrievably tied up with representation. (McRobbie and Thornton 2002: 76)

That is to say, there is an intelligible process in place, by means of which images of disorder are combined and utilised to generate a collective perception of 'threatening youth' (Davies 1986).

This proposition leads us to the notion of 'hegemony' (Gramsci 1971). This, in essence, is the mechanism by which dominant assumptions and norms are integrated to create a shared and conventional view of the 'problem', how it arises and how it should be tackled. Thus, for example, the administration of the youth justice system does not simply reflect the routine delivery of rational processes based on established and shared social norms; it also acts, in combination with other authoritative sources (like the media) to justify and reinforce prior categorisations of acceptable and unacceptable behaviour. It is not just a matter of distinguishing between fixed and immutable categories of 'right' and 'wrong', but the exercise of judicial, organisational and professional authority also acts to legitimise this distinction as it applies in any given social milieu. Behind this process, however, lies the question of which interests are represented in these apparently neutral and objective processes.

Gramsci (1971) observes that the key factor here is the extent to which particular forces can establish the general legitimacy of their own interests and thereby claim the authority to police these. Legitimacy has to be earned, and the exercise of authority has to gain the consent of citizens in order to secure their active engagement in maintaining social control. The smooth and effective running of social institutions essentially depends on a widely-shared commitment to the principles and structures on which they are based (for example, the police need the 'consent' of the community in order to be able to carry out their functions effectively; Scarman 1982).

The authority to govern is gained in two ways, according to Gramsci: by the achievement of the 'spontaneous' consent of the population; or by the direct invocation of the 'apparatus of state coercive power' in order to 'legally' enforce discipline on those who do not conform. The latter option, though, should be seen as a kind of reserve power, only brought to bear when rule by consent has failed. It cannot become the norm because it implies at least a partial breakdown of consensual norms and becomes increasingly difficult to sustain. The explicit use of state power in this way is in fact much less efficient or effective than the day-to-day project of earning and sustaining the consent and willing compliance of most, if not all, elements in society. In order to achieve this end, the state therefore prefers to adopt an 'educative and formative' role (Gramsci 1971: 242). This is a specific characteristic of 'liberal democratic [governments] which make a major attempt to secure public support for state criminalisation and crime control through centralised high-profile politics of "law and order" (Lea 2002: 172). Here, we can see again the significance of the media as a vehicle for conveying information and securing consent, borne out by research into public attitudes (Chapman *et al.* 2002).

The 'rule of law' aspires to create an externalised, objective and apparently neutral standard by which behaviour can be judged and by which the line between the law-abiding and the criminal can be drawn. It is not simply a matter of creating effective machinery for crime control and the administration of official sanctions; it is also the function of 'the law' to carry out an 'educative' role in setting the terms for common standards of acceptable behaviour, and generating the only valid criteria by which compliance (or not) with these can be judged.

Althusser (1977) has developed a similar line of argument, agreeing that it is important to distinguish the ideological function of the law from its practical purposes. His useful, but over-deterministic and monolithic, characterisation of the exercise of social control depends on the notion of 'state apparatuses'. These can be subdivided into 'Repressive State Apparatuses' and 'Ideological State Apparatuses', which share the same objectives but operate rather differently. In the judicial context, some bodies can be thought of as primarily repressive, such as the courts and the prisons, while others, including the range of community justice agencies, can be seen to perform a more ideological function depending on their credibility to establish legitimacy for their interventions and gain consent for the administration of justice. In this way, 'the law belongs both to the [Repressive] State Apparatus and to the system of ISAs [Ideological State Apparatuses]' (Althusser 1977: 137).

This distinction helps us to appreciate the way in which legal institutions and judicial processes operate both directly to control certain types of behaviour by coercion and indirectly by creating the conditions under which certain acts are defined as unlawful and then dealt with as transgressions. The use of direct means of repression is supported by the ideological project of establishing the limits of what is acceptable.

Althusser also suggests that there is a complementary relationship between the ISAs which support and reinforce one another in sustaining the position of dominant interests. This network includes the educational ISA, the family ISA, the communications ISA and the religious ISA. Building on this kind of argument, Garland suggests that a similar kind of relationship exists between justice agencies and other systems:

Institutions of crime control and criminal justice have definite conditions of existence. They form part of a network of governance and social ordering that, in modern societies, includes the legal system, the labour market, and welfare state institutions. They refer to, and are supported by, other social institutions and social controls, and are grounded in specific configurations of cultural, political and economic action. (Garland 2001: 5)

In the context of youth justice, the way in which such elements coalesce to establish and maintain an interlocking system of social control was classically illustrated by Hall and colleagues (1978). Their extensive study, based on the emergence of the phenomenon of 'mugging' in the 1970s and associated public concern, shows how perceptions of criminal behaviour can be generated and then intensified by a network of social institutions, including the media, political interests and the judiciary, intervening in public debates in such a way as to amplify fears and create an overwhelming sense of lawlessness and threat about which something had to be done (see also Hearne 2003). The consequence of this interactive process was, indeed, a heightened level of public sensitivity to a particular form of behaviour, street robbery (or 'mugging', in its popularised form), and therefore also a readiness to endorse draconian interventions by the judicial system. Thus we can see how amplificatory spirals of this kind operate to support and strengthen ideological assumptions about the nature of offending behaviour and its perpetrators, and the way they should be dealt with – compounded in the case of 'mugging' by issues of 'race' and racism, another recurrent motif, as Garland (2001) confirms.

A more contemporary reflection on the relationship between the repressive and ideological functions of state apparatuses might lead us to consider the example of the Youth Justice Board itself. The YJB, as previously observed, operates in a number of spheres of policy and practice, but is clearly driven by a particular set of assumptions about the offending behaviour of young people and 'what works' in dealing with this. It is also constituted as an, apparently, independent body representing a diverse range of relevant interests. It thereby also lays claim to authority based on its collective credentials of expertise, knowledge and experience, which puts it in a privileged position to lead thinking, innovation and delivery. This standing, in turn, provides the YJB with sufficient credibility and 'clout' to be able to determine what counts as 'good practice' and what principles should underpin practitioners' activities. One model of 'restorative justice' has thus been privileged, at the expense of alternative approaches in this relatively new and contested field (Haines 2000; Haines and O'Mahony 2006).

However, the 'ideological' function of the Board in shaping our understanding of appropriate forms of intervention is complemented by rather more 'repressive' aspects of its operation, such as the introduction of ISSPs, its role in policing Referral Orders and its acquisition of responsibility for placing children in secure facilities. The YJB's independence and professional standing will, of course, help to provide legitimacy for these activities; for instance, its claims to have made improvements in conditions and services for young people in custody (Youth Justice Board 2005e) might help to make such an option more tolerable to those who might otherwise baulk at the idea of sending a 12-year-old to prison (Pitts 2003).

Cohen (1985) is particularly critical of the 'humanisation' of apparently oppressive forms of treatment in the name of progress. He argues that this represents no more than the extension of the network of coercion made possible precisely because of the appearance of reasonableness and solicitude. He also fears that this 'softly, softly' approach may pervade the entire criminal process:

> At the shallow end, the generation of new treatment criteria and the pervasiveness of the social welfare and preventive structures, often ensure an erosion of traditional rights and liberties. In a system of low visibility and accountability, where a high degree of discretion is given to administrative and professional bodies ... there is often less room for such niceties as due process and legal rights. (Cohen 1985: 70)

This observation may have predated ASBOs, Acceptable Behaviour Contracts, Final Warnings and Referral Orders by 15 years or so, but his critique is clearly still valid.

On the other hand, Cohen takes issue with the fact that 'heavy end' intensive community options (such as ISSP) are justified largely on the grounds that they are not custody. Thus at both ends of the spectrum increased levels of control and coercion are imported into community disposals while apparently representing liberal alternatives to repressive measures:

> Meanwhile, there is no problem in finding criminologists, psychologists, social workers and others who will justify all these community alternatives as humane, kindly and even 'therapeutic'... This is the particularly wondrous advantage ... of those programmes which use the explicit rationale of behaviourism. (Cohen 1985: 75)

The rationale of humanitarian and personally beneficial behaviour change (anger management, for example) provides strong support for 'community corrections': 'Deviance must be "brought back home". Parents, peers, schools, the neighbourhood, even the police should dedicate themselves to keeping the deviant out of the formal system' (Cohen 1985: 77). But of course this does not mean that nothing happens. Instead, 'the primary institutions of society', such as schools, family or neighbourhood groups, are expected to take responsibility for scrutinising and controlling the behaviour of young people who are 'at risk' of getting into trouble.

However, this kind of close attention may be counter-productive and lead to unintended consequences:

> Thus, if a youth is already under the surveillance of the system – even a preventive program serving a non-offending youth from a 'high risk' neighbourhood, but particularly an offender supervised intensively – he or she is far more likely to be caught offending and sanctioned sooner, and more often. (Kempf-Leonard and Peterson 2002: 438)

As already noted, for example, the ASBO breach rate had reached 42 per cent by 2003, and this may well be explained in part by the increased level of scrutiny associated with the order.

Cohen's vision seems remarkably prescient. The language of being 'tough on crime, tough on the causes of crime', of linking 'rights' with 'responsibilities', of 'targeting' and of promoting 'parental responsibility' – in sum, the New Labour vision – fits well with his articulation of a correctional approach extending the machinery and techniques of the justice system into the community.

Thus even the family becomes a 'correctional resource' (see also Donzelot 1979), which has become a 'site for expert invasion and penetration' (Cohen 1985: 79). Clearly, the Parenting Order is one highly explicit manifestation of this, first introduced under the Crime and Disorder Act 1998, but subsequently extended to become available in tandem with an ASBO and in truancy cases.

Schools and neighbourhoods are also identified as sites for the development of sophisticated methods of surveillance, supervision and correction – Cohen was perhaps anticipating the development of Pupil Referral Units and mentoring schemes (Tarling *et al.* 2001). Youth Inclusion Projects (Eccles 2001) and Summer Splash Schemes (Loxley *et al.* 2002) were both explicitly targeted at 'at risk' young people in areas identified as crime 'hot spots' – although their reported success in achieving reductions in crime is limited (Loxley *et al.* 2002; Morgan Harris Burrows 2003). As well as seeking to improve the efficacy of local social control measures, these schemes also carry out an important ideological function, focusing concern on specific young people in designated areas and thereby shifting attention away from the wider questions of disadvantage, inequality and discrimination, and from the structural factors which, as we have seen, are equally viable explanations of the incidence of youth offending (Anderson *et al.* 2001). Indeed, as Cohen observes, with the move towards a greater emphasis on managerial and technical solutions to the problems of crime, causes become of less importance – the logic being that 'if we can control crime, we don't really need to understand the causes', which epitomises the 'what works' philosophy (Cohen 1985: 176). Hence, perhaps, New Labour's lack of interest in the broader 'causes of crime', which have been supplanted by a limited number of 'indicators' of social exclusion (Social Exclusion Unit 2001), justifying interventions targeted at specific 'at risk' populations, such as those excluded from school, teenage parents and their children, and drug users.

In concluding this discussion, it may be helpful to recapitulate the means by which this sleight of hand is carried out. A particular and 'situated' ideology of crime and disorder is reconstituted as representing the natural order of things, which in turn necessitates a specific intervention strategy based on identifying and targeting those responsible and controlling their behaviour. Other (structural) issues are no longer viewed as relevant. However, this is just a partial image, and in reality what is defined as youth crime derives from both the actions of young people and the *ideological* process by which their behaviour is defined as criminal. This behaviour may be unacceptable, but whether or not it should be criminalised remains a matter of judgement, not fact. This is perhaps a key point for those who feel trapped in a routinised, irrational and vicious cycle of surveillance, classification and regulation of young people to no beneficial purpose.

Foucault and the techniques of justice

Following this theme, it may also be helpful to consider the extent to which contemporary youth justice practices are, indeed, essentially based on techniques of measurement, management and control, often associated with the work of Foucault. His thesis is that the modern era (late eighteenth century onwards) is characterised by a significant shift from forms of punishment based on 'spectacle' and example to an approach to intervention based on measures designed to ensure discipline and compliance. Thus he suggests that the last 200 years have witnessed a reduction in 'penal severity' and a 'displacement in the very object of the punitive operation' (Foucault 1979). Punishment can no longer be seen in terms of a direct physical operation inflicting pain and suffering on the body, but a more insidious activity, acting, in his words, 'on the soul'. Thus ideas of correction and treatment have been incorporated into penal discourse, with a focus on controlling and changing behaviour.

Foucault associates these changes with a range of other transformations, such as the development of the legal concept of contract and a 'new economy'. Crime control was thus driven by a new emphasis on rationality and uniformity of treatment, based on 'new principles for regularizing, refocusing, universalizing the act of punishment. Humanize its application. Reduce its economic and political cost by increasing its effectiveness and by multiplying its circuits' (Foucault 1979: 89). The criminal, by breaching the terms of her/his contract with the communal interest, becomes liable to punitive intervention and must accept the rational and calculated consequences that follow. Punishment will therefore be justified, reasonable and proportionate to the offence.

It follows that the machinery of justice and its coercive practices must be clearly and precisely specified and applied, rather in the manner of Weber's (1957) 'legal-rational' organisation of administrative procedures. Thus 'the new arsenal of penalties ... must be as unarbitrary as possible' (Foucault 1979: 104), and must be clearly calculable as the interventions merited by specific acts. This emphasis on precision and the routinisation of judicial processes suggests certain similarities between the 'scientific' strategies suggested by Foucault and the kind of actuarial techniques (Smith, R. 2006) embedded in youth justice practices:

> Actuarial justice presents a theoretical model of criminal justice processing in which the pursuit of efficiency and techniques that streamline case processing and offender supervision replace traditional goals of rehabilitation, punishment, deterrence and incapacitation ... (Kempf-Leonard and Peterson 2002: 432)

'Incapacitation', however, may sometimes be dictated by scientific calculations of appropriate means of controlling behaviour.

Foucault elaborates two further aspects of the technologisation of punishment which are significant: the forms and conduct of disciplinary mechanisms themselves, and the development of professional specialisms for the assessment and management of individual offenders:

ultimately what one is trying to restore in this technique of correction is not so much the judicial subject ... but the obedient subject, the individual subjected to habits, rules, orders, and authority that is exercised continually around him and upon him ... (Foucault 1979: 129)

Standardised procedures (such as ASSET) are applied to young people reported for offences in such a way as to discount many of the factors which are relevant or important to them. Christie comments that in many cases:

The defendant might as well not have been in court ... When such attributes are eliminated, a seemingly 'objective' and impersonal system is created ... in full accord with normal bureaucratic standards, and at the same time extraordinarily well-suited for power-holders. (Christie 2000: 163)

In this way, a standardised process can be applied to produce 'tailored' interventions based on only those characteristics which are deemed relevant (the limited range of predetermined 'risk' factors already identified; Social Exclusion Unit 2001, 2002).

The kind of disciplinary techniques to be applied in Foucault's analysis include prescribed regimes for ordering and controlling the individual's day-to-day activities, thereby ensuring conformity ('tagging' is a contemporary example of this). Thus a 'timetable' is established in order to regulate behaviour and monitor compliance (such as the 25-hour ISSP attendance requirement). The timetable itself is a means of exerting power over the individual concerned, as well as providing a means of micro-managing her/his behaviour on a daily or even hourly basis. Every aspect of the day is structured and planned according to the logic of control.

Christie (2000: 127) suggests that such developments are predictable for other reasons, too, given wider trends towards the standardisation and commercialisation of forms of technological behaviour control and surveillance. Thus aspects of the overall package can be parcelled up and contracted to the most appropriate provider. He offers the contemporary examples of electronic bracelets and voice verification as means by which this level of technologised coercive scrutiny can be achieved. The development of these means of behaviour management and monitoring has made possible 'the integration of a temporal, unitary, continuous, cumulative dimension in the exercise of controls and the practice of dominations' (Foucault 1979: 160). This process culminates in the emergence of 'disciplinary networks', which involve experts in the fields of 'medicine, psychology, education, public assistance (and) social work'. These will assume quasi-judicial powers of assessment and programme delivery (as with the Referral Order), so that a wide range of professional interventions in the field of welfare will acquire the characteristics of penal and disciplinary power. As Lea (2002: 29) puts it, the establishment of a wide-ranging coalition of agencies with a crime control function (such as Youth Offending Teams) is part of a process of securing the widest possible 'collaboration in the task of regulating society'.

Donzelot (1979) takes this an important stage further by linking the development of these disciplinary structures and mechanisms with changes in the way in which intervention in the family is pursued. He suggests that similar processes can be identified in the ways in which families are pathologised and made subject to statutory interventions, especially where one (or more) family member is defined as delinquent. This is of particular relevance when we come to consider the new measures aimed at 'improving' the way in which parents bring up their children and control their behaviour. Donzelot suggests that this represents a shift in the 'modes' of social discipline, such that government *of* the family is replaced by government *through* the family:

> the modern family is not so much an institution as *mechanism* ... A wonderful mechanism since it enables the social body to deal with marginality through a near-total dispersal of private rights, and to encourage positive integration. (Donzelot 1979: 94)

In other words, parents themselves are to be persuaded or coerced (by means such as the Parenting Order or imprisonment for allowing their children to truant) into accepting and then exercising as private obligations disciplinary techniques to ensure conformity among their children. It has been suggested elsewhere that the New Labour reform programme reflects this kind of agenda, targeting young people *and* their parents:

> The 'new' professional practices in the form of cognitive-behavioural treatment, reparation and mediation and mentoring all strive to make good these defects in the behaviour, beliefs and attitudes of young offenders and their parents, and to instil in them a new, disciplined, capacity for self-regulation. (Pitts 2000: 10)

The limits of functionalism

Foucault's arguments have been criticised on a number of grounds, not least the functionalism which appears to run through them, incorporating monolithic visions of unified structures and machinery of state power and control. Giddens (1991), for example, suggests that Foucault overgeneralises to the extent that he cannot provide a plausible explanation for the variety of state institutions and their inherent contradictions and conflicts; nor is it possible to account for change over time:

> Foucault's conception of the disciplinary world view, the *savoir* as he calls it, effectively forecloses on the possibility that the *savoir* itself was a site of contradiction, argument and conflict. (Ignatieff 1985: 95).

Garland (1990) takes the criticism of Foucault further, suggesting that his thesis is open to challenge both on historical and sociological grounds. He, too, takes issue with Foucault's 'functionalism', which, he states, leads to a narrow view that all aspects of the penal system are determined by the pursuit and exercise of power, and, in 'this sense, Foucault's conception of power is strangely apolitical. It appears as a kind of empty structure, stripped of any agents, interests or grounding, reduced to a bare technological scaffolding' (Garland 1990: 170). This seems to imply that the ostensible purposes of custody and other penal machinery have been confused with their real and lived impact, which is much more uneven and unpredictable. Conflicts between purposes and practice are commonplace. The problem for Foucault is that the prison and other apparatuses of control do not always perform in the prescribed manner, or achieve the outcomes specified (as we have observed throughout this book). They are actually quite inefficient, and their effectiveness as direct instruments of discipline is quite limited as we are repeatedly reminded (see Lyon *et al.* 2000; Goldson 2002).

Foucault himself acknowledges that the relations of power themselves generate opposing currents, distorting the patterns of social order. These 'resistances' are:

> Distributed in irregular fashion: the points, knots of focuses of resistance are spread over time and space at varying densities, at times mobilizing groups or individuals in a definitive way, inflaming certain points of the body, certain moments in life, certain types of behaviour. (Foucault 1981: 96)

In the context of the penal system, these counter-currents will manifest themselves in specific modifying effects on the machinery of justice:

> The orientation of the agents involved, their ideologies, their resources or lack of them, the legal limits placed on their powers, the rights of clients and the resistance that they offer, can all moderate the extent to which the sanction's power is actualised. (Garland 1990: 168)

On the one hand, Foucault's analysis provides a thoroughgoing account of the means and mechanisms by which disciplinary power is organised, exercised and legitimised in order to control the behaviour of the young. On the other hand, his critics, in common with Harris and Webb (1987), demonstrate that the complex realities of intervention are much less unilinear and predictable than these frameworks might suggest. Christie notes that legal structures should not be seen purely as rational instruments of 'utility'. Rather, law-in-practice has to elaborate and resolve competing aims, purposes and values: For example, courts:

> cannot function as instrumental tools for management without sacrificing their greatest strengths in the protection of values: spelling them out, evaluating them against each other, and also seeing to it that single-minded goals in some institutional settings are not given undue weight in the totality. (Christie 2000: 198)

This might, optimistically, be interpreted as a call to the judicial system to act independently to resist either routinised measures of oppression and denial of the rights of children and young people, or populist calls for ever more intense forms of surveillance and control.

Power will be, and should be, modified by practice. This leads to the relatively positive conclusion that it is always possible to modify, resist or even transform some of the more repressive routinised and intrusive aspects of the contemporary youth justice system.

Youth justice: the value of theory

This brief and somewhat superficial excursion into the theoretical terrain of youth crime, ideology and the machinery of youth justice has been intended to open up some alternative perspectives on what has become a rather narrowly conceived contemporary preoccupation with effective system management, which itself is nonetheless infused with ideological assumptions. In bringing together ideas about 'youth' and 'crime', theories of power and legitimacy, and accounts of the 'machinery of control', I have attempted to show that our understandings of these phenomena need to be well-grounded and thorough. The interactions between these conceptual areas need to be addressed clearly and explicitly for us to develop a rounded appreciation of what is both necessary and practical in developing a progressive and responsive approach to the problems associated with youth offending.

As this chapter has illustrated, adolescent transitions are a feature of most societies, but their specific nature and the way in which the behaviour of the young is classified are contextually determined. Thus the particular form taken by contradictory expectations, challenge and conflict (Merton 1957) depends on the social context within which these are played out. For example, the rapid emergence of mobile phone theft as an aspirational crime is clearly specific to the developed world in the early twenty-first century, but it is also linked to recurrent themes about culturally accepted goals and the availability (or not) of the means to achieve these.

At the same time, conflict of this kind can be reframed in terms of the aim of dominant interests to establish hegemonic forms of control (Gramsci 1971), which will sustain their dominance whilst legitimising disciplinary forms of intervention, exercised through the justice system. This strategy is exemplified by the establishment of structures that are able to function repressively, but are still able to secure consent by ideological means (Althusser 1977; Cohen 1985). Foucault's (1979) analysis elaborates this process by illustrating the way in which the state's control strategies are depoliticised and reconstituted as a managerial and technical question, essentially concerned with efficient delivery (Clarke *et al.* 2000). Relevant and instructive research findings (Farrington 1996; Rutter *et al.* 1998; Anderson *et al.* 2001) are decontextualised and tentative causal connections are reproduced as 'soundbite' explanations such as 'poor parenting' (Muncie 2000). In this way, the highly problematic nature of youth justice and the injustices perpetrated in its name are subsumed by what appears to be a natural, logical and scientifically grounded approach to quantifying and responding to a fixed and readily intelligible phenomenon.

However, this apparent uniformity of purpose and function also contains the seeds of its own destruction, for two reasons. Firstly, as Foucault's critics have observed, in practice the machinery of justice is not actually very good at identifying, quantifying and dealing with youth crime – in fact, it is remarkably inefficient. Secondly, it may simply be unsustainable in resource terms, in light of the consequences of implementing an increasingly costly and 'top-heavy' regime for dealing with the infractions of the young, including those which are pre-criminal, and trivial matters. By the autumn of 2002, for example, the Treasury was expressing real concern about the costs of penal sanctions for young people (*Guardian* 9 October 2002).

9. The consumer view

What do we want from the youth justice system?

Having taken a brief diversion into the realms of theory, it may also be helpful to take a much more grounded approach to the question of youth crime and what should be done about it. There is no doubt that this is an area of practice which is particularly susceptible to public perceptions and political manoeuvring (Jamieson 2006), and this suggests that any intervention strategy must take account of these particular influences:

> The dissatisfaction that people express with youth justice is real, whether or not it is grounded in the realities of current sentencing practice. There has to be *some* response to these public views. (Hough and Roberts 2004: xi)

While theorising helps us to understand the meaning and dynamics of young people's behaviour and the way this intersects with the machinery of youth justice at the same time as suggesting some of the ways in which social attitudes and beliefs on the subject are formed, consideration of the practical steps to be taken must also address the expectations of 'stakeholders'. An exploration of some of these perspectives here will both give us a grasp of the range of viewpoints to be taken into account, and some idea of what may be seen as practical, realistic and achievable solutions to this perennial issue.

In reality, we must recognise that key influences and interest groups will have a powerful effect at all levels of debate and decision-making in youth justice. Indeed, the message of the previous chapter, in terms of hegemony and the power to determine what is 'reasonable' and acceptable, is that these are unavoidable factors 'in the mix'. Thus a clearer understanding of the views and aspirations of some at least of the relevant constituencies will shed more light on the question 'what is to be done?'

The victim's perspective

The first interest group to be considered will be victims of crime, not least because their interests have progressed steadily up the political and operational agenda in recent years. Indeed, concern for victims has become somewhat totemic, if at the same time, rather tokenistic. As already noted, Williams (2000) has suggested that victims have become something of a 'political football', with the initial publication of the *Victim's Charter* in 1996 and subsequent moves to strengthen the entitlements this bestowed. It has been suggested that as a result the 'balance' between offenders and victims may have shifted (Williams 2000: 176; 2005: 215).

We have already seen evidence of the readiness of policy-makers to respond to these developments in the form of innovations such as the Referral Order, which mandates youth justice services to involve victims in formal interventions. The expectation here, and elsewhere, is that victims' views and wishes will be routinely incorporated into youth justice decision-making:

> Yots must establish a protocol with the police in consultation with other relevant agencies for the exchange of information relating to victims at the earliest appropriate stage ...
>
> Yots must ensure that all work with victims accords with ... the following general principles:
>
> - The wishes of victims in relation to their involvement in restorative justice processes must be respected by Yot staff at all times;
> - the need of victims to feel safe;
> - victims should be given sufficient information to enable them to make informed choices about whether, and at what level, they wish to be involved in restorative justice processes ... (Youth Justice Board 2004: 32)

But what does this increasing sensitivity to the needs of victims tell us about the best ways of responding to young people who offend? Of course, it is important to avoid falling into the trap of stereotyping victims or their views, just as we must not stereotype young offenders (Dignan 2005: 87). For instance, the British Crime Survey now regularly reminds us that the risk of becoming a victim of crime is not evenly distributed (Kershaw *et al.* 2001: Salisbury and Upson 2004; Upson 2005). Indeed, it has been observed that it is young people themselves, and especially young men, who are most at risk of becoming victims of violence (Kershaw *et al.* 2001: 31). Figures from the 2003 Crime and Justice Survey suggest that 21 per cent of 10–15 year olds had been assaulted during a twelve month period (Wood 2005: 3), higher than any other age category. Worryingly, perhaps, the interest in young people as victims of crime is comparatively recent, with official statistics on victimisation of under 16 year olds being unavailable prior to 2003.

The evidence is complicated by findings that the experiences of being a victim and a perpetrator of crime appear to overlap to a substantial degree.

MORI (2002) has found that groups which are more likely to offend ('children who are excluded from school') are at the same time more likely to be victims of crime. In fact, they were more likely to be victims (82 per cent) than offenders (64 per cent). Wood (2005: 5) observes that the strongest predictor of 'personal crime victimisation' among 10–15 year olds was '[c]ommitting an offence in the previous year', with the odds being 2.5 times those for non-offenders. David Smith (2004) has also explored this relationship, arguing that there is a demonstrable interaction between delinquency and victimisation, even over a three-year period, with one predicting the other. In addition: 'The more often victimization is repeated, the more strongly it predicts delinquency' (Smith, D. 2004: 3). Smith argues that this correlation is so strong as to suggest a possible causal link, also in both directions. Thus any simplistic assumption which opposes 'offenders' and 'victims' is clearly neither accurate nor helpful.

The tendency to reify the idea of 'victimhood' must be avoided, although this is not to minimise the damaging and distressing consequences of being victimised. As Lea and Young (1984) demonstrated some time ago, the impact of crime on people and areas already disadvantaged in other ways is likely to have a powerful and demoralising effect. People are more worried about crime where its incidence is most often identified (Upson 2005: 101). As Rock has pointed out, the concern for victims has represented a substantial shift in criminological thinking over a relatively short space of time: 'Until the late 1970s victims were almost wholly neglected in criminology and criminal justice' (Rock 2002: 1). While, as he notes, there is an association between this growing awareness and a strong populist tide, there have also emerged more thoughtful analyses:

> We know that our earlier assumptions about the impact, quantity and spread of crime have had to be replaced not only by an appreciation of its deep, persistent, pervasive and often unexpected effects, but also by an awareness of its capacity to confound typifications of who the victim and offender might actually be. (Rock 2002: 11).

As a consequence, he says, there needs to be a more sensitive appreciation of 'the victim' and what it means to her/him to be offended against and how s/he comes to terms with the experience. It is not simply a matter of following a predetermined script, despite the best efforts of some: 'What else do crime series and shows such as *Kilroy* and *Oprah* achieve if not to offer public representations of wounded sentiment' (Rock 2002: 18)?

One implication of these reflections is that victims' perceptions of offenders' level of responsibility are likely to vary, as are their views about the best way of dealing with the offence. Their responses are not limited by conventional measures of the nature and seriousness of the crimes committed either. A further level of complication is introduced when we consider the position of 'corporate victims' who may well have a distinctive agenda, while they will also be seen in a rather different way by offenders (Young 2002). Of course, too, many of us are victims, often unknowingly, of corporate *crime* (Dignan 2005: 21).

These reflections, added to the evidence that very few offenders are ever 'matched' with their victims (see Chapter 7), must lead us to express some caution about the global impact of the new restorative measures introduced as part of the New Labour reform package. While it is helpful to consider how victims perceive their participation and treatment in this context, it can only convey a highly selective impression. It will, nonetheless, be helpful briefly to consider some of the evidence emerging from recent initiatives to develop a more central role for victims in youth justice processes (see Holdaway *et al.* 2001; Hoyle 2002; Newburn *et al.* 2002; Young 2002; Crawford and Newburn 2003; Dignan 2005).

The introduction of the Referral Order, for example, has provided a good opportunity to consider at close hand just what happens when the justice system seeks to involve victims more fully. However, it should be noted that problems arise from the outset, given that securing victims' participation at all is often problematic (Holdaway *et al.* 2001; Crawford and Newburn 2003). Thus those who reach the point of attendance at Youth Offender Panels are a relatively small fraction of an already highly selective group. Nevertheless, for those who do attend, evidence has been obtained of their motives for attending (see Table 9.1). It is interesting, for example, that it was found to be more important to them to express their feelings or to have a direct say in how the offence was dealt with than ensuring that they would be compensated or that a suitable punishment would be imposed.

Thus, although this a partial view, it seems that those victims who take up the opportunity to attend panel meetings are very much concerned with engaging with the offender and solving the problems that the offence has caused. Hoyle's study of the Thames Valley restorative justice project also appears to support this observation; for example: 'I just wanted to get the message across to him that if it happened to him how would he feel, basically, I mean, for him to put himself in my shoes' (victim, quoted in Hoyle 2002: 120). Even 'helping the offender' appears to have come higher up victims' list of priorities than seeking redress (Newburn *et al.* 2002: 45).

Table 9.1 Victims' motivating factors for attending panel meetings

Motivating factor	Strength of factor			
	Not at all	Not very	Somewhat	Very
Expressing feelings	4%	9%	7%	78%
Offence resolution	22%	4%	28%	43%
Helping the offender	28%	13%	26%	28%
Seeking compensation	33%	13%	15%	35%
Ensuring appropriate penalty	52%	11%	20%	15%

Adapted from: The Introduction of Referral Orders into the Youth Justice System: Final Report (Newburn *et al.* 2002: 45).

Exploring victims' views in more detail, researchers have found that their generally positive views of the process were somewhat tempered by the limited nature of their involvement and their inability to secure the outcomes they required in the form of compensation or apologies. Dignan (2005: 154), too, suggests that victims may be beneficially involved in restorative processes, but still be left dissatisfied with the outcomes. Victims appeared to want a greater sense of involvement in the entire process rather than merely attending the formal panel meeting alone. In particular, they wanted to know what happened afterwards and 'if the young person had managed to stay out of trouble. One of the most important factors for many of the victims was "has it worked?"' (Newburn *et al.* 2002: 47).

Nonetheless, the evidence seems to suggest that for those victims who were involved in Youth Offender Panels, the process was generally viewed in very positive terms. Thus there appears to be some indication that there is an aspiration on the part of victims of youth crime towards an approach based on offence resolution rather than simply on retribution. In the case of the Referral Order research, this was clearly a small and self-selected sample, whose very involvement may have indicated a predisposition towards negotiated solutions.

The partial nature of victim involvement is borne out by other evidence, both more generally (Dignan 2005) and specific to the field of youth justice. Thus Holdaway *et al.* (2001) have reported 'low consent rates' for victims approached to participate in Reparation and Action Plan Orders, with only half of those asked agreeing to either direct or indirect means of making amends by the offender. Victims were much more likely to participate if they were not asked to 'opt in' to the process, that is where they were specifically encouraged to participate, rather than left to make up their own minds. The conclusion drawn is that there is limited enthusiasm among victims for more direct engagement with young offenders and, indeed, a feeling that in some cases their interests might be subsumed under those of the justice system or even young offenders themselves (Holdaway *et al.* 2001: 81). In some cases, too, this perception has been borne out by experience:

> The impression I got from [the facilitator] was that ... he was wanting to get them off as lightly as possible ... He was looking after them. It was outrageous ... It was a very one-sided thing and we just had to go along with it ... (Mother of victim, quoted in Burnett and Appleton 2004: 48)

These observations are supported by other findings (Davis *et al.* 1988; Hoyle 2002; Dignan 2005). For some, this is unsurprising, given that victims will, inevitably, have their own priorities. We should be more ready to doubt the 'often unquestioned assumption that victims want to assume a role in the state response to "their" offender ... most restorative justice schemes find that by no means all victims wish to be fully involved' (Hoyle 2002: 104). This certainly coincides with the present author's experience in a juvenile diversion project during the 1980s, where the lack of pressure to involve victims meant that they could be approached on their own terms.

Victims' unwillingness to get involved clearly has a number of origins, including the fear of retaliation ('secondary victimisation'; Dignan 2005: 85) and the belief that it is and should be the job of the police and the justice system to deal with the offence – in the same way, perhaps, as we might ask a plumber simply to come and mend a leak, rather than be 'engaged' in the process. For others, it may be that they do not have a particularly favourable view of the justice process itself: 'I have to say if I was a victim of a similar crime again … I've got a feeling I would administer my own justice and not involve the police …' (quoted in Hoyle 2002: 125).

This again acts as a salutary reminder that we should not draw overoptimistic conclusions from positive accounts of victim involvement in restorative programmes. Hoyle concludes that to focus solely on improving restorative processes risks overlooking the more important challenge of 'empowering victims generally' (Hoyle 2002: 130). The interests of victims can be seen to range well beyond the question of appropriate engagement in youth justice interventions to wider considerations of safety, security and community participation. Restorative justice initiatives may offer positive benefits to *some* victims, but they are ill-suited to dealing with the much larger questions of the complex relationship between offending and victimhood. Indeed, arbitrary separations between the interests of 'victims' and 'offenders' may be conceptually inaccurate and ultimately unhelpful in obstructing the pursuit of 'inclusive' forms of criminal and social justice (Dignan 2005: 187).

The community: conflicting needs or common agendas?

Following the line of argument which suggests that it is extremely difficult and, in fact, unhelpful to seek to create arbitrary distinctions between overlapping interests, it may be helpful now to move on to consider the broader concerns of neighbourhoods and communities in relation to anti-social behaviour, youth crime and youth justice. As Dignan (2005) observes, the interests of 'the community' may stand in a complex relationship to both victims and offenders, which may lead us in the direction of rather different models of restorative justice to that currently prevalent in England and Wales.

The backdrop for any such innovations, however, is not propitious. Concerns about the behaviour of young people are connected with wider and extensive fears about deteriorating standards of living, neighbourhood decay, abandonment and moral decline. There is said to be a close link between 'disorder', fear of crime and a progressive cycle of neighbourhood decline and increasing criminalisation (Hancock 1999). There appears to be a direct and cumulative relationship between perceptions and experience, so that the sense of a community 'going downhill' is reinforced by observable events and changes in the landscape:

There are lots of young people hanging around at weekends … There is a *lot* of litter. People throw their litter down as they walk past. We have also had problems with broken windows. Buildings have deteriorated …

pride in the area has gone down. (Elderly resident of Edgebank, quoted in Hancock 2001: 92)

Indeed, the elision of young people with the problem of disorder and decline appears to be commonplace, and it is often assumed that it is their anti-social behaviour which causes 'distress in neighbourhoods' irrespective of other contributing factors (Hancock 2006: 176). The British Crime Survey (Budd and Simms 2001) has revealed a substantial degree of concern about anti-social behaviour, which appears to be linked in people's minds with 'teenagers hanging around on the streets'; we are reminded again that this is nothing new when we reflect on Corrigan's (1979) study of young people 'doing nothing' on the streets of Sunderland in the mid-1970s.

By 2000, over half those surveyed thought that young people 'hanging around' was 'very or fairly common', and 32 per cent identified this as a problem in itself. At the same time, 31 per cent of respondents thought that this was having a 'negative impact' on the quality of life in their neighbourhoods (Budd and Simms 2002: 2); this was the single biggest factor mentioned in this respect. Furthermore, a fifth of those interviewed cited specific examples of 'young people being rude or abusive' to them in the previous twelve months (Budd and Simms 2001: 4), once again the most common example of problem behaviour cited. It should perhaps also be noted that it was people living in poorer areas and those from black and minority ethnic groups who were more likely to report being victimised in this way. Young people thus appear to be widely associated with anti-social behaviour and they are blamed for a general sense of disturbance and unease experienced in communities. Detailed analysis of popular concerns about anti-social behaviour identifies 'teenagers hanging around' as a significant cause for concern, with 28 per cent of the population regarding this as a 'very or fairly big problem' in their own area (Wood 2004: 11). Although, as Hancock (2006) points out, forms of anti-social behaviour such as speeding and inconsiderate parking caused concern to the largest numbers of people, other behaviours associated with young people also figured highly in the list of irritations (litter, letting off fireworks, graffiti and 'being drunk or rowdy', for example). As a consequence, we should perhaps expect a fairly punitive public orientation towards young people.

Work based on the British Crime Survey (Mattinson and Mirrlees-Black 2000) sheds further light on this issue. The public is reported to substantially overestimate 'juvenile involvement in crime', with 28 per cent of respondents believing that young people were responsible for most crime, whereas, in fact, 89 per cent of 'known offenders' are aged over 18. This mismatch may, of course, partly be accounted for by different understandings of the term 'young', and by variable perceptions of what counts as 'crime', especially those offences which are not officially recorded as such. For example, this survey suggests that as many of 40 per cent of respondents thought that 'teenagers hanging around' and damage to property were problems in their own area:

Respondents are likely to extrapolate from their own local experience when forming a view about the national crime picture. Certainly, those respondents who said teenagers hanging around was a big problem in their area were significantly more likely to say crime was mainly committed by juvenile offenders. (Mattinson and Mirrlees-Black 2000: 12)

Of course, it is not inevitable that these views will feed straightforwardly into attitudes and beliefs about how to deal with the crimes of the young and with what degree of severity. However, studies have consistently shown that most people feel that the courts are 'too soft' with offenders in general (Hough and Roberts 2004), but that they also underestimate the severity of sanctions actually administered (Hough and Mayhew 1985; Hough and Roberts 1998). Thus demands for more stringent penalties, particularly the greater use of custody for specific offences (Hough and Roberts 1998), are largely based on a misconception about current sentencing practice. Those who have been victims of offences have been reported as being slightly more likely to demand harsher sentences (Hough and Roberts 1998).

As well as having a distorted view of sentencing practice, surveys have also demonstrated repeatedly that the public holds erroneous views about trends in youth crime (Hough and Roberts 1998; Mattinson and Mirrlees-Black 2000), which are likely to be associated with a belief in the need for tougher sentences. Acknowledging that perceptions of the pattern of youth crime are unbalanced, 'media portrayals of persistent juvenile offenders and the continuing influence of the James Bulger murder on the public psyche ... are the most likely cause' (Mattinson and Mirrlees-Black 2000: 14). Of course, the 'hegemonic' role of politicians in both echoing and reinforcing public opinion is also significant (see Chapter 8), although these authors do not comment on this possibility. Further evidence of the mismatch between public perceptions and practice has been provided more recently, and once again the media seem to be largely to blame:

> Three quarters of the population thought that youth crime was rising, when there was little evidence for this. They cited the media as the main source of information that led them to this belief. (Hough and Roberts 2004: 17)

The role of the media in shaping opinions and attitudes about youth crime is supported by other research, too (Allen 2004). The scepticism about crime levels amongst the general population may also be linked with their perception that other aspects of the youth justice system are also performing poorly. One report based on the British Crime Survey has suggested that only 14 per cent of respondents thought that the 'juvenile courts' were doing a good job (Mattinson and Mirrlees-Black 2000: 17), and those who had recently been victims of crime held even more negative views in this respect. This view seems also to be associated with a belief that courts are 'too lenient' – held by 76 per cent surveyed in one study (Mattinson and Mirrlees-Black 2000:

18) and remaining at about this level over time, according to others (Hough and Roberts 2004: 26). Interestingly, it also seems that this belief applies much more strongly to the sentencing of young people who offend than adults. As has been observed, there appears to be a correlation between ignorance of the justice system and a belief that courts perform poorly and are too 'soft'. There also appears to be a correlation between concerns about 'teenagers hanging around' and poor opinions of the court process:

> It may be that physical and social disorder is taken as evidence of a crime problem that is not being adequately contained. Or, perhaps, [this] reflects a belief that the police and courts remit does – or ought to – encompass dealing with such issues. (Mattinson and Mirrlees-Black 2000: 23)

Subsequent investigation of attitudes to anti-social behaviour has confirmed the link between perceived levels of this type of behaviour and fears of crime, particularly violent crime (Wood 2004: 38).

With the extension of the scope of Curfew Orders, and the introduction of ASBOs and Dispersal Orders, it could perhaps be argued that the remit of the justice system has indeed been widened in just this way in order to deal with nuisance as well as criminal behaviour. Whether or not this will have a sustained impact on public confidence remains to be seen, although initial findings are not particularly encouraging in this regard (Smithson 2004). What is evident to researchers is that the link between poor knowledge and negative perceptions suggests the value of providing better and more accurate information to the public about the incidence and impact of youth crime as well as how it is dealt with (Allen 2004; Hough and Roberts 2004).

The British Crime Survey has also explored respondents' views about the best way to enhance courts' powers to deal with young people who offend, and it has found that there is considerable support for the idea of making parents take more responsibility for their children's actions (15 per cent) and greater use of custody (12 per cent); these were the two most popular options among those questioned. There was support also for other options such as corporal punishment, tagging or curfews, community work and restitution. Thus it could be argued that the programme of sentencing reforms introduced from 2000 onwards does, indeed, reflect widely held and punitive public views, although the pressure in this direction appears to be offset to a limited extent by a desire for greater use of restorative and welfare interventions (Mattinson and Mirrlees-Black 2000: 24).

As is noted by these researchers, this reflects a fairly consistent pattern, with previous evidence suggesting that 'increased discipline in the home' (36 per cent) and 'tougher sentences' (20 per cent) were consistently popular strategies for preventing and responding to delinquency (Hough and Roberts 1998: 33). When this question was posed in a different way in 2003, harsher punishment remained the second most popular option (17 per cent), but this time it was 'more discipline in schools' (42 per cent) which proved the most effective option in the public mind (Hough and Roberts 2004: 20).

Taken together, these findings suggest that 'criminal justice' measures are favoured as solutions to the problem of crime by no more than a third of the population; it is therefore suggested that a wider preventive strategy might yet gain significant support:

> Thus although [it has been] established that lenient sentencing is a concern to the British public, four out of five people see the most effective solution to crime as lying outside the criminal justice sphere system, namely in the home, the schools and the workplace. These trends are worth noting, as they contradict the view of the public as being exclusively oriented towards punishment. (Hough and Roberts 1998: 34)

There is also a degree of continuity over time in this respect with both earlier and later studies demonstrating a similar level of willingness among the public to consider more moderate sentencing options for some offenders in some circumstances. Readiness to consider non-custodial options for non-violent offenders, for example, was identified as early as 1984 (Hough and Mayhew 1985: 45) and, some twenty years later, similar sentiments could be observed. Indeed, it seems that the more people know about the offender, her/his circumstances and the range of disposals available, the more likely they are to support a non-custodial option (Hough and Roberts 2004: 43).

More detailed analysis of sentencing preferences suggests that 'the public' do hold some fairly consistent views about 'persistence' and 'seriousness', with over a third (36 per cent) believing that imprisonment is the appropriate disposal for a 3-time 15-year-old male shoplifter (Mattinson and Mirrlees-Black 2000: 28). Burglary, in turn, is seen as more serious than shoplifting, and 59 per cent of those surveyed believed that a similar young person committing a third such offence should be sent to custody. Violence, in any form, is viewed as more serious still, although in all three instances, there remains some support for more lenient measures in response to first-time offenders, including 'cautions' and 'community sentences'. Victims, as noted, are somewhat more punitive than the general population, notably in relation to burglaries (Mattinson and Mirrlees-Black 2000: 33).

These findings led the researchers to suggest some policy implications – in effect, seeking to represent the collective view. They concluded that better public understanding is important; better awareness of the range of non-custodial sentencing options would be helpful; 'persistence' is a significant 'aggravating factor'; concerns about 'disorder' need to be addressed in their own right; and moves towards a more restorative approach might, by engaging both victims and the community, lead to improvements in public confidence (Mattinson and Mirrlees-Black 2000: 45). A subsequent MORI survey demonstrated substantial support for community-based crime prevention initiatives with young people, as well as recognition of the negative impact of custody, and a desire to reduce the general level of imprisonment (MORI 2001). Further work in this area (Hough and Roberts 2004) suggests that, when offences are made 'real' for people through the use of 'vignettes', they are willing to consider a variety of sentencing options, even in cases where custody might initially be indicated:

Even in the case of a robbery committed with violence by an offender with previous convictions – where Court of Appeal guidance indicates a significant custodial sentence – half of respondents would accept a community penalty involving supervision and reparation. (Hough and Roberts 2004: 43)

There is a notable shift of emphasis when questions about the problems and behaviour of young people are reframed, it seems (Allen 2004). Against a generalised picture of fear and alarm and a desire for harsher punishment in the abstract, there appears to be a rather less draconian spirit at large when we consider them as rounded and real individuals and as members of their communities. In this context, for example, concerns tend to be framed in terms of lack of facilities and restricted opportunities (Hancock 1999) rather than on their miscreant activities. Crime prevention initiatives which take an 'inclusive' approach might therefore be expected to find an echo within communities who simply want problem behaviour to stop (Hancock 2006: 176). The relationship between young people and their community is important; young people themselves can be engaged and may be seen as active contributors to crime reduction initiatives (Crime Concern 2001: 5, for example).

The shift of focus away from the stereotypical and demonised individual troublemaker to young people as a group and as members of the community is an important aspect of the process of changing the public mindset (Hancock 1999). The Audit Commission (2002), for example, argues that most people are concerned about crime, especially those who have recently been victimised; at the same time, a MORI survey conducted for the same report indicates very high levels of support for action to improve facilities for young people as a means to promote community safety and to reduce crime. Thus there appears to be a clear contrast between a generalised caricature of the offender who is 'not one of us' and deserves to be treated with severity (Hancock 2006: 177), and a more inclusive notion of young people as part of the community with their own concerns (including being victims of crime) and interests which need to be addressed.

Lea and Young (1984) have suggested that there is a dualistic view of crime and offending and that neighbourhood dynamics are complex, leading to the continual attribution of criminality 'elsewhere', even in areas with an established reputation for high levels of crime. This rather contradictory position finds echoes also in the work of Garland, who elaborates two distinct 'criminologies' which reflect these ambiguities:

There is a *criminology of the self* that characterizes offenders as normal, rational consumers, just like us; and there is a *criminology of the other*, of the threatening outcast, the fearsome stranger, the excluded and the embittered. One is invoked to routinise crime, to allay disproportionate fears, and to promote preventative action. The other functions to demonise the criminal, to act out popular fears and resentments, and to promote support for state punishment. (Garland 2001: 137)

In his view, it is the latter which predominates in public and political discourse, with the result that there is a prevailing view of offenders as representing this kind of stereotype: 'young minority males, caught up in the underclass world of crime, drugs, broken families and welfare dependency' (Garland 2001: 136). Against this view, however, should be noted the complexity and variety of perceptions and experiences, not least amongst those groups which are typically the target for stereotypes and prejudice.

Youth crime and black and minority ethnic groups

It may be helpful to consider the question of complexity and diversity further by addressing the position of those from black and minority ethnic communities who have a particular interest in the interlinked issues of youth and crime for two fundamental reasons. They are, on the one hand, more likely to be victims of crime than the population in general, and, on the other, some of them at least (notably young black men), are disproportionately likely to be processed as offenders, as we have seen (see Chapter 7).

Firstly, in addressing the issue of 'victimisation', the British Crime Survey has repeatedly shown that certain groups are exposed to 'unequal risks' of being offended against (see, for example, Mirrlees-Black et al. 1998; Kershaw et al. 2001; Barclay et al. 2005). Certain types of crime, such as burglary, vehicle-related theft and violent offences, are found to occur to a greater extent in 'multi-ethnic areas' (Mirrlees-Black et al. 1998), and those people living in inner-city areas are likely to be at greater risk of repeat victimisation, which may also account for the higher levels of 'worry' about crime observed among ethnic minority groups (Barclay et al. 2005: 4). Even amongst minority communities, there is considerable variation in the likelihood of becoming a victim with 'risks of almost all crimes' being greater for people of Pakistani and Bangladeshi origin (Percy 1998), a trend broadly confirmed more recently (Barclay et al. 2005).

In a very specific sense, minority ethnic groups are likely to be disproportionately affected by racist crimes (Salisbury and Upson 2004: 3). As Bowling and Phillips (2002) demonstrate, such crimes, from harassment to murder, have been evident throughout the history of black and minority ethnic communities in Britain, while recognition of this, from either criminological or other sources, has been slow to follow. Thus records of 'racial incidents' have only been maintained since the 1980s, and it is only from the 1990s onwards that 'concern about racist violence' has been heightened (Bowling and Phillips 2002: 109), initially in response to the murder of Stephen Lawrence and more recently that of Zahid Mubarek (Keith 2006). The report of the inquiry into the first of these deaths concluded that too little attention was paid by official bodies to 'racist incidents' (Macpherson 1999). In response to this prompt, the number of such incidents recorded increased from 13,878 in the year ending March 1998 to 47,814 in the twelve-month period to March 2000 (245 per cent).

Such statistics are, of course, at best an imprecise indicator of what is happening, but they suggest that one or more of three possible factors are in play. It may be that police and other elements of the justice system are taking such incidents more seriously; they may show that the number of racist crimes is increasing very rapidly; or they may suggest a greater degree of awareness and confidence in the justice system among people from ethnic minorities, and thus a greater willingness to report incidents. Whatever the reason, though, the figures suggest that there is a very substantial level of racist crime taking place in Britain. In one local survey, around one in five of all black and Asian adults in Newham had experienced 'some form of racist victimisation' (Bowling and Phillips 2002: 112). Perceptions about the perpetrators of such offences are similar to those for offences in general, with 'young, white males' being identified as primarily responsible (Percy 1998: 1).

As Bowling and Phillips observe, this evidence helps to explain why minority ethnic communities are more fearful of crime than their white counterparts:

> Although the relationship between fear, crime and victimisation is a complex one, fear of 'ordinary crime' among people from ethnic minority communities is fundamentally shaped by their *fear of racist victimisation.* (Bowling and Phillips 2002: 113)

This is not a uniform pattern, however, for instance in areas with high black populations (Yarrow 2005: 30). Nevertheless, people from ethnic minorities are more likely to be fearful of crime (Percy, 1998; Clancy *et al.* 2001; Barclay *et al.* 2005). Percy (1998: 29), for example, has reported 40 per cent of people from ethnic minorities being 'very worried' about burglary compared to 21 per cent of white people. Indeed:

> Ethnic minorities scored higher than white people on all BCS measures of fear of crime. They perceive themselves to be at greater risk of crime than whites, worry more about falling victim of a crime and feel less safe on the streets or within their own homes at night. To a large extent this is a reflection of their higher risks of victimisation and harassment. (Percy 1998: 1)

Much of this, too, is attributed to young people who are often identified as the perpetrators: 'Young boys shout out racist chants to me as I leave my house or walk in the street' (Chinese woman, quoted in Saini 1997).

As the Stephen Lawrence inquiry forcefully reminds us, black and minority ethnic groups are also often dissatisfied with the official response to crimes against them. The report of the inquiry commented on a pervasive sense of mistrust:

> The atmosphere in which racist incidents and crimes are investigated must be considered since that will condition the actions and responses which may follow. That atmosphere was strongly voiced in the attitude of those who came to our hearings. In the words of David Muir, representing senior Black Church leaders, 'the experience of black people

over the last 30 years has been that we have been over policed and under protected.' (Macpherson 1999: para. 45.7)

Similar feelings have been expressed in local surveys (Saini 1997), revealing a widely held view among victims that involving the police would be pointless. Qualitative research also reveals a degree of suspicion and mistrust amongst certain groups, such as young black men who are victims of crime (Yarrow 2005: 16).

These perceptions are echoed in the level of satisfaction with the police, according to the British Crime Survey; whereas 70 per cent of the white population is reported to be 'very/fairly satisfied', this figure drops to 56 per cent for Pakistani or Bangladeshi respondents. For victims, too, similar disparities were noted (Clancy *et al.* 2001: 3). These are persistent problems (Bowling and Phillips 2002) and can be seen to be related to dissatisfaction with the 'overall performance' of the police, who are found not to show sufficient interest or to be polite, a concern reinforced by Yarrow's (2005) investigation. Such concerns about the nature of the police response support and reinforce more general beliefs about the unfair treatment of certain ethnic groups. The broad perception of inconsistency, lack of interest and second-class treatment by the police seems to be held fairly widely (Bowling and Phillips 2002: 136).

However, there appears to be less concern about *other* aspects of the justice system. Indeed, people from minority ethnic groups appear to be more confident than white respondents that the system is 'effective in bringing people who commit crimes to justice' and that it 'meets the needs of victims of crime' (Mirrlees-Black 2001: 3). In other words, the concerns of black and minority ethnic communities about the operation of the criminal justice process do appear to reflect something more than blanket disapproval. The police and the prisons are seen by these groups as being more likely to be seen as doing a 'poor job' by respondents from these groups than from the white population; however, courts, probation and prosecutors are more likely to be seen by them as doing a 'good job' (Mirrlees-Black 2001: 4). The explanation for these disparities is not obvious, but it does seem that there is a pattern to the views held by ethnic minorities about the justice system and its constituent parts.

It may be that the police are a specific focus for discontent because they are the first point of contact with the judicial apparatus for many, and that this contact has been experienced as inadequate and/or discriminatory by many (Yarrow 2005). The unfair treatment of young black people who are suspected of crime results in low confidence in the police (Clancy *et al.* 2001), and this is compounded by a perception that they do not receive a respectful or committed response when they are victims of crime (Yarrow 2005). Unsurprisingly therefore the solutions favoured by this group are not technical but involve major change. For black and minority ethnic groups the strands of racist crime, victimisation and fear and the experience of discriminatory treatment are intertwined, and lead to the conclusion that a systematic strategy aimed at (re)building mutual trust and respect is required (Macpherson 1999; Lawrence Steering Group 2004).

At a local level, a number of such initiatives can be identified; for example, the Black Community Safety Project produced its own agenda for change, focusing on the interests of victims and young people as well as the wider community (Saini 1997). Those people surveyed on behalf of the project wanted 'more police patrolling the streets', but they also wanted police to treat them with more respect and wanted more police officers to be recruited from ethnic minorities. They also expected the police to improve the service offered to those affected by crime and to work on improving their relations with young people. Despite such initiatives, by 2004 little progress appeared to have been made in improving the confidence of black communities in the police and criminal justice system (Lawrence Steering Group 2004: 16).

In addition to police-specific improvements, local projects have also identified a desire to see greater emphasis on community safety and crime prevention, including prevention of racially-motivated attacks. The education system, for example, should bear some responsibility for teaching respect for people and property, and promoting greater 'parental control'. The attention given to changes *within* the youth justice system may be quite limited, focusing on issues such as the need for better support for black people within the court setting (Saini 1997: 40). These aspirations were reflected in some of the recommendations arising from the Stephen Lawrence Inquiry (for example, Recommendations 35–37 directed at the Crown Prosecution Service and Recommendations 67–69 intended for the education system; Macpherson 1999).

Britton, too, has suggested that from the perspective of black and minority ethnic communities a holistic approach is needed: 'Statutory organisations should place tackling institutionalised racism at the centre of their policy agendas ... statutory organisations should have their policies and daily practice rigorously monitored' (Britton 2000: 108).

Bowling and Phillips (2002) broaden this argument to include the impact of social variations and structural inequalities on criminal justice practices and procedures. Thus, for example, account should be taken of the way in which family circumstances impact on bail decisions, whereby apparently neutral rules of decision-making produce inequitable outcomes, with a greater number of young black people liable to be remanded to custody. It is concluded that it is unacceptable to allow the continuation of practices which 'marginalise, criminalise and socially exclude ethnic minority communities in England' (Bowling and Phillips 2002: 260).

For these groups, then, calls for harsher treatment of young offenders (Hough and Roberts 2004) are highly problematic, since any unfairnesses built into the system will only result in more acute levels of discrimination. Indeed, consistent with our earlier observations, solutions must be found, not just or even primarily within youth justice processes, but in wider structural reforms which promote inclusion and anti-discrimination in general. The technical and managerial preoccupations of New Labour with crime control and behaviour management seem greatly misconceived by comparison (see Bowling and Phillips 2002: 258); indeed, they are likely to produce contradictory outcomes. By 2005, clear concerns were beginning to emerge about the limited achievements of the substantial programme put in place following the Stephen Lawrence Inquiry and the continuing sense of injustice felt by some communities (Foster *et al.* 2005).

'What about us?' Young people's views

Another (overlapping) group that is both 'over-policed' and 'under-protected' is young people themselves. We should perhaps take a little time to consider how they feel about youth crime, punishment and the justice system.

The context in which young people form their views about crime and punishment is one in which they are more likely than the general population to be victimised or experience 'anti-social behaviour' (Haines and Drakeford 1998; Budd and Simms 2001; Kershaw *et al.* 2001; Armstrong *et al.* 2005). Many children feel unsafe; for example, 42 per cent feel unsafe 'walking around their local area alone in the dark' (MORI 2002), although those identified as potential offenders appear rather more confident (MORI 2004: 48). Levels of concern about becoming a victim of crime are high, with 45 per cent of children in mainstream education reported as fearing theft, with 47 per cent worrying about being physically assaulted, while 53 per cent of 'Asian' young people and 42 per cent of 'black young men' are fearful of experiencing racism (MORI 2004: 49). Young people who are 'excluded' from school and therefore assumed to be more likely to offend are somewhat less worried about being victimised (23 per cent fear theft and 26 per cent physical assault, for example). In other studies, too, children consistently express apprehension about the behaviour of older children and 'teenagers' (Hine 2004). As children get older, perhaps unsurprisingly they become less fearful (MORI 2004: 48).

Their fears are not baseless, as we have seen. MORI's Youth Surveys have consistently shown high levels of victimisation, with 49 per cent of 'mainstream' children stating that one or more offences had been committed against them in the previous year, including being threatened (26 per cent), bullied (23 per cent), experiencing theft (15 per cent), or having property damaged (14 per cent). Those who are 'excluded' are more likely to be victimised (55 per cent) than mainstream children. Of those who had an offence committed against them, 74 per cent of 'mainstream' and 59 per cent of 'excluded' children reported that another young person had been responsible (MORI 2004: 54). Where young people tell anyone about the offence, it is usually parents whom they inform, then friends or teachers, and only 13 per cent report the matter to the police (21 per cent for the 'excluded' group). A significant proportion try to 'sort it out' themselves (26 per cent mainstream, 39 per cent excluded; see also Haines and Drakeford 1998: 22). The picture here is one of routine victimisation of young people and at the same time little reliance on the formal machinery of the justice system to resolve offences.

Although young people are at least as likely as adults to experience crime, their views on the justice system appear to differ somewhat. In comparing the views of adult respondents with those of 'juveniles', researchers have expressed the opinion that the determining factor for differences of attitude is age rather than offending (Mattinson and Mirrlees-Black 2000: 20). Those aged 12–17 appear considerably less likely to believe the courts too lenient (29 per cent) than adults in general (76 per cent). However, even young people appear to believe that the youth justice system is too lenient overall. Young offenders (12–17 years old) are somewhat more likely than non-offenders to state that the police and courts are 'too tough' (15 per cent compared with 7 per cent), but even for this group there are at least twice as many who believe the system is too soft as those who do not. Thus, while young people may be more likely than adults to see the justice system as too punitive, all age categories still tend to see it as too lenient.

A number of exercises to ascertain young people's views tend to support the view that young people are in favour of tough punishment; 'thus: if somebody is caught [for an offence] they should be punished severely' (12-year-old boy, quoted in Children and Young Persons Unit 2001), and 'tougher penalties for young people' were also requested by young people surveyed in Greater Manchester (Greater Manchester Police Authority 2002). On the other hand, young people do appear more likely than adults to believe that the police and courts' treatment of offenders is 'about right'. The reasons for this are not entirely clear, although it may be that young people are inevitably somewhat closer to the actual workings of youth justice and do not therefore share the unrealistic beliefs of the adult population. Young people might also be less willing to support punitive measures, partly because they are more 'understanding' of those who commit crime: 'Some people in gangs get involved because they could have a bad life at home, and ... [they're] pressured into it. That's how people join gangs, they're pressured into it. Having a lot of trouble at home and that' (quoted in Willow 1999: 52).

However, there is no evidence that young people take a less serious view of 'delinquent acts' than the population overall (Smith, D. *et al.* 2001). They appear to share a common view of a continuum of criminal behaviours, from minor infringements such as fare-dodging, through to 'quite serious' acts such as shoplifting and graffiti, and 'very serious' offences such as housebreaking, joy-riding and fire-raising (see also MORI 2002). However, there appears to be some evidence of 'neutralization' (Matza 1964), whereby minor infringements can be viewed as acceptable. Those who have engaged in 'less serious' criminal behaviour are less likely than their law-abiding peers to see these as significant transgressions (Smith, D. *et al.* 2001), and Hine reports an age factor in this respect:

> The younger age groups are sure that stealing any item is wrong. The older groups presented more tolerance, and even approval of stealing minor items of little value, but when the item involved is more valuable (such as a CD player) there is general disapproval here too. Children and young people clearly have a moral code which they can articulate and apply. (Hine 2004: 41)

The overall picture suggests that young people share many of the moral judgements and rules of behaviour of the community in general, expressing similar concerns about personal safety and the fear of crime (for example, Greater Manchester Police Authority 2002; Hine 2004), and holding similar views about the need for criminal sanctions and tougher punishment. This assessment finds support from wider surveys of the values and attitudes of young people which have also found that 'young people's values did not differ significantly to those documented for adults' (Thompson *et al.* 1999: 5). Despite this, it would appear that young people are not always well served by the formal justice system, with many offences going unreported, as we have seen, and a general sense of 'not being listened to', especially for black young people (Yarrow 2005).

Young people in Manchester have identified a need for 'more interaction by the police with young people; serious treatment of young people when reporting a crime; treating young people with respect; not being judgemental' (Greater Manchester Police Authority 2002: 1). These concerns about not being taken seriously are echoed elsewhere: 'I don't trust the police cos ... Like when someone stole my scooter. And he goes, "have you got it back?" And, he goes, "yes". "But can you find the person who done it?" and he goes "Sorry, sort it out yourself" (8/9-year-old quoted in Hine 2004: 31).

The apparent contradictions between young people's beliefs and their experiences may thus account for their rather ambiguous views about authority figures and the legitimacy of the powers they are ascribed (Thompson *et al.* 1999). As active participants in the social world (Smith, R. 2002c), young people do not simply take existing structures and systems of power as given; indeed, respect and recognition must be earned:

> Traditional authority figures such as the police, religious leaders and the royal family received very little automatic respect from young people. They explained that respect must be earned, authority won and merit proven ... While young people did not always invest teachers with moral authority, they watched them closely to see if they were worthy of it. (Thompson *et al.* 1999: 6)

Young people seem to be looking for certain characteristics in those who claim authority over them, in order to evaluate the legitimacy of these claims – characteristics such as 'consistency, care, the ability to listen and practical skills' (Thompson *et al.* 1999: 6).

It is perhaps important here to distinguish between the broad consensus to be found about what is appropriate behaviour and the means by which this is enforced on the one hand, and the experience of the application of these normative understandings in practice on the other. The evidence of a disparity is fairly clear. Young people consistently believe that their concerns are not taken seriously and that they are treated unfairly: 'Police ... don't make us feel safe and take their time getting to the crime scene' (14-year-old girl), and 'I have had police harassment on the streets for no reason other than being young' (16-year-old male) (both quoted in Children and Young

People's Unit 2001). That these concerns are not new is graphically conveyed by a previous study: 'I fuckin' hate coppers. They've just tried to do us for robbing some fuckin' sword or something. Murky and me were walking up the hill. Up they screeched, pulls us into the back of the car and start acting hard' (quoted in Parker 1974: 162).

This kind of perception creates some difficulties for the youth justice system in laying claim to legitimacy and the authority to impose sanctions for wrongful behaviour. Moral rectitude clearly does not lie only on one side, especially for young people who are identified as offenders. While Parker's study identified the police as the initial source of distrust and hostility, the resentment of unfairly imposed authority also extended to other aspects of the justice system, including probation and social services: 'Tank was extremely disillusioned to find that the social worker who had always helped out with his rather chaotic family had finally recommended him for a period of detention' (Parker 1974: 173).

Moving forward in time again, it seems that legitimacy and fair treatment remain significant areas of concern for those processed as young offenders. In terms of system effectiveness alone, it is likely that rates of non-compliance and even reoffending may be influenced by their perceptions of what is 'just', but these issues also raise more fundamental questions about what sort of youth justice system we want. An important study carried out with young people in custody (aged 15 to 21) sheds some light on this (Lyon et al. 2000). These young people talked first about the contextual factors relating to their criminal activities:

> They talked about growing up in bad areas, with high levels of crime and drug use; being labelled by education as a 'problem' and subsequently being excluded; they gave explanations for beginning offending; and they were critical of the way they had been treated by the criminal justice system. (Lyon et al. 2000: 7)

Their complaints focused on the police, the courts and other players in the justice system. The police, for instance, were seen to be 'taking advantage of their power ... the majority of young people did not have respect for the police. Nor did they see them as any deterrent against becoming involved in crime' (Lyon et al. 2000: 23). These views extended to the courts, where judges were seen as both racist and biased against young women; sentencers were criticised for 'not caring'. Youth justice professionals were seen as indifferent and lazy: 'The probation officer doesn't know what's going on. They should know you – they're your probation officer. They should know that you're going down again – they should know what's happening in your life shouldn't they?' (quoted in Lyon et al. 2000: 27). The experience of custody itself was seen as a poor preparation for a law-abiding life outside. For most, 'prison was a dislocating experience ... It was a "whole other life", not connected to their everyday lives before entering custody, and often not preparing them at all well for release ...' (Lyon et al. 2000: 29).

Despite their overwhelmingly negative experiences, the young people in this study appeared to have a real commitment to avoid offending in the future, and it was in this light that they made a number of suggestions for improving the justice system in order to address issues both of effectiveness and legitimacy. They supported ideas for preventing crime by targeting children at risk of social exclusion; they argued for improved peer support (mentoring) programmes; they emphasised the importance of continuing education; and they identified the need for continuity and stability for those in local authority care.

Specifically in relation to the justice system, these young people argued for tougher treatment of drug dealers, improved relations between police and young people, and fairer and explicitly anti-racist practice at all stages of the judicial process. They were also supportive of ideas such as mentoring, reparation and citizenship education, which they felt might reduce reoffending. In addition, they argued for better and more consistent welfare support to enable them to be reintegrated effectively into the community. Above all, it was found, young people processed by the justice system wanted to be treated with respect, something which they felt had not been accorded to them in many cases.

The authors of this report concluded positively that:

> Many of the young people's concerns about lack of professionalism are being tackled by the Government's agenda for reform of the youth justice system and the work of the Youth Justice Board ... The young people highlighted the need for complex solutions to complex problems. Their views support the Government's joined-up approach to tackling social inequalities as a way to reduce crime. (Lyon *et al.* 2000: 80–1)

A subsequent and rather more comprehensive study of young offenders' views has confirmed many of the concerns reported by these young people, especially about their treatment by the police, discrimination, the adverse effects of custody and the need for suitable support in the community (Hazel *et al.* 2002).

It seems to be the case that young people (offenders and non-offenders) share a detailed and nuanced understanding of youth offending, which means that simplistic responses are unlikely to be effective. Young people resent being targeted simply because of their age, and they feel that they have something to offer in constructing realistic solutions to perceived social problems (for example, the 'Young Voices' initiative in Liverpool; Hancock 2006: 178). Interventions and policies need to be holistic and focus on the social context and the social construction of crime (and anti-social behaviour) as a problem as well as – and, arguably, to a greater extent than – its immediate manifestations. To concentrate on dealing with their behaviour alone and out of context is not seen as justified by young people and may well be viewed as unfair and discriminatory. The possibility of a more inclusive and socially grounded approach has at least been signposted by the analysis and strategy developed by the Social Exclusion Unit (2002).

The answers are complex

The perceptions and attitudes of those with an interest of one kind or another in the youth justice system, far from reflecting simplistic judgements and identifying simple solutions, provide ample evidence that the issue is multi-faceted and demands careful analysis and considered action. Attitudes appear to be shaped partly in a context of limited and skewed knowledge (Mirrlees-Black and Allen 1998; Hough and Roberts 2004). Thus, for example, the public believes the youth justice system to be far more lenient than it actually is and seeks tougher punishments in the light of this erroneous belief. Despite this, popular sentiment is not uncompromisingly punitive (MORI 2001). Even among victims, there is support for approaches based on restorative principles (Mattinson and Mirrlees-Black 2000), and more detailed information and understanding generate a less punitive response from the public at large (Hough and Roberts 2004). Young people, including those who offend, appear to share widely held views about 'right' and 'wrong' (MORI 2002), but they are concerned about the inadequacies and injustices of the criminal process, feeling that it does not take their wishes and needs seriously, and that it is a source of racist and oppressive practice (Lyon *et al.* 2000; Bowling and Phillips 2002; Children and Young Person's Unit 2002; Yarrow 2005).

Although perceptions differ quite widely, it seems that all are agreed that the system as currently constituted 'doesn't work' (Mattinson and Mirrlees-Black 2000). It also seems that there is substantial support for the view that the most effective strategies must concentrate on securing wider social change outside the relatively narrow confines of the justice system itself. Despite this, there is a need for new and imaginative developments within youth justice in order to circumvent some of its perceived shortcomings. If these are pursued vigorously, they might even incur public approval:

> When public opinion is complex and multilayered ... there can be no policy justification for privileging people's unconsidered desire for tougher punishment and ignoring other dimensions to their views ...
> there is clearly potential for building on public support for new approaches to sentencing young offenders ... (Hough and Roberts 2004: xi)

10. Making sense of it all: looking ahead

Another fine mess?

The previous chapters have demonstrated in a number of ways the complexities and anomalies to be found in the workings of the youth justice system in the early part of the new millennium. This concluding chapter will seek to re-evaluate the key issues highlighted thus far in order to sketch some ideas about how we can move on from this fundamentally flawed and unsustainable state of affairs (see also Goldson and Muncie 2006).

We should not underestimate the scale of the problem or the pressures which impact on everyone involved in youth justice. It is located at a particularly uncomfortable conjuncture, where the perennial question of how to socialise or control our young people is addressed in the full glare of the media, community concerns and political interests. This will always be a controversial and hotly contested area of social practice. Ultimately, indeed, the failings of the system can be traced back to the complex dynamics arising from this unstable brew of high drama and loud voices. Inevitably, contradictory and counter-productive outcomes are generated in this unstable and conflict-ridden context.

As already observed, the development of present-day structures and processes can be seen to derive from the state's objectives of achieving its policy goals in terms of maintaining social cohesion, exercising control of deviant behaviour, and reproducing the existing structure of social relations (Althusser 1977). The construction of 'youth' as the source of a range of social problems, including crime and disorder, is also important in this project, to the extent that it contributes to and sustains 'consent' (Gramsci 1971; Hall *et al.* 1978). Underlying social factors associated with deviant behaviour are de-emphasised and the focal point of concern becomes the stereotypical 'threatening youth' (Davies 1986). It would be wrong to suggest that the behaviour of young people is never problematic, but the criminalisation of their activities ensures that its origins, and indeed its purposes, fade into the background. An effective separation is achieved in contemporary discourse between the 'criminal' and the causes of criminality.

It is this false distinction which lies at the heart of most of our difficulties in arriving at a clear understanding of youth offending and the consequent failure to devise and put into practice appropriate interventions. It is debatable as to whether the separation of the problem behaviour of young people from its social context is deliberate or misguided, and we are likely to encounter a cocktail of beliefs and attitudes among those concerned with the administration and delivery of youth justice. Althusser's (1977) argument that the judicial apparatus is simply a vehicle by which powerful interests impose their will is oversimplistic, while Foucault's (1979) characterisation of the machinery of justice as systematic and coherent attributes a greater degree of logic and consistency than is apparent to many who work within it. On the other hand, certain patterns and trends suggest a degree of consistency and even intent behind recent developments, such as the sustained increase in the use of custody from the mid-1990s onwards, or the 'demonising' effects of anti-social behaviour policies and initiatives (Squires and Stephen 2005).

We may gain a better insight into the complexities of current debates by considering analyses, such as Cohen's (1985), which identify competing strands of thought and capture the sense of youth and criminal justice as contested territory, where alternative views and disparate motives are played out in the construction and delivery of concrete practices. Indeed, it is suggested elsewhere that there is a 'melange' of different principles and provisions which demonstrate 'fundamental contradictions' in youth justice (Muncie 2002: 156).

Cohen, however, suggests that three main ideological strands can be detected in the changing shape and shifting dynamics of criminal justice. First, there are those who believe that its history and development can be characterised in terms of steady, if sometimes uneven, progress. The justice system, according to this view, can be (and is) improved consistently by the application of increasingly refined 'scientific' methods of research, management and practice, which will progressively improve the 'targeting' and impact of service delivery. There will thus be a continually enhanced understanding of 'what works', reflected in increasingly effective interventions and outcomes. Thus, 'although we are not at the end of the journey in the quest to find out what works ... there is now a rapid accumulation of understanding and knowledge in this field' (Burnett and Roberts 2004: 11). The development of National Standards for Youth Justice, the implementation of performance management and the adoption of specific practice tools such as ASSET (Baker 2004) are all represented as part of a process of advancement and refinement of good practice. Not only is there consensus around means, but there also appears to be common ground in terms of the ends to be achieved, that is crime reduction, pure and simple. The use of more sophisticated and intrusive means of monitoring and control such as surveillance and tagging is not problematic from this perspective, if it can be shown to contribute to lowering offending rates (Moore 2004: 170). At the same time, the entire project is depoliticised, becoming simply a matter of finding the best technical solutions to a commonly agreed problem. Changes in the political sphere, such as the election of a new government in 1997, are thereby reduced in significance (see, for instance, Pitts 2001b: 42), since the continuing task for penal experts remains unchanged, that is to improve the machinery for prediction, monitoring and managing the behaviour of those young people who are at risk of (re)offending.

Cohen's second category is characterised by the phrase 'we blew it', and this perspective views the progress of youth justice as a process of action and reaction, with each successive era offering evidence of apparently drastic attempts to put right the mistakes of the previous phase. This model of change fits well with the impression sometimes created of a history of continuing debates between opposing and irreconcilable positions. Specific initiatives can be linked to the ascendancy of one or other of these positions. Thus, historically, the 'welfare'-led reforms of the Labour government of the late 1960s could be seen as a reaction to the oppressive, class-based institutional regime that preceded them, represented by Approved Schools and Borstals in particular. As time progressed, however, these welfare reforms themselves generated a backlash, reflecting the views of a wide-ranging coalition of academics, politicians, sentencers and practitioners. This resulted in the 'back to justice' movement of the late 1970s/early 1980s (Morris *et al.* 1980; Thorpe *et al.* 1980). The 'justice model' then became the dominant paradigm of the following decade. As we have seen, however, aspects of this orthodoxy themselves generated a further reaction, notably in response to the liberalising trends associated with it, and a corresponding reduction in the use of punitive interventions including custody. Thus the 1990s saw a further 'backlash', this time leading to a prioritisation of punishment and control over rights and minimum intervention, epitomised by the 'prison works' mantra (Howard 1995). This shift of emphasis, politically rather than practice led, produced a new coalition concerned with 'protecting the community' and provided legitimacy for the package of reforms introduced in the latter part of the decade. On the face of it, then, there seems to be some support for the notion that youth justice is subject to periodic reappraisals leading to significant transformations in policy and practice. Pitts (2002), for example, argues that the recent history of juvenile/youth justice can indeed be seen in terms of distinctive paradigm shifts (Kuhn 1970), with four specific 'eras' represented: welfarism, back to justice, systems management and correctionalism. This portrayal also coincides quite neatly with a political context dominated by two political parties who seek to create a sense of distance between each other. Thus much of the New Labour rhetoric of the late 1990s emphasised the alleged failures of the previous Conservative government.

Cohen's third position – 'it's all a con' – reflects a rather more critical view that the kind of changes represented by the other positions are more or less superficial, disguising, and indeed contributing to, underlying attempts to legitimise the exercise of social control. Thus even favourable developments may be treated with suspicion. For example, Pratt's (1989) dismissal of juvenile diversion as an exercise in 'corporatist' control represents a wholly cynical view of what may have been viewed as an example of progressive practice. Goldson (2000a), more recently, has advanced a similar critique of the Referral Order, on the grounds that it creates an illusory form of 'contract' which is merely a cipher for the expropriation of children's rights. The problem posed by this perspective for practitioners is that it offers little scope for working in ways that are genuinely inclusive and progressive; it may, indeed, appear virtually impossible to practise in a way that 'prefigures' positive transformations (Smith, R. 1989). Thus, within this position, two contrasting strands of thought have developed – 'radical pessimism' and 'radical optimism' – which have become associated with rather different orientations to practice. For those holding the former view, it may be better not to intervene at all, than to muddy the waters by trying to act in children's interests in a hostile environment; 'radical non-intervention' is the preferred strategy (Schur 1973). On the other hand, those taking a proactive view would argue for a selective approach to practice, concentrating on those areas which provide for the promotion of children's rights (Scraton and Haydon 2002), such as diversion, remand rescue, community justice and anti-racist initiatives (for example, Right Track in Bristol). This, at least, appears to offer a progressive and practical agenda, but the challenge for this position lies in working within and according to the requirements of a structure which is fundamentally flawed and unjust (Corrigan and Leonard 1978).

While the differing perspectives identified by Cohen can be seen to exercise variable influences on the management and practice of youth justice, each can clearly be seen to contribute to a composite picture which is confused and sometimes contradictory. Indeed, it is the interplay of diverse viewpoints which results in the particular (and yet inherently unstable) form of the youth justice at any given point in time.

By the early 2000s, the balance seems to have moved in favour of those seeking to promote a routinised model of management, surveillance and control, based on assumptions of the perfectibility of the instruments and techniques for identifying risk and changing behaviour ('uneven progress'). This appears to coincide with broader currents associated with the concept of 'managerialism' (Clarke *et al.* 2000) and the ultimate 'infallibility of science' (Beck 1992). This also fits well with a political agenda which is attuned to the search for quick and certain solutions which will meet popular demands. Thus external pressures to produce instant results and guaranteed successful outcomes coincide with emerging practice orthodoxies, linked with a detailed analysis of 'what works'. Methods of prediction, surveillance and control are believed to be susceptible to continual improvement (see, for example, Baker 2005) and therefore routinised measures of intrusion and coercion are justified, even *in anticipation* of any possible offence:

> What is noticeable in this gamut of management restructuring and evaluation is that all aspects of young people's lives are now potentially open to official monitoring and scrutiny. (McLaughlin and Muncie 2000: 180)

We should note, however, that these developments are all based on the problematic and one-sided assumption that such improvements are both technically possible and desirable. Others might reflect that in the absence of any real evidence to support this belief, what in fact emerges is a combination of oppressive and divisive measures which at the same time fail to achieve the outcomes to which they aspire.

It should be noted here that the other positions identified by Cohen are also to be identified in various aspects of youth justice policy and practice in the present era, but to a less influential degree. It is politically expedient, for example, for policy-makers to be able to claim that each new initiative represents a radical departure from previous failures. Thus, as late as 2006, after nine years in power, the Prime Minister was reported to be promising a 'rebalancing' of the justice system 'in favour of the decent, law-abiding majority who play by the rules' (*Guardian* 23 June), acknowledging perhaps that he 'blew it'. However, in speaking at the same time of analysing 'where the shortcomings are' and putting in place 'systems to remove them', he appeared to be reverting to the language of the existing technocratic consensus rather than setting out an agenda for radical change.

The radical perspective, on the other hand, has likewise failed to exercise much influence in recent years, and has not offered an effective bulwark against the managerial tide. Part of the explanation for this stems back to the mood of complacency associated with the successes of the 1980s (diversion, offence resolution and reduced use of custody) and co-option by an apparently 'friendly' government after 1997 (McLaughlin and Muncie 2000); however, Pitts (2001b) also argues that the weakness of the radical position can be linked to its unwillingness to be explicit about the structural factors associated with youth offending – often, in the arena of practice, it might appear to make more sense, tactically, to avoid direct challenges to dominant assumptions. Thus, for example, court reports would not be constructed in a way which addressed the contextual issues relating to specific offences, such as poverty and institutional discrimination; arguments against excessively punitive sentences would be more likely to advance individual needs or 'mitigating factors'. As a result, the underlying rationale of due process, risk assessment and coercive interventions would remain unquestioned. The problem of a pragmatic strategy such as this is that it offers a weak base from which to develop principled and generalised arguments against either populist calls for tighter control over young people or technocratic measures aimed at generating a greater sense of certainty in tackling the threat they apparently represent.

The product of converging interests

The disastrous consequences of this convergence of populist ideologies, political opportunism and technocratic management are evident in the outputs of the youth justice system, of course. In many ways, these were both predictable and predicted (Goldson 1999, for example). The move towards creating 'wider, stronger and different nets' (Austin and Krisberg 2002) has been complemented by further steps to ensure that they are also deeper and more finely meshed. The system became increasingly efficient at processing and punishing young people, developing its own fearsome and inexorable logic

(Pratt 2000). The concrete evidence of this process is clearest at the apex of the structure, with a dramatic and sustained rise in the use of custody which has become firmly entrenched (Simes and Chads 2002; Youth Justice Board 2005d). Government appears to have taken the view that the actions of the courts in increasing demand for custodial places through their remand and sentencing practices should be endorsed and even encouraged, by taking steps to create ever more secure provision (Home Office Press Release 1 May 2002; *Guardian* 27 July 2006). This approach can be contrasted with other countries which have an active commitment to keeping the use of custody to a minimum (in Scandinavia, for example; Goldson and Muncie 2006b), or 'capping' its use (as in the Netherlands and Ireland; *Irish Examiner* 21 August 2002).

The outcomes observed in England and Wales are not just the result of populist gestures to increase the availability of custody[21]. The machinery of youth justice, too, has contributed to the emergent trends. Despite a static or falling crime rate (and at odds with popular beliefs fanned by government rhetoric; see, for example, Blunkett quoted in Home Office Press Release 20 March 2002; *Daily Mail* 24 June 2006), the greater resources invested and the increasingly sophisticated mechanisms of control applied have produced more and more oppressive outcomes. Even before they commit offences, young people are subject to ever closer scrutiny and targeted for interventions – first through preventive programmes such as Youth Intervention Projects and Summer Splash, born out of 'fear not need', according to one commentator, and subsequently through the use of Anti-Social Behaviour Orders, Dispersal Orders and Curfew Orders.

As they move into the criminal sphere, more young people are being formally processed (rather than receiving informal sanctions); they are being drawn into the justice system younger, for relatively more minor offences (Jennings 2002); and they are experiencing formal and recordable disposals earlier in their offending careers. The loss of the option to administer second and subsequent cautions following the 1998 legislation almost certainly ensures quicker progression to court, where the option of a Conditional Discharge is effectively removed, and more demanding and intrusive programmes are imposed at an earlier stage, effectively compressing the sentencing tariff. At the same time, the opportunities for non-compliance, failure and breach action are inevitably increased.

The principle of 'voluntarism' has been squeezed out at all stages of the process, for example through the contractual nature of the Referral Order (Crawford and Newburn 2003), which contrasts significantly with the negotiated and informal diversionary approaches of the 1980s. Failure to comply or the commission of further offences will speed young people towards categorisation as 'persistent young offenders', qualifying them for yet more intrusive forms of constraint and surveillance (almost irrespective of the gravity of their actions). These sentencing trends are complemented by an increasing array of bail conditions which are equally likely to lead to an increase in the number of breaches and subsequent custodial remands.

Managing 'risk'

Associated with the emergence of these highly developed and intrusive mechanisms of control has been a concern with the management of risk, and this has also been reflected in the tools and strategies of youth justice. ASSET, for example, represents an ideal instrument for systematising apparently objective measures of likelihood of reoffending, based on 'actuarial' principles (Lea 2002; Smith, R. 2006). Despite the rather overstated claims for its predictive accuracy (Youth Justice Board 2002; Baker *et al.* 2005), the form is of little value in identifying welfare needs (Roberts *et al.* 2001) or assisting in the construction of inclusive intervention programmes – welfare is written out of its remit (hence its incompatibility with the Common Assessment Framework; Youth Justice Board 2006b). As youth justice practitioners have repeatedly commented, ASSET is highly unbalanced and selective. Indeed, the preoccupation with risk is almost bound to prompt a predisposition to 'see the worst in people' and to focus unduly on the potential for negative outcomes. Is it entirely a coincidence that its adoption as a key assessment tool was accompanied by a surge in custodial sentencing?

However, such developments are not uniform, giving further cause to doubt the objectivity of the procedures in place. There have been consistent indications of wide variations in sentencing practices and the use of custody (Youth Justice Board Press Releases 22 August 2001, 3 November 2003, 10 December 2004). Evidence of 'justice by geography' also gives grounds for cautious optimism, suggesting that in some areas at least it has been possible to reduce the level of punitive interventions and to maintain a commitment to rather more inclusive forms of youth justice practice. On the other hand, such models have not always gained official approval, with the hint of veiled threats in some cases, and signs that increases in the number of young people being 'dealt with' have been applauded on occasion (Youth Justice Board Press Release 19 May 2002; McMahon 2006).

In the midst of all this, a number of important issues are raised. Perhaps of greatest weight is the argument that increased reliance on custody actually runs counter to the core aim espoused for the youth justice system which is to prevent offending by young people, since incarceration is known to be among the most effective mechanisms for promoting recidivism (Goldson and Peters 2000). In addition, as already noted, a concentration on the 'risk of failure' is likely to have a sensitising effect, creating both a greater predisposition to finding evidence of non-compliance and a greater likelihood that this will be officially recorded, which in turn is liable to generate an increasingly punitive response. The lessons of 'labelling theory' (Becker 1963) have clearly not been learnt, as the Chair of the Youth Justice Board has belatedly reminded us (*The Independent* 23 April 2006). Furthermore, increased investment in the machinery of youth justice, including expensive secure provision and cost-intensive community surveillance, will also contribute to a growing obsession with controlling the problematic behaviour of the young – generating a further spiral of increased fear and renewed demands for 'quick-fix' solutions. In the autumn of 2002 the Youth Justice Board announced the establishment of 'pre-crime panels' for children as young as eight years old, who would be marked out as potential offenders, and therefore liable to correctional interventions. Following the 'successful' piloting of the Youth Inclusion and Support Panel aimed at 8–13 year olds, the Youth Justice Board was funded by the Home Office to invest in 122 such schemes (Home Office 2004d). Beck's (1992) portrayal of the consequences of a preoccupation with things going wrong in a 'risk society' appears to be borne out by this kind of development. As he points out, a greater emphasis on the potential for failure will be associated with an 'actuarial' response based on the principle of identifying the possibility of damaging events and taking action to control this. This, however, has certain associated effects, such as a heightening of public fear and a sense of loss of control, as it becomes increasingly apparent that there is no way of providing absolute guarantees of security and personal safety. Indeed, some of the measures undertaken may actually generate new risks, for example by the creation of new forms of infringement (*The Independent* 16 August 2006).

The final irony to be noted here is the contrast between the emphasis, in one policy strand, on promoting social inclusion and a sense of belonging and the opposing pressures emerging from the criminal justice sphere to mark out young people as different, to exclude them from mainstream activities and to isolate them in 'targeted' programmes or settings. Thus the inclusive intent of programmes such as New Deal and Connexions, which focus on creating opportunities and building a spirit of community, is substantially undermined by the impact of parallel developments which depend for their very rationale on creating and sustaining a sense of 'the other' (Garland 2001). This permeates not just youth justice, but other settings such as education where differentiation and segregation appear to be endemic. The use of techniques which classify young people and their behaviour on negative grounds and then insert them into specialised forms of intervention can only intensify their sense of rejection and separation (Berridge *et al.* 2001), as well as confirming for the community in general that their special treatment is justified (Fionda 2005: 266). This aspect of the policy agenda has even permeated ostensibly preventive programmes, such as the Youth Inclusion Projects and Summer Splash schemes, which have been evaluated partly on the basis of how many 'at risk' young people they reach. We might ask, 'at what point do inclusive measures themselves become exclusive?'

Looking ahead: an alternative framework

The problems arising from the current organisation and delivery of youth justice are clear. They are essentially derived from the intertwined strands of populist authoritarianism and managerialist operational strategies which pervade the practice arena. This is not to suggest, though, that nothing can be done, rather that we should be clear about the size and nature of the task. In many ways, the prospectus for change is not new, because the key elements of a just and liberal youth justice system have been elaborated often enough (see, for example, Schur 1973; Smith, R. 1989; Scraton and Haydon 2002; Fionda 2005; Goldson and Muncie 2006). However, with each new development, the task of moving from 'where we are' to 'where we want to be' also becomes transformed, and the practical and political questions of achieving progressive reforms must be addressed rather differently. Nonetheless, it is important to set out certain central principles that ought to underpin the realisation of a fair and inclusive youth justice system.

Rights – not justice

This might seem a somewhat unusual distinction to make, but the underlying issue concerns the application of formal models of justice in unequal and unjust circumstances. In this sense, the administration of 'justice' actually compounds existing *injustices*, as is the case with institutional racism, for example (Bowling and Phillips 2002).

Thus, as Williams (1999) argues, merely setting the 'rights' of victims against the obligations of young offenders creates a false and simplistic opposition which does not reflect wider social, community or interpersonal dynamics. For example, the ambiguous position of young offenders who may also have been victims (MORI 2002) is likely to have an impact on their perceptions and attitudes (Smith, D. *et al.* 2001). The distinction between the idealised offender on the one hand and the victim on the other is therefore blurred.

Furthermore, in the context of specific offences, moral judgements, too, may be inconsistent or conflictual. The 'offender' may not accept unqualified responsibility for an offence, even when the facts of the matter appear relatively clear cut. This again is the predictable consequence of the unfolding of complex social and personal relationships. Young people may well be unwilling to accept the blame, for instance, for incidents that arise out of long-standing local disputes if these are taken out of context.

Rights, then, are not one-sided or pure. Despite this, the concept is powerful, and there does appear to be some value in seeking to apply the abstract principle itself in concrete circumstances:

> In established, 'mature' democracies, the conceptualisation, definition and formulation of commonly held and institutionally applied rights would seem straightforward ... Yet rights discourses are complex – reflecting a long history of contestation. Rights can be defensive in nature proclaiming the 'right' not to be on the receiving end of the actions of others ... Also, they can be proactive or positive ... providing the right to something ... (Scraton and Haydon 2002: 312)

It should be added here that rights are not fixed and determinate, and that they are subject to re-evaluation and modification over time. Thus they can be seen as negotiable and related to the specific context and networks of social relations relevant to the matter under consideration. It is thus inappropriate to think in terms of a static system of justice which invokes standardised procedures and fixed penalties to deal with all forms of problematic behaviour, which themselves originate in unique and variable circumstances. We may have to consider 'sacrificing due process', as Fionda (2005: 270) advocates. Apparently rational and logical frameworks for decision-making and sentencing must therefore be called into question. The apparent benefits offered by standardised and logical methods of identifying, processing and dealing with offenders must be set against the unjust consequences, in terms of 'the "loss" to the offender of relevant mitigating circumstances. It is a significant loss, given the consequences inherent in the determining contexts of class, "race", gender, sexuality and age inequalities' (Scraton and Haydon 2002: 315).

In order to deal with the problem of institutionalised unfairness, Bowling and Phillips (2002) propose a strategy of building into the decision-making process of the justice system an 'equalising' function, which adapts outcomes to take account of disadvantages which impact disproportionately on specific groups such as those from ethnic minorities. Thus, as already discussed, the uneven impact of differing family circumstances on remand decisions should be allowed for in order to avoid compounding prior social inequalities through the judicial process (Bowling and Phillips 2002: 260).

It is clear that a sophisticated and nuanced conception of rights is required, which incorporates a recognition of prior experiences, inequalities and power imbalances. What is needed here is 'substantive' rather than 'formal' justice. (Fionda 2005). The starting point for the incorporation of this principle into youth justice is provided for us by international frameworks such as the UN Convention on the Rights of the Child, the Beijing Rules on the Administration of Juvenile Justice and the European Convention on Human Rights. If followed conscientiously, these should ensure that the administration of justice incorporates a recognition of the distinctive position of children, especially those who experience disadvantage or discrimination.[22] Clearly, the justice system should take the utmost care not to compound the negative and damaging experiences which some children and young people endure, and which may well be relevant factors in their offending behaviour.

Problem-solving

In light of this, it is suggested that the primary focus of any form of intervention to deal with offending behaviour should adopt a 'problem-solving' approach. To some extent, this is consistent with the ideas associated with 'restorative justice' (Strang and Braithwaite 2001; Johnstone 2002), although it also extends more widely to incorporate the principle that any problem associated with an offence should be addressed, including those issues which might be thought of as 'welfare' needs.

Whereas the starting point is inevitably the 'trigger' incident, with a focus on 'putting right the wrong to the extent that it is possible for *both* victim and offender' (Gelsthorpe and Morris 2002: 242), this should not be an isolated aim, but should be incorporated in a more far-reaching strategy, encapsulated in the phrase 'responsibility, restoration and reintegration'. Indeed, this kind of approach is reflected in the objectives of some recent practice developments such as Community Restorative Justice in the North of Ireland (see http://www.extern.org/restorative/CRJI.htm, for example).

These objectives point towards a pragmatic and situated approach, drawing on ideas of social learning (Bandura 1976), and they clearly call into question punitive and exclusive modes of intervention. Thus, for example, the extent to which problem-solving interventions such as family group conferences (Jackson 1999) and restorative panels (Haines 2000) are subsumed by the formalities of the justice system will play a substantial part in determining their efficacy. If they are seen merely as an adjunct to the criminal process, then their meaning and impact are likely to be compromised (Newburn and Crawford 2003: 237). As a result, 'there have been questions about whether restorative justice principles can work when reparation orders are *imposed* on offenders without their consent' (Gelsthorpe and Morris 2002: 247). Rather, to be genuinely constructive, methods of resolving the difficulties arising from the offences of young people need to ensure, as far as possible, that 'the key participants in all of this – offenders, victims and their families – actually ... take charge' (Gelsthorpe and Morris 2002: 249). The contradictory measures and conflicting signals of the Crime and Disorder Act 1998 are expected to compromise restorative principles in the absence of further reforms to promote mutually determined arrangements for addressing the consequences of the offence and putting things right.

A problem-solving approach will also need to be more broadly based than simply focusing on 'making amends'. The one-dimensional preoccupation with the offender *as an offender*, reflected in the one-sided emphasis of instruments such as ASSET, creates an arbitrary and unsustainable separation between the young person concerned and her/his circumstances, needs and perspective.[23] The commission of an offence does not simply represent an atomised interaction between free-standing individuals, where one is in the wrong and the other is simply wronged. It is rather the culmination of a series of interconnected dynamics and influences, including family background, peer group expectations, cultural norms, personal experiences, educational needs and mental health, not to mention structural factors such as racism and poverty. Whether we think in broad systemic terms or in terms of immediate contextual influences, these are all relevant and therefore need to be addressed in any response.

Voluntarism

As youth justice has moved to progressively more prescriptive and mandatory interventions at all levels, so we are losing sight of an important principle which follows from the previous discussion. At the heart of progressive and inclusive practice, we must seek to engage young people on their own terms, ensuring their active and explicit commitment to resolving the problems associated with their wrongdoing. It is not therefore merely a technical question as to whether restorative measures can 'work' when they are imposed rather than negotiated; it is also an important defining feature of the overall character of the youth justice system. The attraction of imposing swift and certain solutions cuts across the opportunities available for achieving social inclusion and reconciliation wherein the offender genuinely accepts responsibility.

As already observed, serious doubts must be raised about the value and meaning of measures that might claim to be restorative but which depend for their implementation on coercion and threat. Thus, where 'the courts ... *direct* personal apologies, [this] may lead to grudging or insolent attitudes being displayed when young offenders meet their victims' (Gelsthorpe and Morris 2002: 247). The impression gained is that reparation has not always been particularly meaningful, whether to offenders or to victims (Holdaway *et al.* 2001), with routine and demeaning tasks being required of young offenders in the name of making good (Haines and O'Mahony 2006) and with 'letters of apology being rehearsed by hard-pressed YOT workers anxious to get young people through' (Gelsthorpe and Morris 2002: 248).

While some (Masters 2005) have suggested that young people's consent is unimportant, others (Haines and O'Mahony 2006) take the view that their commitment to the process is crucial, both in relation to the genuineness of their efforts to make amends, and also in terms of their perceptions of the justice system and 'their wider social situation' (Haines and O'Mahony 2006: 122).

It should perhaps be recalled from earlier chapters that, while most young offenders do not take issue with the need for rules and sanctions, they are often antagonistic to the manner in which these are applied (Lyon *et al.* 2000). It may seem, on the face of things, that the consent of the young person is irrelevant in a context where their criminal behaviour means that they forfeit the right to be consulted. However, this point is implicitly conceded in the (limited) incorporation of the young person's viewpoint in the ASSET exercise; at the same time, securing compliance without commitment seems of limited value in terms of gaining active consent or lasting change.

It is also important to consider the wide question of legitimacy and the extent to which young people are encouraged or dissuaded from according this to the criminal process. As the previous chapter shows, there is a substantial degree of mistrust directed towards youth justice agencies, not just among those who offend but among the wider population of young people – and this is felt even more acutely among specific subgroups, including young black people.[24] The problem here is that loss of trust, in broad terms, is likely to be exacerbated by an overemphasis on coercion within the machinery of the justice system. In this respect, to ignore the need for consent is merely to compound a wider sense of injustice.

In light of this, it may be relevant to note that a range of community sentences (Probation Orders, Community Service Orders and Supervision Orders) actually required the consent of the offender before they could be imposed until quite recently. Clearly, 'consent' in these circumstances is very heavily circumscribed, but it does indicate a historic acceptance within the justice system of the need to engage with those responsible for offences and to secure their agreement to the disposals proposed, in turn suggesting a principled commitment to notions of personal responsibility and social solidarity. Assuming that at some level these aspirations remain feasible as well as desirable, they might point towards a broader refocusing of the principles of youth justice. As Lea argues, given the right social conditions, we should be entitled to expect that:

> communities could take the law into their own hands again ... Relations of trust and solidarity will be enabled to replace those of risk and unpredictability. Social inclusion will enable robust communities to sort out a large proportion of their own disputes. (Lea 2002: 189)

For this to be achieved, however, the state needs to take a lead role in promoting, rather than circumscribing, personal and social responsibility through pursuing voluntarism as a fundamental principle of youth justice.

Minimum (state) intervention

These aspirations also help to generate a persuasive logic in favour of the principle of pursuing the least intrusive and coercive means of intervention achievable, since this is clearly consistent with the agenda of rights, problem-solving and voluntarism already set out here. While the UK government has committed itself to this principle since 1991 through its adoption of the UN Convention on the Rights of the Child (Articles 37 and 40 in particular) along with other international instruments (Goldson and Muncie 2006), it has repeatedly been taken to task for failing to comply with this obligation (UN Committee on the Rights of the Child 2002).

On purely pragmatic grounds, of course, it is extraordinarily wasteful to rely on expensive, ineffective and excessive machinery of control (Smith, R. 2001). The relatively high cost of custody as compared with community disposals has been repeatedly demonstrated (Goldson 2006: 150). However, as community sentences, too, become progressively 'toughened up', these will also become more expensive to administer, and it would therefore seem to make good economic sense not to use them unless stringent criteria are met.[25]

Regrettably, the expansion of available custodial options and the dilution of safeguards against their use, stemming from the mid-1990s onwards, have ensured that the thresholds for the use of prison for young people have clearly been lowered, as is confirmed by the statistical evidence (Simes and Chads 2002). The sustained increase in the use of custody over a number of years (Goldson 2006: 145) suggests a system 'out of control' rather than one that is rigorous and rational in setting limits to the use of extreme measures such as the deprivation of liberty.

Not only is the excessive use of measures of containment and control inefficient in economic terms, it is also ineffective in terms of the 'principal aim' specified for the youth justice system of reducing youth crime. The evidence of the failure of custody to reduce further offending is compelling (Muncie 1999; Goldson 2006); this is perhaps unsurprising, given that a period of incarceration represents a severe rupture in the lives of those who are locked up (Goldson 2006: 147), and that the experience itself is often oppressive and demoralising (Goldson and Peters 2000).

Of course, a rather more important consideration than the inefficiency and ineffectiveness of such measures in terms of system goals is the damage caused to young people, for which there is copious evidence (Lyon *et al.* 2000; Goldson and Coles 2005; Carlile 2006). The most dramatic and severe injustices perpetrated in the name of youth justice, and its most divisive and discriminatory impact, are inevitably experienced through the needless use of custody. There is no excuse for this, and persistent failures to address it must raise serious questions about the intentions of government and the capability of the Youth Justice Board. Ironically, rather than learn the obvious lesson that custody does not work (and is not necessary), the drive of policy-makers has been to extend its availability while also exporting its techniques (surveillance, monitoring, behaviour management) into the community.

Inclusion

Rather than seeing historic failures compounded through ill-conceived coercive measures, the core of youth justice practices should be informed by the principle of inclusion, ironically one which has been promulgated extensively by government in recent times. It is an attractive notion, suggesting the possibility of achieving a greater sense of social solidarity and mutuality, and in this respect the government's aspirations should be applauded. Garland (2001), too, provides theoretical justification for this by contrasting it with the kind of 'exclusionary' criminology to which it is opposed. As he puts it, those policies which set offenders apart, representing them as 'the other', are likely to have divisive consequences on a broader scale. They are likely to institutionalise oppressive and discriminatory practices which are both based upon and sustaining of inequality. By contrast, an inclusive approach to youth justice will seek to reintegrate those who are on the outside with their communities and the wider society, to promote their acceptance as fellow citizens and to ensure that their offences are dealt with constructively. A forward-looking strategy based on personal and social development should be emphasised.

However, this distinction between ways of thinking about the justice system leads us to the central contradiction of the New Labour project, which has attempted to keep a foot in both camps, adopting policies geared towards inclusion in some respects (see Chapter 3) while at the same time pursuing policies and practices which mark out and exclude those who do not comply with normative expectations, who do not behave responsibly or who reject the opportunities available to them.

Even within the field of youth justice these contradictions are apparent, with 'inclusive' measures borrowed from France (Pitts 2001b) such as the Youth Inclusion Projects competing for both resources and ideological legitimacy with the 'exclusive' model of justice associated with the United States (electronic monitoring, surveillance and behavioural programmes). Ultimately, these two positions are incompatible, and the evidence we have considered here demonstrates unquestionably that the inclusive agenda must be prioritised (Hughes and Follett 2006).

The way ahead: working at different levels

Beyond setting out the foregoing set of principles to inform future developments in youth justice, it is also important to propose some concrete suggestions by which these aspirations could be realised, or at least to suggest some practical steps along the road. In order to do so, it may be helpful to follow the structure introduced earlier and suggest options to be pursued at each of the 'macro', 'mezzo' and 'micro' levels.

Implicit in this, of course, is an assumption about the power relationships between these levels, and the extent to which there is a hierarchy of influence stemming from the level of government and policy ('macro') through the intermediate structures and agencies ('mezzo') to the level of practice and first-line management ('micro'). While some have suggested that this model may underestimate the extent to which 'street-level bureaucrats' are able to work independently and creatively to develop good practice (Crawford and Newburn 2003: 236), the evidence we have considered suggests that this remains an uneven relationship, as these authors also seem to acknowledge (Crawford and Newburn 2003: 222).

Global coalitions – pie in the sky?

As globalisation becomes more of a reality, and as international frameworks become more firmly established (Goldson and Muncie 2006a), there may be some value in beginning our exploration of the 'macro' level with a consideration of the potential for change offered by these developments. If we do not look beyond the national context, it may seem that suggestions such as the 'decriminalisation' of childhood wrongdoing are too far-fetched. However, it is possible to look to other states not too far away, to see that they may have a quite different view of crime and criminality in relation to young people (Belgium, for example, has set the age of criminal responsibility at 18; Goldson and Muncie 2006: 219).

In a rather different vein, Lea (2002) also argues that a global perspective is important, suggesting that a major restructuring of social relations is a necessary prerequisite of a fair and humane justice system:

> There must be a fundamental redistribution of economic and welfare resources to poor communities, both within advanced capitalist countries and on a global scale. This will enable the disconnection from dependence on criminality, violence and the violation of the rights of others like oneself as a survival necessity ... But [despite this] there will be a need for criminal justice agencies to facilitate dispute resolution by providing legal resources to track people down and bring disputants together and to furnish legal frameworks for handling disputes. (Lea 2002: 189)

Thus social transformation will not remove the need for criminal justice systems and processes, but these will be driven democratically by the emergence of a broad global coalition of 'social groups, political and voluntary organisations

[and] non-governmental organisations' (Lea 2002: 191), which might include those already engaged in the delivery of youth justice, with the skills and experience to develop the new problem-solving legal frameworks envisaged. So, in Lea's view, broad transformations at the global level must be mirrored by practical initiatives at the level of communities and individuals. This is an important connection to make, although it clearly leaves unexplored the intermediate steps by which such changes can be achieved.

Youth justice and social inclusion

Opportunities are provided, for example in the political rhetoric currently being espoused and the policy agendas being pursued. As already suggested, it is important that consistency is achieved between youth justice strategies and the broader aim of ending social exclusion and promoting a more cohesive society. It is clearly important that the specific policies and structures that underpin youth justice do not contradict or undermine these aspirations. Thus those shortcomings of policy which have been identified previously will need to be addressed, not just because they are not effective, but also because they are not consistent with the goal of achieving social inclusion. Thus there is a need to bring an end to measures which set offenders apart, and create barriers between them and the wider community, such as the Anti-Social Behaviour Order, segregated education provision and 'targeting' of potential offenders from an early age.

Curbing custody

On revisiting the first edition of this book (Smith, R. 2003), I would probably acknowledge that it should have been stronger in its support of an 'abolitionist' approach to youth custody (Mathiesen 1974; Fionda 2005; Goldson and Muncie 2006a). Given that this is unlikely to be achieved instantaneously, however, it also seems reasonable to suggest interim measures which might support this goal, however. For example, as in other countries, a clear limit could be set for the number of secure places available for young people. The Children's Society (1988, 1993) has calculated, for example, that the number of secure places required for those under 17 throughout England and Wales is no more than 500. At the same time, despite some limited progress in this direction (ADSS *et al.* 2003), all secure settings for children and young people should be brought unequivocally under the protections, standards and operational requirements of the Children Act 1989 (see Goldson and Coles 2005).

Minimum intervention and children's rights

Again, in terms of immediate policy objectives, it is important to re-emphasise those objectives to which national government is committed in principle but which are not being honoured in practice, such as minimum intervention. The use of informal means of dealing with offences should be pursued more robustly (Fionda 2005) and greater flexibility in the use of pre-court diversion utilised. At the same time, it is important to revisit the long-standing argument for the raising of the age of criminal responsibility in line with international norms. Ireland has made recent moves in this direction and it has been considered by previous governments.[26]

The criticisms of the UK's performance made by the UN Committee on the Rights of the Child are stringent, and would seem to necessitate some form of positive response. Indeed, 'the Committee notes with serious concern that the situation of children in conflict with the law has worsened' (UN Committee on the Rights of the Child 2002: 15). If the UK government was serious about its international obligations in this context, it would also ensure adherence to the Beijing Rules for the Administration of Juvenile Justice (United Nations 1985) and the Human Rights Act 1998.

These instruments, if incorporated into the judicial process, should ensure that family life is not disrupted by the imposition of intrusive and punitive orders, whether these are ASBOs or custodial sentences, only allowing children's liberty to be curtailed as a 'last resort' (UN Committee on the Rights of the Child 2002). Likewise, these measures should ensure that punitive restrictions (bail conditions, surveillance or curfews) would no longer be acceptable to the extent that they impose sanctions on young people prior to a finding of guilt.

Problem-solving and policy

A problem-solving approach to youth crime could complement a rights-based minimum intervention strategy quite well. Relatively small-scale legislative and policy changes could facilitate this quite substantial reorientation of the shape of youth justice. For example, removal of the arbitrary ceilings placed on the use of reprimands and 'Final' Warnings would create space for a much more flexible approach to pre-court disposals, as would explicit approval of the use of non-recordable informal measures where appropriate. Similarly, extension of the availability of Referral Orders would ensure greater scope for mediated settlements while also reducing the dominance of the retributive sentencing tariff. It is worth noting that government has made modest steps in this direction by proposing 'a limited extension to Referral Orders to allow them on a later court appearance, for example where the young person has not previously received one, or did so at least two years ago' (Home Office 2004b: 11); at the same time, however, the government resisted calls for increased use of informal pre-court disposals. It should be noted that 'diversion' has been an explicit centrepiece of policy in the past (Home Office 1985) and appears to play an important role in other jurisdictions such as Italy (Nelken 2006). Such approaches are also associated with the emergence of a broader range of interventions which concentrate on resolving the problems associated with an offence, whether these relate to the feelings of the victim or the offender's needs (Smith, R. 1989; Rutherford 1992). In Italy, this is made quite explicit:

> These are all youths with big problems and dealing with these must be the best way of solving the problems youths represent for the legal system. (Juvenile court judge, quoted in Nelken 2006: 173)

Government is clearly in a position to initiate moves towards a youth justice system that is inclusive which, in the case of England and Wales, would bring this aspect of its programme into line with a broader agenda; at the same time, this could open up possibilities for the development of a greater sense of order and cohesion within communities (Haines and O'Mahony 2006; Hancock 2006).

Of course, such steps depend on finding the political will to move away from the attractions of inflammatory and misleading populist rhetoric and on recognising the need for 'joined up' policies:

> *No More Excuses* promised that the Crime and Disorder Bill would establish prevention as a statutory aim of the youth justice system … That is radical and encouraging – as long as preventive policies are not seen as solely the responsibility of the youth justice system and as long as its strategies are genuinely proactive, preventive and not simply reactive in the face of emergent problems of delinquency. Crime prevention has to be a concern of all public policies. (George and Wilding 1999: 194)

Of course, all the available evidence (see previous chapters) suggests that the youth justice system itself is particularly poorly placed to do much about preventing or reducing crime. Socially inclusive crime prevention measures could, indeed, be much better resourced if the decision was taken to shift funding into the community and away from the expensive and ineffective machinery for processing and punishing young offenders currently in place. Reducing the throughput of the system would, of course, enable this kind of constructive refocusing to take place.

Oiling the wheels: the 'mezzo' level

Naturally, change cannot be achieved simply by putting the right policies in place and then 'rolling them out' to achieve the desired outcomes, despite the sometimes rather naive assumptions of policy-makers themselves:

> The Government's reforms of the youth court in England and Wales will help to shape a more effective youth justice system for the next century. The approach combines the principles of restorative justice with more traditional punitive measures, which must be available to the courts to protect the public. The overall result should be a more streamlined and effective system, with a clearer focus on preventing offending. (Home Office 1997b: 34)

By the same token, it should also be noted that poor policies do not necessarily lead to bad practice and undesirable outcomes. The history of youth justice is, in fact, littered with misguided policies, unrealistic expectations, unintended consequences and unresolved contradictions, all of which can be traced back to the limitations of the underlying strategy itself. There is, therefore, a substantial task facing those whose responsibility it is to organise and make possible the delivery of effective interventions, both practitioners and those at the 'mezzo' level responsible for interpreting and adapting policy and delivering systems and strategies, including the Youth Justice Board, local partnerships, agencies, the courts and penal institutions. At this level rests the responsibility for making sense of national policy and translating it into operational guidance.

At the same time, an important responsibility for those at this intermediate level is sometimes overlooked, and that is to pass messages in the other direction as well, as Pitts (2002) reminds us. It is important that those responsible for administering youth justice also recognise their obligations to represent the concerns of those engaged in direct practice as well as those on the receiving end, that is those who offend or are affected by the problematic behaviour of young people (Brown 2005: 126). This role, as a conduit for ideas, evidence, opinion and critical feedback, appears to be underplayed, except perhaps where the message can be taken as affirmative. Equally, there appears to be some evidence of 'selective listening' from those on the receiving end of such comment (see *YJ*, formerly *Youth Justice Board News*, as a prime example of this).

The new Youth Justice Board – shameless collaborator or 'critical friend'?

Since its establishment as an arm's length quango, the position of the Youth Justice Board has been problematic; indeed, it is bound to be wrought with tension, and this has been reflected in its ambiguous and changing approach. In its early days, it seemed to be concerned primarily with 'franchising and McDonaldising' youth justice services and overlooking its evaluative and critical responsibilities. With a change of leadership, it appeared subsequently to show signs of taking on more diverse and representative functions, as indeed it should if it is to serve a useful purpose. These include acting as:

- a 'buffer' between government and the field, encouraging diversity and ironing out inconsistencies in government policy;

- an 'informed advisor' to government and other policy-makers on best practice, rather than purveying simplistic and erroneous assumptions;

- a 'champion of rights' of young people and their families as well as victims of crime (especially those groups which experience consistent forms of discrimination);

- a consistent 'purveyor of advice' to practitioners, the judiciary and other interests;

- a 'developer and supporter' of professional youth justice practice, rather than simply promoting a 'homogeneous, offence-oriented' culture; and

- a commissioner and disseminator of wide-ranging and independent research designed to broaden understanding rather than simply to confirm prior assumptions.

(Based on Pitts 2002)

All this suggests a shift of emphasis from a managerial perspective, based on securing routinised compliance with targets, performance indicators and specified measures of 'success' towards a more developmental approach, which encourages and builds on professional innovation and creativity, encourages debate and risk-taking, funds critical and exploratory research, and acts as a 'knowledgeable friend' to those in the field.

Some signs of attempts to take up an independent position were initially apparent in tentative expressions of concern over excessive use of custody (Youth Justice Board Press Release 22 August 2001, 5 September 2002), and the promotion of community alternatives. However, these were limited and muted until the board's second chair began to take a more explicitly critical view of certain aspects of government policy such as the use of ASBOs (*The Independent* 23 April 2006), the unnecessary 'criminalisation' of young people and the unacceptable conditions in some custodial settings (*Guardian* 16 August 2006).

The courts and sentencing bodies as opinion formers

Of course, the YJB is not the only 'middle-range' body with considerable power and influence in the youth justice arena. For instance, the impact of judicial pronouncements (for good or bad) was demonstrated graphically by the imposition of an 'exemplary' custodial sentence by the Lord Chief Justice for the theft of a mobile phone in 2002. The immediate consequence was a rapid sequence of copy-cat sentences around the country (for instance, a 16-year-old was sentenced to a 3½-year jail term for robbery of a phone on 8 February 2002 at Sheffield Crown Court). One of the consequences, clearly, is that the specific circumstances and characteristics of the offender concerned become subsumed under the wider imperative of 'stamping out' a certain type of behaviour. Such effects are not new, as Hall and colleagues (1978) have demonstrated.

However, the courts need not simply be a source of pressure for more severe sentencing, and their direct contribution to the more lenient ethos within which 'alternatives to custody' came to thrive is significant. Rutherford (1992) documented the role of the local magistracy in supporting and promoting the development of one such initiative in Basingstoke, the Woodlands centre. This is a good example of the ability of local networks of agencies, sentencers and practitioners to achieve positive change, even in a punitive climate:

> There was growing despair that the juvenile court did not have local alternatives to incarcerative institutions, and a powerful determination to do something about it. The main initiative was taken by Margaret Baring, chairperson of the juvenile court. She and other magistrates, the clerk to the court and other local people wanted a programme which did more than pack young people and canoes into a mini-bus. (Rutherford 1992: 136)

It is perhaps no coincidence that Hampshire was one of the pioneers of the 'custody-free zones' which became a feature of significant numbers of local youth justice systems throughout England and Wales in the 1980s.[27]

A more recent example of the progressive use of judicial influence can be found in the Lord Chief Justice's attempt to encourage his colleagues to consider non-custodial options for first- and second-time burglars (Woolf 2002) – somewhat ironic in view of his earlier pronouncements on mobile-phone theft. The Sentencing Guidelines Council established in 2004 may also have an increasing role in influencing practice in this respect, too, and it is of interest that this body has sought to resist what it perceives as unhelpful media influence (Phillips 2006).

Effective agency coalitions

Progressive developments in other aspects of the youth justice process have been identified, for example in Northamptonshire, where the achievement of consistently high levels of diversion for young offenders was attributable to close and committed inter-agency collaboration (Smith, R. 1989). Interestingly, the police were prime movers for this initiative. It seems almost inevitable that the emphasis on partnership and inter-agency working that has permeated youth justice since the 1998 reforms (and now through *Every Child Matters*, too) will give rise to similar opportunities. However, this will also depend on the ability to establish a degree of independence and meet the essential requirements of a shared vision and collective commitment. Poulantzas's (1978) notion of 'relative autonomy' provides theoretical support for the argument that specific coalitions of interest can emerge, even within highly centralised and frameworks of power and bureaucracy, and that these groups will have the capacity to set their own terms of reference and act independently. Clearly, different practices do arise in different areas given our knowledge of the substantial geographical variation in practices and outcomes (Feilzer and Hood 2004: 95). The task is to build upon the experience of those which demonstrate a consistently progressive approach in this respect (see, for example, Youth Justice Board Press Release 3 November 2003).

The power of the inspectors

Other significant actors at the 'mezzo' level are the regulatory bodies, including the various inspectorates and auditing bodies which have an interest in youth justice, and whose impact on policy and practice can be significant (Audit Commission 1996, for example). The work of the Prison Inspectorate has been of particular interest in this respect, with a series of strongly critical reports challenging the unacceptable treatment of young people in custody, and a clear underlying commitment to promote the human rights of children who are locked up. The extent to which these criticisms will have a cumulative effect is perhaps unclear, given the other influences at play, but they have clearly affected the behaviour of individual regimes (Travis 2002).

Further evidence of the potentially valuable contribution of the inspectors has been provided by the report of a collaborative exercise, *Safeguarding Children*, which found that:

> the welfare needs of young people who commit offences were not being adequately addressed by those services responsible for their welfare. There were no national minimum standards for the work of YOTs, and there was no regular inspection of their work. They were operating largely in isolation from other services in most areas. (Joint Chief Inspectors 2002: 69)

Given the importance of collaboration, as set out above, and given that YOTs were established precisely to encourage joint working, this was particularly damning criticism.[28] Although the combined inspectorates appeared to suggest that some improvements had been made subsequently (Joint Chief Inspectors 2005), this view was not shared by all those responsible for monitoring practice standards (Commission for Social Care Inspection 2005).

The report concluded that young people in custody were still seriously at risk, and that youth justice services generally were paying insufficient attention to the protection and safeguarding of children's welfare. A more proactive role for Area Child Protection Committees was recommended (see also, Smith, R. 2002c), and the report's conclusions were at least partly responsible for the increased emphasis on collaboration reflected in the *Every Child Matters* reform agenda.

Campaign groups and collective interests

It is also important to acknowledge the role of a rather different kind of middle-range organisation, that is the various representative bodies, trade unions, lobby groups and voluntary organisations who all perform an important function in casting a critical gaze over areas where change may be required. Such networks act as collective whistle-blowers, as well as a site for risk-taking and innovation which would not otherwise be sanctioned or financially supported. The role of bodies such as the National Association for Youth Justice is particularly important, for example, through its work in formulating and disseminating a clear philosophical base and manifesto for action (National Association for Youth Justice 2002a, 2006).

The extent to which these alternative sources of power, knowledge and influence might lead to change over time is always unpredictable, but they do provide a focal point for critical thinking and practical opposition to prevailing norms and practices. We should not be as pessimistic as those left-wing 'functionalists' such as Althusser (1977) who saw power as flowing only in one direction. Resistance is possible, and others have suggested that 'institution-building' at the local and community level is a central part of any strategy to create an inclusive and just society (George and Wilding 1999). The experience of communities in Northern Ireland in trying to develop their own frameworks and practices to deliver youth justice is a strong case example in support of this proposition, despite the problematic aspects of these initiatives which have also been acknowledged (Schrag 2003; Eriksson 2006).

Local agencies and community and professional interests, therefore, have a key role to play in generating approaches to youth crime that engage those who are affected and attract their commitment.

Following Scarman's (1982) prescription for the police, it seems that we should be pursuing active strategies to secure 'youth justice by consent'. Crawford and Newburn (2003: 236), for example, suggest that whatever its shortcomings the Referral Order provides one such opportunity to engage with communities in the process of 'reworking' youth justice to promote 'the principles of "inclusivity, reciprocity, appreciation and tolerance"'.

The search for progressive practice at the 'micro' level

It is probably right to conclude with some observations about the possibilities for working to deliver constructive and effective practice within youth justice, according to the principles outlined earlier. Obviously, these ideas have been developed more fully elsewhere (see, for example, Crawford and Newburn 2003; Bateman and Pitts 2005) but here the aim will be to concentrate on a few areas of significant potential and certain key themes.

Informal justice

As noted previously, the principle of 'voluntarism' is crucially important, not just because it can lead to a reduction in the use of punitive measures, but also because it aims to secure the active engagement of young people rather than their passive compliance. This leads, in turn, to a renewed emphasis on promoting diversionary approaches (Goldson and Muncie 2006a) and informal action – given that they represent a non-criminalising, quick and cheap way of resolving minor infractions. In some parts of England and Wales, it appears that informal action remains an acceptable option, and this probably represents another example of 'justice by geography'. Wherever the opportunity arises, practitioners should seek to pursue offence resolution by this means. Not only does this strategy ensure that young people's misdemeanours are dealt with outside the statutory (and criminalising) framework, but it also creates space for a more genuine engagement with young people, their families and their victims to reach mutually agreed solutions, without unnecessary pressure to contrive a 'happy ending'.

Equally, in terms of system efficiency, this approach to minimum intervention removes a substantial and needless burden from youth justice agencies, and notably the police. This would, of itself, contribute substantially to other objectives such as 'speeding up' youth justice, purely by removing large numbers of cases from the formal system – allowing more time to be devoted to other matters of public concern (such as lack of community policing and low clear-up rates). The challenge here is to confront at all points the relentless logic (Foucault 1979) which requires that all infractions are recorded, accounted for and processed in the cause of routinised discipline and control. Both Italy (Nelken 2006) and Ireland (Seymour 2004), for example, seem able to incorporate these diversionary objectives within their youth justice processes.

Making sense of restorative practice

Given that 'restorative justice' has become the dominant discourse under which problem-solving and negotiated interventions are subsumed, it is important to consider the implications for progressive practice of this development. It is clearly a contested term, and the argument here is that the quality of the process is more important than meeting prescribed targets, such as specified participation rates for victims (Masters 2005). Interventions based on the principles of reconciliation and 'making good' are most likely to be effective when they are carefully planned and have genuine meaning for those involved, that is the offender, victim and other interested parties (Smith, R. 1985; Dignan 2005), and where the issues to be resolved are mutually agreed and clearly understood. In many cases, these conditions simply cannot be met, for example where the young person's formal 'guilt' is mediated by a history of mutual hostility between different groups within the community.

The constraints of the justice system do not easily lend themselves to dealing with ambiguity and unfinished business, but restorative processes need to avoid the tendency to abstract criminal matters from their personal and social context (see Bradley *et al.* 2006, on the New Zealand experience, too); rather, they must ensure that these are factored into the proceedings – this means ensuring that offenders and victims are enabled to influence the restorative 'agenda', for example, as well as determining more practical issues such as where and when meetings will take place and who should attend.

As well as being largely meaningless for offenders, contrived 'restorative' solutions are also often unsatisfactory for victims, as the initial evaluation of Referral Orders amply demonstrated (Newburn *et al.* 2001). The position of 'corporate' (private or public sector) victims is also problematic, as is the perspective young people may have of such bodies. Thus, for practitioners, the challenge is one of thinking widely and creatively about how to achieve 'restoration' within the constraints of tightly prescribed operational parameters, such as those established by Final Warnings, Referral Orders or Reparation Orders. In contrast to Masters (2005), I would argue that it is clear that a consultative approach is required, which relies on developing a clear understanding of the participants' perspective on the offence, and the ideas young people themselves may have about how to deal with the problems arising from it. They are, indeed, often remorseful, apologetic and willing to make amends, sometimes perhaps because of their own experiences of being victimised, but these responses cannot be extorted from them; it is a process of engagement and dialogue which may, necessarily, take time.

Managing the system and avoiding the tariff

While the introduction of a range of highly prescriptive new orders appears to impose additional constraints on both young people and practitioners, it has also created possibilities for 'system management' (Smith, R. 2002a). The espousal of restorative principles, as well as the 'principal aim' of reducing offending, also appear to have generated support for approaches to intervention which are less tariff-based than in the immediate past. Further steps, such as the proposal to replace the array of community sentences with one 'all-purpose' option – an expanded Action Plan Order (Home Office 2003) also suggest a gradual loosening of the idea that sentences should be progressively more intrusive and punitive.

The principle that sentencing should be 'proportionate' (Youth Justice Board 2000), allied with the range of requirements of sentencers proposed by the Home Office (2003: 4) indicates that the rationale for progressively more severe sentences might have been eroded somewhat. However, this sits rather oddly with the government's apparently continuing 'expansionist' (Fionda 2005: 172) commitment to high levels of custody, and its increasingly 'actuarial' approach to the gradation (Foucault 1979) of risk and seriousness which is a central pillar of sentencing policy (Home Office 2001a; Home Office et al. 2002), and which ensures that young people progress swiftly and surely to the status of 'persistent young offender' with all the implications associated with that particular label.

Despite these tensions, the emerging recognition of the value of 'restorative' approaches does provide some support for alternatives to the narrow actuarialism which pervades much of the youth justice system (Kempf-Leonard and Peterson 2002). It is important that practice reflects this orientation and avoids the tendency to regard 'failure' (such as non-compliance with the terms of a specific order) as an automatic justification for a further escalation of the sanctions applied to any young person. Rather, we should adopt Rutherford's (1992) approach of 'holding on', showing support and commitment to young people in trouble, and offering them opportunities to 'grow out of crime'.

Refocusing: welfare and rights

An intervention strategy that is based on dealing with young people holistically and considering the factors underlying the offence also implies an approach to assessment, planning and intervention that is not driven by the spurious scientific accuracy offered by instruments such as ASSET (Baker et al. 2005). Rather, we should reassert the importance of 'causes', and at the same time reinsert a proper concern with the 'welfare' principles that have been crowded out of the youth justice system (Joint Chief Inspectors 2002).[29]

As well as rediscovering 'welfare', we should also be driven by socially based notions of 'justice' that take proper account of factors such as inequality, poverty and discrimination. Bowling and Phillips (2002), as we have seen, argue that to be genuinely fair, interventions must take account of prior factors such as institutional racism and disadvantage. It is not simply a matter of applying standard rules and procedures even-handedly, but of adjusting these to offset their impact on young people from particular origins. Legislative attempts to introduce equalising principles into judicial processes (such as 'day fines' under the Criminal Justice Act 1991) have not been successful, but it remains open for practitioners and provider agencies to incorporate notions of social as well as criminal justice into their work.

In line with this approach, consideration should be given to bringing 'rights' more explicitly into the practice arena, even where this might prejudice smooth-running and efficiency. As young people become exposed to an ever-increasing armoury of intrusive interventions, some of these applying at pre-trial (and even pre-criminal) stages, agencies must be concerned with the consequences in terms of net-widening (and net-strengthening; Austin and Krisberg 2002). The certainty and security offered by the imposition of ever more stringent bail conditions, tags or curfews should not be gained at the expense of 'proportionality' or basic rights, especially at the pre-trial stage where questions of guilt and responsibility have not been determined. Home visits, for example, are a better, more natural and less oppressive option than electronic tags, and they are certainly less likely to represent a breach of the UN Convention on the Rights of the Child or the Human Rights Act 1998. We must avoid contributing to the furtherance of the 'technologies of control' envisaged by Foucault (1979), and instead pursue an agenda of 'welfare-rights' (Scraton and Haydon 2002) which engages with young people, linking their offending to other aspects of their lives, establishing sensitive and effective working relationships with them and their families.

As we have seen throughout this book, the youth justice system is poorly equipped to do many of the things it claims to, such as preventing crime, meeting victims' needs or administering fair and effective punishment. Those of us concerned with effective practice must recognise these limitations in order to put forward alternative strategies which prioritise bridge-building and solution-finding, rather than social division and oppression. This is not about criminalising young people who offend, but addressing the problems associated with their crimes, both individual and social, in order to find mutually beneficial ways forward.

Lessons from elsewhere

Briefly, before concluding, it will be helpful to reflect on the growing body of evidence from elsewhere which offers some optimistic signs. Buckland and Stevens (2001) suggest, for example, that there are 'significant differences' of approach, even among European countries. These differences are to be found, it seems, at the level of culture, philosophy and purpose, as much as in direct practice (see also Lappi-Seppala 2006; Nelken 2006), even though there is a common fear of increasing punitiveness (Muncie and Goldson 2006).

Some fundamental variations in orientation can be identified. France is held to be less inclined to use custody than England, and the Netherlands has a history of being resistant to the use of imprisonment (Christie 2000), although in both cases these predispositions are under threat, it would seem (Beijerse and Swaaningen 2006; Gendrot 2006). Pitts (2001b) has explicitly contrasted the inclusive philosophy informing youth crime policy and 'Specialised

Prevention' in France and what he calls the 'politics of blame' that underpin New Labour's approach.

Spain and Belgium are identified as being strongly committed to 'welfare approaches' (Buckland and Stevens 2001) which have generally held firm against the punitive drift evident elsewhere (Muncie and Goldson 2006). Diversion of children towards 'social welfare methods', as opposed to punishment, is observed to be the starting position for interventions in Scandinavian countries (Goldson and Muncie 2006b).

Interestingly, too, there is clear evidence of increasing divergence between the countries of Britain and Ireland, with 'diversion' remaining central to strategies in Scotland (Scottish Executive 2002) and Ireland (Seymour 2004; Fionda 2005), and 'welfare' re-emerging as a central theme in Wales (Cross *et al.* 2003). Similarly, the emphasis on community-based justice and locally supported interventions is also evident in both policy and practice in Scotland and Northern Ireland:

> We need youth justice teams to listen to the concerns of local communities to tackle youth crime and to work with communities to identify solutions to reduce crime and the fear of crime. All those who work with young people who offend will know that many young people can be diverted from crime if effective programmes are in place to tackle their behaviour. (Jamieson 2002)

Under the 'unique' non-criminal children's hearings, Scotland has been able to establish a wide range of interventions to deal with youth offending outside the courts (Scottish Executive 2004). In Northern Ireland, long experience of conflict and division has generated a greater willingness to seek communal solutions based in notions of reconciliation (Schrag 2003). As a result, there has been considerable impetus behind a range of imaginative community-based restorative initiatives which have, in turn, received positive initial evaluations (Beckett *et al.* 2005).

While we must not allow ourselves to become too idealistic about positive alternative approaches in evidence elsewhere (for example, the age of criminal responsibility in Scotland is 8, the lowest in Europe, and the custody rate is the highest in Europe; Muncie and Goldson 2006), other countries are able to demonstrate successful outcomes based on principles of diversion and informal offence resolution, just as England and Wales did in the 1980s. In the Netherlands and Germany, there have been long-established mechanisms for dealing with the issues arising from young people's offences outside the court setting (Buckland and Stevens 2001), associated with the higher age of criminal responsibility applying in these countries. Evaluations of such programmes suggest that they are successful on a number of conventional criteria, such as reduced reoffending rates, satisfactory compliance, victim satisfaction and reductions in the use of formal proceedings and punishment measures (Buckland and Stevens 2001).

We must be cautious about the quality of such evidence and we must also avoid drawing lessons uncritically from elsewhere ('criminological tourism'), but this does provide international support for approaches which we already know to have been effective domestically. Such evidence offers further validation for the principles of youth justice outlined in the present book; however, we cannot underestimate the cultural and political barriers to securing progressive change:

> Despite being a universal problem, policies and practices to deal with juvenile delinquency are related to the social, political, historical and cultural context of the countries in which they are located. This is therefore likely to impact upon the extent to which they can be transformed. (Buckland and Stevens 2001: 6)

While recognising the obstacles, I have sought to set out here some creative possibilities for intervention at all levels of the justice system to promote inclusive, anti-oppressive and rights-based practice. The aim of the first edition was 'to generate some inspiration for reinventing' diversionary, problem-solving, negotiated forms of youth justice which would act as the touchstone for all aspects of the process, and in this context I referred to the lessons of earlier years. To these can be added the emergent models of good practice from elsewhere, and on this basis, I can only express again my belief that what is most needed now is for us to 'reinvent the wheel'.

Notes

1. Prior to its abolition by section 31 of the Crime and Disorder Act 1998, the common law presumption of *doli incapax* was that children aged between 10 and 14 involved in criminal proceedings were not fully aware of the difference between right and wrong, and were thus incapable of acting with criminal intent unless it could be proved otherwise.
2. Superseded subsequently by sections 90/91 of the Powers of Criminal Courts (Sentencing) Act 2000.
3. More recent evidence (Kemp *et al.* 2002) re-examines and questions this perception, suggesting that action short of a prosecution is likely to be more effective than prosecution itself in reducing reoffending by young people, irrespective of any other potential benefits, even when administered for offences committed subsequent to their third or fourth criminal 'proceedings'.
4. One example of an increasing divergence between England and Wales in terms of social policy developments has been the growing use of different terminology to describe apparently similar programmes. The Welsh equivalent of the Connexions Service was launched under the heading 'Extending Entitlement' (National Assembly for Wales 2000).
5. Although this provision was implemented under the Crime and Disorder Act 1998, the Children Act 2004 modified the Child Safety Order so that care proceedings could no longer be instituted for failure to comply – on the basis that it contravened the principles and procedures of the earlier Children Act 1989.
6. A study carried out by Graham and Bowling (1985).
7. 'Speeding up' youth justice was one of the five core pledges made by Labour in its 1997 election campaign.
8. Replacing Community Service and Probation Orders under the Criminal Justice and Court Services Act 2000.
9. Sections 90/91 Powers of Criminal Courts (Sentencing) Act 2000 provide crown courts with the power to make longer custodial sentences where deemed appropriate.
10. These became Youth Offender Panels under the subsequent legislation.
11. Although note recent concerns about a possible 'punitive turn' in the youth justice sphere, even in Scotland (Piacentini and Walters 2006).
12. The extent to which the countries of the United Kingdom are now characterised by markedly different philosophies, policies and practices in youth justice, as in other policy areas, is an important issue, it should be acknowledged.

13. The first edition of these standards in 2000 was issued on behalf of the Youth Justice Board, Home Office, Department for Education and Employment (as it was then), Department of Health, Lord Chancellor's Department and the National Assembly for Wales (now the Welsh Assembly Government).

14. At the time of publication of the revised standards (2004), this list included: Referral, Reparation, Action Plan, Parenting, Supervision, Community Punishment and Rehabilitation, Attendance Centre, Drug Treatment and Testing, Curfew, Anti-Social Behaviour and Child Safety Orders.

15. Community Safety Partnerships in Wales.

16. This was subsequently amended under the Children Act 2004 for England, to include 'a person with experience of social work' and 'a person with experience in education' both to be nominated by the Director of Children's Services.

17. The gravity factor system is a basic scoring device to determine whether an offence merits a Reprimand, Final Warning or, in some cases, prosecution (Home Office 2000b).

18. It was later consolidated in the Powers of Criminal Courts (Sentencing) Act 2000.

19. In this context, 'reoffending' covers offenders who received a subsequent formal disposal of any kind for an offence.

20. While such associations have been found, it is much harder to demonstrate causal connections (Anderson *et al.*, 2001), although these are sometimes assumed with limited justification.

21. It is worth reminding ourselves here that the abolition of custody for children and young people seemed a realistic possibility as recently as the early 1990s.

22. Regrettably, successive reports by the UN Committee on the Rights of the Child suggest that the UK government has not met its obligations in relation to youth justice under the UN Convention (Fionda 2005: 170).

23. The 'What do you think?' section in the revised ASSET represents little more than an afterthought.

24. We might expect, too, that increased attention directed by justice agencies recently towards young Muslims will be a matter of concern in this respect (see http://www.ihrc.org.uk/show.php?id=1149).

25. Indeed, in 2005 the criteria for admission to the ISSP were strengthened somewhat.

26. The Children and Young Persons Act 1969 included provisions which would have effectively raised the age of criminal responsibility to 14, but these were never implemented.

27. It is also interesting to note that the Audit Commission (2004: 34) has identified a positive relationship between courts' level of confidence in local youth justice services and low use of custodial sentences.

28. Despite these critical comments, it was perhaps surprising that YOTs were applauded for their collaborative practice only a short while later by the Chief Inspector of Probation (Bridges 2004).

29. Although it is noteworthy that the *All Wales Youth Offending Strategy* issued jointly by the Welsh Assembly Government and the Youth Justice Board in 2004 was much more welfare-oriented than anything comparable in England.

Bibliography

Abel, R. (1982) 'The contradictions of informal justice', in Abel, R. (ed.), *The Politics of Informal Justice, Vol. 1*. London: Academic Press, pp. 267–320.

Allan, R. (2001) 'Why ASSET must be a real asset for Yots', *Youth Justice Board News*, June, p. 3

Allen, R. (2004) 'What works in changing public attitudes: lessons from rethinking crime and punishment', *Journal for Crime, Conflict and the Media*, 1 (3): 55–67.

Althusser, L. (1977) *Lenin and Philosophy and Other Essays*. London: NLB.

Anderson, B., Beinart, S., Farrington, D., Longman, J., Sturgis, P. and Utting, D. (2001) *Risk and Protective Factors Associated with Youth Crime and Effective Interventions to Prevent It*. London: Youth Justice Board.

Annison, J. (2005) 'Risk and protection', in Bateman, T. and Pitts, J. (eds), *The RHP Companion to Youth Justice*. Lyme Regis: Russell House Press, pp. 119–24.

Armstrong, D., Hine, J., Hacking, S., Armaos, R., Jones, R., Klessinger, N. and France, A. (2005) *Children, Risk and Crime: The On Track Youth Lifestyles Surveys*. London: Home Office.

Ashton, J. and Grindrod, M. (1999) 'Institutional troubleshooting: lessons for policy and practice' in Goldson, B. (ed.), *Youth Justice: Contemporary Policy and Practice*. Aldershot: Ashgate, pp. 170–90.

Association of Directors of Social Services, Local Government Association and Youth Justice Board (2003) *The Application of the Children Act 1989 to Children in Young Offender Institutions*. London: ADSS.

Audit Commission (1996) *Misspent Youth*. London: Audit Commission.

Audit Commission (2002) *Community Safety Partnerships: Learning from Audit, Inspection and Research*. London: Stationery Office.

Audit Commission (2004) *Youth Justice 2004*. London: Stationery Office.

Austin, J. and Krisberg, B. (2002) 'Wider, stronger and different nets: the dialectics of criminal justice reform', in Muncie, J., Hughes, G. and McLaughlin, E. (eds), *Youth Justice: Critical Readings*. London: Sage, pp. 258–74.

Bailey, R. and Williams, B. (2000) *Inter-Agency Partnerships in Youth Justice: Implementing the Crime and Disorder Act 1998*. Joint Unit for Social Services Research, University of Sheffield.

Baker, K. (2004) 'Is ASSET really an asset? Risk assessment of young offenders', in Burnett, R. and Roberts, C. (eds), *What Works in Probation and Youth Justice?* Cullompton: Willan, pp. 70–87.

Baker, K. (2005) 'Assessment in youth justice: professional discretion and the use of Asset', *Youth Justice*, 5 (2): 106–22.

Baker, K., Jones, S., Appleton, C. and Roberts, C. (n.d.) *Assessment, Planning Interventions and Supervision*. London: Youth Justice Board.

Baker, K., Jones, S., Merrington, S. and Roberts, C. (2005) *Further Development of ASSET*. London: Youth Justice Board.

Baker, K., Jones, S., Roberts, C. and Merrington, S. (2002) *Validity and Reliability of Asset*. London: Youth Justice Board.

Baker, K., Jones, S., Roberts, C. and Merrington, S. (2003) *ASSET: The Evaluation of the Validity and Reliability of the Youth Justice Board's Assessment for Young Offenders*. London: Youth Justice Board.

Bandura, A. (1976) *Social Learning Theory*. New York: Prentice Hall.

Barclay, G. and Mhlanga, B. (2000) *Ethnic Differences in Decisions on Young Defendants Dealt With by the Crown Prosecution Service*. London: Home Office.

Barclay, G., Munley, A. and Muntom, T. (2005) *Race* and the *Criminal Justice System: An Overview to the Complete Statistics 2000–2004*. London: Home Office

Batchelor, S. and McNeill, F. (2005) 'The young person-worker relationship', in Bateman, T. and Pitts, J. (eds), *The Russell House Companion to Youth Justice*. Lyme Regis: Russell House, pp. 166–71.

Bateman, T. (2005a) 'Reducing child imprisonment: a systemic challenge', *Youth Justice*, 5 (2): 91–104.

Bateman, T. (2005b) 'Court reports' in Bateman, T. and Pitts, J. (eds), *The RHP Companion to Youth Justice*. Lyme Regis: Russell House Press, pp. 113–18.

Bateman, T. (2006) 'Youth crime and justice: statistical "evidence", recent trends and responses', in Goldson, B. and Muncie, J. (eds), *Youth Crime and Justice*. London: Sage, pp. 65–77.

Bateman, T. and Pitts, J. (2005) 'Conclusion: what the evidence tells us', in Bateman, T. and Pitts, J. (eds) *The RHP Companion to Youth Justice*. Lyme Regis: Russell House Press, pp. 248–58.

Beaumont, C. (2005) 'Work with young people whose offending is persistent: Intensive Supervision and Surveillance Programmes', in Bateman, T. and Pitts, J. (eds), *The RHP Companion to Youth Justice*. Lyme Regis: Russell House Press, pp. 137–43.

Beck, U. (1992) *Risk Society*. London: Sage.

Becker, H. (1963) *The Outsiders*. New York: Free Press.

Beckett, H., Campbell, C., O'Mahony, D., Jackson, J. and Doak, J. (2005) *Interim Evaluation of the Northern Ireland Youth Conferencing Scheme*. Belfast: Northern Ireland Office.

Beijerse, J. u. and Swaaningen, R. v. (2006) 'The Netherlands: penal welfarism and risk management', in Muncie, J. and Goldson, B. (eds), *Comparative Youth Justice*. London: Sage, pp. 65–78.

Bell, A., Hodgson, M. and Pragnell, S. (1999) 'Diverting children and young people from crime and the criminal justice system', in Goldson, B. (ed.), *Youth Justice: Contemporary Police and Practice*. London: Ashgate.

Benedict, R. (1961) *Patterns of Culture*. London: Routledge.

Bentley, M. (2000) 'An English magistrate's view of Scottish youth justice', in Pickford, J. (ed.), *Youth Justice: Theory and Practice*. London: Cavendish Publishing, pp. 189–216.

Berridge, D., Brodie, I., Pitts, J., Porteous, D. and Tarling, R. (2001) *The Independent Effects of Permanent Exclusion from School on the Offending Careers of Young People*. London: Home Office.

Blagg, H. (1985) 'Reparation and justice for juveniles', *British Journal of Criminology*, 25: 267–79.

Blagg, H., Derricourt, N., Finch, J. and Thorpe, D. (1986) *The Final Report on the Juvenile Liaison Bureau Corby*. Lancaster: University of Lancaster.

Blair, T. (1993) 'Why crime is a Socialist issue', *New Statesman*, 29 January, pp. 27–8.

Blair, T. (1997) Speech at Stockwell Park School, 8 December.

Blair, T. (2002) 'Rebalancing of criminal justice system', Speech, 18 June.

Blunkett, D. (2002) Statement on street crime, 20 March.

Bottoms, A. (1977) 'Reflections on the renaissance of dangerousness', *Howard Journal*, 16: 70–96.

Bottoms, A. (1995) *Intensive Community Supervision of Young Offenders: Outcomes, Process and Cost*. Cambridge: University of Cambridge Institute of Criminology.

Bottoms, A. (2005) 'Methodology matters', *Safer Society*, Summer, pp. 10–12.

Bottoms, A., Brown, P., McWilliams, B., McWilliams, W. and Nellis, M. (1990) *Intermediate Treatment and Juvenile Justice*. London, HMSO.

Bowling, B. and Phillips, C. (2002) *Racism, Crime and Justice*. Harlow: Longman.

Bradley, T., Tauri, J. and Walters, R. (2006) 'Demythologising youth justice in Aotearoa/New Zealand', in Muncie, J. and Goldson, B. (eds), *Comparative Youth Justice*. London: Sage, pp. 79–95.

Bridges, A. (2004) *Joint Inspection of Youth Offending Teams: The First Phase Annual Report 2004*. London: HM Inspectorate of Probation.

Bright, M. (2002) 'Suicide fear for teen victims of Blunkett's get-tough rules', *Observer*, 7 July, p. 12

British Institute for Brain Injured Children (2005) *Ain't Misbehavin'*. London: BIBIC.

Britton, N. (2000) *Black Justice? Race, Criminal Justice and Identity*. Stoke-on-Trent: Trentham Books.

Brown, S. (1998) *Understanding Youth and Crime*. Buckingham: Open University Press.

Brown, S. (2005) *Understanding Youth and Crime*, 2nd edn. Buckingham: Open University Press.

Buckland, G. and Stevens, A. (2001) *Review of Effective Practice with Young Offenders in Mainland Europe*. Canterbury: European Institute of Social Services.

Budd, T. and Sharp, C. (2005) 'Offending in England and Wales: first results from the 2003 Crime and Justice Survey', *Findings 244*. London: Home Office.

Budd, T. and Sims, L. (2001) *Antisocial Behaviour and Disorder: Findings from the 2000 British Crime Survey*. London: Home Office.

Budd, T., Sharp, C., Weir, G., Wilson, D. and Owen, N. (2005) *Young People and Crime: Findings from the 2004 Offending, Crime and Justice Survey*. London: Home Office.

Burnett, R. and Appleton, C. (2004) 'Joined-up services to tackle youth crime', *British Journal of Criminology*, 44: 34–54.

Burnett, R. and Roberts, C. (2004) *What Works in Probation and Youth Justice*. Cullompton: Willan.

Burney, E. (2002) 'Talking tough, acting coy: what happened to the Anti-Social Behaviour Order?', *Howard Journal*, 41 (5): 469–84.

Burney, E. (2005) *Making People Behave*. Cullompton: Willan.

Cadman, S. (2005) 'Proportionality in the youth justice system', in Bateman, T. and Pitts, J. (eds), *The RHP Companion to Youth Justice*. Lyme Regis: Russell House Press, pp. 59–64.

Campbell, S. (2002) *A Review of Anti-Social Behaviour Orders*. London: Home Office.

Carlile, L. (2006) *An Independent Inquiry into the Use of Physical Restraint, Solitary Confinement and Forcible Strip Searching of Children in Prisons, Secure Training Centres and Local Authority Secure Children's Homes*. London: Howard League.

Chapman, B., Mirrlees-Black, C. and Brawn, C. (2002) *Improving Public Attitudes to the Criminal Justice System: The Impact of Information*. London: Home Office.

Charman, J. and Savage, S. (1999) 'The new politics of law and order: Labour, crime and justice', in Powell, M. (ed.), *New Labour, New Welfare State?* Bristol: Policy Press, pp. 191–212.

Cheetham, J. (1985) 'Juvenile offenders and alternatives to custody in Northamptonshire: the views of magistrates and social workers', unpublished.

Children and Young People's Unit (2001) *Building a Strategy for Children and Young People*. London: Children and Young People's Unit.

Children and Young People's Unit (2002) *Children's Fund*. Available online at: http://www.cypu.gov.uk/corporate/childrensfund/ontrack.cfm.

Children's Society (1988) *The Line of Least Resistance*. London: Children's Society.

Children's Society (1992) *Education for Citizenship: A Schools' Pack*. London: Children's Society.

Children's Society (1993) *A False Sense of Security*. London: Children's Society.

Children's Society (2004) *Response to the Youth Justice Board for England and Wales 'Strategy for the Secure Estate for Juveniles: Building on the Foundations'*. Available online at: http://www.the-childrenssociety.org.uk/media/pdf/FINALYJBStrategyTCSresponse.pdf.

Christie, N. (2000) *Crime Control as Industry*. London: Routledge.

Cicourel. A. (1968) *The Social Organisation of Juvenile Justice*. London: Heinemann.

Clancy, A., Hough, M., Aust, R. and Kershaw, C. (2001) *Ethnic Minorities' Experience of Crime and Policing: Findings from the 2000 British Crime Survey*. London: Home Office.

Clark, T. (2002) 'New Labour's big idea: joined-up government', *Social Policy and Society*, 12: 107–17.

Clarke, J. (2002) 'Whose justice? The politics of juvenile control', in Muncie, J., Hughes, G., and McLaughlin, E. (eds), *Youth Justice: Critical Readings*. London: Sage, pp. 284–95.

Clarke, J., Gewirtz, S. and McLaughlin, E. (eds) (2000) *New Managerialism New Welfare?* London: Sage.

Cohen, S. (1972) *Folk Devils and Moral Panics*. London: Paladin.

Cohen, S. (1985) *Visions of Social Control*. Cambridge: Polity Press.

Commission for Social Care Inspection (2005) *Making Every Child Matter*. London: Commission for Social Care Inspection.

Conservative Party (1979) *General Election Manifesto*. London: Conservative Party.

Corrigan, P. (1979) *Schooling the Smash Street Kids*. London: Macmillan.

Corrigan, P. and Leonard, P. (1978) *Social Work Practice Under Capitalism: A Marxist Approach*. London: Macmillan.

Craine, S. (1997) 'The "Black Magic Roundabout": cyclical transitions, social exclusion and alternative careers', in MacDonald, R. (ed.), *Youth, the 'Underclass' and Social Exclusion*. London: Routledge, pp. 130–52.

Crawford, A. and Burden, T. (2005) 'Involving victims in referral orders and Youth Offender Panels: an evaluation of Leeds Youth Service', in Centre for Criminal Justice Studies, *Criminal Justice Review 2004–2005*. Leeds: Centre for Criminal Justice Studies.

Crawford, A. and Newburn, T. (2003) *Youth Offending and Restorative Justice*. Cullompton: Willan.

Crime Concern (2001) *Reducing Neighbourhood Crime*. Swindon: Crime Concern.

Cross, N., Evans, J. and Minkes, J. (2003) 'Still children first? Developments in youth justice in Wales', *Youth Justice*, 2 (3): 151–62.

Crowley, A. (1998) *A Criminal Waste*. London: Children's Society.

Davies, B. (1986) *Threatening Youth*. Milton Keynes: Open University Press.

Davis, G., Boucherat, J. and Watson, D. (1988) 'Reparation in the service of diversion: the subordination of a good idea', *British Journal of Criminology*, 27: 127–34.

Davis, G., Boucherat, J. and Watson, D. (1989) 'Pre-court decision-making in juvenile justice', *British Journal of Criminology*, 29: 219–35.

Department for Education and Skills (2003) *Every Child Matters*. London: DfES.

Department for Education and Skills (2004) *Every Child Matters: Next Steps*. London: DfES.

Department for Education and Skills (2005) *Youth Matters*. London: DfES.

Department for Education and Skills (2006) *The Common Assessment Framework for Children and Young People: Practitioners' Guide*. London: DfES.

Department of Health (2000) *Framework for the Assessment of Children in Need and Their Families*. London: Stationery Office.

Department of Health and Social Security (1983) *Further Development of Intermediate Treatment*, Local Authority Circular 83(3). London: DHSS.

Dignan, J. (1992) 'Repairing the damage: can reparation work in the service of diversion?', *British Journal of Criminology*, 32: 453–72.

Dignan, J. (2000) *Interim Report on Reparative Work and Youth Offending Teams*. London: Home Office.

Dignan, J. (2005) *Understanding Victims and Restorative Justice*. Maidenhead: Open University Press.

Dominelli, L. (1998) 'Anti-oppressive practice in context', in Adams, R., Dominelli, L. and Payne, M. (eds), *Social Work: Themes, Issues and Critical Debates*. Basingstoke: Macmillan, pp. 3–22.

Donzelot, J. (1979) *The Policing of Families*. Baltimore, MD: Johns Hopkins University Press.

Drakeford, M. and McCarthy, K. (2000) 'Parents, responsibility and the New Youth Justice', in Goldson, B. (ed.), *The New Youth Justice*. Lyme Regis: Russell House, pp. 96–114.

Eadie, T. and Canton, R. (2002) 'Practising in a context of ambivalence: the challenge for youth justice workers', *Youth Justice*, 2 (1): 14–26.

Earle, R. and Newburn, T. (2002) 'Creative tensions? Young offenders, restorative justice and the introduction of Referral Orders', *Youth Justice*, 1 (3): 3–13.

East, K. and Campbell, S. (2000) *Aspects of Crime: Young Offenders 1999*. London: Home Office.

Eccles, P. (2001) *Youth Inclusion – The Programme Most Likely?* Discussion paper, University of Huddersfield, Huddersfield.

Erikson, E. (1995) *Childhood and Society*. London: Vintage.

Eriksson, A. (2006) 'The politicisation of community restorative justice in Northern Ireland'. Available online at: http://www.restorativejustice.org/editions/2006/april06/erikssonarticle.

Ernst & Young (1999) *Reducing Delay in the Criminal Justice System: Evaluation of the Pilot Schemes*. London: Home Office.

Esping-Andersen, G. (1990) *The Three Worlds of Welfare Capitalism*. Oxford: Polity Press.

Evans, R. and Ellis, R. (1997) *Police Cautioning in the 1990s*. London: Home Office.

Everitt, A. and Hardiker, P. (1996) *Evaluating for Good Practice*. London: Macmillan.

Family Rights Group, Family Welfare Association and Parentline Plus (2003) *Every Child Matters: A Joint Response*. London: FRG/FWA/Parentline Plus.

Farrington, D. (1996) *Understanding and Preventing Youth Crime*. York: Joseph Rowntree Foundation.

Farrington, D., Ditchfield, J., Hancock, G., Howard, P., Jolliffe, D., Livingston, M. and Painter, K. (2002) *Evaluation of Two Intensive Regimes for Young Offenders*. London: Home Office.

Feilzer, M. (2002) *Cognitive Behavioural Projects in Youth Justice*. Oxford: Centre for Criminological Research.

Feilzer, M. and Hood, R. (2004) *Differences or Discrimination?* London: Youth Justice Board.

Feilzer, M., Appleton, C., Roberts, C. and Hoyle, C. (2004) *Cognitive Behaviour Projects: The National Evaluation of the Youth Justice Board's Cognitive Behaviour Projects*. London: Youth Justice Board.

Fionda, J. (2005) *Devils and Angels: Youth Policy and Crime*. London: Hart.

Fletcher, H. (2005) *ASBOs: An Analysis of the First 6 Years*. London: ASBOConcern/ Napo.

Foster, J., Newburn, T. and Souhami, A. (2005) *Assessing the Impact of the Stephen Lawrence Inquiry*. London: Home Office.

Foucault, M. (1979) *Discipline and Punish*. Harmondsworth: Peregrine.

Foucault, M. (1981) *The History of Sexuality, Vol. 1, The Will to Knowledge*. London: Pelican.

Fox Harding, L. (1997) *Perspectives in Child Care Policy*, 2nd edn. Harlow: Longman.

France, A. and Crow, I. (200) *CTC – The Story So Far*. York: Joseph Rowntree Foundation.

Gamble, A. (1988) *The Free Economy and the Strong State*. Basingstoke: Macmillan.

Garland, D. (1990) *Punishment and Modern Society*. Oxford: Clarendon Press.

Garland, D. (2001) *The Culture of Control*. Oxford: Oxford University Press.

Gelsthorpe, L. and Morris, A. (2002) 'Restorative youth justice: the last vestiges of welfare?', in Muncie, J., Hughes, G. and McLaughlin, E. (eds), *Youth Justice: Critical Readings*. London: Sage.

Gelsthorpe, L. and Sharpe, G. (2006) 'Gender, youth crime and justice', in Goldson, B. and Muncie, J. (eds), *Youth Crime and Justice*. London: Sage, pp. 47–61.

Gendrot, S. (2006) 'France: the politicization of youth justice', in Muncie, J. and Goldson, B. (eds), *Comparative Youth Justice*. London: Sage, pp. 48–64.

George, V. and Wilding, P. (1999) *British Society and Social Welfare: Towards a Sustainable Society*. Basingstoke: Macmillan.

Giddens, A. (1991) *Modernity and Self-Identity*. Cambridge: Polity.

Gilroy, P. (2002) 'Lesser breeds without the law', in Muncie, J., Hughes, G. and McLaughlin, E. (eds), *Youth Justice: Critical Readings*. London: Sage, pp. 50–67.

Goldblatt, P. and Lewis, C. (eds) *Reducing Offending: An Assessment of Research Evidence on Ways of Dealing with Offending Behaviour*. London: Home Office.

Goldson, B. (1997) 'Children, crime, policy and practice: neither welfare nor justice', *Children and Society*, 11: 77–88.

Goldson, B. (1999) 'Youth (in)justice: contemporary developments in policy and practice', in Goldson, B. (ed.), *Youth Justice: Contemporary Policy and Practice*. Aldershot: Ashgate, pp. 1–29.

Goldson, B. (2000a) 'Whither diversion? Interventionism and the new youth justice', in Goldson, B. (ed.), *The New Youth Justice*. Lyme Regis: Russell House, pp. 35–57.

Goldson, B. (ed.) (2000b) *The New Youth Justice*. Lyme Regis: Russell House.

Goldson, B. (2002) *Vulnerable Inside*. London: Children's Society.

Goldson, B. (2005) 'Taking liberties: policy and the punitive turn', in Hendrick, H. (ed.), *Child Welfare and Social Policy*. Bristol: Policy Press, pp. 271–87.

Goldson, B. (2006) 'Penal custody: intolerance, irrationality and indifference', in Goldson, B. and Muncie, J. (eds), *Youth Crime and Justice*. London: Sage, London, pp. 139–56.

Goldson, B. and Chigwada-Bailey, R. (1999) '(What) justice for black children and young people?', in Goldson, B. (ed.), *Youth Justice: Contemporary Policy and Practice*. Aldershot: Ashgate, pp. 51–74.

Goldson, B. and Coles, D. (2005) *In the Care of the State?* London: Inquest.

Goldson, B. and Muncie, J. (2006a) 'Critical anatomy: towards a principled youth justice', in Goldson, B. and Muncie, J. (eds), *Youth Crime and Justice*. London: Sage, pp. 203–31.

Goldson, B. and Muncie, J. (2006b) 'Rethinking youth justice: comparative analysis, international human rights and research evidence', *Youth Justice*, 6 (2): 91–106.

Goldson, B. and Peters, E. (2000) *Tough Justice: Responding to Children in Trouble*. London: Children's Society.

Gordon, P. (1983) *White Law: Racism in the Police, Courts and Prisons*. London: Pluto Press.

Graham, J. and Bowling, B. (1995) *Young People and Crime*. London: Home Office.

Gramsci, A. (1971) *Selections from Prison Notebooks*. London: Lawrence & Wishart.

Gray, E., Taylor, E., Roberts, C., Merrington, S., Fernandez, R. and Moore, R. (2005) *Intensive Supervision and Surveillance Programme: The Final Report*. London: Youth Justice Board.

Greater Manchester Police Authority (2002) *Consultation for Best Value: Young People*. Available online at: http://www.gmpa.gov.uk/consultation/young_people.htm.

Green, D. (2004) *The Intensive Supervision and Surveillance Programme*. Available online at: http://www.civitas.org.uk/pdf/issp.pdf.

Haines, K. (2000) 'Referral Orders and Youth Offender Panels: restorative approaches and the new youth justice', in Goldson, B. (ed.), *The New Youth Justice*. Lyme Regis: Russell House, pp. 58–80.

Haines, K. and Drakeford, M. (1998) *Young People and Youth Justice*. London: Macmillan.

Haines, K. and O'Mahony, D. (2006) 'Restorative approaches, young people and youth justice', in Goldson, B. and Muncie, J. (eds), *Youth Crime and Justice*. London: Sage, pp. 110–24.

Hall, S., Critcher, C., Jefferson, T., Clarke, J. and Roberts, B. (1978) *Policing the Crisis: Mugging, the State and Law and Order*. Basingstoke: Macmillan.

Hancock, L. (1999) 'Community and state responses to crime and disorder: conflict, compromise and contradiction', in *The British Criminology Conferences: Selected Proceedings*, Vol. 2. Papers from the British Criminology Conference, Queens University, Belfast, 15–19 July, 1997. Available online at: http://www.britsoccrim.org/volume2/002.pdf.

Hancock, L. (2001) *Community, Crime and Disorder: Safety and Regeneration in Urban Neighbourhoods*. Basingstoke: Palgrave.

Hancock, L. (2006) 'Urban regeneration, young people, crime and criminalisation', in Goldson, B. and Muncie, J. (eds), *Youth Crime and Justice*. London: Sage, pp. 172–86.

Harris, R. and Webb, D. (1987) *Welfare, Power and Juvenile Justice*. London: Tavistock.

Harvey, R. (2002) 'The UK before the UN Committee on the Rights of the Child', *Childright*, 190: 3.

Hazel, N., Hagell, A. and Brazier, L. (2002) *Young Offenders' Perceptions of their Experiences in the Criminal Justice System*. London: Policy Research Bureau.

Hearne, B. (2003) Speech to Nacro Annual Conference, Loughborough University, 10 April.

Hine, J. (2004) *Children and Citizenship*. London: Home Office.

Hine, J. and Celnick, A. (2001) *A One Year Reconviction Study of Final Warnings*. Sheffield: University of Sheffield.

Hinks, N. and Sloper, G. (1984) 'How to divert in practice', in Fox, H. and Williams, R. (eds), *Diversion – Corporate Action with Juveniles*. Northampton: Northamptonshire County Council, pp. 30–4.

HM Chief Inspector of Prisons (2001) *Annual Report 1999–2000*. London: Stationery Office.

HM Chief Inspector of Prisons (2002) 'Preface', in HM Inspectorate of Prisons, *Report on an Unannounced Follow-Up Inspection of HM Prison Eastwood Park*. London: HM Inspectorate of Prisons, pp. 2–5.

HM Chief Inspector of Prisons (2004) *Report on an Announced Inspection of HMP Eastwood Park 22–26 September 2003*. London: Home Office.

Hodgson, P. and Webb, D. (2005) 'Young people, crime and school exclusion: a case of some surprises', *Howard Journal*, 44 (1): 12–28.

Holdaway, S. and Desborough, S. (2004) *The National Evaluation of the Youth Justice Board's Final Warning Projects*. London: Youth Justice Board.

Holdaway, S., Davidson, N., Dignan, J., Hammersley, R., Hine, J. and Marsh, P. (2001) *New Strategies to Address Youth Offending: The National Evaluation of the Pilot Youth Offending Teams*. London: Home Office.

Home Affairs Committee (1993) *Juvenile Offenders*. London: HMSO.

Home Office (1968) *Children in Trouble*. London: HMSO.

Home Office (1980) *Young Offenders*. London: HMSO.

Home Office (1984) *Cautioning by the Police: A Consultative Document*. London: Home Office.

Home Office (1985) *The Cautioning of Offenders*, Home Office Circular 14/1985. London: Home Office.

Home Office (1988) *Punishment, Custody and the Community*. London: HMSO.

Home Office (1990a) *The Cautioning of Offenders*, Home Officer Circular, 59/1990. London: Home Office.

Home Office (1990b) *Crime, Justice and Protecting the Public*. London: HMSO.

Home Office (1992) *National Standards for the Supervision of Offenders in the Community*. London: Home Office.

Home Office (1994) *The Cautioning of Offenders*, Home Office Circular 18/94. London: Home Office.

Home Office (1995) *Strengthening Punishment in the Community*. London: HMSO.

Home Office (1997a) *Consultation Paper: Tackling Youth Crime*. London: Home Office.

Home Office (1997b) *No More Excuses*, Cm 3809. London: Home Office.

Home Office (1998) *Youth Justice: The Statutory Principal Aim of Preventing Offending by Children and Young People*. London: Home Office.

Home Office (2000) *Crime and Disorder Act 1998 – Community-Based Orders*. London: Home Office.

Home Office (2001a) *Criminal Justice: The Way Ahead*, Cm 5074. London: Home Office.

Home Office (2001b) *Criminal Statistics England and Wales 2000*. London: Stationery Office.

Home Office (2001c) *Establishing Referral Order Schemes: A Guidance Note for Youth Offending Teams*. London: Home Office.

Home Office (2002a) *Criminal Justice and Police Act 2001: Electronic Monitoring of 12–16 Year Olds on Bail and on Remand to Local Authority Accommodation*. London: Home Office.

Home Office (2002b) *Criminal Justice and Police Act 2001 Section 130 Guidance – Secure Remands*. London: Home Office.

Home Office (2002c) *Race and the Criminal Justice System*. London: Home Office.

Home Office (2002d) *A Guide to Anti-Social Behaviour Orders and Acceptable Behaviour Contracts*. London: Home Office.

Home Office (2003a) *Respect and Responsibility – Taking a Stand against Anti-Social Behaviour*. London: Home Office.

Home Office (2003b) *Youth Justice – The Next Steps*. London: Home Office.

Home Office (2004a) *Every Child Matters: Change for Children in the Criminal Justice System*. London: Stationery Office.

Home Office (2004b) *Every Child Matters: Next Steps*, Annex B. Available online at: http://www.homeoffice.gov.uk/justice/sentencing/youthjustice/index.html.

Home Office (2004c) *Statistics on Women and the Criminal Justice System*. London: Home Office.

Home Office (2004d) *Confident Communities in a Secure Britain*. London: Home Office.

Home Office (2005a) *Criminal Statistics*. London: Stationery Office.

Home Office (2005b) *Sentencing Statistics*. London: Stationery Office.

Home Office, Department of Health, Department for Education and Employment and Welsh Office (1998) *Establishing Youth Offending Teams*. London: Home Office.

Home Office, Lord Chancellor's Department, Attorney General's Office (2002) *Justice for All*, Cm5563. London: Stationery Office.

Hope, T. (1998) 'Community crime prevention', in Goldblatt, P. and Lewis, C. (eds), *Reducing Offending: An Assessment of Research Evidence on Ways of Dealing with Offending Behaviour*. London: Home Office, pp. 51–62.

Hough, M. and Mayhew, P. (1985) *Taking Account of Crime: Key Findings from the 1984 British Crime Survey*. London: Home Office.

Hough, M. and Roberts, J. (1998) *Attitudes to Punishment: Findings from the British Crime Survey*. London: Home Office.

Hough, M. and Roberts, J. (2004) *Youth Crime and Youth Justice*. Bristol: Policy Press.

Howard, M. (1995) Speech to Conservative Party Conference.

Howard League (2002) *Children in Prison: Provision and Practice at Ashfield*. London: Howard League for Penal Reform.

Hoyle, C. (2002) 'Securing restorative justice for "non-participating" victims', in Hoyle, C. and Young, R. (eds), *New Visions of Crime Victims*. Oxford: Hart, pp. 97–128.

Hudson, B. (1987) *Justice Through Punishment*. Basingstoke: Macmillan.

Hudson, B. (1996) *Understanding Justice*. Buckingham: Open University Press.

Hughes, G. and Follett, M. (2006) 'Community safety, youth and the "anti-social"', in Goldson, B. and Muncie, J. (eds), *Youth Crime and Justice*. London: Sage, pp. 157–71.

Hughes, G., Pilkington, A. and Ruchira, L. (1996) *An Independent Evaluation of the Northamptonshire Diversion Unit*. Milton Keynes: Open University.

Ignatieff, M. (1985) 'State, civil society and total institutions: a critique of recent social histories of punishment', in Cohen, S. and Scull, A. (eds), *Social Control and the State*. Oxford: Blackwell.

Jackson, S. (1999) 'Family group conferences and youth justice: the new panacea?', in Goldson, B. (ed.), *Youth Justice: Contemporary Policy and Practice*. Aldershot: Ashgate.

Jamieson, C. (2002) *Youth Justice in Scotland: A Progress report for All Those Working for Young People*. Available online at: http://www.scotland.gov.uk/library5/justice/tycs-oo.asp.

Jamieson, J. (2005) 'New Labour, youth justice and the question of respect', *Youth Justice*, 5 (3): 180–93.

Jeffs, T. (1997) 'Changing their ways: youth work and "underclass" theory', in MacDonald, R. (ed.), *Youth, the 'Underclass' and Social Exclusion*. London: Routledge, pp. 153–66.

Jenks, C. (1996) *Childhood*. London: Routledge.

Jennings, D. (2002) *One Year Juvenile Reconviction Rates: July 2000 Cohort*. London: Home Office.

Jennings, D. (2003) *One Year Juvenile Reconviction Rates: First Quarter of 2001 Cohort*. London: Home Office.

Jessop, B. (n.d.) *From Thatcherism to New Labour: Neo-Liberalism, Workfarism, and Labour Market Regulation*. Available online at: http://www.lancs.ac.uk/fss/sociology/papers/jessop-from-thatcherism-to-new-labour.pdf.

Johnson, K. and colleagues (2001) *Cautions, Court Proceedings and Sentencing*. London: Home Office.

Johnstone, G. (2002) *Restorative Justice: Ideas, Values, Debates*. Cullompton: Willan.

Joint Chief Inspectors (2002) *Safeguarding Children*. London: Department of Health.

Joint Chief Inspectors (2005) *Safeguarding Children: The Second Joint Chief Inspectors' Report on Arrangements to Safeguard Children*. Newcastle: Commission for Social Care Inspection.

Jones, D. (2001) 'Questioning New Labour's youth justice strategy: a review article', *Youth Justice*, 1 (3): 14–26.

Keith, B. (2006) *Report of the Zahid Mubarek Inquiry (Vol. 1)*. London: Stationery Office.

Kelly, R. (2005) 'Foreword', in Department for Education and Skills, *Youth Matters*. London: Stationery Office.

Kemp, V., Sorsby, A., Liddle, M. and Merrington, S. (2002) *Assessing Responses to Youth Offending in Northamptonshire*. London: Nacro.

Kempf-Leonard, K. and Peterson, E. (2002) 'Expanding the realms of the new penology: the advent of actuarial justice for juveniles', in Muncie, J., Hughes, G. and McLaughlin, E. (eds), *Youth Justice: Critical Readings*. London: Sage, pp. 431–50.

Kershaw, C., Chivite-Matthews, N., Thomas, C., and Aust, R. (2001) *The 2001 British Crime Survey: First Results, England and Wales*. London: Home Office.

Kinsey, R., Lea, J. and Young, J. (1986) *Losing the Fight Against Crime*. Oxford: Blackwell.

Kuhn, T. (1970) *The Structure of Scientific Revolutions*. Chicago: University of Chicago Press.

Landau, S. and Nathan, G. (1983) 'Selecting delinquents for cautioning in the London Metropolitan Area', *British Journal of Criminology*, 23: 128–49.

Lappi-Seppala, T. (2006) 'Finland: a model of tolerance?', in Muncie, J. and Goldson, B. (eds), *Comparative Youth Justice*. London: Sage, pp. 177–95.

Lawrence Steering Group (2004) *5th Annual Report 2003–2004*. London: Home Office.

Lea, J. (2002) *Crime and Modernity*. London: Sage.

Lea, J. and Young, J. (1984) *What Is to Be Done about Law and Order?* Harmondsworth: Penguin.

Leicester Youth Offending Team (2001) *Leicester Youth Justice Plan 2001–02*. Leicester: Leicester City Council.

Leonard, P. (1984) *Personality and Ideology*. London: Macmillan.

Lipsky, M. (1980) *Street-Level Bureaucracy*. New York: Russell Sage Foundation.

Loxley, C., Curtin, L. and Brown, R. (2002) *Summer Splash Schemes 2000: Findings from Six Case Studies*. London: Home Office.

Lyon, J., Denison, C. and Wilson, A. (2000) *'Tell Them So They Listen': Messages from Young People in Custody*. London: Home Office.

MacDonald, R. (1997) 'Youth, social exclusion and the new millennium', in MacDonald, R. (ed.), *Youth, the 'Underclass' and Social Exclusion*. London: Routledge, pp. 167–97.

Macmillan, J. (1998) 'In whose interests? Politics and policy', in Brown, S. (ed.), *Understanding Youth and Crime*. Buckingham: Open University Press, pp. 53–78.

Macpherson, W. (1999) *The Stephen Lawrence Inquiry*, Cm 4262-1. London: Stationery Office.

Masters, G. (2005) 'Restorative justice and youth justice', in Bateman, T. and Pitts, J. (eds), *The RHP Companion to Youth Justice*. Lyme Regis: Russell House, pp. 179–85.

Mathiesen, T. (1974) *The Politics of Abolition*. Oxford: Martin Robertson.

Mattinson, J. and Mirrlees-Black, C. (2000) *Attitudes to Crime and Criminal Justice: Findings from the 1998 British Crime Survey*. London: Home Office.

Matza, D. (1964) *Delinquency and Drift*. New York: Wiley.

McAra, L. (2003) *Negotiated Order: Gender, Youth Transitions and Crime*. Available online at: http://www.britsoccrim.org/volume6/005.pdf.

McLaughlin, E. and Muncie, J. (2000) 'The criminal justice system: New Labour's new partnerships', in Clarke, J., Gewirtz, S. and McLaughlin, E. (eds), *New Managerialism New Welfare?* London: Sage pp. 169–85.

McMahon, W. (2006) *The Politics of Antisocial Behaviour*. Available online at: http://www.crimeandsociety.org.uk/articles/polantisocial.html.

McRobbie, A. and Thornton, S. (2002) 'Rethinking moral panic for multi-mediated social worlds', in Muncie, J., Hughes, G. and McLaughlin, E. (eds), *Youth Justice: Critical Readings*. London: Sage, pp. 68–79.

Merton, R. (1957) *Social Theory and Social Structure*. Glencoe, IL: Free Press.

Milne, S. (2004) *The Enemy Within*. London: Verso.

Ministère de la Justice (2001) *La Justice des Mineurs*. Paris: Ministère de la Justice.

Mirrlees-Black, C. (2000) *Confidence in the Criminal Justice System: Findings from the 2000 British Crime Survey*. London: Home Office.

Mirrlees-Black, C. and Allen, J. (1998) *Concern about Crime: Findings from the 1998 British Crime Survey*. London: Home Office.

Mirrlees-Black, C., Budd, T., Partridge, S. and Mayhew, P. (1998) *The 1998 British Crime Survey: England and Wales*. London: Home Office.

Moore, R. (2004) 'Intensive supervision and surveillance programmes for young offenders: the evidence base so far', in Burnett, R. and Roberts, C. (eds), *What Works in Probation and Youth Justice*. Cullompton: Willan, pp. 159–79.

Moore, S. and Peters, E. (2003) *A Beacon of Hope: Children and Young People on Remand*. London: Children's Society.

Moore, S. and Smith, R. (2001) *The Pre-Trial Guide*. London: Children's Society.

Morgan Harris Burrows (2001) 'Youth inclusion programme: evaluation overview', unpublished.

Morgan Harris Burrows (2003) *Evaluation of the Youth Inclusion Programme*. London: Youth Justice Board.

MORI (2001) *Rethinking Crime and Punishment Survey*. London: MORI.

MORI (2002) *Youth Survey 2002*. London: Youth Justice Board.

MORI (2004) *MORI Youth Survey 2004*. London: Youth Justice Board.

Morris, A., Giller, H., Geach, H. and Szwed, E. (1980) *Justice for Children*. London: Macmillan.

Muncie, J. (1999a) 'Institutionalized intolerance: youth justice and the 1998 Crime and Disorder Act', *Critical Social Policy*, 19 (2): 147–75.

Muncie, J. (1999b) *Youth and Crime: A Critical Introduction*. London: Sage.

Muncie, J. (2000) 'Pragmatic realism? Searching for criminology in the new youth justice', in Goldson, B. (ed.), *The New Youth Justice*. Lyme Regis: Russell House, pp. 14–34.

Muncie, J. (2001) 'Policy transfers and "What Works": some reflections on comparative youth justice', *Youth Justice*, 1 (3): 27–35.

Muncie, J. (2002) 'A new deal for youth? Early intervention and correctionalism', in Hughes, G., McLaughlin, E. and Muncie, J. (eds), *Crime Prevention and Community Safety: New Directions*. London: Sage, pp. 142–62.

Muncie, J. (2004) *Youth and Crime*, 2nd edn. London: Sage.

Muncie, J. and Goldson, B. (2006) 'States of transition: convergence and diversity in international youth justice', in Muncie, J. and Goldson, B. (eds), *Comparative Youth Justice*. London: Sage, pp. 196–218.

Muncie, J. and Hughes, G. (2002) 'Modes of youth governance: political rationalities, criminalisation and resistance', in Muncie, J., Hughes, G. and McLaughlin, E. (eds), *Youth Justice: Critical Readings*. London: Sage, pp. 1–18.

Muncie, J., Hughes, G. and McLaughlin, E. (eds) (2002) *Youth Justice: Critical Readings*. London: Sage.

Murray, C. (1996) 'The emerging British underclass', in Lister, R. (ed.), *Charles Murray and the Underclass: The Developing Debate*. London: IEA Health and Welfare Unit, pp. 23–54.

Nacro Cymru/Youth Justice Board (2001) *Guide to the National Standards for Bail Supervision and Support Schemes*. London: Youth Justice Board.

Nacro/ACOP (1995) *A Crisis in Custody*. London: Nacro.

National Assembly for Wales (2000) *Extending Entitlement*. Cardiff: National Assembly for Wales.

National Association for the Care and Resettlement of Offenders (1987) *Time for Change: A New Framework for Dealing with Juvenile Crime and Offenders*. London: Nacro.

National Association for the Care and Resettlement of Offenders (2001) *Lessons from Pilots: A Summary of the National Evaluation of the Pilot Youth Offending Teams*. London: Nacro.

National Association for the Care and Resettlement of Offenders (2005) *A Better Alternative: Reducing Child Imprisonment*. London: Nacro.

National Association for Youth Justice (2001) *Remands to Local Authority Accommodation with a Security Requirement and Placement in the ex-Secure Training Centres (per S133 Criminal Justice & Police Act 2001) – A Position Statement from the National Association for Youth Justice*. Leicester: NAYJ.

National Association for Youth Justice (2002) *Working with Children in Trouble: The Philosophical Base*. Available online at: http://www.nayj.org.uk/website/index.php?module=ContentExpree&func=display&ceid=1.

National Association for Youth Justice (2006) *Manifesto for Youth Justice*. Available online at: http://www.nayj.org.uk/website/index.php?module=ContentExpree&func=display&ceid=2.

National Audit Office (2004) *Youth Offending: The Delivery of Community and Custodial Sentences*. London: Stationery Office.

Nelken, D. (2006) 'Italy: a lesson in tolerance?', in Muncie, J. and Goldson, B. (eds), *Comparative Youth Justice*. London: Sage, pp. 159–76.

Newburn, T. (1998) 'Tackling youth crime and reforming youth justice: the origins and nature of "New Labour" policy', *Policy Studies*, 19 (3/4): 199–211.

Newburn, T., Masters, G., Earle, R., Goldie, S., Crawford, A., Sharpe, K., Netten, A., Hale, C., Uglow, S. and Saunders, R. (2001a) *The Introduction of Referral Orders into the Youth Justice System: First Interim Report*. London: Home Office.

Newburn, T., Earle, R., Goldie, S., Campbell, A., Masters, G., Crawford, A., Sharpe, K., Hale, C., Saunders, R., Uglow, S. and Netten, A. (2001b) *The Introduction of Referral Orders into the Youth Justice System: Second Interim Report*. London: Home Office.

Newburn, T., Crawford, A., Earle, R., Goldie, S., Hale, C., Hallam, A., Masters, G., Netten, A., Saunders, R., Sharpe, K. and Uglow, S. (2002) *The Introduction of Referral Orders into the Youth Justice System: Final Report*. London: Home Office.

Nicholas, S., Povey, A., Walker, A. and Kershaw, C. (2005) *Crime in England and Wales 2004/2005*. London: Home Office.

Northamptonshire Youth Offending Team (2001) *Northamptonshire Youth Justice Plan 2000–01*. Northampton: Northamptonshire County Council.

PA Consulting (2002) *Reducing Delays*. Available online at: http:// www.reducing-delays.org.

Pandya, T. (2006) *Average Time from Arrest to Sentence for Persistent Young Offenders*. Available online at: http://www.dca.gov.uk/statistics/statpub.htm.

Parker, H. (1974) *A View from the Boys*. Newton Abbott: David & Charles.

Patten, J. (1988) Speech to conference, 'Juvenile Justice – Diversion from Custody', London, 18 March.

Pearson, G. (1983) *Hooligan: A History of Respectable Fears*. Basingstoke: Macmillan.

Percy, A. (1998) *Ethnicity and Victimisation: Findings from the 1996 British Crime Survey*. London: Home Office.

Percy-Smith, J. (2000) 'Introduction: the contours of social exclusion', in Percy-Smith, J. (ed.), *Policy Responses to Social Exclusion*. Buckingham: Open University Press, pp. 1–21.

Peterborough Youth Offending Team (2001) *Youth Justice Plan 2001–02*. Peterborough: Peterborough City Council.

Phillips, L. (2006) 'Foreword', in Sentencing Guidelines Council and Sentencing Advisory Panel, *Annual Report 2005–06*. London: Sentencing Guidelines Secretariat, p. 2.

Piacentini, L. and Walters, R. (2006) 'The politicization of youth crime in Scotland and the rise of the "Burberry Court"', *Youth Justice*, 6 (1): 43–60.

Pickford, J. (2000) 'Introduction: a new youth justice for a new century', in Pickford, J. (ed.), *Youth Justice: Theory and Practice*. London: Cavendish.

Pierpoint, H. (2004) 'A survey on volunteer appropriate adult services', *Youth Justice*, 4 (1): 32–45.

Pitts, J. (1988) *The Politics of Juvenile Crime*. London: Sage.

Pitts, J. (1999) *Working with Young Offenders*, 2nd edn. Basingstoke: Macmillan.

Pitts, J. (2000) 'The new youth justice and the politics of electoral anxiety', in Goldson, B. (ed.), *The New Youth Justice*. Lyme Regis: Russell House, pp. 1–13.

Pitts, J. (2001a) 'Korrectional Karaoke: New Labour and the zombification of youth justice', *Youth Justice*, 1 (2): 3–16.

Pitts, J. (2001b) *The New Politics of Youth Crime*. Basingstoke: Palgrave.

Pitts, J. (2002) 'Amnesia and Discontinuity', speech to National Association of Youth Justice Conference, Milton Keynes, 14 June.

Pitts, J. (2003) Speech to Nacro Annual Conference, Loughborough University, 10 April.

Poulantzas, N. (1978) *Political Power and Social Classes*. London: Verso.

Pragnell, S. (2001) 'Report to Northamptonshire Youth Offending Team Steering Group'. Unpublished.

Pragnell, S. (2005) 'Reprimands and Final Warnings', in Bateman, T. and Pitts, J. (eds), *The RHP Companion to Youth Justice*. Lyme Regis: Russell House Press, pp. 77–82.

Pratt, J. (1989) 'Corporatism: the third model of juvenile justice', *British Journal of Criminology*, 29: 236–54.

Pratt, J. (2000) 'The return of the wheelbarrow men; or, the arrival of postmodern penality?', *British Journal of Criminology*, 40: 127–45.

Pratt, J. (2002) 'Corporatism: the third model of juvenile justice', in Muncie, J., Hughes, G. and McLaughlin, E. (eds), *Youth Justice: Critical Readings*. London: Sage, pp. 404–12.

Reconviction Analysis Section, RDS-NOMS (2004) *Juvenile Reconviction: Results from the 2001 and 2002 Cohorts*. London: Home Office.

Rees, G. and Wilson, D. (2006) 'Introduction', in Wilson, D. and Rees, G. (eds), *Just Justice*. London: Children's Society, pp. 1–4.

Reynolds, F. (1985) 'Juvenile offending in Northamptonshire 1982–3'. Unpublished.

Roberts, C., Baker, K., Merrington, S. and Jones, S. (2001) *Validity and Reliability of ASSET: Interim Report to the Youth Justice Board*. Oxford: Centre for Criminological Research.

Rock, P. (2002) 'On becoming a victim', in Hoyle, C. and Young, R. (eds), *New Visions of Crime Victims*. Oxford: Hart, pp. 1–21.

Rutherford, A. (1992) *Growing Out of Crime: The New Era*. Winchester: Waterside Press.

Rutherford, A. (1996) *Transforming Criminal Policy*. Winchester: Waterside Press.

Rutter, M., Giller, H. and Hagell, A. (1998) *Anti-Social Behaviour by Young People*. Manchester: Fields Press.

Saini, A. (1997) *'So What's the Point of Telling Anyone?'* Lecicester: De Montfort University.

Salford Youth Offending Team (2001) *Salford Youth Justice Plan 2001–02*. Salford: Salford City Council.

Salisbury, H. and Upson, A. (2004) 'Ethnicity, victimisation and worry about crime: findings from the 2001/02 and 2002/03 British Crime Surveys', *Findings 237*. London: Home Office.

Scarman, L. (1982) *The Scarman Report*. Harmondsworth: Penguin.

Schrag, L. (2003) *Restorative Justice in Northern Ireland: An Outsider's Perspective*. Paper to Best Practices in Restorative Justice Conference, Simon Fraser University, 1–4 June.

Schur, E. (1973) *Radical Non-Intervention*. Englewood Cliffs, NJ: Prentice-Hall.

Schweinhart, L. (2003) *Validity of the High/Scope Preschool Education Model*. Available online at: http://www.highscope.org/Research/preschoolvalidity.pdf, accessed 11 April 2006.

Scottish Executive (2002) *National Standards for Scotland's Youth Justice Services*. Edinburgh: Scottish Executive.

Scottish Executive (2004) *Getting It Right for Every Child*. Edinburgh: Scottish Executive.

Scraton, P. (2003) *13 Streets of Terror: Marginalisation, Criminalisation and Authoritarian Renewal*. Paper to European Group for the Study of Deviance and Social Control (Britain and Ireland) Conference, Chester, April.

Scraton, P. and Haydon, D. (2002) 'Challenging the criminalisation of children and young people: securing a rights-based agenda', in Muncie, J., Hughes, G. and McLaughlin, E. (eds), *Youth Justice: Critical Readings*. London: Sage, pp. 311–28.

Seymour, M. (2004) *Juvenile Justice in the Republic of Ireland*. Available online at: http://www.esc-eurocrim.org/files/juvenile_justice_in_the_republic_of_ireland.doc.

Shapland, J., Johnstone, J., Sorsby, A., Stubbing, T., Jackson, J., Hibbert, J. and Howes, M. (2001) *Evaluation of Statutory Time Limit Pilot Schemes in the Youth Court*. Sheffield: University of Sheffield.

Sharp, D. (2006) 'Serve and protect? Black young people's experiences of policing in the community', in Wilson, D. and Rees, G. (eds), *Just Justice*. London: Children's Society, pp. 5–13.

Simes, J. and Chads, K. (2002) *Prison Population Brief England and Wales: May 2002*. London: Home Office.

Smith, D. (1999) 'Social work with young people in trouble: memory and prospect', in Goldson, B. (ed.), *Youth Justice: Contemporary Policy and Practice*. Aldershot: Ashgate, pp. 148–69.

Smith, D. (2000) 'Corporatism and the new youth justice', in Goldson, B. (ed.), *The New Youth Justice*. Lyme Regis: Russell House, pp. 129–43.

Smith, D. (2004) *The Links Between Victimization and Offending*. Edinburgh: Centre for Law and Society, University of Edinburgh.

Smith, D., McVie, S., Woodward, R., Shute, J., Flint, J. and McAra, L. (2001) *The Edinburgh Study of Youth Transitions and Crime: Key Findings at Ages 12 and 13*. Edinburgh: University of Edinburgh.

Smith, R. (1985) 'The catch-all term of reparation', *Community Care*, 25 July, p. 8.

Smith, R. (1987) 'The Practice of Diversion', *Youth and Policy*, 19: 10–14.

Smith, R. (1989) *Diversion in Practice*, MPhil thesis. University of Leicester, Leicester.

Smith, R. (1995) 'Margaret Thatcher: soft on crime'. Unpublished.

Smith, R. (2000) 'Order and disorder: the contradictions of childhood', *Children and Society*, 14: 3–10.

Smith, R. (2001) 'Foucault's law: the Crime and Disorder Act 1998', *Youth Justice*, 1 (2): 17–29.

Smith, R. (2002a) 'Evaluation of Northampton Youth Offending Team'. Unpublished.

Smith, R. (2002b) *Relearning Old Lessons: Diversion and Restorative Justice*. Paper to Effective Restorative Justice Conference, De Montfort University, Leicester, 20 March.

Smith, R. (2002c) 'The wrong end of the telescope: child protection or child safety?', *Journal of Social Welfare and Family Law*, 24 (3): 247–61.

Smith, R. (2003) *Youth Justice: Ideas, Policy Practice*, 1st edn. Cullompton: Willan.

Smith, R. (2006) 'Actuarialism and early intervention in contemporary youth justice', in Goldson, B. and Muncie, J. (eds), *Youth Crime and Justice*. London: Sage, pp. 92–109.

Smithson, H. (2004) *Effectiveness of a Dispersal Order to Reduce ASB amongst Young People: A Case Study Approach in East Manchester*. Sheffield: Sheffield Hallam University.

Social Exclusion Unit (1998) *Bringing Britain Together: A National Strategy for Neighbourhood Renewal*. London: Stationery Office.

Social Exclusion Unit (1999a) *Bridging the Gap*. London: Stationery Office.

Social Exclusion Unit (1999b) *Teenage Pregnancy*. London: Stationery Office.

Social Exclusion Unit (2000) *The Social Exclusion Unit Leaflet*. London: Cabinet Office.

Social Exclusion Unit (2001) *Preventing Social Exclusion*. London: Stationery Office.

Social Exclusion Unit (2002) *Preventing Re-offending by Ex-prisoners*. London: Social Exclusion Unit.

Social Exclusion Unit (2003) *A Better Education for Children in Care*. London: Office of the Deputy Prime Minister.

Soothill, K., Francis, B. and Fligelstone, R. (2002) *Patterns of Offending Behaviour: A New Approach*. London: Home Office.

Squires, P. and Stephen, D. (2005) *Rougher Justice*. Cullompton: Willan.

Statewatch (2006) *ASBOwatch*. Available online at: http://www.statewatch.org/asbo/ASBOwatch.html.

Stevens, M. and Crook, J. (1986) 'What the devil is Intermediate Treatment?', *Social Work Today*, 18 (2): 10–11.

Strang, H. and Braithwaite, J. (eds) (2001) *Restorative Justice and Civil Society*. Cambridge: Cambridge University Press.

Straw, J. (1997) 'Foreword', in Home Office, *No More Excuses*. London: Stationery Office.

Straw, J. and Michael, A. (1996) *Tackling the Causes of Crime: Labour's Proposals to Prevent Crime and Criminality*. London: Labour Party.

Sure Start (2000) *What is Sure Start?* London: Sure Start.

Tarling, R., Burrows, J. and Clarke, A. (2001) *Dalston Youth Project Part II (11–14): An Evaluation*. London: Home Office.

Thompson, R., Holland, J., Henderson, S., McGrellis, S. and Sharpe, S. (1999) *Youth Values: A Study of Identity, Diversity and Social Change*. London: South Bank University.

Thornton, D., Curran, C., Grayson, D. and Holloway, V. (1984) *Tougher Regimes in Detention Centres*. London: HMSO.

Thorpe, D. (1984) 'Does the Northamptonshire model work? Some preliminary results', in Fox, H. and Williams, R. (eds), *Diversion – Corporate Action with Juveniles*. Northampton: Northamptonshire County Council, pp. 40–2.

Thorpe, D., Smith, D., Green, C. and Paley, J. (1980) *Out of Care*. London: George Allen & Unwin.

Travis, A. (2002) 'Youth jail taken off the critical list', *Guardian*, 15 October.

United Nations (1985) *The United Nations Standard Minimum Rules for the Administration of Juvenile Justice (Beijing Rules)*. Geneva: United Nations.

United Nations (1989) *Convention on the Rights of the Child*. Geneva: United Nations.

United Nations Committee on the Rights of the Child (2002) *Concluding Observations of the Committee on the Rights of the Child: United Kingdom of Great Britain and Northern Ireland*. Geneva: United Nations.

Upson, A. (2005) 'Patterns of crime', in Nicholas, S., Povey, D., Walker, A. and Kershaw, C. (eds), *Crime in England and Wales 2004/2005*. London: Home Office.

Vickerstaff, S. (2003) 'Apprenticeship in the golden age: were youth transitions really smooth and unproblematic back then?', *Work, Employment and Society*, 17 (2): 269–87.

Walklate, S. (2004) *Gender, Crime and Criminal Justice*, 2nd edn. Cullompton: Willan.

Walsh, C. (2002) 'No more hanging around', *Youth Justice*, 2 (2): 70–81.

Walther, A. (2006) 'Regimes of youth transitions', *Young*, 14 (2): 119–39.

Warner, N. (2001) 'Foreword', in Youth Justice Board, *The Preliminary Report on the Operation of the New Youth Justice System*. London: Youth Justice Board.

Weber, M. (1957) *The Theory of Social and Economic Organisation*. Glencoe, IL: Free Press.

Webster, C. (2006) '"Race", youth crime and justice', in Goldson, B. and Muncie, J. (eds), *Youth Crime and Justice*. London: Sage, pp. 30–46.

Webster, C., Simpson, D., MacDonald, R., Abbas, A., Cieslik, M., Shildrick, T. and Simpson, M. (2004) *Poor Transitions: Social Exclusion and Young Adults*. Bristol: Policy Press.

White, M. (2002) 'Anti-crime plan for urban youth under threat', *Guardian*, 16 August.

Whiting, E. and Cuppleditch, L. (2006) *Re-offending of Juveniles: Results from the 2004 Cohort*. London: Home Office.

Whyte, B. (2000) 'Youth justice in Scotland', in Pickford, J. (ed.), *Youth Justice: Theory and Practice*. London: Cavendish, pp. 169–88.

Wilcox, A. (2002) *National Evaluation of Restorative Justice Projects*. Oxford: Centre for Criminological Research.

Wilcox, A. (2003) 'Evidence-based youth justice? Some valuable lessons from and evaluation for the Youth Justice Board', *Youth Justice*, 3 (1): 21–35.

Wilcox, A. (2004) *The National Evaluation of the Youth Justice Board's Restorative Justice Projects*. London: Youth Justice Board.

Williams, B. (1997) *Working with Victims of Crime: Policies, Politics and Practice*. London: Jessica Kingsley.

Williams, B. (2000) 'Victims of crime and the new youth justice', in Goldson, B. (ed.), *The New Youth Justice*. Lyme Regis: Russell House, pp. 176–92.

Williams, B. (2005) 'Working with victims in youth justice', in Bateman, T. and Pitts, J. (eds), *The Russell House Companion to Youth Justice*. Lyme Regis: Russell House, pp. 210–15.

Willis, P. (1977) *Learning to Labour*. Farnborough: Saxon House.

Willow, C. (1999) *It's Not Fair*. London: Children's Society.

Wilson, D. (2006) '"Playing the game": the experiences of young black men in custody', in Wilson, D. and Rees, G. (eds), *Just Justice*. London: Children's Society, pp. 14–21.

Wilson, D. and Rees, G. (eds) (2006) *Just Justice*. London: Children's Society.

Wood, M. (2004) 'Perceptions and experiences of antisocial behaviour', *Findings 252*. London: Home Office.

Wood, M. (2005) *Perceptions and Experience of Antisocial Behaviour: Findings from the 2003/2004 British Crime Survey*. London: Home Office.

Worrall, A. (1999) 'Troubled or troublesome? Justice for girls and young women', in Goldson, B. (ed.), *Youth Justice: Contemporary Policy and Practice*. Aldershot: Ashgate, pp. 28–50.

Yarrow, S. (2005) *The Experiences of Young Black Men as Victims of Crime*. London: Criminal Justice System Race Unit.

Young, R. (2002) 'Testing the limits of restorative justice: the case of corporate victims', in Hoyle, C. and Young, R. (eds), *New Visions of Crime Victims*. Oxford: Hart, pp. 133–71.

Youth Justice Board (1999) *Speeding Up Youth Justice*. London: Youth Justice Board.

Youth Justice Board (2000) *National Standards for Youth Justice*. London: Youth Justice Board.

Youth Justice Board (2001a) *Youth Justice Board for England and Wales Corporate Plan 2001–02 to 2003–04 and Business Plan 2001–02*. London: Youth Justice Board.

Youth Justice Board (2001b) *Youth Justice Board Review 2000/2001: Delivering Change*. London: Youth Justice Board.

Youth Justice Board (2001c) *The Preliminary Report on the Operation of the New Youth Justice System*. London: Youth Justice Board.

Youth Justice Board (2002) *Youth Justice Board Review 2001/02: Building on Success*. London: Youth Justice Board.

Youth Justice Board (2004a) *National Standards for Youth Justice*, 2nd edn. London: Youth Justice Board.

Youth Justice Board (2004b) 'Written Evidence to the House of Commons Home Affairs Select Committee'. Available online at: http://www.publications.parliament.uk/pa/cm200405/cmselect/cmhaff/80ii/80we51.htm.

Youth Justice Board (2004c) *Race Audit and Action-Planning Toolkit for Youth Offending Teams*. London: Youth Justice Board.

Youth Justice Board (2005a) 'Supplementary written evidence to the House of Commons Home Affairs Select Committee'. Available online at: http://www.publications.parliament.uk/pa/cm200405/cmselect/cmhaff/80/80we28.htm.

Youth Justice Board (2005b) *Strategy for the Secure Estate for Children and Young People*. London: Youth Justice Board.

Youth Justice Board (2005c) *Corporate and Business Plan 2005/06 to 2007/08*. London: Youth Justice Board.

Youth Justice Board (2005d) *Annual Report and Accounts 2004/05*. London: Youth Justice Board.

Youth Justice Board (2005e) *Bail Supervision and Support*. London: Youth Justice Board.

Youth Justice Board (2005f) *Strategy for the Secure Estate for Children and Young People.* London: Youth Justice Board.

Youth Justice Board (2006a) *Youth Justice Annual Statistics 2004/05.* London: Youth Justice Board.

Youth Justice Board (2006b) *Common Assessment Framework: Draft Guidance for Youth Offending Teams.* London: Youth Justice Board.

Youth Justice Board (n.d.) *ASSET Assessment Profile.* London: Youth Justice Board.

Youth Justice Board and Welsh Assembly Government (2004) *All Wales Youth Offending Strategy.* London: Youth Justice Board.

Index

Acceptable Behaviour Contract 50, 75, 77
acquisitive crimes 164
Action Plan Orders 55, 58, 59, 121–3, 128, 153, 186, 227
actuarial regimes/techniques 39–40, 176, 209–10, 226–7
adaptability 163–4
administrative justice 8–9, 49
adolescence 160, 180
African-Caribbean men 16
Aggravated Vehicle-Taking Act 1992 25–6
All Wales Youth Offending Strategy 69
Althusser, L. 172, 204, 224
America 40, 44, 51, 163–4
Anderson, B. 167
anti-social behaviour 166–7, 169, 204
    perceptions and experience 188–90
Anti-Social Behaviour Order 50, 55, 58, 63, 68, 72–7, 101, 190
    consequences 75–7
    credibility 76
    discrimination 76
    net-widening 76–7
    oppression 76
    use of 73–5
Antisocial Behaviour Act 2003 50, 63
Appleton, C. 106
approach 42–3, 64–70
Area Child Protection Committees 224
ASBO *see* Anti-Social Behaviour Order
Ashfield Young Offenders Institution 101
Asian origin 133–7
Asperger Syndrome 76
assessment 88–9
ASSET assessment 57, 89, 90–1, 107, 112–15, 204, 209, 213, 214

utilisation 127–8, 177, 209
    and Youth Offending Teams 112–15
Association of Chief Police Officers 12
Attendance Centre Order 58, 121
Audit Commission 34–5, 37, 40, 67, 111, 112, 192

Bail Act 1976 27, 32, 62
bail support/conditions 32–4, 126, 219
Barclay, G. 135
Bateman, T. 78, 157
behaviour
    and left realism 165–6
    management 7, 9–10, 64, 87
    and social control 174–5, 187
    typology of adaptability 163–4
Beijing Rules on the Administration of Youth Justice 27, 35, 212
Belgium 229
Benedict, R. 160
bifurcation 5, 17, 23, 40, 140
Black Community Safety Project 196
Black Prisoners Support Group 96
Blair, Tony 25, 42, 44, 51, 61, 65, 67
Blunkett, David 61, 72
boot camps 28
Bottoms, A. 152
Bowling, B. 193, 194, 196, 212, 227
Bristol 206
British Crime Survey 77–8, 188, 190, 193, 195
British Institute for Brain Injured Children 75
Buckland, G. 228
Bulger, James 25, 189
bureaucracy 84

Burnett, R. 106
Burney, E. 63, 73, 74

Cambridge Intermediate Treatment study
   15
campaign groups 224–5
Canton, R. 107
carceral continuum 56
case management approach 128
Catch 'em Young 48
cautioning 4, 12, 27, 154
   rates 37, 77
change programmes 117
Chigwada-Bailey, R. 134
Child Safety Order 54, 58
Child Support Act 1991 2, 26
Children Act 2004 64
Children in Trouble 6
Children and Young Offenders Act 1969
   3, 52
Children and Young Persons Act 1933 27
Children's Fund 98
children's rights 35, 41, 94, 212, 215,
   218–19
Children's Society 11, 12, 30, 32, 33, 218
Christie, N. 169–70, 177
Cicourel, A. 159
Clarke, Charles 61
Clarke, J. 170
Clarke, Kenneth 25, 26
cognitive impairment 167
Cohen, S. 41, 170, 173–5, 204–6
Coles, D. ix
collective interests 224–5
colour blind 83
Commission for Racial Equality 135
*Common Assessment Framework for
   Children and Young People* 113
Communities that Care 167
community 187–93
   perception and experience 187–9
Community Charge 2
Community Punishment and
   Rehabilitation Orders 58, 126
Community Restorative Justice in the
   North of Ireland 212
Community Service/Combination Orders
   23
community-based interventions 5, 18, 29,
   39, 99
   impact 15–16

supervision programmes 34–5
compound social dislocations 44
Conditional Discharge 57–8, 79–80, 82
Connexions 47, 210
continuum treatment 58
control culture ix, 85
   see also social control
Corby 6, 8
corporatism 40, 41, 102, 107–8, 205
Corrigan, P. 161, 188
costs 181
courts 88, 91–2
   as opinion formers 222–3
Craine, S. 164
Crawford, A. 225
credibility 76
crime control 55, 61–2
Crime and Disorder Act 1998 32, 40,
   57–9, 68, 72, 85, 95, 105, 109, 111,
   118–19, 157, 175, 213
Crime, Justice and Protecting the Public 18,
   23
crime prevention
   individualised 49–50
   and national standards 87
   objectives 53–4
   options 157–8
   perceptions and experience 190–1
   pre-delinquent 54–5, 58
   serious/persistent offenders 56–7
   targeted 47–9
Criminal Justice: The Way Ahead 61, 62
Criminal Justice Act 1982 18
Criminal Justice Act 1991 5, 12–13, 23–4,
   25, 26, 40–1, 133, 227
Criminal Justice Act 1993 26
Criminal Justice Act 2003 63
Criminal Justice and Police Act 2001 50,
   62
Criminal Justice and Public Order Act
   1994 27
criminogenic influences 42–3, 51
criminologies of self/other 192–3
curfew provisions 47–8, 50, 55, 58, 190,
   219
custody
   alternatives 9–10, 222–3
   avoidance 19–20, 33
   as disciplinary framework 56–7
   increased use 204, 208, 209–10, 215–16
   limits on 218

and prison works 27, 41, 205
and racism 136
rates 14–15, 16, 18, 38–9, 78–80, 127
secure accommodation 93
voluntary sector 30
and young women 139–40, 141–2
and Youth Justice Board 100–1

Daily Mail 208
Daily Mirror 140, 142
Davies, B. 160
day fines 227
delay reduction 111–12, 148–9
délits v *crimes* 58
depoliticisation 29–30, 40, 204–5
detection trends 37
Detention Centres 18, 26
Detention and Training Order 56, 58, 126
Dignan, J. 121, 186–7
disabilities 76
disciplinary techniques 177
discretionary alternatives 57, 96–7
discrimination 76
Dispersal Orders 50, 55, 58, 157, 190
diversion 1, 6–9, 20, 34, 64, 97, 105, 223
    impact 36–9
doli incapax 25, 157
dominant goals 163–4
Dominelli, L. 158
Doncaster 48
Donzelot, J. 53, 178
Drakeford, M. 10–11, 13, 30, 40, 146
due process 207

Eadie, T. 107
Eastwood Park Prison 141–2
electronic tagging systems 63, 99, 169,
    177
equalising function 212
Erikson, E. 160
Ernst & Young 111
ethnicity *see* minority ethnic groups
Every Child Matters 64, 223, 224

Falklands' War 2
family 175, 178
Farrington, D. 166, 167
Feilzer, M. 136
Feltham Young Offender Institution and
    Remand Centre 31
Final Warnings 55, 57, 58, 68, 76, 77, 82,

90, 117–18, 128, 135, 149–50, 153, 219,
    226
Fionda, J. 212
Foucault, M. 53, 55, 85, 137, 153, 176–80,
    204, 228
    limits to functionalism 178–80, 181
    techniques of justice 176–8
*Framework for the Assessment of Children
    in Need* 112–13
France 48, 58, 216, 228–9
fraud 164
functionalism 178–80

Garland, D. 172–3, 178–9, 192, 216
gate-keeping 19
Gateshead 48
gender *see* young women
Germany 229
Gilroy, P. 165
girls *see* young women
globalisation 217–18, 228–30
Goldson, B. ix, 40–1, 78, 80, 82, 134, 154,
    157–8
graffiti 47
Gramsci, A. 171–2
Guardian 101, 181, 208

Haines, K. 10–11, 13, 30, 40, 145, 146
Hall, S. 173
Hancock, L. 188
Harris, R. 83, 158, 159, 179
Headstart programme 44
hegemony 171, 180
Hine, J. 198
Holdaway, S. 116, 186
Home Secretaries 17, 61
Hood, R. 136
Howard, Michael 26, 27
Hoyle, C. 185, 187
Hudson, B. 4, 9–10, 39, 40
human rights 35, 41, 94, 212, 215, 218–19
    see also rights
Human Rights Act 1998 133
hyperactivity 167

ideal types 127
Ideological State Apparatuses 172
incapacitation 176
inclusion *see* social inclusion
Independent 101, 222
indicators 175

indictable offences 38
Individual Support Orders 63, 75, 77
individualised crime prevention 49–50,
    169–70
informal disposals 150, 151, 219
informal justice 225–6
inspectors 223–4
institutional racism 98, 132–7
institutionalised unfairness 212
integrated approaches 43–4
Intensive Supervision and Surveillance
    Programmes 13, 50, 58, 61–2, 64, 80,
    92–3, 99, 125–7, 153
    eligibility 126
    and social control 174, 177
inter-agency co-operation 23, 30, 101–2,
    223
Intermediate Treatment 4, 6, 9–11, 18, 20
intra-group crimes 51
Ireland 226, 229
ISSP see Intensive Supervision and
    Surveillance Programmes
Italy 226

Jeffs, T. 162
Jenks, C. 160
joined up problems/policies 43–4, 46, 48,
    102
    see also problem-solving
joy-riding 25–6
just deserts 23, 80
justice see youth justice
Justice for All 65
justice model 205
juvenile justice 158
Juvenile Liaison Bureaux 6–9, 18–19,
    145–6

Kent 34

labelling theory 67–8, 209–10
laissez-faire 17
Lawrence, Stephen 132, 134, 193, 194–5,
    196, 197
Lea, J. 165, 177, 184, 192, 217
learning difficulties 75
Learning Support Units 46
left realists 51, 165–6
legitimacy 171–2, 199–200, 214
Leicester 143
Leonard, P. 169

liberal democracy 172
Lipsky, M. 107, 159
local authority secure units 63
local child curfew 47–8

MacDonald, R. 162, 163, 164, 166
Macmillan, J. 27
Major, John 24, 25, 28
managerialism 29, 30, 56–7, 66, 80, 84,
    148–9, 175, 196
Manchester Youth Bail Support 32–4, 136
masculinity 137, 162–3
media 189–90
Merton, R. 163–4, 165, 169
mezzo/macro levels 158–9, 217, 220–1,
    223
Mhlanga, B. 135
micro level 159, 217
micro-management 57–9
Miners' Strike 2
minimum intervention 17–18, 215–16
minority ethnic groups 13, 193–7
    see also racism
    and police 194–6
    victimisation 193–4
monitoring, electronic see electronic
    tagging systems
MORI Youth Surveys 197
Mubarek, Zahid 193
multiplier effect 134
Muncie, J. 40, 81, 82, 84, 152, 157–8,
    161–2, 168–9

naming and shaming 76
National Association for Youth Justice
    224
national objectives/standards 85–93
National Remand Rescue/Review
    Initiative 32, 36
National Standards for the Supervision
    of Offenders 29
National Standards for Youth Justice 85–94,
    112, 204
    aim/objectives 86–7
    assessment 88–9
    and corporatism 107
    court ordered interventions 91–2
    Detention and Training Order 93
    Final Warnings 90
    Intensive Supervision and Surveillance
        Programmes 92–3

Pre-Sentence Reports 90–1
preventive work 87
remand management 88
Section 90/91 Order 93–4
secure accommodation 93
and victims 89, 146
work in courts 88
National Strategy for Neighbourhood
Renewal 47
negotiated justice 8
neighbourhood decline 187–8, 192
net-widening 19, 33, 76–7, 108, 127, 147,
207–8
Netherlands 228
New Deal programmes 210
New Labour
approach 42–3, 64–70, 169
individualised crime prevention 49–50
integrated strategy 64–6
intensification process 61–3, 154–5
policy refinements 59–61
prevention initiatives 45–7
reform approach 50–4
social contract 81–2
targeted crime prevention 47–9, 81–2
victim perspective 143
welfare and behaviour 63–4
New York 51
New Zealand 146
Newburn, T. 225
No More Excuses 49, 51, 52–7, 65, 94, 111,
220
Northamptonshire 6–7, 19, 20, 27, 145–6,
223
Northern Ireland 212, 224

Offending, Crime and Justice Survey 77
On Track 48
opinion forming 222–3
oppression 76
other/self, criminologies of 192–3

Parenting Orders 50, 58, 63, 175, 178
Patten, J. 17
Pearson, G. 170
Percy-Smith, J. 67
persistent offenders 24–5, 56–7, 111,
125–7, 149, 153
Phillips, C. 193, 194, 196, 212, 227
Pitts, J. 10, 18, 66, 67, 95, 110, 157, 205,
207, 221, 228–9

police
clear-up rates 16
detection trends 37
and Dispersal orders 157
informal disposals 150, 151
and minority ethnic groups 194–6
and persistent offenders 24–5
and young people 199–200
Police Reform Act 2002 72
policy
changes 17–18
outcomes 71, 77–80
patterns 80–2
and practice 83–5
political agenda 16–17, 28–9
Poll Tax 2
populism 22, 81
and politicians 23–6
Positive Action for Young People 98
post-sentencing
see also sentencing
supervision and surveillance 56–7
Poulantzas, N. 223
poverty 2, 44, 207
Powers of Criminal Courts (Sentencing)
Act 2000 60, 123
practice
new disposals 115–16
and policy 83–5
prescription 85–93
and theory 157–63
practitioner-led initiatives (1980) 18–19
practitioners 28–30
Pratt, J. 29, 84, 205
pre-delinquent crime prevention 54–5,
58, 210
Pre-Sentence Reports 23–4, 90–1, 111, 114, 143
predictors 167–8, 175, 206
preventive detention 157
see also crime prevention
Prison Inspectorate 223
prison works 20, 26, 205
problem-solving 212–13, 219–20
see also joined up problems/policies
proceduralism 56–7
progressive sanctions 68
proportionality 17–18, 23, 96–7, 227
Protective Orders 58
public opinion 16, 187–93
Punishment, Custody and the Community 5
Pupil Referral Units 46, 175

Race Relations (Amendment) Act 2000 133

racism
  see also minority ethnic groups
  and crime/violence 193–4
  institutional 98, 132–7
  stereotyping 67, 83, 165
radical ideas 206–7
reconviction see reoffending
Referral Orders 55, 58, 59–61, 63, 69, 79–80, 82, 92, 135, 153, 177, 183, 205, 208, 225
  and problem-solving 219–20
  as restorative justice 123–5, 143, 144, 145, 185, 226
regulatory bodies 223–4
Rehabilitation Orders 58
reintegration 59
relative autonomy 223
remand management 88
Remand Rescue/Review Initiative 32, 36, 98–9
reoffending 50, 124–5, 128, 151–2, 153
reparation 7–8, 20, 60, 96, 122, 146–7
Reparation Orders 58, 118–21, 128, 143, 186, 226
Repressive State Apparatuses 172
Reprimands 57, 58, 68, 77, 82
Residential Care Order 3
Respect and Responsibility 63, 65
responsibilities 54, 59
restorative justice 59–61, 81, 119, 120, 226
  and problem-solving 212–13, 219–20
  Referral Orders 123–5
  victim-orientated 146–7, 185–7
  and voluntarism 30, 208, 213–15
revenge justice 28
Right Track 206
rights
  see also human rights
  approach 211–12
  and responsibilities 54, 81–2
  and welfare 227–8
riots 24, 31
risk factors 66, 80–1, 88–9
Rock, P. 184
routinization 206
rule of law 172
Rutherford, A. 17, 222, 227
Rutter, M. 166–7

Safeguarding Children 224
Safer Cities projects 47
Safer Schools Partnerships 98
sanctions 86
  progressive 68
savoir 178
Scarman, Lord 225
schools
  exclusion 46
  and social control 175
Scotland 229
secondary victimisation 187
Section 90/91 Order 58, 93–4
secure accommodation/Training Centres 26, 27, 33, 63, 78, 83, 93, 99, 99–100, 136, 140, 208
self/other, criminologies of 192–3
sentencing 23, 25
  see also post-sentencing, custody
  community 39
  and opinion forming 222–3
  patterns 78–80
  punitive 26–8
  tariff 41, 68, 123
Sentencing Guidelines Council 223
serious/persistent offenders 56–7
shoplifting 164
short, sharp, shock regime 3, 18
single-issue legislation 26
Smith, D. 10, 15, 20, 41, 85, 184
social control 170–5
  legitimacy 171–2, 199–200, 214
  limits to functionalism 178–80
  state apparatuses 172–4
  techniques of justice 176–8
social exclusion 66–7, 216
  indicators 175
Social Exclusion Unit 43, 44–5, 46, 48–9, 102, 168, 201
social inclusion 43–5, 53, 216, 218
social information processing 167
Social Inquiry Reports 23
social learning 213
society, dominant goals 163–4
South East Kent Bail Support Scheme 34
Spain 229
Specific Sentence Reports 90–1, 111
Speeding Up Youth Justice 111
  see also delay reduction
Splash 48
Squires, P. 68, 73

stakeholders 143, 154, 156, 182, 202
standards 29, 85–93, 129, 177
state
    minimum intervention 17–18, 215–16
    rolling back 17
Stephen, D. 68, 73
Stevens, A. 228
stop and search 134
Straw, Jack 51, 61, 69, 72
structured interventions 35–6
success
    meaning 15–16
    reasons 16–19
Summer Splash 10, 98, 175, 208
Supervision Order 28, 34, 39, 58, 79,
    85–6, 122, 126, 159
Sure Start 46
systems management 19, 20, 39, 205,
    226–7

tagging see electronic tagging systems
targeted crime prevention 47–9, 67, 75,
    137
tariffs 41, 59
techniques of justice 176–8
technologisation of punishment 176–7
Thames Valley Restorative4 Justice
    project 185
Thatcher, Margaret 2–3, 4, 16–17, 24
theory
    context 156
    multi-faceted analysis 158
    and practice 157–9
    and social control 170–5
    typology of adaptability 163–4
    value 180–1
tracking 9
Treasury 181
Troubleshooter Project 31–2, 33, 36, 136
truancy sweeps 46, 66
typology of adaptability 163–4

U-turn
    explanation 39–41
    impact 36–9
UN Convention on the Rights of the
    Child 35, 41, 212, 215
unintended outcomes 67–8, 84, 108, 148,
    174
USA see America

victims 8, 89, 119–21, 123–5, 143–8, 154,
    183–7, 211
    at risk groups 183
    corporate 184
    impact of crime 184
    minority ethnic groups 193–4
    as perpetrators 183–4
    and restorative justice 185–7
    Victim's Charter 183
violent crimes 138
voice recognition systems 169, 177
voluntarism 30, 208, 213–15
vulnerability provisions 32, 88

Waddington, David 24
Wales 229
Warner, Lord 100
Webb, D. 83, 158, 159, 179
Weber, M. 127, 176
Webster, C. 162, 164, 165
welfare
    approaches 228–9
    benefits, restructuring 2
    issues 96, 122
    needs 148
    reforms 205
    and rights 227–8
    and young women 140
Wellingborough 6–7
what works 109–10, 157, 204–5
Whitelaw, William 4
Williams, B. 121, 146, 147, 183, 211
Willis, P. 160, 162
women see young women
Wood, M. 184
Worrall, A. 139–41
Wrexham 48

Young, J. 165, 184, 192
Young Offenders 3, 4, 17–18
young people 159–63
    attitudes to youth justice 200–1
    and authority 199–200
    constraints 162–3
    control preoccupation 161–2, 170–1
    criminalisation 203–4, 222
    as next generation 160–1
    and police 199–200
    and public opinion 187–93
    views on crime/punishment 197–201,
        202

and voluntarism 30, 208, 213–15
young women 11, 12, 99, 137–43
    offending behaviour 138
    offending rates 140
Youth Custody 3
Youth Inclusion Programmes/Projects 10,
    48, 98, 141, 175, 216
Youth Justice: The Next Steps 64
youth justice
    see also youth offenders
    alternative approach 127–9, 210–16
    contradictory evidence/pressures
        109–10, 127–30, 203–97
    converging interests 207–8
    informal justice 225–6
    institutional racism 133–7
    intensification process 61–3, 154–5
    lessons from past 19–21
    limits to functionalism 178–80
    measurement of impacts 131–2
    periodic reappraisals 205
    policy changes 17–18
    policy and practice, impact 36–9
    political influences 16–17
    practitioner-led initiatives 18–19
    and problem-solving 212–13, 219–20
    procedural change 110–12
    progress model 204–5
    reforms, critique 148–53
    and social control 205–6
    social inclusion 43–5, 53, 216, 218
    and standardisation 129–30
    techniques 176–8
    voluntarism 30, 208, 213–15
    young people's attitudes 200–1
    and young women 139–43
Youth Justice Board 75, 78–9, 83, 84, 93,
    94–5, 110, 112, 132–3, 210, 221–2
    and ASSET assessment 113–15
    behavioural interventions 168
    as champion of change 100–1
    and Final Warnings 118, 150
    funding strategy 98–100
    independent functions 221–2
    institutional racism 133
    pre-crime panels 210
    and social control 173
    and victims 144
    and young women 141–2

youth justice plans 95–8
Youth Justice and Criminal Evidence Act
    1999 57, 60
youth justice plans 95–8
Youth Offender Panels 92, 123–4, 144–5
    and victims 186–7
youth offenders 1–2
    see also youth justice
    educational opportunities 47
    and left realism 165–6
    offending rates, decline 153–4
    outcomes 10–15
    prevention initiatives 45–7
    propensity factors 166–70
    and proportionality 96–7
    public opinion 16
    punitive approach 3–5
    responses 55–60
    trends 36–9
    typology of adaptability 163–4
Youth Offending Teams 57, 85–94, 101–7
    Action Plan Order 121–3
    and ASSET assessment 112–15
    case management approach 128
    corporatist strategy 106
    court ordered interventions 91–2
    delay reduction 111–12, 148–9
    Detention and Training Order 93
    establishment 102–4
    Final Warnings 90, 117–18
    independence 103–4
    Intensive Supervision and Surveillance
        Programmes 126
    introduction 104–7
    joint working commitment 103, 104,
        128, 224
    objectives 95–8
    Pre-Sentence Reports 90–1
    preventive work 87
    Referral Order 124–5
    remand management 88
    Reparation Orders 118–21
    Section 90/91 Order 93–4
    and social control 177
    and victims 89, 143, 183
    work in courts 88
    and young women, case study 142

zero tolerance 52